CW00950752

Trade Unions and
Socialist Politics

Trade Unions and Socialist Politics

JOHN KELLY

VERSO

London · New York

First published by Verso 1988
© 1988 John Kelly
All rights reserved

Verso
UK: 6 Meard Street, London W1V 3HR
USA: 29 West 35th Street, New York, NY 10001 2291

Verso is the imprint of New Left Books

British Library Cataloguing in Publication Data

Kelly, John E. (John Edward), 1952-
    Trade unions and socialist politics.
    1. Trade unionism. Theories, to 1980
    I. Title
    331.88′01

ISBN 0–86091–206–X
ISBN 0–86091–924–2 Pbk

US Library of Congress Cataloging in Publication Data

Kelly, John E., 1952-
    Trade unions and socialist politics/John Kelly.
        p. cm.
    Includes index
    ISBN 0–86091–206–X: $42.50 (U.S.). ISBN 0–86091–924–2 (pbk.):
$14.95 (U.S.)
    1. Trade-unions and communism.   I. Title.
HX544.K46 1988
322′.2--dc 19

Typeset by Falcon Graphic Art Ltd
Wallington, Surrey
Printed in Great Britain by Biddles Ltd, Guildford

To Caroline

Contents

Acknowledgements

Many people either commented on earlier drafts of this book or contributed to discussions of its ideas and arguments, and I would like to thank the following: Tony Benn, Robin Blackburn, Kevin Davey, Andrew Glyn, Mike Hayes, Ed Heery, Caroline Kelly, Nick Lewis, John McIlroy, Ralph Miliband, Jim Mortimer, Brendan O'Leary, Hilary Wainwright and Ellen Meiksins Wood. Parts of the manuscript have been typed and retyped by the following and my gratitude to them is doubtless matched by their relief that the job is at last finished: Sue Allen, Lucille Bailey, Yvonne Curtis, Pam Hodges, Anne Morris, Allison Reid, Joan Wilson, Jon Whittle.

Introduction

For more than a decade after 1968 the advanced capitalist world was shaken by a wave of strikes on a scale that had not been seen for fifty years. The effects were dramatic: two British governments went down to election defeat, in France and Italy governments quickly enacted major concessions to restore social order, many workers' parties swung to the left, and issues of workers' control and self-government re-emerged into public debate after years of neglect. Across Europe the heads of union federations were regularly consulted by government ministers in the social partnerships that marked the zenith of trade union power.

Yet by 1978 Eric Hobsbawm was already speaking of a crisis in the labour movement as its 'forward march' ground to a halt. Ten years on, unions have lost members in almost every capitalist country: in Britain, three million have been lost since 1979, whilst in America just 17% of the civilian workforce now belong to a union. Strike totals have fallen to their lowest levels for many years, and well-organised groups of workers have suffered spectacular defeats: American air traffic controllers, French steel and car workers, British coalminers and printers, Italian car workers. Trade union divisions have opened up sharply: the austerity policies of European 'socialist' governments have pitted Communist and non-Communist union federations against each other in France, Italy, Spain and Greece; the concessions offered to employers by the American UAW and the British EETPU have stirred up fierce debates and criticism. Politically, the 1980s has on the whole been a period of retreats: the British Labour vote in 1983 slumped to its lowest level for fifty years and recovered only a little in 1987; 'socialist' governments across Europe have been cutting public expenditure, shaking out labour and trying to restrain the growth of wages. Many Communist Parties have lost membership, votes and influence, some of them have split, and the far-left is in a state of disarray, particularly in Britain, following a series of schisms, regroupings and expulsions.

Writing of Britain, one commentator offered this scenario:

> The choice before the labour movement could be stark. Either there will be greater 'Americanisation' of British trade unions through no-strike deals and aggressive management techniques . . . or Britain's unions can try to overcome their historic limitations by constructively politicising their activities, broadening their sectional interests into community-wide ones, . . . and most important, campaigning for industrial democracy as a step towards *real* workers' control (Hain, 1986, p.322; and see also Coates and Topham, 1986).

In this view of the world the British miners' strike of 1984-1985 represented 'the last of an old wave of industrial struggles' (Coates, 1985), an archaic form of class politics that failed to connect with contemporary trends:

> reliance on the actions and approach of yesteryear as models for today's struggles and victories, are counterproductive and only go to help Thatcher gain a tighter grip on the reins (Carter, 1985, p.30).

'The working class', to which Scargill turned for support, no longer resembled the traditional image. Restructured, reorganised and relocated through the years of recession, and increasingly heterogeneous in its make-up, interests and outlooks, 'the working class' of old is said to have vanished.

This 'Eurocommunist' or post-industrial vision of the decline and transformation of the old working class, and its search for new models of trade unionism, has been taken even further by right-wing intellectuals in the British labour movement. John Lloyd and Philip Bassett, past and present Labour Editors of the London *Financial Times*, have openly praised the business unionism of the EETPU as a realistic and credible response to the crisis of the labour movement (Adeney and Lloyd, 1986; Bassett, 1986).

But these gloomy prognostications have not gone unchallenged and they have conjured up an entirely opposed line of argument, which emphasises a pattern of continuity and stability through recession, not discontinuity and turmoil. According to Harman, a prominent intellectual in the Socialist Workers' Party (SWP),

> What I have attempted . . . is to show what the objective situation really is. And it is not all that different to that which in the early 1970s enabled the organised sections of the manual working class to enter into struggles whose victories brought down a government (Harman, 1986, p.30).

Or as two fellow party members put it, 'Capitalism has reshaped the working class, not abolished it' (Callinicos and Simons, 1985, p.237). And the claim that recession has not precipitated a crisis in trade unionism and industrial relations has been buttressed by the findings of several large scale British surveys:

> Many of the findings that we have summarised in this final chapter have been concerned with changes through time. Many of these changes have been marginal when set against the general picture of industrial relations structures and practices which the two sets of results [1980 and 1984] portray (Millward and Stevens, 1986, p.316; see also Batstone, 1984; Batstone and Gourlay, 1986).

Others have disputed the connections often made between shifts in working-class composition and working-class attitudes and values (Hyman, 1984b; Westergaard, 1984). And if the working class has *not* changed radically in its outlook and interests ten it may be premature to abandon traditional tactics and strategies. So the miners' strike was not the final, tragic act of the old working class, but an awe-inspiring exemplar of the class struggles of the future (WRP, 1985; Socialist Organiser, 1985). These competing assessments of the working class in the 1980s raise fundamental questions about socialist theory and practice, about the ways in which workers can acquire political class consciousness, and about the role of trade unions in the transition to socialism.

In early 1983, when I first began to prepare the lecture course out of which this book evolved, I would have placed myself firmly within the 'Eurocommunist' wing of the British Communist Party, and shared many of its ideas on trade unionism: its critique of wages militancy; its desire to promote forms of trade union organisation that transcended sectionalism; and its attempt to steer unions in a more 'political' direction through a commitment to industrial democracy and 'political exchange' or 'social contracts' with future Labour governments. I developed a strong affinity with the ideas of Gramsci and saw no reason to disagree with the generally negative assessment of Trotsky that is commonplace in most Communist Parties.

Much has happened over the past few years, both within the Party and beyond, and the process of writing this book has inevitably reflected and been influenced by the intense and bitter ideological struggle within the British CP and the European left as a whole. During this period I have examined more critically than before the 'Eurocommunist' thinking on trade unions, and whilst I still believe that some of its insightes are valid, I now regard many of them as one-sided and inadequate. The fashionable distaste for wages militancy is one that I no longer share for reasons I will explain in the course of this book. I have become considerably more sceptical about the prospects for effective regulation of capital through schemes of industrial democracy, and more doubtful about the capacity of highly fragmented and decentralised trade union federations to sustain a political exchange with government for more than a few years. Moreover, some 'Eurocommunist' writing about 'new social forces' and 'political trade unionism' is so vague and ill-defined it is difficult to know just what to make of it.

In this book I have deliberately concentrated on Marxist analyses of trade union actions and strategies, on the attempts of organised workers to change their world and develop their own class consciousness. Marxists have produced numerous critiques of 'institutionalist', 'pluralist', 'neo-liberal' and other non-marxist approaches to industrial relations and politics. And they have often written very acutely about the barriers to class consciousness: the sectional divisions amongst workers, the impact of dominant ideologies, the incorporation of union leaders, the capacity of capitalism to satisfy basic wants. But they have been much less adept at mapping out the conditions under which class consciousness could reasonably be expected to flourish. This however is a crucial task because few people believe that the removal of these barriers would be enough to facilitate an upsurge of class consciousness. For that to happen the organisations of the labour movement must pursue appropriate strategies and tactics. It is the strategies for trade unions that provide the focus of this book. In particular I have concentrated on two major questions that are central for Marxists who want to change the world, as well as to interpret it. Firstly, what types of trade union strategy would be most likely to develop political class consciousness amongst workers? And second, what role will such strategies play in the transition to socialism?

To answer these questions Marxism must generate propositions about trade unions, class consciousness and the transition to
socialism that are sufficiently clear and precise to be tested
against empirical evidence. Too often Marxists have fallen prey
to the easy options of predicting the past and describing the
present in terms that have no obvious implications for the future.
Whatever the virtues of these activities they do not justify
Marxism's often-repeated claim to be scientific. The scientific
status of a theory is measured largely by its explanatory and
predictive power, something Marxists have too often disregarded.

The book is organised in the following way. In Part One I
examine the analyses of trade unionism developed by the classical
Marxists, starting with Marx and Engels (Chapter 1), then
proceeding through Lenin, Luxemburg and Trotsky (Chapter 2),
to Gramsci (Chapter 3). This is not out of a sense of reverence for
the classical Marxists, but because all of them were intimately
connected with trade union and socialist organisations and their
struggles. Classical Marxist theory was invariably an attempt to
grasp the significance of the real movements of workers in the
nineteenth and early twentieth centuries. Chapter 4 summarises
the strengths and weaknesses of the classical Marxist tradition
and argues there is considerable merit in Luxemburg's theory of
the mass strike. The chapter then sets out two broad strategies for
socialist advance that are assessed in Part Two. One strategy is
based on the mobilisation of workers through strikes in order to
promote the common interests of labour against capital and
overcome sectional divisions and leadership inertia.

Therefore Chapter 5 examines the relationship between strikes
and class consciousness concluding that under the conditions
specified by Luxemburg, economic struggle by trade unions can
have a major impact on workers' class consciousness and contribute significantly to socialist advance. Chapter 6 examines the
problem of sectionalism, and concludes that the scale of the
problem has been exaggerated and its character misunderstood.
Chapter 7 assesses the classical Marxist critiques of trade union
bureaucracy as a conservative social force and argues that a vast
body of contemporary empirical evidence contradicts them.

The second strategy for trade unions owes something to
Gramsci, as well as to Bernstein, and consists of attempts to
encroach on the prerogatives and powers of capital. Chapter 8
therefore assesses this strategy at the level of the enterprise, and
argues that 'industrial democracy' is unlikely to make any

significant impact on capital unless trade union resources are backed up by tough sanctions wielded by the state. Consequently, Chapter 9 evaluates Marxist theories of the capitalist state and looks in particular at the 'Swedish road to Socialism' as an application of the 'class struggle' theory of the state. I argue that Swedish labour's use of the state reflects circumstances peculiar to that country which are so far absent in other advanced capitalist countries.

Chapter 10 returns to some of the issues raised in the opening quotations of this introduction. It sets out to evaluate the current state and future prospects of the labour movement since this will be a major influence in people's assessments of the feasibility of different trade union strategies. I conclude that whilst the organised labour movement clearly faces a series of acute problems, these are by no means terminal in character, as some believe. In the concluding chapter (Chapter 11) the themes of the book are drawn together and summarized; finally I try to answer some of the most powerful objections to the Marxist account of trade unions that I have considered in the book.

PART ONE

The Classical Marxists

1

Marx and Engels: the Trade Union as Revolutionary Agency

Marx and Engels were close observers of British trade unionism in its most formative period and commented frequently on its development and struggles for over fifty years. For the short lifespan of the First International they were indeed active partici-pants in an organisation whose main function was the coordina-tion of solidarity actions with striking workers, and which was kept alive financially, if not always politically, by the English trade unions. Yet despite their contact with, and interest in, trade unionism they left behind no systematic or coherent analysis of the limits and possibilities of trade union action—certainly nothing that compares with Lenin's *What is to be done?* or Luxemburg's essay *The mass strike*.

This certainly cannot be explained by lack of knowledge or experience, for nineteenth-century Britain provided an ideal setting for the analysis of working-class organisation and politics. As early as 1844 Engels used his position as a factory owner in Manchester to study at first hand the conditions of the working class and the beginnings of collective organisation. The cam-paigns by the Chartists for basic political and civil rights were closely followed by Marx and Engels, who were acquainted with their most prominent leader, Ernest Jones. After the wave of European revolutions in the late 1840s Marx and Engels were able to observe the economic expansion and political stabilisation of Britain, then the world's leading industrial power. It was in this period, lasting from the 1850s into the 1860s, that the trade union movement began to assume its distinctly modern shape. Craft trade unionism expanded, despite continued legal harassment, and more and more employers were forced to discuss wages (and some conditions) with their 'men'. National organisation emerged as expanding unions began to centralise their finances, and establish permanent officials.

In 1864 London was the venue for the foundation of the First International (officially titled the International Workingmen's Association), a body which was heavily reliant on the British trade unions, at that time the largest and most powerful in the world. Four years later many of these unions came together to create the Trades Union Congress, and then lobbied successfully for the legalisation of trade union organisation and activity in the 1870s. The Depression of those years gave way to the socialist revival of the 1880s, with the creation in 1884 of the Fabian Society and the Social Democratic Federation. As the economy revived towards the end of the decade it was wracked by a wave of strikes by semi-skilled workers and labourers who joined in large numbers the so-called 'New Unions' of the unskilled.

Throughout their lives, then, Marx and Engels were able to observe a wide range of critical events in the development of the British working class, and of its trade union and political organisations. Yet from this wealth of experience they produced an array of seemingly contradictory insights and arguments. At times they adhered to the view that capitalist economic development would of itself inexorably drive trade unions, the 'schools of war', down the road to revolutionary politics. At other times they seemed almost to despair of the British unions, with their narrow craft mentality and their conservative leaderships.

Careful study of the writings of Marx and Engels reveals that their analyses of trade unionism did not follow a simple linear evolution from an uncomplicated revolutionary optimism of the 1840s to a more subtle, critical, even pessimistic analysis of the 1880s and 1890s (Draper, 1978). What Hyman (1971) calls the 'optimistic' thesis—that unions would evolve, more or less automatically, into revolutionary organisations—came to the fore in Marx's and Engels' writings during periods of intense industrial and/or political militancy. It registered most clearly in the turbulent years of the 1840s up to and shortly after the revolutions of 1848; it re-emerged in the 1860s and early 1870s, as British trade unions moved into overtly political campaigns to secure the franchise, to legalise trade unions, and to express solidarity with the Italian unification struggles led by Garibaldi; and it re-emerged once more with the birth of the New Unionism

in 1889 and the massive wave of strikes that marked the final
years of the Great Depression.

The reservations about the politics of trade unionism followed
an equally clear pattern, coming to the fore during periods of
downturn in class struggle, associated with the economic growth
of the 1850s and early 1860s, and with the economic stagnation in
the late 1870s and early 1880s. It was in these periods of relative
quiescence that we find Marx and Engels giving vent to their
deepest reservations and their most hostile judgements on the
emerging trade unions with their fondness for 'bourgeois respec-
tability'.

In short, Marx's and Engels' analyses of the revolutionary
potential of trade unionism swung back and forth with cycles of
class struggle. They were tremendously impressed by *current*
events—witness Engels' despondent remarks in the 1850s and
contrast them with his exuberant welcome for the 'New Unions'
of the 1880s. Writing to Marx in 1858, he noted that

> . . . the English proletariat is actually becoming more and more
> bourgeois, so that this most bourgeois of all nations is apparently
> aiming ultimately at the possession of a bourgeois aristocracy and a
> bourgeois proletariat *alongside* the bourgeoisie (Engels to Marx, 7
> October 1858, in *MECW, 40*).

And in 1889, he stated:

> Formally, the movement is first of all a trade union movement, but
> utterly different from that of the *old* Trade Unions of skilled labour,
> the labour aristocracy . . . Moreover, the people regard their immedi-
> ate demands as only provisional, although they themselves do not yet
> know toward what final goal they are working. But this vague notion
> has a strong enough hold on them to make them elect as leaders *only*
> downright Socialists (Engels to Sorge, 7 December 1889, in Marx and
> Engels, 1975a).

This heightened susceptibility to current events contrasts dramatically with Marx's own analyses of the capitalist economy, and
his constant endeavour to penetrate beneath the 'surface appearances' of capitalism to its underlying essence, its 'inner laws of
motion'. Such theoretical penetration is rarely evident in their
writings on trade unionism—instead it is the 'surface appearances', current events and struggles, which occupy the most
prominent place in their writings. This fact seems to me sufficient
indication that Marx and Engels never developed a single, *coherent*

and *rigorous* theory of trade unionism which enabled them to promote and develop a line of analysis through the ups and downs of class struggle (*pace* Chernyayev et al., 1980; Lozovsky, 1935; Stocking, 1978). Had they possessed such a theory we would not have expected their analyses of trade union actions and struggles to swing back and forth so dramatically between periods of militancy and periods of quiescence.

The Early Writings: Capitalist Society as Base and Superstructure

If asked to provide a succinct and lucid summary of the basic Marxist theory of the structure of society, many Marxists would probably reproduce the following quotation, from Marx's 1859 'Preface' to *A Contribution to the Critique of Political Economy*:

> The general result at which I arrived and which, once won, served as a guiding thread for my studies, can be briefly formulated as follows: In the social production of their life, men enter into definite relations that are indispensable and independent of their will, relations of production which correspond to a definite stage of development of their material productive forces. The sum total of these relations of production constitutes the economic structure of society, the real foundation on which rises a legal and political superstructure and to which correspond definite forms of social consciousness. The mode of production of material life conditions the social, political, and intellectual life process in general. It is not the consciousness of men that determines their being, but on the contrary, their social being that determines their consciousness (Marx, 1859, p.503).

In the early writings of the 1840s Marx and Engels were just beginning to construct the outlines of these ideas, and consequently their formulations were often stark and forceful, tendencies reinforced by the polemical nature of many of these works. Against their Hegelian contemporaries who emphasised the role of ideas and values in the explanation of political and economic structures and the genesis of historical change, Marx and Engels sharply counterposed the determining role of the economy. This, they said, comprised productive forces (means of production, or technology broadly defined) and relations of production (e.g. the relationships between employers and employees under capitalism). On top of this economic base there rested a legal and political superstructure whose content was 'conditioned' by the base. In the early writings, Marx and Engels wrote as if this relationship was a relatively straightforward causal one, as in their assertion that 'the ruling ideas in society are the ideas of the ruling class' (Marx and Engels, 1845). The legal system, for instance, reflected and supported property rights. In the *Communist Manifesto* they referred to the modern state as but the 'executive committee of the whole bourgeoisie' (Marx and Engels, 1848). Ideologies and legal and political institutions corresponded to the dominant property relations in the economic base.

The structure of capitalist society was analysed in the same way, and the major forces in society were formed out of the two class locations in the economy, exploiter and exploited, capitalist and worker. With the development of capitalism these two great social classes came to dominate the political arena, and intermediate classes and strata, such as the petit bourgeoisie, were destined to vanish (Marx and Engels, 1848).

Moreover these two social classes increasingly came to pursue economic and political interests that were directly derived from their position in the relations of production. As Marx wrote in 1847,

> The domination of capital has created for this mass a common situation, common interests. This mass is thus already a class as against capital, but not yet for itself. In the struggle, of which we have pointed out only a few phases, this mass becomes united, and constitutes itself as a class for itself. The interests it defends become class interests (Marx, 1847, p.211).

The capitalist economy itself created the working class, in an objective sense (class-in-itself), whilst the struggles of the class served to develop its consciousness and prepared it for the decisive confrontation (class-for-itself). These struggles turned on the fundamental economic interests of the two major social classes: workers strove at first to regulate the wages system, but ultimately to abolish it altogether, whilst capital strove to maintain 'its' mode of production and extraction of surplus value.

All politics was *class* politics in two senses: that the only significant political actors were social classes (recall the opening line of the 1848 *Communist Manifesto*—'All history is the history of class struggle'); and that the content of politics was given exclusively by objectively determined class interests. These same interests *inevitably* drove workers repeatedly into struggle with capital, or as Marx wrote in *The Holy Family*,

It is not a question of what this or that proletarian, or even the whole proletariat at the moment regards as its aim. It is a question of *what* the proletariat *is*, and what in accordance with this *being*, it *must* historically be compelled to do. Its aim and historical action is visibly and irrevocably foreshadowed in its own life situation . . . (Marx, 1845, p.37).

Marx and Engels were supremely confident of the revolutionary character and interests of the early proletariat. The *Communist Manifesto*, written in 1848, went so far as to declare that the 'fall' of the bourgeoisie and the victory of the proletariat were 'equally inevitable'. Their political writings on the Chartist campaign for universal suffrage in the 1840s and 1850s evinced a similar belief. As the working class constituted the majority of the population, and their interests lay in the abolition of capitalism, then universal suffrage would amount to political power for the working class and the enactment of its revolutionary abolition of capitalism (Engels, 1845, p.518; Engels, 1850, pp.298-9; Marx, 1852, pp.335-6).

The Early Analysis of Trade Unionism

What were the implications of this model of capitalist society for the analysis of trade unions? By bringing workers together in large factories, capitalist development itself helped to create combinations of workers, or trade unions. The accumulation of capital also deskilled and degraded work, reducing the worker to 'an appendage of the machine' (Marx and Engels, 1848, pp.490-1), and produced poverty amongst the working class, a poverty that was vividly documented by Engels in *The Condition of the Working Class in England*. Competition between workers would prevent trade unions from raising wages above a minimum subsistence level, and as instruments of economic improvement strikes were therefore useless (Engels, 1845, pp.505, 507-8, 510; Marx, 1849; 1853, p.169; see also Rowthorn, 1980).

It was precisely because unions were *not* economically effective that they would be forced to engage in political struggles against the wages system. In the meantime the spread of trade unions and the prosecution of strikes would prepare workers for the major confrontation that was to come: hence Engels' description of trade unions as 'schools of war' (Engels, 1845, p.512).

By the 1860s it had become clear to Marx and Engels that the actual trajectory of trade unionism was rather more complex than they had originally anticipated, and they offered a variety of explanations as to why the British working class and its trade unions appeared to have entered a period of political quiescence, marked by an accommodation between labour and capital and a disinterest in revolutionary political organisation (what Engels later referred to as 'forty-years of slumber': Engels, 1890, p.401).

The first line of attack, within the ambit of a 'simple economic determinism', was that economic crisis would drive workers and unions into revolutionary politics, but that during the intervening periods of growth little could be expected from trade unions. As Engels wrote in 1858, the British working class needed to be shaken up by 'a few thoroughly bad years' (Engels to Marx, 7 October 1858, in *MECW*, 40), a sentiment echoed some years previously by Marx himself (1855). But the absence of revolutionary political action and consciousness after the crises of 1857 and 1866-68 convinced Marx and Engels that life was more complicated.

Closer contact with trade unions during the economic growth of the 1860s, and deeper reflection on the development of British capitalism and its international empire, led them to elaborate a slightly more sophisticated version of the crisis argument, whilst preserving the idea of a close correspondence between economic situation and class consciousness. According to this argument, generally known as the labour aristocracy thesis, Britain had acquired such a dominant position amongst the capitalist nations that it had accumulated enormous wealth. Its rulers could therefore afford to make limited economic (and sometimes political) concessions to sections of the working class during periods of economic growth, particularly those organised in trade unions and employed in large factories (Engels, 1885; see also Engels, 1874; 1881; Engels to Sorge, 24 October 1891 in Marx and Engels, 1975; Draper, 1978). These sections of the working class therefore developed an interest in the preservation of capitalism, but sooner or later the inevitability of economic crisis would erode even their attachment to capitalism, by forcing a reduction in their wages. Through trade unions workers would then be compelled to challenge capital and in doing so would prepare the way for the final, political struggle between the two major social classes.

This is not to say that Marx and Engels were forerunners of syndicalism, the doctrine that the political sphere or level of society could be bypassed and that the working class required no independent political organisation other than trade unions. Even at the height of their revolutionary optimism about trade unions, in the 1840s, Marx and Engels always argued for political organisation to run alongside or in tandem with trade unions. In 1847 they founded the League of Communists, and the Manifesto, written just a year later, refers to 'this organisation of the proletarians into a class, and *consequently* into a political party . . . ' (my italics, *MECW*, 6, p.493). In 1864 Marx and Engels founded an organisation, the First International, to which trade unions and political parties were affiliated, but whose tasks were none the less separate from those of the unions. Within the framework of what I have called a simple economic determinism, Marx and Engels regarded trade unions and political parties as organisations working in parallel towards the same, revolutionary objectives. But the precise role of the working-class political party, and its precise relationship to the trade unions, was not adequately theorised before the 1860s. Until then (and occasionally afterwards) Marx and Engels concentrated on the development of the economy as the primary means by which workers and trade unions would be hurled into revolutionary politics. What became increasingly clear was that the relationship between economics and politics was far more complex and subtle than they had originally thought.

Complex Economic Determinism

Let us consider to begin with what evidence there is that Marx and Engels ever seriously moved away from the simple economic determinism sketched out earlier, before dealing with the reasons for this shift and its implications for their analysis of trade unionism. During the 'socialist revival' of the 1880s there began a controversy over the precise content of Marx's and Engels' historical materialism, with a number of Marxists placing considerable emphasis on the economic determination of social phenomena in a rather simple and mechanical fashion. In this context Engels wrote an important and much quoted letter in which he said:

> According to the materialist conception of history, the *ultimately* determining factor in history is the production and reproduction of real life. Neither Marx nor I have ever asserted more than this. Hence if somebody twists this into saying that the economic factor is the *only*

determining one, he transforms that proposition into a meaningless, abstract, absurd phrase. The economic situation is the basis, but the various elements of the superstructure . . . also exercise their influence upon the course of the historical struggles and in many cases determine their *form* in particular. There is an interaction of all these elements in which, amid all the endless host of accidents, . . . the economic movement is finally bound to assert itself (italics in original, Engels to Bloch, 21-22 September 1890, in Marx and Engels, 1975).

Notice that we are still firmly within the realm of economic determinism, or historical materialism, but by contrast with the earlier formulations of a simple correspondence between base and superstructure, a simple determination of the latter by the former, we are now dealing with economic determination of the superstructure only 'in the last instance' (the phrase comes from a letter written by Engels to Schmidt, 27 October 1890, in Marx and Engels, 1975). Not only do we have Engels' word for this, in his many letters on historical materialism written mostly in the last five years of his life (Engels to Schmidt, 27 Oct 1890; Engels to Mehring, 14 July 1893; Engels to Borgius, 25 Jan 1894: all in Marx and Engels 1975), we have the evidence of the *political writings* of Marx and Engels from 1848 onwards (see Hall, 1977b).

The revolutions of 1848 provided Marx and Engels with a major opportunity both to 'apply' and 'test' their theory of the relation between economics and politics, and the class content of politics and ideology. It was in the *18th Brumaire* and other texts that Marx and Engels began to work out and unravel the many complex connections between economics and politics, and the range of factors which intervened between them, and which made the economic level determinant only 'in the last instance'. It was in these texts that a range of *specifically* political concepts made their appearance—'alliances, blocs, constitutional forms, regimes, political representatives, political ideologies or "ideas", fractions, factions, etc.' (Hall, 1977a). The political and ideological 'levels' (to use Althusser's term, 1979a) have their own internal dynamics and contradictions which interact with the 'ultimately determining' properties of the economic base. Politics and ideology cannot simply be read off, or deduced from, economics; as levels in the social formation they consequently enjoy a degree of 'relative autonomy' from the economic base.

How then can we characterise the 'complex economic determinism' of Marx and Engels? The central point was that in order to explain a particular phenomenon, let us say the level of working-class consciousness, it was not sufficient to examine the state of the economy, the level of wages or the imminence of economic crisis. Working-class consciousness was *also* determined by specifically political and ideological factors, such as the presence, size, influence, and policies of working-class parties; the character of the political system; the policies of the ruling class; the types of alliance forged between political forces. The economy was determinant 'in the final analysis', but short of that point many other factors were important.

Nor could we assume that classes constituted in the economic base of society would necessarily correspond to political, class forces at another level in society. Between a class of wage-labourers in the economy and a politically organised and unified proletariat there existed a range of mediating factors—the divisions in the working class generated by the economy, skilled and unskilled, manual and non-manual; the sectional organisation of workers in trades; differences in employer strategies between trades; the role of the State: these and other factors rendered the emergence of a political proletariat *always* problematic, and indeed, in a strict sense, allowed for the possibility that at a given point in time the proletariat might be politically unorganised, despite its economic situation and its economic organisations such as trade unions. Or as Przeworski put it,' . . . political class struggle is a struggle *about* class before it is a struggle among classes' (1977, p.372).

Only within this framework can we make *any* sense of Engels' repeated statements of the late 1870s and early 1880s that England had 'no labour movement', that although England had the strongest trade unions anywhere in the world, the politics of the English workers were the politics of their employers. Invited by Eduard Bernstein to write a number of articles on the British labour movement for a Socialist newspaper published in Zurich, he turned down the invitation with the following words, written in 1879:

> For a number of years past the English working-class movement has been hopelessly describing a narrow circle of strikes for higher wages and shorter hours, not, however, as an expedient or means of propaganda and organisation, but as the ultimate goal. The Trades Unions even bar all political action on principle and in their charters, thus excluding all participation in any general activity of the working class as a class. . . . One can therefore speak of a labour movement only in so far as strikes take place here, which, whether they are won

or not, do not get the movement one step further. To inflate such strikes . . . into struggles of world importance . . . can, in my opinion, only do harm. No attempt should be made to conceal the fact that at present no real labour movement in the Continental sense exists here, and I therefore believe you will not lose much if for the time being you do not receive any reports on the doings of the Trades Unions here (Engels to Bernstein, 17 June 1879, in Marx and Engels, 1975. See also Engels to Kautsky, 12 September 1882; Engels to Bebel, 30 August 1883, all in Marx and Engels, 1975).

Marx and Engels developed an increasingly sophisticated account of working-class politics, moving away from the position that all economic struggles were *ipso facto* class struggles, and towards a position in which the very *existence* of class struggle was seen as problematic. In 1871, in a letter to Bolte, Marx wrote that

. . . the attempt by strikes, etc., in a particular factory or even in a particular trade to compel individual capitalists to reduce the working day is a purely economic movement. On the other hand the movement to force through an eight-hour, etc., *law* is a *political* movement, that is to say, a *class* movement, with the object of enforcing its interests in a general form, in a form possessing general, socially coercive force (Marx to Bolte, 23 November 1871 in Marx and Engels, 1975).

Here (and elsewhere) the terms 'class' and 'political' were used interchangeably, and *contrasted* with the economic struggles waged by trade unions (or workers) against their employers. Class struggle was now defined more precisely as struggle by the whole class directed against the State, a body whose significance now loomed large in the writings of Marx and Engels, especially after the Paris Commune, brutally suppressed in 1871.

The theory of working-class interests was also subjected to considerable refinement as Marx, in particular, shifted away from his early classical schema: capitalist development → equalisation of working-class conditions → class struggles → revolutionary class consciousness. The pages of *Capital* (1887) are filled with acute observations on the *contradictory* tendencies of capitalist development, simultaneously unifying and fragmenting sections of the working class, an economic process whose outcome is over-determined by the 'divide-and-rule' tactics of both employers and State (Hall, 1977a).

Complex Economic Determinism and Trade Unions

The shift from a simple to a complex economic determinism in the analysis of trade unions emerged most clearly in the explanations offered by Marx and Engels for the 'narrowness' of English trade unions, a subject on which they had complained frequently as far back as 1844. In their earlier writings the limited objectives of the unions had been considered unproblematic because sooner or later economic crises would erode whatever gains unions had made and would force them onto the path of revolution. But increasingly Marx and Engels came to view economic crisis as only a *necessary* but not a *sufficient* condition for the radicalisation of the working class and their trade unions. For between the state of the economy and the consciousness of workers there intervened a host of political and organisational factors, to which they paid ever more attention.

The Inaugural Address to the First International offered a complex explanation for the political quiescence of the British working class after 1848. According to Marx (1864) it had been demoralised by the defeats of fellow-workers on the continent, deprived of some of its best activists by their emigration, and its leaders had been unable to develop sustained political organisation, in the face of widespread rank-and-file apathy. Ten years later, after two elections fought under an extended suffrage, Engels commented critically on the continued success of the bourgeois parties, and stressed the debilitating effects on class consciousness of the continued alliance between the working class and the Liberals (Engels, 1874). He also noted the ways in which English manufacturers had come to terms with trade unions and learned to use collective bargaining to regulate wages to their own advantage (Engels, 1881: see also Engels, 1885; Engels to Sorge, 29 November 1886; Engels to Sorge, 7 December 1889; Engels to Sorge, 18 January 1893; Engels to Sorge, 10 November 1894: all in Marx and Engels, 1975).

Related to this last point was an important shift in Marx's and Engels' views on the economic effects of trade unions. By the 1860s they had moved away from the idea that wages were exclusively regulated by the relationship between the supply and demand for labour, and that trade unions were therefore economically useless. In his famous debate with Citizen Weston, Marx elaborated a number of economic conditions under which trade union struggles could raise wages above a subsistence minimum, though he also argued there was a definite upper limit beyond which wages could not be pushed (Marx, 1865; see also Mandel, 1971; Rowthorn, 1980). Even this limited effectiveness of unions helped to reconcile workers to life under capitalism, although Marx and Engels nevertheless continued to insist that the economic struggle of workers was an indispensable means of promoting class organisation and consciousness (Draper, 1978, Chap.14).

The First International and After

In principle, to grant a degree of relative autonomy to politics and ideology opened up a theoretical and political space within which it was possible to conceive of radically different types of trade unionism. It was their work in the First International which brought this point home most forcefully to Marx and Engels (Marx, 1974; see also Bambery, 1985).

Created in 1864, the International, under the guidance of Marx and Engels, devoted much of its time and resources to assisting trade union economic and political struggles throughout Europe. It was still common practice in Europe for employers faced with a strike to import blacklegs from as far afield as other countries, or simply to sit tight and starve their employees back to work. The International took action against both these tactics, encouraging their members throughout Europe to agitate against and obstruct blackleg labour, and to raise cash for beleaguered strikers. The third major area of activity was general agitation and propaganda, mostly condemning government actions (or lack of them) in particular, and the capitalist system in general, although the last-mentioned was hardly prominent in the affairs of the International. Asked to explain the 'restriction' of the International's work to 'narrow trade union issues' such as wages, hours of work, blacking, strikes, etc., Marx himself gave one reason, which was purely tactical. As Fernbach (1974) notes, the English trade union movement was, in 1864, easily the largest and most powerful in Europe. An International which did not include it was doomed from the start, and Marx therefore went out of his way to present his Inaugural Address in a manner that would meet with its acceptance, toning down the revolutionary phrases and fervour that were the hallmark of the *Communist Manifesto* whilst dwelling at length on the achievements of trade union economic struggle (Marx, 1864). But tactical considerations aside, Marx and Engels had, by this period, begun to register some of the specific strengths and weaknesses of trade unionism, and their period in the International was notable above all for the emphasis increasingly placed on the importance of a specifically political organisation *alongside* the trade unions. Indeed the more they came into contact with trade unionists and trade unionism through the International, the more they emphasised the need for a political party.

Now in one respect this was not a new departure. As early as 1847 Marx and Engels had after all founded the League of Communists, which was certainly not a trade union! But although the *idea* of a party was present from the early writings, its role in revolutionary struggle, and in particular its relation to trade unions, was very hazy. In 1871 the crushing of the Paris Commune led Marx and Engels not only to revise the *Communist Manifesto*'s position on the State, but also to place renewed emphasis on the countervailing power of the working-class political party. In a resolution to the 1871 London Congress of the International they declared that '. . . this constitution of the working class into a political party is indispensable in order to ensure the triumph of the social revolution and its ultimate end—the abolition of classes' (Marx and Engels, 1871, p.270). But if the party was 'indispensable', what was the role of the union? The resolution continued:

> The combination of forces [i.e. the trade unions] which the working class has already effected by its economic struggles ought at the same time to serve as a lever for its struggles against the political power of landlords and capitalists (Marx and Engels, 1871, p.270).

Here Marx and Engels departed from the 1840s model of a simple parallelism between party and union, each acting directly as a revolutionary organisation, and shifted to a model of complementarity. The union exercised its power against capital at the point of production, but the seizure of power, and the overthrow of capitalism, required a separate organisation, operating on the political terrain and directly confronting the State. Each form of action was to complement the other, and in this sense they were 'indissolubly united'.

We have already said, however, that the theoretical model of complex economic determinism permitted, in principle, a variety of trade union politics and ideology, both revolutionary and non-revolutionary, since not all unions will conform in their outlook to the revolutionary interests of the proletariat. Non-revolutionary trade unionism was increasingly explored by Engels from the late 1870s onwards as he observed the gradual, peaceful evolution and consolidation of the English trade unions. From 1879 he delivered a series of sharp and caustic judgements on the English trade unions in his private correspondence, repeatedly informing anyone who asked that England had no labour movement at all, and that the politics of the working class were bourgeois politics. Despite the proliferation of socialist propaganda and socialist societies in the 1880s the political scene remained under the hegemony of the two bourgeois parties, the Whigs (or Liberals) and the Tories. In an important article in the *Labour Standard* in 1881 he noted that trade union economic struggle was confined to dealing only with the effects of the wages system, but lacking any political vision it was repeatedly subject to successful counterattacks by the employers during economic recessions (Engels, 1881; see also Marx, 1865). This lack of political vision in turn was a function of workers being organised by *trade* rather than by a *class* political organisation. In 1886 Engels remarked that 'the first great step of importance for every country newly entering the movement is always the constitution of the workers as an independent political party, no matter how, so long as it is a distinct workers' party' (Engels to Sorge, 29 November 1886, in Marx and Engels, 1975) and this was a theme that echoed through his correspondence until his death (Engels to Kautsky, 4 September 1892; Engels to Sorge, 10 November 1894: in Marx and Engels, 1975).

Its corollary, however, was a profound and growing awareness of the limitations of trade union organisation and action. In 1894 he observed that the socialist and trade union leader John Burns '. . . acts as if he despaired of the political organisation of the workers and set his hopes *solely* on the trade unions' (my italics: Engels to Sorge, 10 November 1894, in Marx and Engels, 1975). A few months later he wrote that

> The socialist instinct is getting stronger and stronger among the *masses*, but as soon as it is a question of translating the instinctive impulses into clear demands and ideas people at once begin to disagree. Some go to the Social-Democratic Federation, others to the Independent Labour Party, still others go *no further than the trade union organisation* etc., etc. (my italics: Engels to Schluter, 1 January 1895, in Marx and Engels, 1975).

In these later writing Engels increasingly moved towards a model of party-union relations which was *antagonistic*, rather than simply *complementary*. In other words he stressed the limitations of trade union organisation and action, their limited effects on living standards and on class consciousness, and the over-riding necessity for a political party to transcend these limitations and lead the struggle for revolution. This is Leninism in all but name—the key components of Lenin's analysis of trade unionism in *What is to be done?* are all present in Engels' later writings.

Some Problems

Despite the reservations of the later Engels, it has to be said that neither he nor Marx ever abandoned their belief in the inevitability of socialism, and by implication in the emergence of a proletariat organised in trade unions and a revolutionary political party. Periodic economic crises coupled with the existence of an independent working-class party would provide workers with both the incentive and the resources to challenge capitalism root and branch. 'In the last analysis [Marx and Engels] did not believe that reformism could take serious and systematic root in the working class' (Fernbach, 1974, p.64).

It was the 'revisionist' (sic) Eduard Bernstein (1909) who noted certain changes in world capitalism since the 1840s and who posed the most awkward and telling questions for this vision of the revolutionary assault by the proletariat. To begin with, he argued, it was simply not true that living standards were declining—despite occasional falls during economic crises, they had risen considerably since the 1840s. Furthermore, reformist politics and trade union economic struggle had played a considerable part in curbing the worst excesses of capitalism. And nor was it the case that the crises of capitalism were becoming more severe, as Marx had predicted. It was these facts, said Bernstein, which explained why the *normal* path taken by the working class under capitalism was the development of trade union organisation and reformist political parties, for experience taught that these organisations were effective. The creation of revolutionary organisations and revolutionary consciousness was less common, more difficult, and absolutely *not* inevitable. The revisionist challenge in the 1890s, mounted by Bernstein and others, went to the Achilles heel of contemporary Marxism in all its forms. If the proletariat *could* from time to time wrest concessions out of capitalism despite occasional falls in living standards, why should they ever want to overthrow the system? In other words under what conditions would revolutionary class consciousness develop and revolutionary political action occur?

Conclusions

Armed with the simple economic determinism of their early writings, Marx and Engels confidently anticipated the full flowering of revolutionary trade unionism from the early combinations of workers against capital, and the economic struggles in which they engaged. This same determinism also gave them an initial purchase on the *failure* of trade union development in Britain to follow the predicted path, in the form of the theory of the labour aristocracy. But throughout their lives Marx and Engels gradually moved towards the view that the emergence of non-revolutionary trade unionism and reformist politics was not an abnormal development, a by-product of British imperialism and therefore unique to British society, but a powerful form of trade unionism and politics created and sustained by a variety of political as well as economic factors.

The major achievement of Marx and Engels was to have argued forcefully that the earliest proletarian organisations were potentially revolutionary organisations, and in that respect they kept alive their (and others') socialist faith when the actual development of trade unions in the Victorian era provided socialists with little or no encouragement. It was to Engels' credit in particular (rather than Marx's) that he began to explore the organisational and political determinants of non-revolutionary trade unionism in a way which almost wholly anticipated Lenin.

Yet in true dialectical fashion, this emerging strength of Marx and Engels, their willingness to explore actual trade unionism and its organisations, served to expose their critical weakness. For if the development of the capitalist economy could not be relied on to 'deliver' a revolutionary, organised proletariat, and if, indeed, non-revolutionary trade unionism was 'over-determined' by a variety of political and ideological, as well as economic factors, under what conditions, if any, would trade unions become revolutionary organisations and their members develop revolutionary class consciousness? To this question, Marx and Engels gave no satisfactory answer.

2

Lenin, Luxemburg, Trotsky: the Limits of Trade Unionism and the Problem of Class Consciousness

The last chapter established the fact that by the 1890s Engels had arrived at a quite complex theory of trade unionism. He stressed the many obstacles that lay in the path of revolutionary working-class organisation and action, and placed overwhelming emphasis on the necessity of a working-class political party to push unions in a radical direction. Yet it was Lenin who sharply crystallised these scattered ideas into a clear and precise theory of trade unionism, and whose name is often associated with Marxist ideas about trade unions (e.g. Anderson, 1967). Consequently this chapter begins with a brief exposition of the context within which Lenin worked and an outline of his general political theory, before proceeding to a more detailed analysis of his ideas on trade unions. But the importance of Lenin's ideas should not detract from the claims of two of his Marxist contemporaries, Rosa Luxemburg and Leon Trotsky, both of whom remain extremely influential to the present day. Though they were influenced by Lenin in their own time, they advanced rather different propositions and in certain respects, as we shall see, went beyond the framework laid down by Lenin.

Lenin and Politics

Lenin was effective leader for twenty years of the Bolshevik Party, prime instigator and organiser of the 1917 Revolution, founder of the Third Communist International (Comintern) and head of the world's first socialist state for some five years. Interspersed and deeply connected with his political activity went a series of major theoretical contributions: on the revolutionary party, on class consciousness, on the State and on imperialism—writings which retain their clarity and pertinence even today. One of Lenin's strengths lay in his capacity to combine rigour and orthodoxy in Marxist revolutionary theory with tactical and strategic flexibility in politics, in what Lukacs (1970) once so aptly called 'revolutionary real-politik'. What is essential for understanding Lenin's general theory and practice, and his specific analyses of trade unionism, is the political and ideological context within which he worked, a context in which the German Social Democratic party loomed large.

By 1910 the German party was the largest socialist party in the world, with 110 parliamentary deputies, 720,000 members, and over 70 newspapers and periodicals (Geary, 1981, p.91). Intellectually it was the centre of the world socialist movement, counting among its ranks the most prestigious of the contemporary Marxists—Kautsky, Liebknecht, Bebel, Bernstein, Luxemburg, Mehring and Hilferding to name only a few. Much of Lenin's writing was, implicitly or explicitly, directed against the Marxism of the Second International and its most powerful member, the German party. At that time (c.1900), under the theoretical influence of Karl Kautsky, the German Social Democratic Party adhered to a particularly mechanical interpretation of historical materialism, an interpretation closely akin to what I have called simple economic determinism (see Salvadori, 1979; Kautsky, 1983). The development of the capitalist economy was analysed as a growing and sharpening contradiction between the forces and relations of production, resulting in ever more severe crises. Yet this same process also developed a growing, more powerful and more confident proletariat through its expansion of commodity production in industry, and its destruction of the peasantry and the 'middle layers' of employment, who slumped into the proletariat. Guided by the Party, the unique depository of a scientific understanding of the objective laws of history, the proletariat prepared itself for the ultimate and decisive struggle against the bourgeoisie. But *meanwhile*, it bided its time, consolidating its strength and influence and refusing to be drawn into premature and adventurist actions that would only dissipate its forces. Inscribed in the Marxism of the Second International, then, was a simple economic determinism, which asserted a necessary correspondence between economics, politics and ideology, and which foresaw socialism as inevitable, guaranteed by the laws of history.

In the previous chapter we saw that Marx and Engels had begun to dismantle this model of capitalist society in general, and of the working class and its organisations in particular. Their later writings were characterised by an attempt to theorise the specific and peculiar determinants of politics and ideology, and of the revolutionary process. This movement away from simple economic determinism was both continued and yet transformed by Lenin. In the words of Laclau and Mouffe,

> Leninism represents a critical point in the disintegration of the economistic model and in the move towards a new conception of Marxism centred on the primacy of the political. Lenin no longer conceives of the revolutionary rupture as a necessary and predetermined point in the unfolding of a single contradiction, but as a *specific critical conjuncture* dominated by a displacement in the relation of forces between classes (1981, p.18).

For Lenin the capitalist system in general was 'ready' for revolution, and his political practice was, in Lukacs' (1970) words, dominated by the 'actuality of revolution' (see also Harding, 1983). But it was precisely because Lenin recognised that there was no *necessary* correspondence between economics, politics and ideology, no simple growth of revolutionary class consciousness, that he took political and ideological struggle so seriously. It was necessary to combat 'deviations' from Marxism because such ideas *did* have real and dramatic effects, and the laws of history could not be relied upon to dissolve them and promote in their place revolutionary ideology and consciousness. Revolutionary class consciousness had to be created and reproduced, day in, day out, by ceaseless struggle *for* Marxism and against all shades of non-Marxist opinion in the working-class movement. This unrelenting struggle against non- and anti-Marxist ideas runs like a red thread through Lenin's life as he sought to demarcate revolutionary from reformist ideology, and it provides further proof (if it were needed) of Lenin's belief in the relative autonomy of politics and ideology from the economic infrastructure of society. Indeed, without such a model of society, Lenin's unremitting political and ideological struggles become quite incomprehensible. The aim of these struggles was to forge a revolutionary consciousness in the advanced ranks of the proletariat, organised in and by the revolutionary party. It was this objective which informed Lenin's work on trade union organisation and trade union action.

Lenin's Analyses of Trade Unionism

What is to be done? (1902) is Lenin's key text on trade unions, though by no means his only one, and it has given rise to a considerable amount of controversy and misunderstanding. For some writers the text is simple and clear: it argues that revolutionary class consciousness does not, and cannot, develop out of the spontaneous economic struggles of trade unions, but must be brought to the working class from outside the sphere of production relations, by intellectuals (who may themselves be workers) (Anderson, 1967; Zagladin et al., 1981). Hence the idea that Lenin was above all a theorist who stressed the 'inevitable limitations' of trade unionism. Some writers have gone even further, and asserted that Lenin simply 'had no use' for trade unions at all, as evinced in his behaviour towards them after the Revolution (Crouch, 1982, p.31; Hammond, 1957). Lenin did in fact defend the necessity for independent trade unions to protect workers against abuse and exploitation (see Lenin, 1920b), and opposed those who saw no role for trade unions in a socialist society. Although contemporary Soviet trade unions have few collective bargaining rights, they are extensively involved in individual grievance handling and in the administration of a wide range of welfare benefits and provisions. Others have argued that there is a contradiction between the tough criticisms of trade unions in *What is to be done?* and the enthusiastic pro-trade union, pro-strike sentiments to be found in some of Lenin's other writings (Hyman, 1971, pp.41-2; Cliff and Gluckstein, 1986, pp.25-6).

I want to argue that Lenin did *not* believe in the inevitable limitations of trade unionism *in general*; that there *are* contradictions within and between his writings; and that his texts are neither simple nor clear. But these 'contradictions' in Lenin are not *simply* inconsistencies—they arose in part because, in different contexts, Lenin was tackling different questions.

What is to be done? was produced, as Lenin himself later remarked, in a specific context, with a specific purpose. It was written for the Second Congress of the Russian Social Democratic Labour Party (RSDLP) in 1902 as an attack on the theoretical and political tendency known as economism. In all essential respects the economists were simple economic determinists who believed that trade union economic struggle would of itself develop revolutionary class consciousness, with a little educational assistance from the revolutionary party. Lenin's reply to this thesis was forceful and direct:

> The history of all countries shows that the working class, exclusively by its own effort, is able to develop only trade union consciousness, i.e. the conviction that it is necessary to combine in unions, fight the employers, and strive to compel the government to pass necessary labour legislation, etc. . . . The theory of socialism, however, grew out of the philosophic, historical, and economic theories elaborated by educated representatives of the propertied class, by intellectuals (Lenin, 1902, p.375).

In one respect this formulation is similar to those of the later Engels, who had observed the growth of political reformism and of trade unionist politics and consciousness in a number of countries from the 1840s to the 1890s. Yet still he endeavoured to 'explain away' these departures from the classical Marxist schema of the *Communist Manifesto*, by a variety of *specific* factors— composition of the working class, role of the State, nature of political representation. etc. Lenin *completely* overturned the classical arguments of Marx and Engels, describing as absolutely normal what they held to be exceptional, and vica versa. In Lenin's analysis, trade union consciousness was not an aberration from the normal path of revolutionary development—it *was* the normal path taken 'in all countries' by the working class.

But if trade union struggle and organisation did not embody and promote socialist ideology, to what type of ideology did they correspond? Lenin's answer was stark and simple: since all ideology was the worldview of a social class that expressed its fundamental economic and political interests; since in capitalism there were only two major social classes, proletariat and bourgeoisie; and since the ideology of the proletariat was revolutionary socialism (Marxism); *then* it followed that trade union ideology and consciousness departing from Marxism '. . . means the ideological enslavement of the workers by the bourgeoisie' (Lenin, 1902, p.384). Explaining why bourgeois ideology dominated trade unionism, Lenin advanced three reasons: it was older, it was more developed as a set of ideas, and it had vastly more resources available for its diffusion than its socialist rivals.

Did these arguments imply that the role of trade unions in revolutionary class struggle and the development of class consciousness was therefore minimal or limited? The answer, even from Lenin's own texts, is no. To begin with, the domination of trade unions by bourgeois ideology was not an *inevitable*, but a purely *contingent* feature of trade unions under capitalism, since it could be challenged by the revolutionary party. In a letter written just a few years later to the secretary of the Odessa Party Committee, Lenin made it clear that his strictures entailed no thesis of inevitable limits on *all* forms of trade unionism. Criticising a suggestion in the Committee's resolution that all trade unions were 'narrow' in their outlook, he asked:

> What about Social-Democratic trade unions which are linked with the political organisation of the proletariat? The crux of the matter is not that trade unions are narrow, but that this one aspect . . . should be bound up with others (Lenin to Gusev, 13 October 1905, in Lenin (1970).

This theme of party-union relations informed Lenin's political struggles at the time, preoccupied as he was with the growing movement, particularly in Germany, to separate trade unions from political parties under the guise of trade union neutrality. Lenin argued strongly for Social-Democratic 'influence', even control, in the trade unions, thereby indicating his belief in the possibility of a revolutionary trade unionism as distinct from a non-revolutionary or bourgeois trade unionism (see Lenin, 1905, 1906, 1907a, 1908).

It is also vital to appreciate the *purpose* of *What is to be done?* Like much of Lenin's writing, it was directed *against* a theoretical-political current, in order to *demarcate* revolutionary from reformist politics, and above all to assert the over-riding necessity for a vanguard party of professional revolutionaries. In *this* context, Lenin later observed, *What is to be done?* was '. . . a controversial correction of Economist distortions and it would be wrong to regard the pamphlet in any other light' (1907b). It was designed to map out the terrain on which revolutionaries had to operate, to distinguish the peaks of revolutionary ideology and consciousness from the troughs of reformism and trade unionism. What it was *not* designed to do was to pose and try to answer the question of *how* revolutionaries might traverse this terrain with the proletariat. In other words, it was not designed to trace the dynamics of class consciousness. In distinguishing revolutionary and reformist politics Lenin went to great lengths to emphasise the *differences* between trade unionist politics and Marxist or revolutionary politics, going so far as to declare that 'trade unionist politics of the working class is precisely bourgeois politics of the working class' (Lenin, 1902, p.426). What Lenin meant by this

sharp formulation was *not* that trade unions were traitorous
organisations which failed to promote any of the proletariat's
interests, but that in pursuing the economic struggle and parliamentary reform they were engaging in a type of politics that
was wholly compatible with bourgeois rule. Trade union politics
was working-class politics, and *did* promote a form of class
consciousness, but it was not revolutionary politics and did not
promote revolutionary class consciousness.

The dynamics of class consciousness

But if there *was* such a sharp divide, a chasm, between the two
types of politics and consciousness, how did workers pass from
one to the other, from reformism to revolution? In other words,
what was Lenin's theory of the dynamics of class consciousness?
Lenin frequently emphasised the role of the Party in the formation of worker-intellectuals, and the waging of ideological struggle against the bourgeoisie. But Lenin was not a product of the
Enlightenment, and did not believe that knowledge could be
brought to workers for their passive absorption. Workers became
receptive to Party propaganda under certain conditions, notably
during economic struggles. And whilst Lenin attacked the Economists for their belief that trade union struggle was *sufficient* for
the formation of revolutionary class consciousness, he also repeatedly emphasised, even in *What is to be done?*, that it was
nonetheless *necessary*. When Lenin discussed the dynamics of class
consciousness he therefore emphasised the points of contact, or
similarity, between trade union economic struggle and revolutionary struggle. These points of contact were mentioned even in
What is to be done?, which referred to 'the sparks of political
consciousness' generated by economic struggles (Lenin, 1902,
p.416). In other texts Lenin went much further, giving rise to
some of his most misinterpreted phrases:

> This struggle [for higher wages, etc.] develops the workers' political
> consciousness . . . [and] spurs the workers on to think of State,
> political questions, questions of how the Russian State is
> governed . . . (1896, p.115).

> Every strike brings thoughts of Socialism very forcibly to the worker's
> mind . . . (1899, p.315).

> The working class is instinctively, spontaneously Social-
> Democratic . . . (1905, p.32).

At every step the workers come face to face with their main ememy—the capitalist class. In combat with this enemy, the worker becomes a socialist . . . (1910, p.302).

Some of these formulations were undoubtedly influenced by current events, notably the strike wave of 1896-97 and the revolution of 1905, but they did not in themselves reveal a major inconsistency in Lenin's thought. Every one of these phrases has been taken out of context, and the texts in which they belong are replete with arguments which also point to the limitations of trade union economic struggle as well as their political potential (Lenin, 1896, p.112; 1899, p.319; 1905, p.32. Contrast Cliff, 1975a, and Hyman 1971, pp.40-3). Yet this potential was invariably to be realised through the actions of the political party, whose job it was to 'develop' class consciousness, conduct and lead political class struggle against the State, and transform 'spontaneity' into consciousness (Lenin, 1920c).

On the dynamics of class consciousness Lenin operated within a broad and uncharted territory, marked at one extreme by a simple economic determinist model of the inevitable growth of revolutionary consciousness through trade union struggle, and at the other by the vague presentiment that such struggle had *a* role to play, in conjunction with other factors. But what were these other factors, or conditions? Lenin never clearly formulated a theory on this question, and lacking such a theory his ideas shifted about within a large and open territory, veering sometimes towards a 'spontaneist' praise of economic struggle, sometimes towards a harder 'limitations-of-trade-unionism' view.

Equally unsatisfactory was Lenin's analysis of 'the labour aristocracy', the most well-paid and secure strata of the proletariat. In *Imperialism and the Split in Socialism*, Lenin (1916) argued that there was an intimate connection between relative economic privilege for a section of the proletariat, and that group's open support for opportunist and chauvinist politics, viz. support for the Imperialist war (see also Lenin, 1912, 1913, 1915, 1920a). Just three months later Lenin was warmly praising the leading role played in the 1905 Russian revolution by the metalworkers, who were not only 'the best paid' but also 'the most class-conscious' of the Russian proletariat (Lenin, 1917a). Economic privilege, apparently, was associated with reactionary politics . . . *and* with revolutionary politics (cf. Polan, 1984, pp.67-70, 166-73). Now to argue that a worker's economic situation has contradictory implications for class consciousness is in itself a

perfectly reasonable and thoroughly Marxist proposition, so far
as it goes. But under what conditions do well-paid workers play a
reactionary role, and under what conditions a progressive role?
On this question Lenin was unclear. What does seem clear is that
like Marx and Engels before him, and like his contemporaries
Trotsky and Luxemburg, Lenin did not believe in the long-run
stabilisation and growth of capitalism, and with it the living
standards of the workers. In the short term, economic struggle by
trade unions could raise living standards, but it did so only
against a backcloth of long-term stagnation and decline of
capitalism in the imperialist era. It was this process of decline
and its effects on workers' living standards that would ultimately
push them into support for socialism.

So how can we summarise Lenin's contribution to the theory of
trade unionism? His principal achievement was to point out that
trade union action and organisation rarely posed any challenge to
the capitalist system of production. Nor did such action develop
amongst workers a revolutionary class consciousness that would
prepare them for the ultimate battle to seize State power. For
these tasks a revolutionary political party was necessary to
educate workers and instil in them a realisation of their true
interests. But this line of argument led to the principal weakness
of Lenin's view which was his inability to explain under what
circumstances and in what types of action revolutionary class
consciousness would be developed. That task was performed far
more ably and perceptively by one of Lenin's contemporaries, the
Polish Marxist, Rosa Luxemburg.

Rosa Luxemburg: the Mass Strike and the Dynamics of Class Consciousness

Rosa Luxemburg, an influential member of the German Social
Democratic Party (SPD) and a founder member of the Communist Party of Germany, is perhaps best known for her enthusiastic
support for the 'spontaneous mass strike' and her strictures
against democratic centralism and one-party rule in the Soviet
Union (Luxemburg, 1904, 1918). In the wake of the 1984-5
miners' strike there has been a certain revival of British interest in
her work (Cliff, 1985; Coates and Topham, 1986; Cliff and
Gluckstein, 1986), and a film has recently been made of her life.
Despite her direct criticisms of Lenin and 'Leninism', Luxemburg did in fact have much in common with her Russian fellow

revolutionary, not least a penchant for polemic. It was Luxemburg who wrote the sharpest attacks on Eduard Bernstein at the height of the 'revisionist controversy' at the turn of the century (Luxemburg, 1900), and who, ten years later, pronounced the Second International to be dead because of its failure to oppose World War One. A passionate enemy of 'deviations' from orthodox Marxism, she never wavered in her belief in the need for a revolutionary party. Like Lenin she was scathing about the 'parliamentary road to socialism' and all forms of reformism. Like Lenin she was a sharp critic of trade union 'bureaucracy', i.e. the paid and unpaid leaderships of the trade union movement, for their concern with organisational survival, industrial peace, short-term reforms, and their personal careers (1906). She also shared his view that without the influence of a revolutionary party, trade unions could make only a limited impact on workers' conditions under capitalism:

> The scope of trade unions is limited essentially to a struggle for an increase of wages and the reduction of labour time, that is to say, to efforts at regulating capitalist exploitation. . . . But labour unions can in no way influence the process of production itself.

> Trade unions are nothing more than the organised *defence* of labour power against the attack of profit. They express the resistance offered by the working class to the oppression of capitalist economy (1900, pp.50, 71).

Indeed, she was much sharper than Lenin in her attacks on trade union leadership, living as she did in a country with the largest trade union apparatus outside England. In the more repressive climate of Russia, where most trade unions were illegal, the problem of trade union bureaucracy was much less pressing. But it was in her theory of the dynamics of class consciousness and the role of economic struggle that Luxemburg differed from Lenin, and surpassed him. Sharing Lenin's view that the mass strike was one of the most effective means of bringing *masses* into struggle and raising their political consciousness, Luxemburg attempted to theorise the *mechanisms* which brought about changes in consciousness.

As Bonner (1981) correctly noted, 'Rosa Luxemburg placed the "subjective moment" of class consciousness at the very centre of revolutionary action, and it only makes sense that her thought should be situated within this tendency' (p.98).

The mass strike

The starting point in Luxemburg's argument actually appears towards the end of her pamphlet *The Mass Strike* (1906), where she analysed the means by which the bourgeoisie continued to rule in capitalist societies:

> The separation of the political and the economic struggle and the independence of each is nothing but an artificial product of the parliamentary period, even if historically determined. On the one hand, in the peaceful 'normal' course of bourgeois society, the economic struggle is split into a multitude of individual struggles in every undertaking and dissolved in every branch of production. On the other hand the political struggle is not directed by the masses themselves in a direct action, but in correspondence with the form of the bourgeois state, in a representative fashion, by the presence of legislative representation (1906, pp.207-8).

The separation of economics and politics had the effect of 'depoliticising' trade union struggles and of channelling trade union politics into the safe conduit of parliament. The significance of 'the mass strike' was that it shattered this distinction between economics and politics in one of two ways. Either the mass strike, a weapon of the economic organs (trade unions) of the working class, was used for directly political purposes, as in the Belgian strikes of the 1890s for the franchise; or economic struggles spearheaded by mass strikes *acquired* a political character, a process carefully analysed by Luxemburg.

But exactly what did Luxemburg mean by a 'mass strike', and how did the idea relate to the apparently similar concepts of 'general strike' and 'strike waves'? Luxemburg declined to offer a precise definition of the mass strike and indeed in her pamphlet of the same title she refers to at least one particular strike—by St Petersburg textile workers in 1896-7—as both a general strike *and* a mass strike (Luxemburg, 1906, pp.164, 184). The nearest she came to a definition was the enigmatic phrase *'the method of motion of the proletarian mass*, the phenomenal form of the proletarian struggle in the revolution' (1906, p.182). The mass strike, she also wrote, was a 'product of the revolution' (1906, p.187). What Luxemburg meant was that a general strike or strike wave constituted a mass strike (a revolutionary phenomenon) only during periods of revolutionary struggle, but that outside of such periods general strikes, for instance, would tend to assume a quite different and more limited character (cf. Nettl, 1969, p.154).

Figure 2.1   Strikes and class consciousness: Luxemburg's model

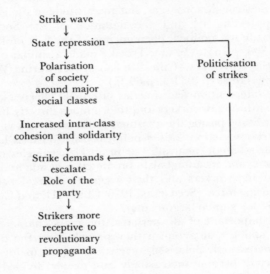

How did Luxemburg arrive at these conclusions? Minutely examining the strikes in Russia from the 1890s until 1903, she noted that the vast majority *began* as strikes over economic issues, mostly wages and the length of the working day, but although

> the earlier mass and general strikes orginated from individual coalescing wage struggles . . . , *in the general temper of the revolutionary situation, and under the influence of the Social Democratic agitation,* [they] rapidly became political demonstrations (Luxemburg, 1906, p.170: italics added).

The effect of the situation was crucial—mass strikes did not invariably pass over into political strikes, but only in 'revolutionary situations', for it was in these situations that

> the proletarian is transformed from a provident pater familias demanding support, into a 'revolutionary romanticist', for whom even the highest good, life itself, to say nothing of material well-being, possesses but little in comparison with the ideals of the struggle (Luxemburg, 1906, p.189).

The nature of the situation also defined the actions of the State. The St Petersburg general strike of 1896 'was outwardly a mere economic struggle for wages, but the attitude of the government [in suppressing it] and the agitation of the Social democracy made it a political phenomenon of the first rank' (Luxemburg, 1906, p.165). (In fact Trotsky made a similar observation about the repression of the Russian strikes during World War One: see Trotsky, 1932-3, p.60 ff.).

State intervention had a series of crucial effects (see Fig. 2.1 above): it brought workers and their unions directly into conflict with the State, posing the question (in Luxemburg's view) of who was to rule society; it raised political consciousness by showing the State was not 'neutral', but in all key struggles backed the employers; and its antagonism promoted cohesion and solidarity amongst the workers and their supporters threatened with its over-bearing force. (See Geras, 1976, Chap. III; and Geras, 1987, pp.59-62 for similar arguments).

Most important of all, perhaps, the mass character of these strikes, and the antagonism they provoked on the part of the State, increasingly polarised society around the major protagonists. Society became increasingly and deeply divided into pro- and anti-strikers; into those who backed labour and its demands, and those who supported capital and the capitalist state. In other words politics and political struggle came to be dominated temporarily but overwhelmingly by the reality of *class*. In this situation sectional outlooks by groups of workers were likely to be transcended, and submerged in a class-wide identity (cf. Cliff, 1985, p.6). This rapid escalation of class identity could also help to prevent individual sections of workers returning to work as their own demands were settled. Class loyalty would help to keep some workers out on strike in solidarity with their fellows. More importantly, the propaganda and agitation of the revolutionary party would serve to raise workers' expectations, heighten their sense of grievance still further, and thereby escalate strike demands. Strikes which began over wage issues would, in this context, rapidly develop into political struggles for a wide range of reforms as class consciousness rose in the course of struggle.

An appraisal

By far the most important strength of Luxemburg's analysis was that she distinguished conditions under which trade union economic struggle could be contained by capitalism from conditions under which it could not. In the former, a strike by a group of workers sparked off concessions and/or retaliation by their employers; in the latter it sparked off similar strikes by other groups, in a chain reaction, constituting a mass, general strike. The scale of the actions and the intervention of the State dramatically altered the psychology of workers, and facilitated the transition from purely economic to political demands, under the guidance of a revolutionary party. For Luxemburg, such revolutionary situations were inevitable because of the growing contradictions of capitalism and the inability of the ruling class to salvage their own system (Luxemburg, 1906c, p.83; *pace* Cliff, 1983).

In retrospect we can see that Luxemburg vastly underestimated the capacity of capitalism to survive—not least by virtue of the support it receives from the working class. She also, characteristically, conflated the State and government: State intervention in disputes was thought to call into question the neutrality of the State itself, but did it? Perhaps in Tsarist Russia, with its virtually non-existent parliamentary democracy, or in Germany with its strong State, this scenario was plausible. But eighty years on, with the development of parliamentary democracy and universal suffrage, State intervention in disputes is likely to call into question the authority of the particular government in parliament, rather than the *whole* of the State apparatus, and to lead to calls for a change of government rather than the overthrow of the State.

Luxemburg also tended to conflate two instances or types of class consciousness. In a mass strike, threatened with State intervention, workers might well feel an intense class identification with fellow workers and against the employer-State axis. But a feeling of solidarity and identity with fellow workers in struggle is not at all the same as the revolutionary conviction that the working class must act decisively to end the rule of the employers and their State. A sense of shared class interests (what Gramsci called corporate consciousness) is not the same as a desire to rule society in line with those interests (hegemonic consciousness), and by conflating these two levels of consciousness, Luxemburg may have overestimated the revolutionary potential of the mass strike, as Kautsky (1983, Chap.4) pointed out. A similar tendency is evident in Cliff (1985), who endeavours to distinguish between mass strikes on the grounds of whether they are bureaucratically led from above or democratically led from below by the rank and file. In the latter case, according to Cliff, who cites the

1972 miners' strike, we come close to Luxemburg's model of the revolutionary mass strike. Although it is true that Luxemburg was violently opposed to 'the trade union bureaucracy', it was the political and economic situation, not the role of bureaucracy, which for her was the *primary* determinant of the revolutionary character of mass strikes.

Nevertheless, Luxemburg's discussion of the dynamics of class consciousness, for all its shortcomings, is undoubtedly one of the best there is in the literature of classical Marxism. It displays above all an enormous sensitivity to the incredible volatility of class conflict and class consciousness and it stands as a cautionary warning to those who are inclined to make a fetish of the distinction between economic and political struggles. The contemporary relevance of Luxemburg's analyses will therefore be pursued in Chapter 5, when we look at the impact of strikes on class consciousness.

Trotsky: Trade Unions in the Epoch of Imperialist Decay

In common with the other classical Marxists, Trotsky actually wrote comparatively little on trade unions, and much of what he did write, particularly in the 1930s, was ephemeral commentary on particular disputes involving his followers. Despite the paucity of his writings, Trotsky's ideas on trade unionism have, directly or indirectly, exerted an enormous influence in the trade unions and elsewhere, and his violent antagonism to 'the trade union bureaucracy' continues to provide a staple, if repetitive, diet of rank-and-file criticism of 'leadership betrayals' and 'sell-outs' (cf. Anderson, 1976; Hallas, 1979). More significantly, some of his ideas about the conduct of militant trade union actions and the role of the General Strike weapon have percolated into the left wing of the Labour Party, and into the leadership of unions such as the National Union of Mineworkers. Finally Trotsky's ideas (in various forms) have provided the major focus of the left-wing challenge to Labourism and the dominant traditions of West European Communism, particularly since 1968. Consequently they merit careful and extensive exposition and analysis.

Political economy and politics

On many general political issues—the nature of imperialism, the capitalist state, the necessity for a revolutionary party, the roots and effects of reformism—Trotsky was basically in agreement with Lenin, certainly from about 1914 onwards. Yet if we look closely at Trotsky's political theory we can see that an understanding of imperialism and its implications loomed much larger than in Lenin's work. Indeed Trotsky attempted to derive, sometimes to *deduce*, specific policies and positions more or less directly from his analysis of 'the imperialist epoch'. The 'epoch', starting around the turn of the century, was always defined by Trotsky as the 'epoch of wars and revolutions'—revolution was directly on the agenda and reformism was vanishing as its material base eroded (see for instance Trotsky, 1922). Trotsky took the idea of 'the epoch of wars and revolution' so seriously that his political writings, especially from the 1920s, were increasingly suffused by a catastrophist vision of imminent capitalist collapse or imminent socialist revolution (Hodgson, 1975). How, in detail, did he conduct his analysis? And what were its implications for trade unionism?

For Trotsky, society's productive forces had then reached the highest level of development consistent with the structure of nation states: henceforth systematic development of these forces would be possible only internationally, through cooperation between socialist states. There might be occasional and short-lived economic booms but these would be superimposed on a general downward trend of decline. Under these conditions the only way for capitalism to prolong itself was through wholesale assaults on the living standards of the working class, to raise the rate of exploitation and increase profitability. Not only living standards, but the working class organisations which defended them—trade unions and political parties—had also to be attacked and their powers undermined, in the most extreme case even abolished under fascism. The problems of capitalism could be solved ultimately only through revolution, as the space for reforms and concessions in a declining crisis-ridden economy was gradually whittled away.

Writing of Britain in 1925, Trotsky said:

> It is just because there are no further prospects for the trade unions within the framework of capitalist society in Great Britain's present situation that the industrial workers' unions are compelled to take the path of the socialist re-organisation of the economy (Trotsky, 1926a, pp.103-4; see also Trotsky, 1919).

But this analysis presented Trotsky with a problem: as a simple economic determinist he inclined to the view that there was a close and necessary correspondence between economics and politics. If the capitalist economy was 'ripe for revolution', why had there been only one successful revolution? Was the Marxist theory of the revolutionary potential of the working class suspect? On the contrary, wrote Trotsky, 'the masses are better, more daring, more resolute than the leaders. The masses wish to struggle' (1938a, p.68). In other words the developing capitalist economy *had* nurtured its own 'grave diggers'. It is true that in the particular case of Britain Trotsky was not quite so impressed with the class consciousness of the mass of workers, and frequently noted the popularity of bourgeois, liberal, religious and other non-Marxist ideas in their ranks (e.g. Trotsky, 1924). And it is also the case that during his days as a leading member of the Comintern he frequently commented with great insight on the many splits and divisions within the ranks of the world's working classes (e.g. Trotsky, 1921a, b). But the backwardness and divisions to be found amongst workers in the advanced capitalist economies were themselves explained as the products of inadequate political leadership in the face of sophisticated and wealthy ruling classes (Trotsky, 1924, 1931a).

The trade union bureaucracy

The Transitional Programme of 1938 opened with the claim that 'the world political situation as a whole is chiefly characterised by a historical crisis of the leadership of the proletariat' (Trotsky, 1938b). The leadership of the working class had fallen into the hands of reformists, Stalinists, labour aristocrats and trade union bureaucrats (see also Trotsky, 1924, 1933a). Before explaining just what Trotsky meant by 'bureaucracy', it should be stressed that despite the formal similarity with Lenin's position, Trotsky always placed far greater weight on the role of the bureaucracy in retarding revolutionary trade union struggle and consciousness. In 1929, for instance, he wrote:

> It is thanks to it [the trade union bureaucracy] that the whole structure of capitalism now stands upright, above all in Europe and especially in England. If there were not a bureaucracy of the trade unions, then the police, the army, the courts, the lords, the monarchy would appear before the proletarian masses as nothing but pitiful and ridiculous playthings. The bureaucracy of the trade unions is the backbone of British imperialism (Trotsky, 1929a, p.28).

For all his strictures on trade union bureaucracy, Lenin never assigned it such a crucial role in his political analysis. Why then did Trotsky?

Theoretically, Trotsky believed that the economy was ready for revolution; the masses were politically active, conscious and unified (sectional divisions were discussed in Trotsky's 1920s writings, but gradually disappeared from his later writings), or would quickly become so under the impact of economic crisis and revolutionary propaganda; the political leadership of the working class was, within this schema, the *only* agency that could be blamed for defeats ('It is not the ranks who are to blame but the leaders' Trotsky, 1938a, p.64). Trotsky's emphasis on bureaucracy in particular and leadership in general therefore directly followed from, and was organically part of, his general analysis of 'the imperialist epoch'—without this analysis his concern with bureaucracy and leadership would become incomprehensible.

Trotsky was also able to deploy empirical evidence to back up his view of the 'trade union bureaucracy', in particular from the British General Strike which he wrote about at length. The 1925 TUC Congress had witnessed a significant shift to the left, in terms of policies, the tenor of conference speeches, and the political composition of the General Council. Although most of the 'left leaders' were not members of the CPGB, and contemporary Marxists, Trotsky included, were acutely aware of their limitations, they nonetheless represented a distinctly new trend in the trade union bureaucracy when compared with the old conservative leaderships. Despite this fact, these 'left leaders' capitulated after just nine days of the 1926 General Strike, refused to conduct a political struggle against the ruling class and abandoned the miners to fight on alone for six months. For Trotsky, the capitulation of the 'left wing' of the TUC General Council signified the weakness of trade union bureaucracy in general; it showed that even a 'left wing' bureaucracy would not, and could not, lead a revolutionary struggle. Only a disciplined revolutionary party with roots in the masses could do this. Trotsky's interpretation of the outcome of the General Strike rested on the assumption that Britain in 1926 was faced with a revolutionary situation, since this was after all the epoch of 'wars and revolutions':

> A general strike is the sharpest form of class struggle. It is only one step from the general strike to armed insurrection . . . [but] the General Council of the Trades Union Congress set out with the

ridiculous statement that the present General Strike did not represent a political struggle and did not in any event constitute an assault upon the state power of the bankers, industrialists and landowners, or upon the sanctity of British parliamentarism (Trotsky, 1926b, p.144).

Armed with his assumptions about the imperialist epoch Trotsky *had no need* to analyse the balance of forces in Britain, the ideology of different sections of the proletariat, the bases on which support for the miners was mobilised, in order to determine the actual meaning and significance of a given General Strike. Its meaning was simply 'read off' from the general characteristics of the imperialist epoch, and statements to the contrary were dismissed without argument as 'ridiculous'. Having said this, it should also be noted that the appearance in the 1930s of some of Engels' writings on political strikes led Trotsky to a rather more careful and cautious analysis of General Strikes than he displayed in the 1920s (cf. Trotsky, 1935).

But why did the 'trade union bureaucracy' behave as it did? Trotsky's account of their behaviour constitutes the least satisfactory part of his analysis, resting as it does on a simple economic determinism (see for instance Trotsky, 1921c). As Mandel has summed it up:

> The powerful apparatus of working class functionaries, recruited mainly from the class itself and only in part out of the petit bourgeois intelligentsia, has the tendency to identify itself with the organisation as such, to lose sight of the fact that the organisation is not an end in itself but a means to attain the emancipation of the working class and the building of a classless society . . . . Combined with the material advantages of posts in the labour apparatus—and very often with advantages gained in the bourgeois state apparatus—this change in outlook and motivation indicated the appearance of a new social layer, the labour bureaucracy.
>
> Its very political and social function is to substitute for intransigent class struggle attempts at class conciliation and class collaboration. . . . This labour bureaucracy is in essence conservative and opposed to the revolution which 'threatens the organisation' (Mandel, 1979, p.49).

The 1930s writings

For Trotsky the characteristics of the trade union bureaucracy were powerfully reinforced by active efforts at the incorporation of union leaders into the State apparatus, a tendency to which he assigned growing significance throughout the 1930s. And he linked the analysis of incorporation to his prognosis of the decline of reformism in the imperialist epoch.

> The decay of British capitalism, under the conditions of the decline of the world capitalist system, undermines the basis for the reformist work of the trade unions. Capitalism can continue to maintain itself only by lowering the standards of living of the working class. Under these conditions trade unions can either transform themselves into revolutionary organisations or become lieutenants of capital in the intensified exploitation of the workers. The trade union bureaucracy, which has satisfactorily solved its own social problem, took the second path (Trotsky, 1933b, p.75).

This theme of the twin paths for trade unionism—in the direction of revolution or of naked class collaboration—went back to the 1920s (cf. Trotsky, 1926a), and was expressed with increasing starkness and simplicity as Trotsky watched the world slide into war. By the late 1930s he was talking of the actual absorption of trade unions into the State as he observed the destruction of independent trade unions in fascist Germany and Italy:

> By transforming the trade unions into organs of the state, fascism invents nothing new; it merely draws to their ultimate conclusion the tendencies inherent in imperialism . . . Impossible are the independent or semi-independent reformist trade unions. Wholly possible are revolutionary trade unions which not only are not stockholders of imperialist policy but which set as their task the direct overthrow of the rule of capitalism. In the epoch of imperialist decay the trade unions can be really independent only to the extent that they are conscious of being, in action, the organs of proletarian revolution (Trotsky,1940, pp.69, 72; also Trotsky, 1929b, 1975).

One of the consequences of Trotsky's perspective on 'reformist trade unions' was a tendency to regard trade union economic struggles as revolutionary struggles against the bourgeoisie. As early as 1919 Trotsky had ridiculed the idea that workers joined trade unions to promote their immediate economic interests, forcefully declaring that they were being driven into unions by the revolutionary crisis of world capitalism (Trotsky, 1919, p.101). We have also seen this tendency at work in connection with the 1926 British General Strike (where Trotsky's position is at least debatable), but it took ever more extreme forms as Trotsky became more and more isolated from political activity, shut away in his Mexican exile.

> The unprecedented wave of sit-down strikes and the amazingly rapid growth of industrial unionism in the United States (the CIO) is the most indisputable expression of the instinctive striving of the American workers to raise themselves to the level of the tasks imposed upon them by history . . . Every sit-down strike poses in a practical manner the question of who is boss of the factory, the capitalist or the workers (Trotsky, 1938b, pp.6, 11).

The possibility that these strikes might have been undertaken for purely 'reformist' purposes—trade union recognition, collective bargaining rights, wage increases—was never entertained by Trotsky. In place of serious analysis of reformism Trotsky often substituted acerbic and witty invective:

> [Ramsey] MacDonald . . . is an evolutionist, that is to say, he believes that everything is 'gradually' changing and, with God's help, for the better. MacDonald is an evolutionist, he does not believe in miracles, he does not believe in leaps apart from a single one that took place 1,925 years ago: at that time a wedge was driven into organic evolution by none other than the Son of God and He put into circulation a certain quantity of heavenly truths from which the clergy collect a substantial terrestrial income (Trotsky, 1926a, p.44).

Transitional demands

Trotsky's most interesting contribution to the study of trade unionism was his theory of transitional demands as a mechanism for raising class consciousness. Whilst he recognised 'revolutionary striving', 'instincts', etc. amongst the working class, he also believed (implicitly) that such strivings did not in themselves constitute full-blown revolutionary class consciousness. Indeed in his more sober moments he sharply criticised the 'backwardness' of workers, and their 'petit-bourgeois spirit' (1938c, p.43). He agreed with Lenin on the necessity for ideological struggle against non-revolutionaries but shared Luxemburg's concern to delineate the conditions under which such consciousness was most likely to develop. For Trotsky these conditions were defined by a collision between the economic *potential* of capitalism and the economic *demands* of the working class, a collision that was to be facilitated by the promotion of transitional demands,

> stemming from today's conditions and from today's consciousness of wide layers of the working class and unalterably leading to one final conclusion: the conquest of power by the proletariat. . . . If capitalism is incapable of satisfying the demands inevitably arising from the

calamities generated by itself, then let it perish (Trotsky, 1938b, pp.7, 9).

The best example of such a demand was the sliding scale of wages and hours, adjusted to maintain working-class living standards at the expense of profits and to maintain full employment despite labour surplus. Another example was the slogan 'Open the books' as a way of exposing the machinations of capitalist employers and the fraudulence of their alleged inability to meet workers' demands. For Trotsky the key property of these demands was that they should be unrealisable under capitalism, for otherwise the capitalist system would remain intact, having met demands which it could afford to concede. From the non-achievement of these basic demands workers were supposed, the argument ran, to echo Trotsky's refrain—if the system cannot satisfy our demands, then let it perish. But Trotsky nowhere clearly explained just why he thought workers would draw such a radical conclusion instead of pursuing the obvious alternative strategy of simply scaling down their demands. One suggestion he made was that workers might be more likely to act radically in a revolutionary situation characterised by a political regime of 'dual power' (an idea similar to some of Luxemburg's thinking) but this insight was never systematically developed (Trotsky, 1931b). Indeed there is a profound ambivalence in Trotsky's characterisation of these demands, which were supposed to bridge the minimum programme of short-term reforms and the maximum programme of full socialism. For in one of his few recorded discussions on the Transitional Programme Trotsky said of the 'Sliding Scale of Wages and Hours':

> What is this slogan? In reality it is the system of work in socialist society. The total number of workers divided into the total number of hours. But if we present the whole socialist system it will appear to the average American as Utopian, as something from Europe. We present it as a solution to this crisis which must assure their right to eat, drink and live in decent apartments. It is the programme of socialism, but in very popular and simple form (1938c, p.44).

Here the transitional demand appears as a purely tactical device predicated on the particular nature of the American working class, rather than a universal mechanism for raising consciousness. It was no doubt Trotsky's own ambivalence about the nature of 'transitional demands', coupled with uncertainty about the precise dynamics of their consciousness-raising effect, which led Mandel (1979) to downgrade 'the transitional demand' almost to insignificance in his 1979 study of Trotsky.

Trotsky on trade unionism — a critical approach

Because Trotsky's political thought is highly coherent, it is sensible to start any critique with his master-theme of 'the imperialist epoch' from which so many other views were derived. The most striking feature of Trotsky's understanding of the imperialist epoch was the absence of any developed concept of contradiction. Classically, Marxists have understood capitalist crisis as a contradictory phenomenon, at once both a stressful and unstable process of destruction and a process of restructuring and growth. Trotsky's understanding of his epoch was a one-sided, catastrophist vision from which effective restructuring and regeneration were wholly absent. Contradiction was likewise absent from his analysis of the trade union bureaucracy (conservative), the working class (generally radical or soon likely to become so), and the socialist and Communist parties in the 1930s (reformist or counter-revolutionary). Trotsky, in short, was an old-fashioned theorist of inevitable collapse, and a simple economic determinist with an apocalyptic vision, an understandable position in the context of the 1930s but by no means the only position then available.

Within this framework Trotsky thought he discerned the imminent disappearance of reformist trade unions—after all, if reforms were 'in general' unavailable what role was there for reformist politics? What prevented 'the masses' from acting politically in line with the actual state of the economy was the trade union bureaucracy, firmly set on a policy of compromises rather than revolutionary struggle. But to blame trade union leadership for the nature and policies of trade unionism was and is surely oversimplified. As Thompson and Lewis have written,

> once beyond bargaining over the terms of the sale of labour power and faced with classwide confrontations involving the bourgeois state trade unionism has gone beyond its political limits. The trade union leaders are merely the summit of this weakness and its most obvious manifestation. . . . It is the bargaining function, *not* the existence of trade union bureaucrats as a separate group in the division of labour with their own distinct interests, that creates the conditions for social privileges (1977, p.31).

As the Webbs pointed out many years ago, the growth of trade union officials was as much an *effect* of collective bargaining and arbitration as its cause.

For Trotsky the material privileges of 'the bureaucracy' were a key factor in explaining their behaviour, irrespective of the relations between officials and members, the structure of the trade union, or the nature of relations with the employers. Trotsky then was guilty of simple economic determinism, or *economism*, 'the reduction of all other levels of a social formation to the movement of the economy, which becomes an idealist essence, of which social groups, political institutions and cultural products are merely manifestations' (Krasso, 1967, p.71).

Trotsky's Marxism, however, was also characterised by *sociologism*:

> Here it is not the economy, but *social classes*, which are extracted from the complex historical totality and hypostatised in an idealist fashion as the demiurges of any given political situation. Class struggle becomes the immediate, internal 'truth' of any political event, and mass forces become the exclusive historical agents (Krasso, 1967, p.72).

Trotsky's writings are replete with references to 'the masses' or 'working classes' thinking this, feeling that, doing the other, in a way which is strikingly reminiscent of the early Marx and Engels. Nor should this be surprising, for what Trotsky shared with them (particularly from the late 1920s) was a simple economic determinism in which social classes were formed in the economy and took to the political stage as unified agencies to act out their allotted parts according to the laws of history, undisturbed by sectional or other divisions.

As a simple economic determinist Trotsky was also increasingly inclined to the philosophical tendency of *essentialism*: the real meaning of events was already known in advance, derived from general Marxist theory, and so appearances to the contrary could be lightly disregarded. During the early 1920s, when he was still active in the Comintern, Trotsky showed considerable sensitivity to detailed evidence about the actual state of working-class consciousness and organisation (e.g. Trotsky, 1921b). But his later writings were increasingly characterised by a formal and schematic approach to the analysis of situations and events.

Thus Trotsky was utterly negligent about contradictory trends in working-class living standards in the 1930s (rising for some of the employed, sinking for others and for the unemployed) because he 'knew' that capitalism as a whole was in its epoch of decline. He was negligent about the impact of union and labour movement reforms, such as the American New Deal, because he 'knew' that 'in general' reforms were no longer possible. He was negligent of the real strength of reformist trade unionism in the working class because he 'knew' the masses were revolutionary. He was wholly unaware of the contradictory politics of the trade union bureaucracies because he 'knew' that 'in essence' the bureaucracy was conservative.

This type of essentialist reasoning generates a characteristic, dual attitude towards empirical evidence. Facts which are consistent with the theory of, let us say, bureaucratic conservatism, are cited as 'proof'; facts which are not consistent with the theory are described as 'exceptions' on the grounds that the theory is already known to be true. In short, facts can be used to 'prove' the theory, but never to disprove it; hence the theory remains intact, completely immune from empirical refutation. This is one reason that Trotsky's theories of trade unionism (and much else besides) have lasted so long—there is simply no way in which they can ever be confronted with damaging empirical evidence. The same reason accounts for the remarkably sterile and repetitive nature of much Trotskyist analysis of trade unionism, since any given action or situation is merely the same play being repeated by different actors, usually the 'masses' in struggle, 'sold out', or 'betrayed' by the bureaucracy. In Chapter 7 we shall therefore look in detail at empirical evidence on the behaviour of trade union leaders.

This essentialist quality of Trotsky's analyses of trade unionism also led to their possessing a remarkably abstract air, illustrating his tendency to neglect concrete analysis in favour of 'general principles' (though his writings on German fascism suggest this was not a ubiquitous defect: cf. Mavrakis, 1976). As Lenin remarked, in 1920,

> I find that Trotsky's basic mistake lies in his always dealing with it 'in principle', as a matter of 'general principle'. All his theses are based on 'general principle', an approach which is in itself fundamentally wrong. . . . (Lenin, 1920b, p.22).

Conclusion

It was this combination of properties—absence of contradiction, economism, sociologism, essentialism and over-abstraction— which lent Trotsky's analyses of trade unionism an increasingly arid and one-sided flavour. The very structure of his thought precluded any serious analysis of contradictions within the 'trade union bureaucracy', the survival and growth of reformist ideology in the working class, and the potential benefits of trade union involvement in the capitalist State. This last issue, analysed by Trotsky as a process of active incorporation by the bourgeoisie, is one that we shall pursue when dealing more fully with the capitalist State itself.

Formally speaking, Trotsky shared many of Lenin's views on trade unionism—on its limitations, on the necessity for a revolutionary party, and on the nature of the trade union bureaucracy and labour aristocracy. Yet beneath the surface there were vastly different theoretical frameworks: Lenin's complex economic determinism, and his ability to analyse situations concretely, contrast sharply with the rigidity and constancy of Trotsky's formulae. Indeed Trotskyism, as a theoretical current, can be described as a type of 'ossified Leninism'.

3
Gramsci: Unions, Factory Councils and the Problem of Ideology

Unlike many of the classical Marxists, Gramsci left behind a relatively coherent body of work on the nature of trade unions under capitalism, notably in a series of articles written in 1919 and 1920 in the midst of Italy's major waves of factory occupations and political unrest. Indeed Gramsci's association with trade unions and other workplace organisations was an unusually intimate one for a Marxist intellectual and his intense experiences of that period produced some of the most productive and fertile writings on a wide range of subjects—class consciousness, the relation between Party and unions, the nature of ideology.

Gramsci's active political life was extraordinarily concentrated, spanning just fourteen years from the time when he joined the Italian Socialist Party (PSI) (1913) until his imprisonment in 1926 as General Secretary of the Communist Party of Italy (PCI). He became prominent in the post-war struggles of 1918-22 that brought Italy close to revolution and was a central figure in the Factory Councils movement, supported and guided by the paper New Order (*L'Ordine Nuovo*) of which he was an editor. He was a major protagonist in the disputes which racked the PSI until it split, in 1921, into a reformist party and a revolutionary party, and was equally active in the debates on the relationship between the established trade unions, the newly-emerging Factory Councils and the Socialist Party. Shortly after Mussolini's march on Rome, in 1922, he became General Secretary of the PCI, a post he held for just two years. He spent eleven years in Mussolini's jails before his death in 1937, and it was there that he produced some of his most imaginative and powerful, though at times very difficult, writings on politics and ideology, generally referred to as 'The Prison Notebooks'. (Gramsci, 1971; see also Joll, 1977; Hoare and Nowell-smith, 1971; Simon, 1982).

By the end of the First World War the Italian Socialist movement had already experienced a series of major struggles against the government involving both the trade unions and the party (PSI). The Italian unions at this period were organised into four general federations, of which the biggest was the CGL, claiming almost two million members in 1920 and loosely affiliated to the PSI. It included many agricultural and public sector workers, but its most powerful constituent was the metal-workers' union, FIOM, with its membership concentrated in the big industrial centre of Turin. The CGL also organised the 'Camera del Lavoro', chambers of labour, which were local bodies embracing trade unions, cooperatives, consumer groups and other popular organisations. The trade unions tended to organise the skilled workers, whilst the rapidly growing body of semi-skilled workers in the engineering and other industries remained for the most part outside the ranks of organised labour. Before 1919 the only significant workplace union organisation was the 'internal commission', an elected factory grievance committee, with limited powers, whose numbers grew rapidly in the First World War and which, like the British shop steward committees in the same period, served as a focus for industrial and political agitation, directed both against the government and against the trade union leaderships.

The first year of peace (1919) witnessed a series of economic, political and ideological ruptures in Italian society. Production in many industries fell by as much as 40% below its highest pre-war level; unemployment rose rapidly, swelled by the demobilisation of troops; the numbers of strikes reached an unprecedented level; and in the election of November 1919 the PSI emerged as the largest single party, though without an overall parliamentary majority. That it captured so many seats with a programme that openly proclaimed the party's intention to organise the revolutionary destruction of capitalism goes some way to explaining what two commentators described as 'the Great Fear of the Italian bourgeoisie' (Hoare and Nowell-Smith, 1971, p.xxxvi).

But it was because of this electoral success that the PSI was confronted with a series of crucial political questions which ultimately tore the Party apart. What attitude should the Party adopt to the workplace organisations—the Factory Councils—then beginning to provoke the hostility of the more conservative trade union leaderships? What attitude should it adopt to the waves of strikes and factory occupations which pulsated throughout Italian industry in the 'Red Years'? Behind these issues lay the central question that split the movement in two: was Italy at that period 'ripe for revolution' as the revolutionary wing of the PSI and the factory council movement believed? Or was it ready simply for a series of major structural reforms as the majority of the trade union leadership and the right wing of the PSI maintained? The answer to *this* question provided the key to all the myriad, immediate questions of tactics and strategy, by indicating precisely what it was possible to achieve and to aspire for.

The Limitations of Trade Unions

It was in this context, and as part of the revolutionary wing of the Socialist movement, that Gramsci simultaneously supported and analysed the Factory Councils, comparing and contrasting them with the existing trade unions. From spring 1919 until early in 1920 Gramsci's writings concentrated on the limitations of trade unionism by comparison with the Factory Councils. From early 1920, he became increasingly aware of the limitations of the Councils and incorporated more explicitly into his analyses the role of the revolutionary party. What did Gramsci consider to be the limitations of trade unionism? How did they arise? And how were they to be overcome by the institution of the Factory Councils?

The trade union as a capitalist institution

Historically, trade unions emerged as part of capitalist society, organising the formally free wage-labour whose existence was integral to capitalism. But, Gramsci argued, unions did not develop their organisational forms independently of capitalism: they developed 'under the formidable pressure of events and compulsions dependent upon capitalist competition' (1919b, p.74). The contours of trade unionism were shaped by the contours of capitalist industrialisation, with unions arising separately in one trade after another, each organising the various occupations created within the division of labour. In other words the historical evolution of trade unionism imparted to it a sectional character as workers were organised in terms of their specific employment, not their general class position. Though trade unions were also class organisations by virtue of organising workers but not employers, it was also the case that they organised only a small proportion of the working class whilst the remainder—the casually employed, those in small enterprises, many women, the unemployed, etc.—remained outside the ranks of organised labour (Gramsci, 1919c, e,g; 1920b; 1921c).

The evolution of unions within capitalism, Gramsci argued, had a second major consequence, of an ideological rather than a structural character: it imbued them with an operating ideology that was essentially capitalist:

> *Objectively*, the trade union is nothing other than a commercial company, of a purely capitalistic type, which aims to secure, in the interests of the proletariat, the maximum price for the commodity labour, and to establish a monopoly over this commodity in the national and international fields. The trade union is distinguished from capitalist mercantilism only *subjectively* . . . (1921c, p.76).

The idea of the trade unions as sellers in labour power was one that Gramsci reiterated in many of his writings of this period (see also Luxemburg, 1900 for a similar analysis), in order to emphasise the degree to which their origins had impressed into their behaviour many of the canons of capitalist business practice, notwithstanding their espoused socialist ideology, whether revolutionary or reformist.

Trade unionism was further weakened as a revolutionary force, he believed, by its internal structure, notably the division between a stratum of paid officials and the rest of the membership. Gramsci shared the widespread contempt of his fellow classical Marxists and other militants for the trade union bureaucracy:

> These men no longer live for the class struggle, no longer feel the same passions, the same desires, the same hopes as the masses. Between them and the masses an unbridgeable gap has opened up. The only contact between them and the masses is the account ledger and the membership file. These men no longer see the enemy in the bourgeoisie, they see him in the communists. They are afraid of competition; instead of leaders they have become bankers of men in a monopoly situation . . . (Gramsci, 1921b, pp.17-18).

Gramsci rarely made any reference to the material position of the trade union official—his salary, fringe benefits, job security and so on—by contrast with Trotsky, for whom such factors were pre-eminent in the explanation of bureaucratic conservatism. For Gramsci this conservatism derived not so much from inflated levels of pay and conditions of employment, as from the very function of the trade union itself. Unable directly and unaided to eliminate private property, trade unions concentrated on the improvement of the immediate terms and conditions of employment of their members, not only through the use of strikes, but also through

> oblig[ing] the employer to acknowledge a certain legality in his dealings with the workers, a legality that is conditional on his faith in the union's *solvency* and its capacity to secure respect for contracted obligations from the working masses (Gramsci, 1920b, p.265; also 1919e, f, h)

In other words the recognition of trade unions by employers brought in its wake a requirement for internal discipline within the unions, so that members would respect agreements signed with the employer.

The functional role of trade unions for the employer was a key theme in Gramsci's writings, so much so that he was able to appreciate the continued existence of trade unions under fascism:

> The capitalists, for industrial reasons, cannot want all forms of organisation to be destroyed. In the factory, discipline and the smooth flow of production is only possible if there exists at least a minimum degree of constitutionality, a minimum degree of consent on the part of the workers (Gramsci, 1923b, p.167).

The institution of collective bargaining also had an important consequence for the nature of trade union officialdom and the qualifications required for that role. As collective bargaining widened, both across industries and in the range of issues covered, the trade union negotiator increasingly became a specialist in quasi-legal documents and contracts, and in commercial calculations about wages, production costs, profits and the like.

> A metalworkers' official can pass on indifferently to the bricklayers, the bootmakers or the joiners. He is not obliged to know the real technical conditions of the industry, just the private legislation which regulates the relations between entrepreneurs and labour force (Gramsci, 1921c, p.77).

But instead of regarding this legislation, this state of 'industrial legality', as 'a compromise which had to be made . . . until the balance of forces favours the working class' (Gramsci, 1920b, p.265), the union officials came to see it as a more or less permanent, normal and desirable state of affairs.

The implication of Gramsci's analysis, then, was that the ideology and behaviour of union officials could not be seen apart from the evolving function of trade unions within collective bargaining under capitalism. Altering the material circumstances of the officials' position, by regular election or payment of salaries no higher than the average of the members', might have some influence on their behaviour, but so long as collective bargaining and collective agreements dominated the world of trade unionism, even poorly paid and accountable officials would still have to enter negotiations with employers and reach agreements with them (a line of argument that will be examined more fully in Chapter 7).

In Gramsci's view, the trade unions were an historical product of capitalism, created in its image. They organised only a part of the working class, in trade or occupational associations, and confined themselves to the sale of labour power under terms and conditions negotiated with the employer by a caste of business-like officials divorced in their world-outlook from the militant temper of their members.

Gramsci's analysis of trade unionism had much in common with those of the other classical Marxists and he shared Lenin's assessment of non-revolutionary politics as the normal state of trade unionism, and his assessment of the role and limitations of trade union officials. And although (like Lenin) Gramsci was *later* to emphasise the importance of ideology in the maintenance of reformist and conservative consciousness, his early analyses of trade unionism (1918-22) went beyond Lenin in two respects. Firstly, where Lenin had simply *observed* that the history of trade unions showed them to lack revolutionary objectives, and *suggested* that this was due to the hegemony of bourgeois ideology, Gramsci probed much deeper. He argued that the very structure of trade unionism—organisation of workers by trade, organisation only of a section of the class—and its emergence under the shadow of the newly ascendent bourgeoisie imparted to it a focus on the short-term interests of particular groups of workers, rather than the long-term interests of the whole working class.

Secondly, Gramsci offered a different interpretation of the conservatism of trade union officialdom. Where Lenin, Trotsky and Engels had pointed to the use of imperialist super-profits to 'bribe' the labour aristocracy and trade union bureaucracy and 'induce' in them reformist politics, Gramsci focussed much more on the collective bargaining *function* of the official with its requirements of contractual obligation and legal-commercial expertise. Gramsci was not, as a result, opposed to collective bargaining, or indeed the signing of agreements: he recognised 'industrial legality' as an historic achievement wrested from the bourgeoisie by class struggle, and essential to defend provided it did not become transformed into an end in itself.

Power at the Workplace: the Factory Councils 1919-20

How were these limitations of trade unionism to be overcome? It was in June 1919 that Gramsci and Togliatti issued a programmatic call for the creation of factory-wide councils, representing the whole workforce, to contest the power of capital at the point of production.

> Today the internal commissions limit the power of the capitalist in the factory and perform functions of arbitration and discipline. Tomorrow, developed and enriched, they must be the organs of proletarian power, replacing the capitalist in all his useful functions of management and administration (Gramsci and Togliatti, 1919a, p.66).

In this quotation are embodied the two central themes of Gramsci's analysis of and programme for the Factory Councils: that the power of capital 'resides' essentially within the capitalist enterprise; and that as part of their offensive against capital, the Councils must begin to take over the functions of management, even before a revolution. Gramsci was to be sharply criticised on both counts, and accused respectively of anarcho-syndicalism (for ignoring the power of capital in the State) and class collaboration, points to which we return shortly.

The first contrast between Council and union was their composition: all workers in a single factory, argued Gramsci, should be represented by the Council, and should therefore be eligible to vote in Council elections. This proposal immediately brought Gramsci and his supporters into conflict with the powerful metalworkers' union, FIOM, which at first refused to allow non-unionists the right to vote for unionists. After protracted and difficult negotiations, a compromise formula was produced in the FIAT works: all workers would be eligible to vote, but only union members could stand as candidates in the Council elections, a compromise which paved the way for the rapid spread of Councils throughout Italy's industrial centre in Turin (Williams, 1975, pp.110-23).

For Gramsci the composition of the Factory Council was a key point, and the FIAT formula a major victory.

> The proletarian dictatorship can only be embodied in a type of organisation that is specific to the activity of producers, not wage-earners, the slaves of capital. The Factory Council is the nucleus of this organisation. For all sectors of the labour process are represented in the Council, in proportion to the contribution each craft and each labour sector makes to the manufacture of the object the factory is producing for the collectivity. The Council is a class, a social institution. Its *raison d'être* lies in the labour process in industrial production, i.e. in something permanent (Gramsci, 1919e, p.100).

By organising the whole of a factory workforce in a single body the Factory Council simultaneously transcended both the limited coverage of the trade unions (which organised only part of the workforce) and their sectional organisation (workers organised by trade, or occupation). The novel structure of the Council gave rise to new forms of politics and ideology.

The Factory Councils certainly entered into agreements with capitalists, but, in the spirit of Gramsci's earlier remarks, these were seen as mere breathing spaces, designed to consolidate the workers' hold on new territory before they launched the next advance (Gramsci, 1919e, 1920a,b). By contrast with the unions, the Councils were unashamedly aggressive and offensive institutions, seeking to augment workers' control within the factory and ultimately to render the capitalist superfluous. But wouldn't this constitute a form of class collaboration? Gramsci deftly turned this charge on its head:

> Nor can it be denied that the discipline which will be established along with the new system will lead to an improvement in production—but this is nothing but the confirmation of one of the theses of socialism: the more the productive human forces acquire consciousness, liberate themselves and freely organise themselves by emancipating themselves from the slavery to which capitalism would have liked to condemn them for ever, the better does their mode of utilisation become . . . (1919d, p.95; see also 1926, p.419).

Gramsci was not always clear in his definition of control, as exercised by the Factory Council, but he generally used the term to refer both to the exercise of decisive influence within the labour process (not just over terms and conditions of employment), and to a major incursion into traditional areas of managerial prerogative. How long the separate stratum of managers would survive in the face of this challenge was rarely made explicit, although in the midst of 'the Red Years' Gramsci appeared to have in mind a brief and uneven process of rapid assaults on managerial prerogative, rather than a protracted war of attrition (see Williams, 1975; Hoare and Nowell-Smith, 1971).

What is clear is that in *some* of his writings Gramsci entirely conflated economy and society and reduced all politics to the politics of production: the reality of a separate sphere of politics, linked to but not reducible to the economy, was implicitly denied: 'The revolutionary process takes place in the sphere of production, in the factory, where the relations are those of oppressor to oppressed, exploiter to exploited, where freedom for the worker does not exist, and democracy does not exist' (Gramsci, 1920a, p.261). Even Williams, an otherwise sympathetic biographer, has to admit that Gramsci did at times write as if he were an anarcho-syndicalist, who believed that revolution could be made by workers at the point of production without the need for a separate political organisation and political programme (1975, p.155 ff; cf. Togliatti, 1979a). As the Italian communist Bordiga said, it was little use seizing the factories, if the capitalists could simply encircle them with the armed power of the State (Bordiga, 1920a, b). From the middle of 1920 onwards Gramsci did begin to register more clearly the significance of political organisation beyond the factory walls and the corresponding need for a powerful communist party. Indeed by February 1921 he conceived of the Factory Councils not simply as 'organs of proletarian power', but as the focal point of an anti-capitalist struggle around which would cluster 'all the popular forces in revolt against the capitalist regime . . . ' (Gramsci, 1921a, p.11; see also Togliatti, 1979b).

Revolutionary Strategy, Ideology and Consciousness

How, and why, did Gramsci come to be more critical of the Factory Councils? To understand Gramsci's views we must first outline very briefly the key events in the development of unions and councils in 1920, for it was out of these events that Gramsci began to develop a distinctive analysis not only of trade unionism but of politics and ideology.

In spring 1920 Italy experienced the first of two major waves of factory occupations and employer lock-outs. The first wave was confined largely to Turin and found little support from elsewhere, because of deep political divisions between anarchists, reformists and revolutionary socialists. In August Italy was convulsed by a second wave of factory occupations and lock-outs, as engineering industry pay negotiations broke down, and both workers and employers took militant action to back their demands. Within weeks the occupations had spread throughout the country and a growing number of factories were being run and operated by Factory Councils, much as Gramsci and Togliatti had argued for the previous year.

Troops were out on the streets, surrounding many of the large factories, but the ruling class was divided. Whilst a minority wanted to use force in a major confrontation with the labour movement, the dominant faction, led by Premier Giolitti, believed a negotiated settlement of the conflict was possible. It soon emerged, however, that the labour movement was also divided in its assessment of the situation, and therefore in its strategy and tactics. In early September the PSI leadership refused to decide for or against an insurrection and effectively handed the decision over to the trade unions. Meeting in September the main confederation, the CGL, voted by a narrow majority not to press ahead with a Bolshevik-style insurrection, but to respond positively to Giolitti's offer of negotiations on 'industrial democracy' and new trade union rights. Within days the wave of factory occupations had petered out, often amidst bitter recriminations. The commission on industrial democracy met only a few times and then virtually ran into the ground. The industrialists, back in control of the factories, increasingly turned to the fascists as their new weapon in the struggle to deal a decisive blow to the already weakened and divided socialist movement. The fascist offensive against the movement gathered momentum into 1921, and the following year culminated in Mussolini's triumphant march on Rome.

It was up to and during this period of defeat that Gramsci began to rework his initial ideas about the Factory Councils and to incorporate them into a wider analysis of politics and ideology in the reproduction of capitalism and the transition to socialism. In developing his ideas Gramsci steered away from two dominant responses by the revolutionary left in their assessment of the September 1920 defeat. One response was to 'blame' the reformist leaders of the trade unions and the PSI for betraying the revolution and refusing to lead an insurrection. Although this was an understandable response it left unanswered the important questions as to *why* those leaders acted as they did, and why so many workers followed them (Gramsci, 1971, pp.158-68).

A second and closely related response was to say that there had been no revolution because of the absence of a revolutionary party wielding the power, and possessed of the will, to lead such an event. This was the line taken strongly by the ultra-left Italian Communist Amadeo Bordiga and his followers, and their argument rested on three fundamental assumptions. It was these assumptions that Gramsci increasingly came to question as he tried to develop his own analysis of revolutionary strategy and the role of trade unions in the West.

Firstly, then, Bordiga viewed society in classical Marxist terms as consisting of an economic base and a political superstructure whose institutional expression was the State. The relationship between base and superstructure was deterministic so that a crisis in the economy generated a corresponding crisis within the political superstructure. In the extreme case of sharp divisions within the ruling class and a crisis of their political leadership, then, a revolutionary situation existed. Secondly, Bordiga assumed that the bourgeoisie continued to rule in capitalist society primarily because of the monopoly of force that was concentrated in the capitalist State. Consequently, revolutionary strategy had to be directed towards the seizure of state power, 'the heart of the enemy bourgeoisie' (Bordiga, 1920b, p.236). Thirdly, as society consisted of two social classes, the bourgeoisie and the proletariat (recall the simple two-class model of the *Communist Manifesto*), then it followed that a revolutionary strategy consisted of a struggle for power by the working class against the bourgeoisie. This struggle had however to be led by a revolutionary party which concentrated the forces and energy of the working class and directed it against the power of the capitalist state. According to Bordiga, it was the lack of such a party in Italy that explained the failure of the working class to seize the opportunity afforded by the revolutionary situation in 1920.

Gramsci's critique

Why did Gramsci come to question and to modify these assumptions about revolution and revolutionary strategy? And what were the implications of his arguments for trade unions and class consciousness? Gramsci undoubtedly accepted that the Socialist Party had failed to exercise decisive leadership in 1920, and that this failure was an important element in the defeat of the revolution, but it was only one element. Writing *before* the Italian defeat, he said this:

> In Germany, Austria, Bavaria, the Ukraine and Hungary, [the] revolution as a destructive act has not been followed by the revolution as a process of reconstructing society on the communist model. The presence of these external conditions—a communist party, the destruction of the bourgeois State, powerful trade-union organisations and an armed proletariat—was not sufficient to compensate for the absence of another condition: the existence of productive forces tending towards development and growth, a conscious movement on the part of the proletarian masses to substantiate their political power with economic power, and a determination on the part of these proletarian masses to introduce proletarian order into the factory, to make the factory the basic unit of the new State (Gramsci, 1920c, p.306).

Several years later, he wrote more explicitly about the development of this 'conscious movement':

> . . . this is the main reason for the defeat of the Italian revolutionary parties: not to have had an ideology; not to have disseminated it among the masses; not to have strengthened the consciousness of their militants with certitudes of a moral and psychological character (Gramsci, 1923a, p.171).

This was the key point in Gramsci's argument. The most important and integral part of a revolutionary strategy was the ideological struggle to develop political class consciousness amongst the majority *before* the struggle for power. The success of the revolutionary party depended on securing ideological leadership, or hegemony, over the masses. How was this conception of revolutionary strategy derived from a critique of Bordiga's three assumptions?

For Gramsci society was not usefully divided simply into economic base and political superstructure: the 'superstructure' was itself divided into the State proper (parliament, executive, judiciary, army etc.), and civil society which comprised the domain of 'private' organisations such as trade unions, political parties, consumer cooperatives, women's groups. Most of the population at one time or another participated in and was organised and influenced by organisations of civil society and, for Gramsci, it was above all (though not exclusively) in these organisations that ideological struggle took place, and hegemony (ideological leadership) was secured. These organisations did not simply involve the working class as producers: they were also involved as consumers, as tenants, and in several other roles. Other groups too were involved, such as members of the intelligentsia and, in Italy of 1920, the peasantry (cf. Urry, 1981).

Secondly, Gramsci criticised the idea that the ruling class continued to rule simply through the coercive power of the State, an argument illustrated by the failure of revolutions which had successfully launched an armed assault on State power (Hungary and Bavaria). Nor was this rule exercised solely or primarily through the labour process and the labour market ('the dull compulsion of economic relations', as Marx described it). That was why the mere seizure of the factories in September 1920, even their expropriation, proved insufficient to challenge bourgeois rule successfully.

What Gramsci called the constructive component of revolution was increasingly defined by him in terms of ideology and ideological struggle, not because he was uninterested in economics, or underestimated coercion, but because in 'normal times' it was *through* ideology that bourgeois rule was maintained. He used the term to refer to 'everyday' or 'commonsense' ideas, as well as the ideas of intellectuals, and ideological struggle thus became a struggle to remake, or refashion commonsense (cf. Mouffe, 1979, pp.65-88). But ideology was also embodied in institutions, it took a material form. The structure of a trade union embodied certain ideas about democracy, authority and bureaucracy; the machinery of collective bargaining embodied the idea of two sides who regularly met to exchange bids and demands, and who normally reached an agreement. In other words ideological struggle was not just a struggle at the level of ideas, and about ideas, through books, pamphlets or meetings: it was also a struggle over the institutions and practices of the labour movement and the ideas they embodied, which is why Gramsci promoted the Factory Councils against the trade unions (cf. Simon, 1982, Chaps 8, 10). It is also why contemporary feminists have critically examined hierarchy and bureaucracy in trade unions as the embodiment of non-socialist values (cf. Beale, 1983; Coote and Campbell, 1987; Cockburn, 1987).

Gramsci also examined with particular care the precise content of different ideologies. What was called 'bourgeois ideology' was not a fixed and eternal set of ideas, but a collection of ideas whose form and content was constantly shifting, and being reworked, as sections of the ruling class sought to express and defend their different interests (Mouffe, 1979). Furthermore 'bourgeois ideology' was in fact drawn from a variety of sources, and social classes, and expressed *both* the strategic or hegemonic interests of the ruling class and some of the short-term interests of the subordinate class. A successful bourgeois ideology was one which articulated, or connected, bourgeois and working-class elements and interests, *not* one which simply imposed bourgeois interests *tout court*. For example, the idea of 'equality before the law' certainly involves an element of mystification, concealing the way in which the legal system is systematically and profoundly biassed in favour of property rights. But it *also* involves an historic concession to working-class demands for the legal right to organise in trade unions and take industrial action, in order to match the employer's right to organise labour and to hire and fire workers. The notion of equality before the law protects *both* the hegemonic interests of the ruling class and some of the interests of workers and their organisations (cf. Gramsci, 1971, p.161).

Finally, Gramsci began to explore the complexities of social structure, and to consider the range of groups and social forces that participated in political life. Within the Italian class structure, labour and capital co-existed with an active and influential intelligentsia, a large petit-bourgeoisie, and a substantial peasantry, particularly in the south of Italy. Within civil society was an array of groups and social forces, civic, cultural, religious etc., with whom a revolutionary party had to engage in ideological struggle and whom it must win over to its side if it wished to be effective.

In Gramsci's view, therefore, the Italian Socialist Party had failed to carry through a revolution in 1920 because i) it had underestimated the resilience of a modern capitalist state in the face of deep economic crisis, ii) it had underestimated the degree to which the ruling class obtains 'consent' to its rule through ideological struggle in civil society, and iii) it had underestimated the role of social forces other than the working class in the political process and in shaping the balance of power in society.

Re-appraising the Factory Councils

From this vantage point—hegemony, civil society, variety of subordinate groups in addition to the working class—the limitations of the Factory Councils in Italy of 1920 became even clearer. Lodged in the production process itself, in the economy rather than civil society proper, and organising only the industrial working class, they were vulnerable on two fronts: they could not easily challenge the hegemony of the ruling class in the wider society (though they began that challenge in the factory); and they were susceptible to counter attack by other subordinate groups, notably the peasantry who, acting under the sway of Roman Catholicism, provided willing recruits for the armed forces sent to the North to quell the factory occupations. Nor could these problems have been overcome merely by an armed assault on the State, for as Gramsci observed, the Italian state was incomparably stronger than its Russian counterpart which fell so easily to the Bolsheviks.

> In Russia the State was everything, civil society was primordial and gelatinous; in the West there was a proper relation between State and civil society, and when the State trembled a sturdy structure was at once revealed. The State was only an outer ditch behind which there stood a powerful system of fortresses and earthworks: more or less numerous from one state to the next (Gramsci, 1971, p.238).

On the other hand, the strength of the Factory Councils, as compared with the trade unions, was that they had at least begun the ideological struggle at the point of production, and did not confine themselves to bargaining over terms and conditions of employment. They embodied the capacity and willingness of the working class to reshape society in its interests, in other words they embodied a *hegemonic* rather than a *sectional* or *corporate* consciousness.

These terms were used by Gramsci in the *Prison Notebooks* to distinguish three phases of development of a major social class, corresponding to which were different levels of consciousness and different forms of organisation (Gramsci, 1971, pp.175-85). Sectional consciousness was manifested in the perception of a common interest among members of a particular trade or occupation, e.g. electricians, car-workers, and in the organisation of workers by individual trade unions, e.g. EETPU. Corporate consciousness was reflected in the perception of a common class interest, against that of the employer, and in the organisation of workers as a class, e.g. the TUC, CGT (France), etc. Politically, corporate consciousness was close to what Lenin described as 'trade union consciousness'—the conviction that it was necessary to organise as a class and struggle for progressive legislation, but within the framework of capitalism. Finally, hegemonic consciousness (revolutionary, or political class consciousness) was reflected in the belief that the interests of the working class required the transcendence of capitalism and the construction of a new type of society.

For Gramsci the Factory Councils embodied some degree of hegemonic consciousness since workers had begun to demonstrate how production could and would be organised in a socialist society. The trade unions, by contrast, pursued sectional or corporate objectives but never ventured into the domain of hegemonic struggle. Was this an inevitable limitation of trade unions? Despite his many criticisms of trade union structure and functioning Gramsci certainly believed in 1920 that it would be possible to 'suffuse' trade unions with the spirit of the Factory Councils, implying that their sectional, even corporate character could be changed (Gramsci, 1920b, d). But exactly how this change could be brought about, and under what conditions, were subjects on which Gramsci remained unclear.

Gramsci on Trade Unions: a Critical Evaluation

Gramsci's analysis of trade unionism placed considerable weight on the structures of trade union organisation and their ideological significance. Indeed, for Gramsci, structural forms embodied ideology. The limited coverage of workers by trade unions; their organisation by trade; their involvement in collective bargaining over terms and conditions of employment; and their use of full-time professional negotiators all stamped them with a profoundly capitalist ideological character.

On the basis of this analysis Gramsci was able to propose three properties of working-class organisation that would facilitate hegemonic consciousness: it must embrace workers as members of a class, not a trade or occupation; it must operate at the level of the workplace so that workers could intervene in the labour process; and it must aspire to the complete control of the labour process and not rest content with negotiation over the terms and conditions of labour's exploitation by capital.

It is possible to use these arguments to support a number of specific organisational forms and actions. Industrial unionism could be one way of structurally transcending organisation and consciousness by trade. Gramsci's emphasis on factory or work-place organisation could easily accommodate multi-union shop steward organisation. And the emphasis on the struggle for control over the labour process is easily compatible with the strategy of 'encroaching control', advanced by the Institute for Workers' Control, and explored in Chapter 8 (below). But before taking Gramsci's brief for a number of contemporary forms and policies of British trade unionism it is important to appreciate some of the problems and weaknesses in Gramsci's analysis.

Firstly, and at the most general level, Gramsci's writings on trade unions and Factory Councils suffer from an inadequate appreciation of contradiction as a property of all social systems. Gramsci's enthusiasm for the Factory Councils led him to an over-zealous and uncritical support for them, certainly until his re-appraisal began around the middle of 1920. But this re-appraisal of the Factory Councils was not matched by any corresponding re-assessment of his generally negative view of trade unionism. Even the best of his writings continued to operate with a unions vs. Councils dichotomy, and to underestimate the contradictory character of both. Unions continued to be seen as largely capitalist institutions (by contrast with the Councils) that were the repository of a sectional or corporate consciousness which stopped short of any hegemonic ambition.

Secondly, Gramsci believed that revolutionary action by the working class required as a precondition the attainment of revolutionary, or hegemonic, consciousness by many of its members. Revolutionary action could not successfully proceed on the basis of sectional or corporate consciousness: the conventional trade union demands corresponding to these levels of consciousness could not facilitate the overthrow of capitalism because they did not embody the constructive aspect of revolution, the creation of the elementary forms of 'the new order'.

Now it is worth recalling that the wave of factory occupations of September 1920 did not begin with worker demands of a hegemonic character; it was not in the first instance a dispute over control of the labour process, hiring and firing, investment plans or other key areas of managerial prerogative. The dispute began after *wage* negotiations broke down. In the *first* instance it was the refusal of the employers to grant reasonable wage rises, or to engage in the quite unsubversive process of collective bargaining, that triggered the chain reaction of lock-outs—strikes—occupations. Yet within a matter of weeks many thousands of workers were apparently ready to do away with the bourgeoisie altogether, and to run the factories and society themselves. In August, we find actions consistent with sectional or corporate consciousness . . . and 'suddenly' by September we are on the verge of revolution. Now it may be that the transition in workers' consciousness was more apparent than real. The years of war-time and post-war struggle, through strikes and occupations, and the propaganda of the Socialist Party may have produced a very high level of consciousness amongst masses of industrial workers, which emerged only in response to the employers' refusal to negotiate seriously. Less advanced workers may have taken strike action, or simply abandoned their demands, whereas workers with a more political class consciousness responded with factory occupations and a wholesale challenge to the capitalist system.

But if this is the case (and it does seem a reasonable interpretation of the Italian events) then it suggests Gramsci was wrong to disparage the role of trade unions in bargaining over wages. Because in the context of widespread industrial and political class conflict and profound economic crisis, even wage demands can precipitate a violent reaction from the employers and the State, leading to a revolutionary situation in which workers engage in radical actions such as factory occupations (a line of argument similar to that of Luxemburg). In other words Gramsci may have overestimated the integration of trade unions within capitalism, and underestimated the destabilising and radicalising effects of economic struggle under the crisis conditions then prevailing in Italy. This argument, in turn, places a question mark beside the claim that widespread hegemonic consciousness is a precondition for socialist revolution, an issue that will be considered more fully later on.

Thirdly, if Gramsci's analysis of class consciousness is not without its problems, the same is true for his analysis of the objective of the Factory Councils, the struggle to wrest control of the labour process from the capitalists. What Gramsci could not conceive of was the possibility that the Factory Councils, both as organisational forms and as a political movement, could become institutionalised, in the way that trade unions had become an integral part of the 'government' of the factory, through collective agreements. In other words, Gramsci underestimated the potential for the institutionalisation of new forms of working-class organisation, and underestimated the capacity of the bourgeoisie to adapt themselves to these new and hitherto threatening institutions. In the revolutionary situation of 1920 this was an understandable and perhaps insignificant omission, but in non-revolutionary situations it is a more serious matter because the forces of integration and institutionalisation are likely to be that much more powerful. Consequently the application of Gramsci's ideas to non-revolutionary Western Europe or North America in the 1990s is extremely hazardous, as we shall see in Chapter 8 in the discussions on industrial democracy.

Finally, Gramsci had relatively little to say about the precise relations between trade unions (or other workplace organisations) and political parties. Whilst obviously accepting that a political party should seek to influence trade unions, Gramsci devoted relatively little attention to the precise forms this influence was to take or to any limitations arising from the democratic procedures of trade unions themselves. It seems clear that he was not in sympathy with the complete organisational independence of trade unions from a political party, but it is not clear whether, and under what circumstances, trade unions were to exercise autonomy from the party.

4

The Classical Legacy and the 'Revisionist' Challenge

In this chapter I begin by reviewing the achievements of the classical Marxists in their analysis of trade unions, their effects on working-class consciousness and their role in the transition to socialism. I then consider some of the problems for these early analyses that were posed by the subsequent development of the capitalist economies, by the forms of working-class politics, and by the theoretical challenge from non-Marxist social scientists. Finally, I consider the broad strategies of trade unionism that are currently being debated on the Left and trace their origins in the analysis of the classical Marxists. We shall then be in a position to proceed with a more detailed investigation of these strategies in Chapters 5 through to 9.

The Achievements of the Classical Marxists

Marx and Engels never wavered from their earliest conviction, expressed in the *Communist Manifesto*, that the capitalist mode of production was a powerful and dynamic economic system constantly driven to expand through the accumulation of capital. The process of accumulation was guided only by the criterion of profit, extracted from the surplus labour of the working class and realised in the market sale of commodities. The very dynamism and competitiveness of this system continually impelled it to over-reach itself and, as profit rates fell, to enter a deep slump in which capital was written off, production cut and workers dismissed. In these ways capital prepared itself for the restructuring that would herald the next round of accumulation. The

71

general upward trajectory of economic expansion, visible through slump and boom, created both a class of capitalists and a class of workers whose structural positions in the production process repeatedly brought them into conflict.

The *first* great insight of the pioneers of Marxism was that wherever capitalism put down roots it would conjure up a working class. In time workers would organise themselves against capital, first in trade unions, and subsequently in socialist political parties. The growth of capitalism, of working class organisation and of political class consciousness were inextricably intertwined. Most of the classical Marxists, particularly in this century, were acutely aware of the immense difficulties, pitfalls, detours and reversals that characterised the growth of a politically conscious working class, yet none wavered in their belief that one day such a class would move to the centre of the political stage in all of the advanced capitalist countries. From the vantage point of the late twentieth century it is sometimes difficult to recapture and appreciate the conviction, the sense of certainty, that underpinned such faith. Yet even a brief look at the progress of working-class organisation in the last century provides part of the picture (and cf. also E.M. Wood, 1986, for a theoretical defence of a similar position).

Table 4.1 Development of working-class organisation in nineteenth-century capitalism

Formation of trade union federation	DATE	Formation of working class or socialist party
	1865	
	–	
Great Britain	–	
	–	
	1870	
	–	
	–	
	–	
	–	
Germany	**1875**	Germany
	–	Denmark, United States
	–	
	–	
	–	Spain, Belgium

	1880	
United States	–	
	–	France
	–	
	–	Great Britain
	1885	
	–	
	–	Norway
Spain	–	
	–	Austria, Sweden
	1890	
	–	
	–	Italy
Italy, Austria	–	
	–	
France	1895	
	–	
	–	
	–	
Belgium, Denmark, Sweden	–	
Norway	1900	

Source: Zagladin et al., 1981, pp. 221-43.

In one country after another the political predictions of the *Manifesto* were borne out as socialist parties were formed and began the long struggle for support, often in hostile environments. By the turn of the century, many had begun to make inroads into parliament and to erode bourgeois and aristocratic domination of their national assemblies. By 1900 the German Party (SPD) had 56 parliamentary deputies, the Belgians 31, the Austrians 14, the French 13 (Zagladin et al., 1981). By the eve of the First World War the position had improved still further.

Table 4.2 Socialist and Labour MPs in selected European countries 1900-14

Germany	France	Italy	Great Britain
81 (1903)	51 (1906)	33 (1900)	29 (1906)
110 (1912)	103 (1914)	52 (1913)	42 (1910)

Source: Khromov, 1983, Chapter 7.

The steady onward march of the working class, so crucial in forming and reinforcing the mechanical Marxism of the Second International, was to proceed across the whole of Europe for some decades to come, notwithstanding the horrors, setbacks and defeats of wars and fascism. By 1980 all but three of the OECD advanced capitalist countries (the exceptions being the USA, Canada and Ireland) could boast mass social-democratic parties with deep roots in and links to the organised working class*; all had a Communist Party though in only a few—Italy, France and Sweden—were these parties large or influential; virtually all of the countries contained Trotskyist groups, some of which had footholds in a number of trade unions; and trade union density varied from 18% (France, USA) to 94% (Sweden) (Therborn, 1984a; Bamber and Lansbury, 1987, p.257).

Post-war voting trends for a number of the advanced capitalist countries are shown in the table below.

Table 4.3 Votes cast for Socialist and Labour Parties 1945-84 (as percentage of total)

	Great Britain	Belgium	West Germany	Austria	France	Sweden
1945-49	48.3	31.1	29.2	41.7	20.9	46.1
1950-54	47.5	38.3	28.8	42.1	14.5	46.1
1955-59	45.1	37.0	31.8	43.9	15.3	45.4
1960-64	44.1	36.7	36.2	44.0	14.6	47.6
1965-69	47.9	28.2	41.0	42.6	17.6	50.1
1970-74	39.8	27.0	45.8	49.1	20.0	44.5
1975-79	36.9	25.7	42.6	50.7	22.5	43.1
1980-84	28.3	—	42.9	47.6	37.5	45.6

Source: von Beyme, 1985, adapted from Table 2.3, pp.72-3.

Only the Belgian Socialist Party has witnessed a similar decline to the British, whilst Socialist and Labour parties in the rest of Europe have either retained their electoral share or even increased it. On the other hand the Communist Parties of the advanced capitalist countries have suffered some recent and considerable setbacks. The Italian party has lost ground since the election of 1976, the Spanish and French parties have seen their

* At the time of writing the leftward-leaning New Democratic Party of Canada has grown dramatically and is now a serious contender for government office.

votes halved in the last ten years, and the British and Dutch parties are dwindling perilously close to extinction (von Beyme, 1985).

Figures for trade union density have shown a secular upward trend.

Table 4.4 Average trade union density in 18 OECD countries 1914-80

1914	c.1930	c.1960	c.1980
11%	24%	38%	50%

Sources: Korpi, 1983, Table 3.2; Therborn, 1984a, Table 2.

These figures are unweighted national averages, in other words they are not adjusted to take account of national differences in the numbers of trade unionists. Nonetheless though trade union density has suffered setbacks, during the 1930s and the 1980s, in the long term it has increased steadily to the point where a majority of workers in the OECD countries belonged to trade unions on the threshold of the 1980s recession.

Working-class receptivity to socialist ideas has varied dramatically, and continues to vary, between countries and between industrial sectors and regions within countries; yet even in places such as Britain with a weak and divided communist movement, the core of support and major zone of influence for socialist ideas has generally been found in the organised working class. In several other countries socialist and communist parties are deeply and bitterly divided, and to these divisions can sometimes be added further schisms amongst union federations, and between unions and parties. Yet for all the problems of working-class organisation and consciousness there is no advanced capitalist country in the world (with the possible exception of the USA) where socialist organisations, consciousness and ideals have been to all intents and purposes extinguished. The durability of the socialist idea, one and a half centuries after the *Communist Manifesto*, is a remarkable tribute to the prescience of Marx and Engels.

The *second* important insight of the classical tradition was its insistence that 'class struggle' was a ubiquitous and inevitable corollary of capitalism, and that through such struggle workers would transform themselves and their world. This latter conviction was not only based on theoretical considerations but was derived from observation of the great periods of working-class struggle, with strikes and demonstrations at their heart: the early revolutionary struggles of the 1840s observed by Marx and Engels; the British strikes of 1888-90 closely monitored by Engels; the Russian strikes of 1905 and the earlier mass strikes involving Lenin, Luxemburg and Trotsky; the Italian strikes and factory occupations of 1918-20 in which Gramsci was a major protagonist; the strikes and defeated revolutions in Germany and Hungary of 1918-19; and the Russian revolution of 1917. And to these events could be added the world strike waves of 1910-14, 1916-22, and 1968-74 which have been linked by several analysts to the long waves of capitalist economic development identified by Kondratiev (Cronin, 1979; Screpanti, 1987). Each of these periods of struggle was associated with a significant surge of political class consciousness amongst workers, embodied in the creation or expansion of socialist parties and a heightened interest in and susceptibility to socialist propaganda. Often the numbers of workers radicalised by such struggle were small and the effects more or less rapidly dissipated in the emergent routines of collective bargaining and trade union administration. But however disappointing the scale of radicalisation it was at least consistent with Marxist materialism and with the dictum that 'social being determines social consciousness'; on this basis it was believed that the transformations wrought in the social milieu of strikers would generate corresponding changes in their world outlook.

Furthermore, since class struggle arose from the social relations of capitalist production, it was bound to persist so long as capitalism remained in existence. Now at any one time the actual level of industrial conflict might be particularly low and Marxist predictions of strikes and conflict might appear somewhat inappropriate. All of the classical Marxists lived through such periods of quiescence—in Britain, the 1850s, early 1880s, early 1900s, late 1920s and 1930s—and such periods have continued up to the present day, with periods of low strike frequency in the late 1940s, early 1950s and 1980s. But these fluctuations in strike patterns have always been understood by Marxists as cyclical phenomena, because the exploitation and authoritarianism of capitalist production would inevitably provide the foundation for new rounds of class struggle.

The *third* major insight of the classical Marxists was an appreciation of the profound obstacles that hindered the growth of class consciousness, a subject on which there now exists an enormous literature (cf. Hill, 1981). Numerous factors have been adduced to explain the 'underdevelopment' of class consciousness amongst sections of the working class: the capacity of capitalism to satisfy the basic living requirements of most of its citizens; the distribution of special privileges to an influential section of the working class, the labour aristocracy (cf. Moorhouse, 1978); the dissemination of bourgeois ideology through capitalist-owned means of communication in order to inculcate a 'pragmatic acceptance', if not a positive endorsement of capitalism; the activities of employers at the point of production designed to promote stability and industrial relations harmony (cf. Kelly, 1982a, 1987a; Nichols and Beynon, 1977); and the existence of divisions within the working class on lines of occupation, industry, union, age, gender, race and nationality, often theorised under the rubric of sectionalism (see especially Davis, 1986; and Gordon et al., 1982 on the USA).

The classical Marxists discussed these explanations at length, but their primary legacy focussed on four sets of factors. Firstly, Gramsci explored in depth the connections between the organisation and structure of trade unions and working-class consciousness. Even if he did not employ the term 'sectionalism', its designation as a barrier to political class consciousness owes much to his line of argument. Secondly, Lenin, Luxemburg, and above all Trotsky established the 'Marxist theory of trade union bureaucracy' according to which trade union leaderships will tend to restrain rank-and-file militancy because of its threat to their own privileges and to industrial relations order. Thirdly, it was Gramsci who argued most perceptively that the growth of collective bargaining, with its networks of institutions, rules and procedures, served to envelop trade unions in a suffocating web of bureaucratic routine and regulation. Formal arrangements for grievance handling and dispute settlement injected a degree of order and predictability into the erstwhile tempestuous and occasionally violent relations between labour and capital. If much of this analysis anticipated the theories of institutionalisation of conflict that were to be developed in the 1950s, its Marxist proponents avoided the contemporary error of overestimating the capacity of collective bargaining and disputes procedures to regulate the frequency of industrial conflict. In this respect some of Gramsci's writings displayed a degree of subtlety unmatched in Marxist studies of collective bargaining. Finally, it was Lenin, and in a different way Trotsky, who pioneered the classical

Marxist theory of the State and noted the latter's allegedly baleful influence on working-class organisation and consciousness. We shall return to all of these points shortly.

The *final* achievement of the classical Marxists was the elaboration of a number of elements of a revolutionary strategy for the overthrow of capitalism. For the purposes of the present study, two key issues need to be brought out: the conditions under which trade union actions will generate political class consciousness, and the conditions under which the working class will engage in a socialist transformation of society. On the first issue, the classical Marxists believed that trade union struggles, particularly in the form of strikes, were an essential component in working-class radicalisation. For this reason they were all deeply hostile to the institution of collective bargaining (particularly Gramsci) because of its potential for demobilising workers' struggles, and sceptical of its outcomes for workers. But behind the widespread consensus about the necessity for strikes, normally described as 'class struggles', there were several different analyses of the types of strikes most conducive to radicalisation. Engels and Lenin stressed the educative role of the political party in raising the consciousness of strikers; Luxemburg offered a sophisticated theory of mass strikes; Trotsky emphasised the radical potential of specifically transitional demands; Gramsci stressed the necessity for trade union struggles to control the labour process itself.

The conditions most conducive to socialist transformation were invariably defined in terms of economic crisis. For the early Marx and Engels the inevitable crises of capitalism would reveal its iniquitous and destructive character and provide workers with a powerful incentive to overthrow it. Later in their lives they came to believe that the effects of economic crisis must be mediated through the actions and policies of working-class political parties. From the turn of the century, and with the rise of imperialism, it became common amongst the classical Marxists to write of the inevitable limits of capitalist growth and the imminence of its final collapse. It was from the depths of capitalist crisis that the working class, with nothing more to lose, would rise up to overthrow it, and the tumultuous revolutionary struggles in the aftermath of the First World War seemed to lend weight to this vision of an imminent, anti-capitalist insurrection. Through the 1920s and 1930s Trotsky in particular continued to adhere to the perspective of imminent revolutionary struggle against a capitalist system that was passing through its 'death agony'.

Problems of the Classical Legacy: the Revisionist Challenge

The most coherent challenge to the legacy of 'classical Marxism' was mounted at the turn of the century by two leading members of the German Social Democratic Party, Eduard Bernstein and Karl Kautsky. Bernstein openly proclaimed his 'revisionism' and became the subject of bitter controversy from 1899, but the full scope of Kautsky's theoretical innovations did not become widely apparent until after 1914. Bernstein (1909) attacked 'classical Marxist doctrines' on four central points.

To begin with he rejected the idea that capitalist crisis was inevitable and that socialists could look forward to capitalism's final collapse. The expansion of credit allowed demand to be maintained at high levels, and consequently crises of under consumption could be avoided. The growth of foreign markets had provided further outlets for domestic production, and the growth of cartels meant that the rhythms of the economy could be planned to a degree that was inconceivable in the early period of competitive capitalism described and analysed by Marx.

Furthermore, the steady growth of capitalism had brought in its wake a rise in living standards rather than the immiseration sometimes forecast by Marx. This same period had witnessed the numerical growth of the working class and its organisations, but in its composition the working class was becoming more differentiated, not less. And it was in the largest enterprises, traditionally regarded as the seedbeds of a homogeneous and deskilled proletariat, that occupational specialisation, and therefore working-class differentiation, had been taken furthest of all. Moreover, between the industrial working class and the class of capitalists there was emerging a large and diverse middle class of white-collar workers who were *not* being driven into the ranks of the organised working class as Marx and Engels had predicted.

Finally, Bernstein argued that many improvements in workers' living standards had been obtained through the struggle for rights and the pursuit of reforms within capitalism. Workers had used trade union and parliamentary pressure to press for improvements in terms and conditions of employment and had therefore shown it was possible to derive benefits from 'reformist' activity. The consequence of this, and the above points, was that workers could not be expected to develop revolutionary class consciousness as an inevitable corollary of capitalism's breakdown and its inability to meet their needs. Socialism, argued

Bernstein, would be achieved through progressive reforms struggled for by an increasingly educated, conscious and well-organised working class; it would not be ushered in through an insurrection launched by an impoverished and desperate proletariat that had 'nothing to lose but its chains'.

Though Kautsky rejected much of Bernstein's economic reasoning (see Salvadori, 1979, pp. 59-73) and sided with Luxemburg's attack on him (Pierson, 1986, Chap. 2), he did nevertheless argue for a political strategy that had close affinities with some of Bernstein's own conclusions (Kautsky, 1983). Kautsky accepted much of the classical Marxist analyses, and in particular the claims that capitalist crises would become increasingly severe and would culminate in a revolutionary situation that was ripe for the socialist overthrow of capitalism. But in the meantime he believed it was essential for the working class to bide its time and conserve and expand its resources, through the membership and support of trade unions and the political party. Premature, adventurist assaults against the state, using weapons such as mass strikes, could provide a pretext for the ruling class to crush and break up the organisational resources of labour, so carefully husbanded over many decades. Kautsky therefore argued for what he called the strategy of attrition, as opposed to the strategy of overthrow (Kautsky, 1910). The working class was to build its strength, and engage the enemy in struggle only where there was a reasonable prospect of success. Kautsky's strategy of attrition laid heavy emphasis on the use of the state as an instrument of reform, a question on which he clashed bitterly with Lenin as we shall see later (Chapter 9).

World Capitalism after 1945 and Contemporary Trade Unionism

World capitalism survived the revolutionary struggles of 1917 into the 1920s, the Depression of 1929-33, the rise of fascism, and the Second World War. And as it entered the post-war era and the most sustained economic boom in its history, the legacy of the classical, revolutionary Marxists underwent a series of profound challenges.

Under the shadow of Stalinist socialism in Eastern Europe, Marxist politics in the West made little headway outside of France, Italy and possibly Greece. In the core capitalist countries of Britain, West Germany, Austria, the Low Countries and Scandinavia, it was social democratic parties who increasingly commanded the loyalty of the organised working class. It was true that the British and Belgian parties proved particularly inept at retaining their share of the electorate, but most of Europe's social-democratic parties held or expanded their percentage vote throughout the post-war period. The steady rise in trade union membership, in the context of economic growth, helped to create a solid, powerful and distinctive pattern of labour movement politics that effectively marginalised the revolutionary left in all but a few countries and industrial sectors. The success of this type of reformist politics posed a major challenge to traditional, classical Marxism, at least until the re-emergence of economic crisis and industrial militancy in the late 1,960s and early 1970s.

What were the results of this period for Marxist analyses of trade unions, and their role in the development of class consciousness, and the transition to socialism? Two broad lines of argument and strategy emerged from this period, loosely associated in Britain (though similar divisions emerged in many other countries) with the 'far left' and the Communist Party respectively, and sometimes (inaccurately) described as revolutionary and reformist.

The resurgent Trotskyist tradition, associated in Britain with far-left groups such as the Socialist Workers' Party (International Socialists, as they were known until 1977), emphasised above all the potential radicalisation of the working class through industrial militancy. Sections of the CP argued that the wages struggle had become a political struggle in an era of State incomes policy and economic intervention, and agreed that wages militancy could therefore radicalise the working class by bringing it into conflict with the State. This line of argument was very similar to that of many classical Marxists, although there were important differences about the question of how strikes radicalised people. Did radicalisation come through victory or defeat? Did it depend on how the strikes were led and how much control was wielded by the trade union 'bureaucracy'? Did it matter whether strikes were fought against private employers or the State? Did *all* strikes radicalise workers, or was it only during strike waves that radicalisation occurred?

Periods of industrial militancy, particularly during economic crisis, were thought to provide the foundations for a political challenge to capitalism and to its supporters in the capitalist State, the Conservative Party and the right wing of the Labour Party. Again there were disagreements amongst supporters of industrial militancy about the politics of socialist transition, with some adhering to a classical, insurrectionary road, and others favouring a more gradual accretion of political power through parliament. Many writers and activists in this broad tradition also identified as two major obstacles to working-class radicalisation and power the 'sectionalism' of the working class and the conservatism of the trade union bureaucracy. In examining this strategy for trade unionism in the next three chapters, we shall consider in turn the impact of strikes and strike waves on class consciousness (Chapter 5), the problem of sectionalism (Chapter 6) and the character of trade union leaderships (Chapter 7).

If this first trade union strategy owes much to the classical Marxist emphasis on industrial militancy and economic crisis, the second major strategy to emerge from the 1970s owes far more to the 'revisionist' tradition of Bernstein and Kautsky. Both men had emphasised the growth potential of capitalism and the political and other gains that could be obtained by the working class through parliamentary democracy and through well-organised trade unions. Kautsky in particular regarded the organisational resources of the working class (trade union membership, the political party and its electoral support) as indispensable assets to be preserved at almost all cost. He eventually came to regard revolution in the Leninist sense as a reckless gamble that could destroy these resources and that would only usher in authoritarian forms of rule.

The second, alternative trade union strategy draws partly on this tradition, and partly on a particular reading of Gramsci. It emphasises advance along two fronts. Firstly, at the level of the enterprise there is an insistence on the necessity for trade unions to struggle for control over the labour process. Echoing Gramsci's critique of trade union economic demands in collective bargaining, and supportive of his stress on workers' control at the point of production, theorists in this tradition have argued for the importance of industrial democracy and workers' control. Drawing more explicitly on Bernstein and Kautsky, they have moreover emphasised the use that trade unions can make of the State, via working-class political parties, in securing reforms that will benefit them and their members. Proponents of this type of strategy have often pointed to Sweden as an example of a labour movement deeply sensitive to the costs of major conflict and therefore willing and able to pursue a long-term strategy of structural reforms at the level of the enterprise and of the state. We shall examine the two arms of this trade union strategy in Chapter 8 (Industrial Democracy) and Chapter 9 (The State).

PART TWO

Contemporary Debates

5
Strikes and Class Consciousness

The impact of strikes on class consciousness has been the subject of intense debate amongst Marxists down to the present day, and the British strike waves of 1968-74 and 1977-79 provoked widespread and heated argument on the left, precipitated in the first instance by Eric Hobsbawm's 1978 Marx Memorial lecture *The Forward March of Labour Halted?* Hobsbawm presented a powerful critique of 'economistic militancy', which strongly echoed Lenin's views of trade union consciousness (see Chapter 2 above), and his arguments were subsequently criticised from a variety of quarters. The fundamental issue in dispute was whether such strike waves had radicalised workers, even though, as we shall see, the strikes which composed them were often fought over traditional economic demands. But before we can make any progress with this question we need to clarify what is meant by the concept of 'class consciousness' and how it is to be measured. The first part of the chapter therefore discusses and attempts to define this concept. Next I look at Hobsbawm's critique of 'economistic militancy', and the alternative theories and strategies advanced by his critics, so that we can then set out to compare systematically different interpretations of the strikes—class consciousness relationship. This comparison forms the bulk of the chapter and I shall concentrate on the periods immediately prior to and during major strike waves, though other periods will be looked at briefly and I shall also consider evidence on the impact of individual strikes. I shall then return to the interpretations outlined at the start of the chapter and consider what support the evidence offers for a trade union strategy centred on industrial militancy.

What is Class Consciousness?

The language of class is common in everyday speech, certainly in
Britain and parts of Europe, though less so in North America.
The pervasiveness of the term tells us that many people are aware
of the *existence* of classes, and studies suggest that about three-
quarters of those living in the advanced capitalist countries are
able to identify themselves as members of a social class (Gallie,
1983, p.34; Lash, 1984, p.89). But for Marxists, class identity can
be only one component of class consciousness, because over and
above this individuals must believe class to be a significant factor
in structuring and explaining economic and political life. Such
beliefs can encompass a wide range of views and perceptions and
therefore if we want to talk with some precision about the
development or the dynamics of class consciousness we need to
introduce some analytical distinctions. Marx and Lenin distinguished between reformist or trade union consciousness (class-in-
itself) and revolutionary consciousness (class-for-itself), but the
clumsiness of Marx's couplet, the tendency for 'reform' and
'revolution' to be used as terms of abuse in lieu of any precise and
agreed definition of either, and the difficulty of actually using
Lenin's distinction (see Hyman, 1971, and Luxemburg, Chapter
2 above) all suggest that we should look elsewhere for more
fruitful concepts.

Of the other classical Marxists, Georg Lukacs (1971) wrote at
most length about class consciousness. Much of his work, however, turns on the distinction between the consciousness workers
would have if fully aware of their interests ('imputed', or revolutionary class consciousness) and the actual consciousness displayed in organisation and struggles. He offered no distinctive
theory of the dynamics, phases or specific types of consciousness,
apart from the distinctions used by Lenin (see also McLellan,
1980, Chap. 11).

If we return to the classical Marxist theory of society (see
above, Chapter 1), the term 'class' designated a group sharing a
common relation to the means of production, and in the simple
model two classes were identified, bourgeoisie and proletariat (or
working class). Logically class consciousness can therefore be
thought of as referring i) to the perceived relation between an
individual and his/her own class, ii) to the perceived relation
between his/her own class and the other class.

It is now conventional amongst Marxists to describe the class
structure of advanced capitalist societies in far more complex

ways. Some Marxists talked of a 'new middle class', whilst others spoke of intermediate strata, or class fractions. More recently still, Marxists such as Wright (1985) have elaborated an even more complex three-dimensional model of class based on ownership of means of production, authority exercised within the labour process and possession of credentials. But since Marxist theories of trade unionism are principally concerned with analysing class struggle, it remains legitimate to concentrate on the principal parties in struggle, that is labour and capital, and to chart variations in people's identification with their own social class, and their perception of its relationship to capital. For this purpose some of Gramsci's concepts may prove particularly helpful.

In Gramsci's terms a worker may identify himself and his interests primarily with a *section* of his class with whom he has a common interest (e.g. electricians, members of the EETPU); he may identify himself and his interests with the *corporate* body and the interests of the working class as a whole within capitalism; and finally he may identify the revolutionary interests of the working class with the interests of society as a whole, within what Gramsci describes as a *hegemonic* consciousness.

The relations between classes may be seen in three ways corresponding to Fox's (1973) threefold division of ideologies of the enterprise into unitary, pluralist and radical categories. Relations between workers and employers may therefore be seen as *complementary*: both parties perform different, but essential and interdependent functions within the enterprise or the economy; they may be seen as *conflictual*, with conflicts of interest over wages, workloads and other issues underpinned by a shared interest in procedural agreements and/or economic growth; and finally relations may be seen as fundamentally *antagonistic*, in which case it is the elements of conflict in the relationship, such as capital's exploitation and domination of labour, that constitute its most salient feature. The strictest definition of revolutionary class consciousness would require the attainment of hegemonic consciousness coupled with a belief in the fundamental antagonism between the two major social classes. The different levels of class consciusness are summarised in Table 5.1.

This model of class consciousness deliberately does not focus on *demands* in class struggle, such as wages, job control, workers' control and the like, setting up a distinction between more or less advanced demands, e.g. control vs. wages. This is because any given demand can be articulated and fought for within a wide variety of ideological frameworks: the 'job control' of the exclusive, skilled craftworker may have little in common with that of the assembly-worker (Hyman and Elger, 1981). Therefore it is extremely difficult to draw any clear and unambiguous inference about class consciousness from the stated demands of strikers (Shalev, 1978), though whether certain types of demands, such as sectional wage rises, inhibit the growth of class consciousness is an important issue I shall consider later. I want to suggest that class consciousness should be understood *primarily* in terms of groups and inter-group relations. In other words, with which groups do workers identify, and why? and how do they perceive the relationships between their own and other groups? The popular language of class and class struggle—'sectionalism', collaboration etc.—invariably turns on these issues.

Table 5.1 The structure of class consciousness

	Own class identity	*Relations between classes*
I	Sectional	Complementary
II	Corporate	Conflictual
III	Hegemonic	Antagonistic

Can class consciousness be measured?

How do we assess a phenomenon as complex as class consciousness? Much of the disagreement and dispute among Marxists derives from different ways of measuring class consciousness, which in turn stem from different definitions. Some use numbers of strikes as an indicator—the higher the level of strikes, the higher the level of class consciousness. But the number of strikes can tell us as much about the class consciousness, the ruthlessness or the economic situation of the employer as it can about workers (Mayhew, 1979). Furthermore some strikes will enjoy a high degree of support and commitment, whereas others will be 'led from above', and it seems unreasonable to suggest that similar levels of consciousness are being manifested in these different cases. Other observers have used voting figures, or party membership, but these again can be questioned. It seems unreasonable to suppose that a similar level of class consciousness was manifested in the decision to vote for a right-wing Labour manifesto in 1979, as for a left-wing manifesto in 1974. Yet a crude index of Labour voting trends would overlook such subtleties. Other analysts have used attitudes and opinions as measures of class consciousness, and not infrequently somebody using one index is likely to dismiss other measures as imperfect or inadequate (Fine et al., 1984).

Some may be tempted to conclude that almost every index of class consciousness is so deeply flawed that the phenomenon is quite unmeasurable, or that measurement can only be based on an arbitrary choice of highly imperfect indicators. But if we want to talk about class consciousness at all then we must use the indicators and measures that are to hand and bear in mind their numerous difficulties when interpreting them. The only alternative is a purely speculative or theoretical discussion that will not advance our understanding of strikes and their effects beyond its present meagre state.

In Marxist terms I take 'class consciousness' to refer to theoretically informed practice (praxis), to a fusion of attitudes and behaviour in both the economic and political spheres, and on the basis of this definition we can construct a 2 x 2 matrix yielding four sets of measures. The matrix below contains examples of the measures or indicators most commonly used in debate.

Table 5.2 Indicators of class consciousness

	Attitudes	*Behaviour*
Economic sphere	Attitudes to trade unions, nationalisation, strikes	Trade union membership Trade union policies Strike patterns
Political sphere	Attitudes on general political issues, law and order, women's rights etc.	Voting Party membership Circulation of Party literature Party policies

The discussion so far has suggested ways of describing the structure of class consciousness (relation to own class/relations with other classes) and ways of assessing it (attitudes/behaviour, economics/politics). We can now look in depth at the relationship between strikes and class consciousness. Because of the controversy it generated about this question, the collection of articles on *The Forward March of Labour Halted?* is a fitting place to begin.

The Impact of Strikes on Class Consciousness: Hobsbawm and his Critics

In his famous essay *The Forward March of Labour Halted?* (1981), Eric Hobsbawm argued that the British working class had reached a high-point of unity and consciousness some 25-30 years earlier, since when it had either registered no further advance at all or had actually regressed. How did he reach this conclusion? By looking at changes in trade union membership, political party membership and party voting, he showed that whilst trade union membership had grown in absolute terms between the 1940s and the 1950s, union density was barely higher than in 1945; membership of the Labour, Communist and other socialist parties had fallen from the early 1950s; and the number and proportion of the electorate voting Labour had declined at almost every election since 1951. Whilst admitting these were rough indicators it was, argued Hobsbawm, inconceivable that class consciousness could have *risen* whilst two of these three indicators had fallen and a third remained stationary. Although the numbers of strikes had risen almost continually since 1950, the evidence, he said, showed this militancy to be overwhelmingly of an economistic and sectional character, principally concerned with wages rather than wider issues, and principally conducted by sections of the working class oblivious or indifferent to the damaging effects of their action on other workers and on consumers (see also Hobsbawm, 1984). In other words the stagnation in class consciousness had proceeded hand in hand with the decline of working-class unity and the growth of internal divisions within the class of which sectional (rather than regional or ethnic) divisions were the most conspicuous.

Hobsbawm's sceptical attitude to the 'economic' or wages militancy (he used the terms interchangeably) of the 1970s attracted a barrage of criticism from Marxists, but for all that it was very close to classical Leninism. Militant trade unionism, Lenin argued, produced only trade union consciousness, an awareness of the unavoidable conflict of interests between worker and employer. Under conditions of economic and political crisis, moreover, Hobsbawm observed that trade union militancy tends to be undermined by an unfavourable balance of forces and by rationalisation, restructuring, and the like (see also Kitching, 1983, Chap.5.). Resisting such attacks requires a higher level of political class consciousness and organisation—to be brought about by revolutionary agitation and leadership (for Trotskyist groups such as the WSL), by revolutionary propaganda (RCG, RCP, NCP) or by a strategy and programme for beginning the transformation of capitalism through radical reforms (Hobsbawm, CP, Labour 'Left').

I have presented Hobsbawm's argument in its simplest form, as it came to be understood by his contemporaries, because this will facilitate its confrontation with empirical evidence. But it would be unfair to Hobsbawm to overlook two important qualifications to his argument which appeared in later contributions to the *Forward March* debate. He did acknowledge the political effects of industrial wages militancy between 1915 and 1922, but this admission introduced a critical ambiguity into his argument. For it implied that industrial wages militancy *could* promote political class consciousness under certain conditions, a position very different from the Leninist rejection of economistic militancy that characterised his original 1978 essay (see Hobsbawm, 1981, p.68). For the purposes of exposition, and at the risk of over-simplification, I propose to take the Leninist argument as Hobsbawm's actual position. Secondly, Hobsbawm retreated from his claim that working-class sectionalism had grown during the post-war years (1981, p.69), but this issue will be pursued in the next chapter.

Hobsbawm's negative view of wages militancy entailed a positive view of other forms of trade union action and even though he himself did not clearly describe these alternatives, other writers sympathetic to his analysis attempted to do so. The logic of Hobsbawm's critique of sectional wage struggle was that if trade union action was engaged in by a wider range of forces and directed towards non-wage objectives then it would be more likely to generate class consciousness. Communist Party theoreticians following in Hobsbawm's path have seen affinities between the logic of his argument and some of the positions developed by Gramsci, and described earlier. In particular they have echoed Gramsci's criticism of wage bargaining as an economic exchange that is normally compatible with capitalism, and his advocacy of trade union struggle over the control of the labour process. They have also adopted his emphasis on social forces other than labour and capital, and argued for trade union action in conjunction with groups such as tenants' associations, community groups, environmentalists and peace campaigners.

As the Communist Party's *British Road to Socialism* noted,

> ... the recent period ... has shown that industrial militancy is not enough, and that there is a need to combat the economist outlook which sees the trade union struggle on economic issues as sufficient in itself. That struggle needs to be linked with a political perspective if it is to produce lasting gains for the working class ... Action on social issues ... helps break down the divisions between work, home and community (1977, pp.23-4; see also Carter, 1981, 1986; Lane, 1982; Simon, 1982).

Feminist writers also took up Hobsbawm's critique, arguing that the economistic militancy of the past had primarily benefited well-organised groups of skilled, and hence mostly male workers. Whilst these groups had been able to protect their differentials through 'free collective bargaining' lower paid groups of women had remained at the bottom of the wages hierarchy (Coote and Campbell, 1987, Chap.2; Phillips, 1983, Chap.6). This concern with differentials was indicative of a narrow, sectional outlook which excluded other demands, of particular interest to women, such as creche facilities or shorter working time. Feminists disagreed about the alternative strategies available, with some favouring a comprehensive incomes policy (e.g. Campbell, 1982), whilst others doubted the effectiveness of this and opted instead for specific legislation to counter low and unequal pay (Weir and McIntosh, 1982; Phillips, 1983). There was however a wide measure of agreement on the necessity for womens' groups and other social forces to campaign jointly with trade unions, as this would lead to a broadening of horizons amongst the 'proletarian patriarchs' of the labour movement and expose them to the enriching effects of the very different traditions, methods and objectives of the womens' movement. The emergence of the miners' wives groups and Women Against Pit Closures during the 1984-85 miners' strike provided a test case for this type of practice and was judged by one leading feminist to have been a success (Campbell, 1986).

There is however an ambiguity in the attack on economistic militancy implicit in this argument, which renders its confrontation with evidence a little tricky. Though several weaknesses in trade union struggle have been identified—its 'economism', its sectional character, and its isolation from other political forces—their relative significance remains unclear. For instance, should we expect a positive impact on class consciousness from wage struggles conducted by trade unions in alliance with consumers? Will 'political struggles' by trade unions radicalise their members if they are conducted in isolation from other political forces? There is no obvious way of answering these questions at a theoretical level, though I shall return to them later in the chapter.

Against Hobsbawm, two different positions can be counterposed, one based on a straightforward defence of 'economistic' wage bargaining and the other drawing on Luxemburg's theory of mass strikes.

Economism

The strong Marxist defence of unfettered wage bargaining underwent a resurgence with the development of State incomes policies in Britain from 1960 onwards, and with the emergence of a legislative drive against trade unions which picked up momentum throughout the 1960s, peaking in 1969 (*In Place of Strife*) and again in the 1971 Industrial Relations Act. Against this burgeoning State intervention in collective bargaining, some Marxists counterposed the slogan of 'free collective bargaining', but others went much further. Harrison (1981) claimed, for instance, that '. . . in our time the wages question is being transformed under our eyes from a *sectional* into a *class* question, from an *industrial* into a *political* one' (p.57; cf. Anderson, 1967). Ken Gill agreed: 'The fact is that wages struggles are no longer *pure* wage struggles' (1981, p.22). The reasoning was simple: the State was a political agency; the State now intervened in wage bargaining; therefore trade union militancy over wages was directed against the State and was *ipso facto* 'political'. Harrison, Gill and others argued that the distinction between economic and political struggle had been dramatically, if not entirely, eroded by State intervention, and that, contrary to Hobsbawm, economic or wages struggles *had* radicalised workers in the early 1970s and would do so again.

Luxemburg's Marxism

A second, and related line of argument can be derived from Luxemburg's analysis of the mass strike. For Luxemburg, as we saw in Chapter 2, the consciousness-raising effect of strikes cannot be predicted from their content or demands alone. Economic strikes, over wages or hours of work, do *not* invariably produce only 'trade union consciousness' (as strict Leninists maintain) and nor do they invariably radicalise (as economist Marxists tend to maintain). Under the conditions specified by Luxemburg—large numbers of almost simultaneous strikes, large numbers of strikers, State repression, polarisation of society, revolutionary propaganda by a political party—the class consciousness of strikers can be raised dramatically. In other words, it is the *scale* of strikes, and the response of the State, not the initial demands of the strikers, that are crucial for understanding the link between strikes and consciousness.

Testing the Strikes–Class Consciousness Relationship

In order to test these arguments we therefore need to conduct two

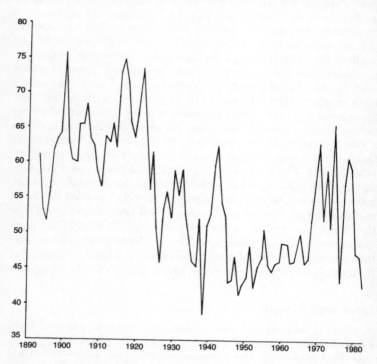

Figure 5.1   Percentage of all strikes conducted over wages and wage-related issues in the UK 1893-1986

types of comparison: firstly between periods of high and low wages militancy, to see whether Hobsbawm is right as against his critics; and secondly, between periods of high and low strike frequency and striker involvement, to evaluate Luxemburg's mass strike thesis. Although most of the ensuing discussion relates to Britain, reference will be made where possible to other countries.

Four historical periods in Britain have witnessed an unusually high proportion of strikes over wages and wage-related issues, as Figure 5.1 shows.

From 1897 to 1914 between 60% and 70% of all officially recorded strikes took place over wages issues, the proportion falling a little below 60% in 1909 and 1910, rising above 70% in 1900, and averaging 63.4% for the whole period. 1915 until 1922 marked the first sustained highpoint of wages militancy, with the

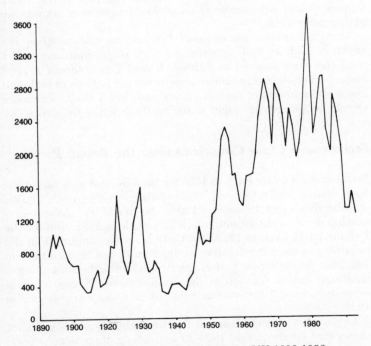

Figure 5.2 Numbers of strikes in the UK 1893-1986

proportion of wage strikes exceeding 70% in four of those eight years. From 1923 until 1940 the proportion of wages strikes fell considerably, rising above 60% only once, in 1924. A second peak of wages militancy occurred during the early years of World War Two, especially in 1941 and 1942. The post-war boom from 1945 to 1967 witnessed an all-time low in wages militancy, with the proportion of wages strikes rising above 50% in only two years, 1955 and 1965. The period from 1968 to 1974 witnessed a third peak in the proportion of wages strikes. Wages militancy peaked again in 1978/79, but from 1980 the proportion of wages strikes fell back to its early post-war figure. Historically therefore the high-water marks of 'economistic militancy' were the periods 1915-22, 1941-42, 1968-74 and 1978-79.

The strike frequency figures follow a similar trajectory (see Figure 5.2 above), peaking during the big strike waves of 1917-24, 1968-74 and 1977-78, with possible strike waves in addition between 1936 and 1946, and 1956-61 (see Screpanti, 1987 and Cronin, 1979 on strike waves). Indeed the two series, strike frequency and percentage of all strikes fought over wages, are highly correlated.

This fact creates an obvious difficulty in disentangling the effects of high strike frequency and high wages militancy and I shall therefore proceed as follows. I shall first compare several indicators of class consciousness between the periods of high and low strike frequency/wage militancy and then I shall focus more closely on periods of wages militancy/high strike frequency.

Strikes and Class Consciousness: the Broad Picture

Strike statistics date back to 1888 for the UK, but only one of the most basic indicators of class consciousness—trade union membership—can be assessed that far back. We have membership data on the Communist Party back to 1922, and for the Labour Party back to 1928, but there is serious doubt about the reliability of the latter figures. Voting figures can be used back to 1922, but for earlier years they can be misleading because Labour contested only a fraction of the existing seats. Finally there is some opinion poll data on trade unions that was first collected in 1954.

Let us start with Communist Party membership. The evidence shows that for the period 1924-79 as a whole, there is no general association between the growth of the CP and any measure of

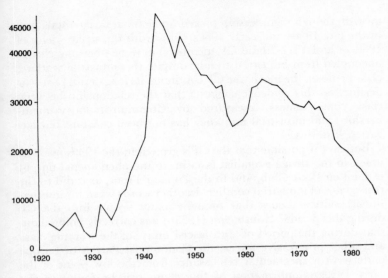

Figure 5.3 Communist Party membership 1924-1987

industrial conflict, either strike frequency, numbers of workers involved, numbers of days lost or proportion of strikes over wages issues.* But closer examination of the evidence suggests a more complex story. There have been three major periods of CP membership growth in Britain (see Figure 5.3): the early 1920s up until the immediate aftermath of the General Strike; the early 1930s until 1942 (in fact the CP grew every year from 1934 to 1942); and 1959 to 1964. Virtually all of the remaining years have witnessed membership decline. To put it another way, the CP grew, on average in three out of every four years until 1942, but it declined in three out of every four years *after* 1942.

Party membership rose in the early 1920s despite the decline in strike frequency after the post-war strike peak of 1918-20. With the recovery of union membership and strike frequency from 1934 the Party once more went into growth, and continued to grow as the numbers of wage strikes climbed steeply (see Figure 5.3 above). As wage militancy receded from 1945 so too did Party

* Communist Party membership figures are those supplied to me by the CPGB Organisation Department in a letter dated 12 July 1984.

growth, though membership picked up again as strike totals rose in the late 1950s and early 1960s. Only with the strike waves of 1968-74 and 1977-79 did CP membership trends become clearly uncoupled from industrial trends: despite the industrial working class being on the move, the CP continued its long-term, post-war decline. So this evidence suggests that the relationship between class consciousness (measured by Communist Party membership) and industrial militancy has not been constant but has varied historically.

But isn't it possible that the CP's growth in the 1930s owed as much to the struggle against fascism, to the phenomenal output of the Left Book Club, and to the Popular Front, as it did to the resurgence of industrial conflict? In other words wasn't it international political issues that brought many people into the CP during this period? Hobsbawm (1985b) has correctly pointed out that during the period of 'anti-fascist unity' of the working class and other progressive forces, the Communist Parties of Europe underwent a spectacular renaissance from the low point of the early 1930s. Confirmation of this claim can be found in the elections held between 1944 and 1946, where nine Communist Parties achieved their highest ever share of the vote either before or since (see also von Beyme, 1985, pp.102-3).

There is almost certainly a degree of truth in Hobsbawm's argument, and a number of famous intellectuals joined the CP in the 1930s as the only organisation capable of preventing the drift towards fascism and war. But Hinton's (1983) judgement is probably closest to the truth:

> . . . renewed growth partly reflected the party's continuing work among the unemployed . . .; partly the influx of intellectuals in the later 1930s; but, most significantly, the party's involvement in militant trade union activity (Hinton, 1983, pp.152-3).

In engineering, aircraft, mining and transport the CP built up powerful rank-and-file and shop steward organisations that played a major role in recruiting militant workers into the Party (see Branson, 1985, Chap.13; Hyman, 1987). It is also the case that CP membership rose again during the strikes of the early 1960s, so that CP advance cannot, in general, be attributed wholly or largely to international factors. At several periods in the past the CP has undoubtedly made substantial membership gains through its support for industrial disputes, many of which were fought over wages.

The second index of class consciousness that we can use is Labour Party voting, even though it was noted earlier that its meaning is extremely problematic. Table 5.3 below shows the Labour Party's share of the total votes cast from 1922 until 1987. The broad pattern is one of reasonably steady growth until 1951, followed by decline, with a resurgence in the mid-1960s, renewed decline through to 1983 and a small recovery in 1987.

Table 5.3 Labour Party votes 1922-87

	Total votes (000s)	As % of votes cast
1922	4241	29.5
1923	4439	30.5
1924	5489	33.0
1929	8390	37.1
1931	6650	30.6
1935	8325	37.9
1945	11995	47.8
1950	13266	46.1
1951	13948	48.8
1955	12404	46.4
1959	12215	43.8
1964	12205	44.1
1966	13065	47.9
1970	12179	43.0
1974 (Feb)	11639	37.1
1974 (Oct)	11457	39.2
1979	11532	36.9
1983	8457	27.6
1987	10034	30.8

Sources: Crewe, 1983; Butler and Sloman, 1980.

Broadly speaking the Labour Party vote shows no clear, overall relationship to industrial militancy over the period as a whole. The Labour vote rose in tandem with industrial militancy in 1924, 1935 and 1945, but fell with a resurgence of strikes in 1955, 1970 and 1979. In the wake of declining strike frequency the Labour vote has sometimes risen (as in 1966) and sometimes fallen (as in 1950). The resurgence of specifically economistic militancy has also been associated with mixed outcomes for

Labour: a rise in its vote from 1918 to 1922, further rises in 1924 and 1945, but declines in 1955, 1970, 1974 and 1979.

The broad pattern is therefore similar to that of the Communist Party, with a pronounced rise in Labour's fortunes pre-World War Two contrasting with an uneven decline after the war. The impact of industrial and economistic militancy has also been similar to its effects on the CP. Pre-World War Two Labour's fortunes rose hand-in-hand with industrial militancy, but after the War the two trends became increasingly disassociated, and Labour tended to be the victim rather than the beneficiary of industrial mobilisation through strikes.

Trade union membership provides one possible measure of class identity, and at the very least indicates an appreciation of the conflicts of interest between worker and employer even if these are not necessarily seen as fundamental antagonisms in the Marxist sense. According to Cronin (1979), fluctuations in trade union membership have been closely associated with the pattern of strike frequency in Britain. Membership rose dramatically during the big strike waves of 1889-92, 1910-13, 1918-21, and 1968-74. And the sharp recovery in strikes from 1934 coincided exactly with the recovery of trade union membership. Even though the militancy of strike waves tends to be highly economistic (at least in Britain) it has repeatedly brought large numbers of unorganised workers into trade unions, affirming their class identity and facilitating conflict with their employer.

Finally, there is opinion poll data on trade union popularity, collected annually by Gallup since 1954. What relationship does this evidence bear to strikes and economistic militancy? Broadly speaking, the proportion of respondents believing trade unions to be 'a good thing' declined slowly and unevenly from the 1960s, falling rapidly during years with a large number of strikes and recovering again quickly. Since 1980 trade union popularity as measured by Gallup has been on an upward trend and now stands at the level it enjoyed in the early 1960s. Trade union popularity tends to decline when strikes are more common, though it doesn't seem to make much difference whether strikes are fought over wage or non-wage issues.

On the face of it this poll data appears consistent with Hobsbawm's claims about the unpopularity of sectional, economistic militancy, at least until we introduce one additional, and puzzling fact. Opinion poll data provides one measure of trade union popularity, but trade union membership provides an even more obvious measure. If union membership is rising, then it seems logical to say that unions must be getting more popular. But if we put the opinion poll data and the union membership figures together, we find a clear negative relationship. In other words, when more people join unions, fewer people say they are a good thing (and vice versa). The explanation for this fact isn't clear, but it could be that a rising number of strikes stimulates both trade union membership amongst one section of society and a reaction against unions by another section.

In general, then, the overall relationship between strike frequency or wages militancy and our indicators of class consciousness is not very impressive. But this poor overall result conceals quite different findings pre- and post-World War Two. From the 1920s to the 1940s both the Labour and Communist Parties grew in association with industrial militancy, even if it was highly economistic as in 1920 and 1940-2. Industrial militancy did seem to 'spill over' into political class consciousness as measured by Labour votes and CP membership. But in the post-war period, the Labour Party in particular has often been the victim of industrial militancy and has twice been ejected from office in the midst of strike waves (1970, 1979). Hobsbawm is therefore wrong to argue that *in general* industrial militancy, and especially economistic militancy, cannot radicalise workers. But if Hobsbawm's general argument is wrong, then so too is the claim of economistic Marxists that the wages struggle *does* radicalise workers. Our evidence suggests that it *can*, but in the post-war period its effects have not been very impressive.

However, the indicators of class consciousness that I have used are not the only ones available; and some of them are ambiguous, whilst others may be too gross or insensitive to smaller changes in workers' consciousness. This suggests that we need to take a closer look at the strike waves in Britain and use a wider variety of ways of assessing class consciousness. There is a second reason for this more detailed exploration of labour disputes, and that is to try and explain *why* their effects appear to have been so different before and after World War Two. In particular I shall consider whether Luxemburg's theory of mass strikes helps account for this variability.

The Strike Wave of 1915-22

On Hobsbawm's basic argument, the economistic strike wave of 1915-22 should have been associated with little or no significant advance in class consciousness, but the evidence shows very much the opposite. Industrially this was a period of tremendous trade union growth, with membership jumping from 4.3 millions in 1915 to a peak of 8.3 millions in 1920 (a figure that would not be reached again until 1946) and falling back in the post-war slump to 5.6 millions just two years later (Cronin, 1979, Table B10). The shop stewards' movement crystallised, with strong bases in the engineering industries of Glasgow, Sheffield and Coventry. The TUC General Council was reorganised as a 'Central Committee' of the trade union movement with the task of overseeing the movement's corporate interests. And the number of small craft and occupational unions was dramatically reduced through the creation by merger of the giant engineering (AEU) and general unions (TGWU, GMWU) in 1920, 1922 and 1924 respectively. The total number of TUC unions was 227 in 1915, and after rising over the next three years to 266, it plummeted to just 194 affiliates in 1922.

Table 5.4   Strike indices for Britain 1915-24

	Strike frequency	Numbers of strikers (000s)	Striker days (000s)	% strikes over wages
1915	672	401	2953	72.8
1916	532	235	2446	74.8
1917	730	575	5647	71.4
1918	1165	923	5875	66.1
1919	1352	2401	34969	63.4
1920	1607	1779	26568	67.1
1921	763	1770	85872	73.4
1922	576	512	19850	66.8
1923	628	343	10672	56.2
1924	710	558	8424	61.4

Sources: Cronin, 1979, Tables B1, B2, B3; Smith et al., 1978, Table 1.

Politically, 1915-22 was the period in which Labour finally displaced the Liberals as the main opposition to the Tories, increasing their vote from 2.4 millions (22% of all votes cast) in 1918 to 4.2 millions (30% of all votes) in 1922 and increasing their parliamentary representation from 63 to 142 seats. The Communist Party came into existence in 1920, formed through an amalgamation of several socialist parties and elements from the shop stewards' movement. Unfortunately we have no systematic evidence on popular attitudes at the time, but it does seem reasonably well-established that war-time deprivation, government controls in the economy and inflation contributed to a fairly widespread discontent amongst citizens during the war and amongst demobbed soldiers at the war's end (Hinton, 1973). In the words of Cronin, 'there seems to have emerged an overwhelming sense that things could and must change' (1984, p.30), and it was this feeling that fed into the Labour Party's 1918 Programme with its vision of a 'new social order'. Trade unionists also displayed a readiness to demand far-reaching changes in the ownership and control of their industries, with the miners leading the way through their call for nationalisation. And when Britain joined with the other capitalist powers in the international struggle against Soviet Russia, it was trade unionists who initiated the 'Hands Off Russia' campaign, and dockers who blacked arms shipments for Polish counter-revolutionaries (Klugmann, 1969; Hutt, 1975).

The phenomenal growth of trade unionism, particularly amongst women workers, signifies at the very least an awareness of employer-worker conflict, and would have constituted for many a new identification with sections of fellow workers. The strengthening of the TUC through the creation of its General Council would seem to mark an advance, or at least an expression, of a strong corporate consciousness in the working class. And hegemonic aspirations were certainly embodied in the CP's foundation in 1920 and arguably expressed in the Labour Party's adoption of a new programme (including the famous Clause Four) two years earlier. These same events, taken together with the strike wave of the period, are testimony to a heightened sense of class identity as well as of class conflict, and to a belief amongst some workers in the fundamental antagonism between labour and capital. Indeed contemporary reports compiled by the police (to be taken therefore with a good measure of salt) declared that workers who wanted a 'social revolution' of some sort 'were by 1920 in the majority' (Cronin, 1984, p.24).

It is certainly true that the strike wave abated rapidly, that trade union membership fell by almost a third in three years (1920-23), that the Labour Party in office was a different animal than might have appeared from its arguably radical constitution and programme, and that CP membership probably fell from 3000 in 1920 to 2000 in 1922 (Klugmann, 1969, pp.331-2).

Moreover the million or so women who had been drawn into factory work to replace the enlisted men found little support for their continued right to work once the War was over. Employers and trade unionists were generally willing to see women return to the home (Boston, 1987, Chap.5, p.109). It is also true, as Hinton (1983, p.109) remarked, that 'Britain remained on the fringes of the international revolutionary crisis of 1917-21', and the weakness of revolutionary politics and organisation in Britain was indicated by the ease with which the Lloyd George government was able to re-establish bourgeois hegemony in the throes of a wave of industrial unrest of unprecedented dimensions (Burgess, 1980). But on balance there does seem to have been an upsurge in political class consciousness in this period, at least some of which was maintained institutionally in the CP, the Labour Party and the shop stewards' movement.

The Strike Wave of 1968-74

Hobsbawm's negative assessment of the outcomes of the 1968-74 strike wave rests in part on his judgement about a long-term decline in working-class consciousness, stretching back to the early 1950s. At about this time, the 'forward march of labour was halted', and the economistic militancy of the 1968-74 period failed to promote political class consciousness because it merely reflected the narrow, sectional outlook that had grown up in the post-war period.

Table 5.5 provides the major statistical data on the 1968-74 strike wave, and shows the substantial increase in strike volume and participation in this period.

The other significant feature of this strike wave is (as in 1915-22) the unusually high proportion of strikes over wages. Let us look in turn then at industrial and political indicators of class consciousness both before and during this wave of unrest.

Trade union membership and organisation

Trade union membership is the most basic indicator of sectional class identification and recognition of worker-employer conflict, and whilst absolute total membership rose from 7.9 millions in 1945 to 10.2 millions in 1968, trade union density was stagnant for most of this period. After the high point of 1948, when 45.2% of workers were organised, union density slipped to 44% where it

Table 5.5 Main strike statistics, UK 1946-76 (annual averages and totals)

	Strike frequency	Workers directly involved (000s)	Striker days (000s)	% strikes over wages
1946-52	1698	444	1887	44.2
1953-59	2093	551	3950	46.5
1960-64	2512	1499	3180	47.5
1965	2354	874	2925	50.1
1966	1937	544	2398	45.6
1967	2116	734	2787	46.5
1968	2378	2258	4690	51.7
1969	3116	1665	6846	57.2
1970	3906	1801	10980	63.1
1971	2228	1178	13551	51.8
1972	2497	1734	23909	59.2
1973	2873	1528	7197	50.9
1974	2922	1626	14750	65.8
1975	2282	809	6012	57.8
1976	2016	668	3284	43.4

Source: Cronin, 1984, Table A2; Cronin, 1979, Table B3.

remained for the next twenty years. But in the following ten years, trade union membership climbed dramatically, as the table below shows, with the total growth equally divided between the period of the strike wave (1968-74) and the period of the Labour government (1974-79).

Trade union density also rose, from 44% in 1968 reaching 50% by 1974. In other words it was during the 1968-74 strike wave that Britain first experienced a new upsurge in union growth, after two decades of stagnation.

One possible indicator of a transition from sectional to corporate consciousness is the decision by a section of workers to affiliate their trade union to the general organisation of unions, the TUC. (It is by no means a sure indicator because unions and their members may affiliate to the TUC merely to gain sectional advantage, and without regard for the interests of other unions or the movement as a whole.) Since 1963 there has been a steady influx of white-collar and public sector unions into the TUC and a recent increase in the proportion of organised workers affiliated

Table 5.6 Trade union membership, UK 1968-79 (millions)

Year	Membership	Year	Membership
1968	10.2	1974	11.8
1969	10.5	1975	12.0
1970	11.2	1976	12.4
1971	11.1	1977	12.8
1972	11.4	1978	13.1
1973	11.5	1979	13.4

Source: Bain and Price, 1983, Table 1, p.5.

to it. The late 1960s and middle-late 1970s witnessed two significant waves of TUC affiliation by unions anxious to secure access to the corridors of TUC power, significantly strengthened in the 1970s through the Social Contract. The two main teaching unions, NAS/UWT and the NUT, affiliated in 1969 and 1970 respectively, whilst the college lecturers' unions (AUT and NATFHE) joined in 1976. Civil Service unions also joined up from the mid 1970s (IPCS 1976, SCPS 1978, FDA 1979) along with a host of smaller unions, invariably organising public sector workers (Eaton and Gill, 1983).

Only the affiliation of the two big teaching unions appears to have been *directly* connected with the 1968-74 strike wave, but the round of later affiliations could be seen as a secondary consequence of the industrial unrest. In other words, the strike wave disrupted Labour trade union relations and led eventually to the Social Contract through which union influence over government was enshrined (see below). Consequently, many public sector unions had a clear interest in obtaining a voice within the TUC because of its increased influence over government.

One result of these affiliations was that the TUC came to speak on behalf of an even higher proportion of the organised working class than ever before and thus consolidated its role as the corporate voice of the working class in Britain. In 1970 the TUC embraced 84.1% of British trade unionists; by 1980 it represented 89.6% (calculated from *TUC Congress Reports* and Bain and Price, 1983, Table 1).

The post-war period also witnessed a decline in the number of trade unions, an important indicator of sectional organisation and possibly of sectional consciousness. In 1988 the TUC had just 85 unions in membership compared with 188 in 1950, 150 in 1970 and 111 in 1975 (*TUC Congress Reports*).

Finally, the industrial militancy of this period laid the basis for several rank and file movements both across and inside the trade unions, a few of which gained a considerable following and consolidated themselves as national, left-wing oppositions. The London Industrial Shop Stewards Defence Committee (later known as the Liaison Committee for the Defence of Trade Unions) was created in 1966 in opposition to the Labour government's incomes policy. By 1968 it was successfully coordinating industrial action through a network of militants against Labour's proposed anti-union legislation, and it played a major role in the strikes and demonstrations against the Conservative 1971 Industrial Relations Act (Hutt, 1975).

Within particular unions several new rank and file groups emerged in the throes of industrial militancy: in the National Union of Teachers in 1968, the NALGO Action Group in 1973, the Redder Tape group in the CPSA, and a group in the NUJ in the early 1970s. The Building Workers' Charter was launched in 1970 with support from Communist and IS (now SWP) stewards, and rank-and-file papers were produced by smaller groups of busworkers, miners, hospital and car workers (Shipley, 1976).

The demands of these groups largely covered improvements in terms and conditions of employment and the democratisation of union organisation by election of officials and strengthening of shop steward organisation. But they also included references to legislative changes, such as the anti-union laws, or calls for health and safety laws, and to wider issues such as nationalisation and public ownership (cf. Goulding, 1975 on the Building Workers' Charter, and Callinicos, 1982). In short, many of these movements and groups sprang from sectional or corporate demands, but some aspired to imbue their supporters with hegemonic aspirations, and the tension between these levels of demands and consciousness often erupted into battles between rival left groups, based around the SWP and the CP (cf. Hallas, 1977; Roberts, 1976).

Industrial action

Another significant feature of this period can be seen in the industrial dispersion of strikes. In the 1950s over 80% of days lost in officially recorded strikes were accounted for by less than 20%

of the workforce—in mining, docks, printing, shipbuilding, vehicles, transport and engineering—and white collar and public sector strikes were comparatively rare. By the mid-1970s a wide range of traditionally moderate and peaceful workers, many of them women, had embarked on strike action, many for the first time in their lives—nurses, doctors, social workers, teachers, local authority manual workers, gasworkers, postal workers and many others (Durcan et al., 1983). Ford women workers had struck for 'equal pay for work of equal value' and along with other women trade unionists had pushed both a reluctant TUC and an apprehensive Labour government into legislation (Boston, 1987, Chap.11). To strike against your employer in a traditionally peaceful industry or sector signifies a major advance in class consciousness on the part of some of the strikers, a recognition, at least behaviourally, that the labour-capital relation contains an element of conflict. This is not revolutionary consciousness, not even, as some socialists would have it, of an embryonic or latent kind, but it does, for all that, represent an advance in class consciousness amongst these groups of (often) public sector workers. But what of higher levels of class consciousness, whether corporate or hegemonic?

1968-74 was not only a period of rising wages militancy, it was also a time in which the political strike returned to Britain after an absence of almost fifty years. The attempts of Labour and Conservative governments to pass and implement repressive legislation curbing strikes and formalising collective bargaining produced a wave of opposition from many sections of the working class. A series of one-day stoppages against the 1971 Tory Industrial Relations Bill culminated in an historic decision by the TUC to *instruct* all of its members not to comply with the Act by refusing to register themselves as trade unions when the Bill became law. At first the General Council had merely wished to *recommend* non-registration, leaving the final decision to constituent unions, but Congress delegates voted to put the corporate interests of the movement above the sectional rights of its affiliated members and carried the day for an instruction (Weekes et al., 1975). The highwater mark of opposition to the Act occurred in 1972 following the jailing of five dockers for contempt of a court order issued in connection with the Act's provisions. A rapidly escalating series of rank-and-file stoppages pushed the TUC into action, and faced with widespread disruption the government backed down and ordered the dockers to be released. This was just one of an upsurge of sympathy strikes that took place after 1968. Further stoppages of work against government policies continued sporadically throughout the 1970s, with strikes-cum-demonstrations against abortion restrictions, public sector spending cuts, and the main thrust of Labour's economic policy. This same period also witnessed some far-reaching challenges to employers' prerogatives in the workplace, with a wave of over 500 factory occupations and sit-ins, mostly asserting the right to work in the face of capitalist rationalisation (cf. Jefferys, 1979; Foster and Woolfson, 1986). None of this data of course is unambiguous: a general stoppage to protest at public sector spending cuts could represent no more than a coalition of sectional interests temporarily united by a common threat (Fryer, 1979).

Labour movement policy and public opinion

There were during this period significant leftward swings in the leaderships of several major trade unions, with the election of Hugh Scanlon in the AEU (1968), Jack Jones in the TGWU (1969) and David Basnett in the GMWU (1973), though only Basnett's election came *after* the strike upsurge from 1968 and can be seen as a product of it. Nevertheless both Scanlon and Jones were left-wing candidates who had risen through the shop stewards' movement and both were at the time of election strong supporters of militant tactics. It was also in this period that many unions came to adopt a more or less radical version of the Alternative Economic Strategy, promoted by the CP and others, and the Labour Party adopted in 1973 a draft manifesto widely described as the most radical since 1945. The heart of the programme was a 'Social Contract' between the trade unions and the Labour government which set out a joint policy covering economic growth, investment, industrial strategy, welfare spending, prices and incomes and industrial relations legislation. (The principles of the policy are covered fully in Chapter 9 on the State). Trade union economic policy had traditionally concentrated on demand management and welfare spending, but by the early 1970s a series of events, including the wave of strikes, had forced trade unions across Europe to rethink their traditional ideas. TUC leaders emphasised the necessity for the State and the unions to exert more control over economic decision-making at both company and State level, but this was not simply a radical *economic* strategy:

... many of the TUC leaders and the Labour Party officials most favourable to these schemes continued to see them less as urgent measures of *economic* policy ... than as steps in a long-range *political* strategy designed to push Britain along the path toward socialism by resuming the reformist endeavour abandoned in the late 1940s (Gourevitch et al., 1984, pp.44-5).

How far were the measures in this strategy reflected in the attitudes and behaviour of Labour supporters and other members of the public? Two of the central planks of the strategy entailed an increase in trade union influence through industrial democracy, and increased state control over firms through a variety of measures up to and including nationalisation. The rightward drift in public opinion on both of these issues notable through the 1960s was temporarily thrown into reverse between 1970 and 1974 amongst Labour supporters, as the following table shows, though unions continued to decline in public opinion polls.

Now the Labour vote declined between 1970 and 1974 (see above) both in absolute and relative terms, and the number of people identifying themselves as Labour supporters declined with it, from 42% to 40% of the electorate (Crewe, 1982). It is therefore possible that the 'rise' in support for unions and nationalisation is more apparent than real, and merely a statistical artefact produced by opponents of these measures opting out of

Table 5.7 Percentage of self-identified Labour supporters and members of the public who believed ...

	1964	*1966*	*1970*	*1974*	*1979*
... trade unions have too much power (Labour supporters)	41	55	60	58	64
... trade unions are a bad thing (members of the public)	12	20	24	27	36
... more industries should be nationalised (Labour supporters)	57	52	39	53	32

Sources: Crewe 1982, Table 1.11; Gallup Political Index, September 1985, Table 10.

Labour support between 1970 and 1974, and not showing up in the figures for 1974. Without more detailed evidence it is difficult to tell whether this is the case.

There is only one reliable data source on *industrial* attitudes amongst trade unionists, namely the Workplace Industrial Relations Surveys carried out in 1966, 1972 and 1973 (McCarthy and Parker, 1968; Parker, 1974, 1975). A representative sample of stewards, members and full-time officials from a range of industries were asked to state under which of four circumstances they thought industrial action was justified. The full results are given in a later chapter (Table 7.3), but they reveal almost no significant differences in attitude over time, contrary to what one might have expected on the basis of the big increase in strikes and trade union membership.

Socialist politics

I have already discussed the broad pattern of Labour Party support in elections (Table 5.3 above), and Communist Party membership (Figure 5.3 above), and the Table (5.8) below shows Communist Party electoral performance over the years.

Table 5.8   Communist Party election results 1945-87

Year	Total votes	Candidates	Votes per candidate
1945	102,780	21	4,894
1950	91,746	100	917
1951	21,640	10	2,164
1955	33,144	17	1,950
1959	30,897	18	1,716
1964	45,932	36	1,276
1966	62,112	57	1,090
1970	37,970	58	655
1974	32,741	44	744
1974	17,426	29	601
1979	15,958	38	420
1983	11,598	35	331
1987	6,078	19	320

Sources: *Communist Focus* 7, June-July 1983; *News and Views*, July 1987; Butler and Sloman, 1980.

The decline of both the Labour and CP votes is clear from the tables, whether measured in absolute or percentage terms, and the votes for other revolutionary left candidates have almost invariably been derisory. It *is* worth noting however that Labour's vote has *not* declined uniformly from the high point of 1951, and in percentage terms its 1966 vote was better than in the landslide of 1945 and not far behind the all-time high 1951 figure. Labour's decline, then, has proceeded in two stages, the first during the long post-war Tory reign from 1951 to 1964, and the second throughout the 1970s and 1980s. It is also worth observing that the secular decline in votes per CP candidate was checked only once after the War, and that was at the tail end of the 1968-74 strike wave, though this was small consolation and could have reflected the more careful placement of a smaller number of candidates. Voting figures, of course, can be notoriously poor indicators of class consciousness, particularly in the case of the Labour Party which has always attracted a broad political constituency of liberals, socialists, pacifists, mild reformers, moderate trade unionists etc.

Furthermore, the British electoral system of first past the post provides little incentive for people to back parties with only a small fraction of the total vote. Support for this interpretation comes from a comparison with other European countries which also experienced strike waves at the end of the 1960s, but whose electoral systems are based on some form of proportional representation. Communist Parties in Belgium, Denmark, West Germany, Finland, France, Italy, the Netherlands, Austria, Sweden and Switzerland all increased their share of the vote between the late 1960s and the middle 1970s, with Norway (and Britain) being the only exceptions to this consistent, if small, trend (von Beyme, 1985, Table 2.5).

If we look at party *membership*, a slightly less depressing and more mixed picture emerges. Individual Labour Party membership fell steadily through the 1950s and 1960s, with an upturn in the mid-1960s (coinciding with an upturn in its vote) and further increases in 1971, 1972 and 1974 (Butler and Sloman, 1980). On the other hand the number of trade unionists affiliated to the Labour Party remained constant at approximately 5.5 million from 1954 until 1974 when it began to rise slowly (Labour Party *NEC Report 1985*, pp.9–78). But as total trade union membership increased rapidly in the 1970s this meant that the *percentage* of trade unionists who were affiliated to Labour actually fell from 67.8% in 1955 to 58.7% in 1970 and to a low of 49.8% in

978 (Labour Party *NEC Report 1985*; *TUC Congress Reports*).
Communist Party membership peaked at 56,000 in 1942 and
part from a short spell of growth between 1959 and 1964 (when
membership rose by almost 10,000), the Party has lost members
n almost all of the remaining post-war years (cf. Figure 5.3).
Though CP membership increased during two of the years of the
big strike wave, 1973 and 1975, the fact remains that between
968 and 1974 the CP experienced a net loss of members, its total
alling from 32,114 to 28,328.

The far left witnessed a spectacular growth in percentage terms
between 1968 and 1974, though it looks minuscule in absolute
numbers. Reliable membership figures are hard to come by for
ny of the revolutionary left groups, but most observers trace any
ignificant growth to the aftermath of the events of 1956, when
he CP lost 7,000 members. Trotskyism gained a new lease of life
n this period, with the substantial inroads made in the Labour
Party Young Socialists by the Socialist Labour League. Whatever
rowth of membership there may have been up to 1964 appears
o have been checked in the first four years of Labour government
as was CP growth), but took off again from 1968. A combination
f student political unrest over Vietnam and industrial unrest in
he face of anti-union legislation and incomes policies precipi-
ated an upsurge of growth for the tiny Trotskyist groups
particularly the International Socialists, IS, now SWP), not only
n Britain but in other West European countries such as France,
taly and West Germany.

Table 5.9 Estimated IS/SWP membership 1966-76

Year	Membership
1966	200
1968	5-700
1970	1000
1972	2000
1974	2500
1976	3500-4000

Sources: Shaw, 1978; Birchall, 1981; Shipley, 1976.

Whilst other groups, such as the Internationalist Marxist
Group (IMG), also recruited in this period, IS was significant
because it alone managed to attract industrial workers active in
disputes, and on this basis to build a network of rank-and-file

groups that would operate throughout the 1970s until their formal closure in 1982 (Callinicos, 1982).

The circulation figures for socialist papers and magazines reveal an even more pronounced renaissance, with *Socialist Worker* increasing its average weekly sale from 8,000 in 1969 to 21,000 in 1972 (a fact that may be partly accounted for by an increased number of sellers) (see Birchall, 1981). A rising volume of socialist paper and magazine sales is hardly conclusive proof for the growth of hegemonic consciousness, but it is consistent with it, and with the figures for rising membership of some socialist organisations. Although the net membership gains of the far left between 1968 and 1974 (approximately 4,000) were offset by a similar decline in CP membership over the same period, far greater numbers flowed through these organisations, staying only for a short while.

Finally, it is worth noting the revival of ideas about workers' control, with the creation of the Institute for Workers' Control in 1968. Over the next few years the IWC held a number of conferences, published a vast number of pamphlets and books and most significantly achieved a hearing for its ideas within the trade union movement. In conjunction with shop stewards and union officials it launched inquiries into industrial democracy in a number of industries, and its meetings and activities were strongly supported by leading trade unionists in the TGWU and the AUEW (see Hyman, 1974, and Chapter 8, below). For a brief period its ideas enjoyed a limited resonance within sections of the trade union movement, particularly where workers were faced with the adverse consequences of rationalisation and technical change.

In summary, then, the 1968-74 strike wave coincided with some limited gains in class consciousness: trade union membership began to grow quickly, inter-union rank-and-file organisation was created and rank-and-file bodies emerged for the first time in a number of unions, reflecting a growth of both sectional and corporate consciousness. Evidence for the growth of hegemonic consciousness is limited and consists of three points. Firstly, there was a leftward shift in union and Labour Party economic strategy away from a purely corporate defence of workers' autonomy and interests within capitalism and towards a desire to intervene in and influence corporate economic decision-making. Secondly, there was a resurgence of far-left political organisation and publications, though on a very limited scale, and even this was virtually offset by a decline in Communist

Party membership. And thirdly there was a limited revival of interest in ideas of workers' control of industry.

The 'Winter of Discontent' 1977-79

The strike wave of 1968-74 began when Labour was in office, with the peaks of strike numbers and workers involved reached in the election year of 1970, but the bulk of the strike wave took place under Edward Heath's Conservative administration. The strike wave at the end of the decade also involved many workers in wages struggles against a government pay norm, only this time the government was Labour.

The table below shows the main statistical indices for the period.

Table 5.10 Strike statistics 1975-80

Year	Strike frequency	Workers directly involved (000s)	Striker days (000s)	Percentage strikes over wages
1975	2282	809	6012	57.8
1976	2016	668	3284	43.4
1977	2703	1166	10142	57.6
1978	2471	1042	9405	61.1
1979	2080	4608	29474	59.1
1980	1330	834	11964	47.7

Sources: Cronin, 1984, Table A.2; Cronin, 1979, Table B.3.

As in 1970, Labour was defeated at the polls in the midst of this wave of industrial unrest. Interestingly, trade union and TUC membership continued to grow; and left-wing policies centred on the Alternative Economic Strategy continued to constitute the official line of the TUC and many of its members. But politically, 1979 witnessed a substantial Tory victory aided by significant rightward swings amongst skilled workers. And overall, whilst the Labour vote remained mainly working class, a majority of manual and a majority of organised workers cast their votes for parties other than Labour (or did not vote at all), a phenomenon not seen since 1922 (Crewe, 1982).

Opinion poll data showed trade unions reaching an all-time low in popularity during the winter of discontent, with 44% of people in February 1979 declaring them to be, in general, a 'bad thing', a view that undoubtedly contributed to the Conservative election victory just three months later.

Individual Strikes and Class Consciousness

Before pulling together the various strands of the discussion on strike waves, it is worth briefly commenting on the impact of individual strikes on workers' consciousness. Many Marxists would probably endorse (albeit with many qualifications) the view recently expressed by Harman (1985a, p.2) when he wrote about the miners' strike that '. . . you can see how once people get involved in such struggles they themselves undergo amazing changes'. The idea that in transforming the world people thereby transform themselves has a long history in Marxist theory and practice. Yet it is an extraordinary fact that the amount of systematic and reliable evidence on the effects of strike involvement is almost nil.

There are quite a number of journalistic accounts of individual strikes, and a few academic studies (see Hartley et al., 1983, for a review), but for the most part these have been primarily concerned with the origins, context and progress of strikes and have said nothing remotely systematic about the effects of strikes on those who took part in them. The few exceptions to this rule include Lane and Roberts (1971), Allen (1981) and Hartley et al. (1983).

Lane and Roberts's epitaph to the Pilkington's dispute has been widely quoted, and on the face of it is consistent with Harman's Marxist thesis quoted earlier: 'By God, this strike has been a bloody education' (1971, p.210). The comment came from a self-confessed militant on the Strike Committee, but did it represent the effects of the strike across the rank and file as a whole? Lane and Roberts continued with the observation that

> a large minority of the RFSC [Rank and File Strike Committee] however continued to think that Britain was basically a fair, just and democratic society. Pilkington's, the police, the press and the GMWU, were just aberrations in a world that was otherwise still fundamentally reasonable . . . For the majority there had been an obvious shift in attitudes from feeling *fairly* optimistic about Britain to feelings of some pessimism . . . (1971, pp.201-2).

But pessimism did not entail fatalism, as many of the strikers expressed their profound dissatisfaction with their own union, the GMWU, by breaking away to form a new (but short-lived) rival body, the Glass and General Workers Union.

It is not clear how this complex mixture of outcomes relates to class consciousness, a point made by Allen (1981) in his informed discussion of the 1972 and 1974 miners' strikes and their aftermath.

> The quality of the consciousness of the miners made the 1972 and 1974 strikes historic ones but it would be mistaken to see revolutionary implications in them. The miners wanted only wage increases on both occasions. They did not aim to threaten the Government, nor did they blame the institution of Government. Indeed they adopted a negative attitude, one of cynicism and irreverence, towards the Government. It was this which was new ... The miners' consciousness did not rise to a consistently higher permanent political plane. Consciousness does not work like that. It goes up and down with circumstances (Allen, 1981, pp.320-21).

What emerges from both of these accounts is that above all else workers acquire through strike action a tremendous sense of confidence in their own, collective power.

This theme also emerges from Hartley et al.'s (1983) account of the thirteen-week 1980 steel strike. On their return to work, South Yorkshire strikers were determined that those haulage firms which had crossed their picket lines would be permanently blacked and banned from British Steel premises. British Steel was equally determined to conduct business with anyone it pleased, and within four hours of the formal resumption of work after the strike, the first dispute arose over a 'blacked' lorry. The workers responded to management's tough-minded approach with an immediate walk-out, and within hours over 10,000 workers were once again out on strike, determined not to be pushed around by their employer.

But the same study also revealed important differences in the effects of the strike as between sections of the workforce. The clear majority of the 535 workers who returned the study's questionnaire believed the strike had made them 'more militant' (a fact demonstrated in their willingness to strike again within hours of being back at work), but manual workers had been affected this way much more than white-collar workers. Furthermore, the experience of picketing during the strike produced much greater effects on the declared militancy of white-collar workers than amongst blue-collar workers (Hartley et al., 1983, pp.155-8,

198-201). The explanation for this, and for the Pilkington results, may be that strike participation has much greater effects on those with relatively little past involvement in or experience of trade unionism and industrial action. Amongst hardened veterans of industrial action, such as the Ford Halewood workers so graphically described by Beynon (1984), the effects of individual strikes may be less because their sense of class identity and consciousness of conflict or antagonism towards the employer has already been formed and reproduced through countless incidents and experiences.

Towards an Assessment

Hobsbawm's critique and the economist defence of wages militancy

Does the evidence in this chapter sustain Hobsbawm's critique of economistic militancy? What it suggests is that the growth of political class consciousness *has* sometimes been associated with periods of high wages militancy, contrary to Hobsbawm's argument. But there have also been periods of such militancy that have produced little sign of politicisation amongst the working class, contrary to some of the economists' arguments. Indeed, what the critics and the supporters of wages militancy have in common is the belief that there exists some general relationship between wages struggle and class consciousness which holds up across a number of historical periods. The evidence from Britain suggests there is *no* such relationship. Wages struggle is a general recipe neither for success in raising class consciousness (as economistic Marxists maintain) nor for failure (as Hobsbawm and Gramscian Marxists tend to maintain). It is therefore quite wrong to attribute the disappointing growth of class consciousness through the early 1970s to the predominance of wage demands in strikes, since this same predominance was associated with quite different outcomes between 1915 and 1922.

Beyond Hobsbawm? Radical demands and 'new social forces'

The obverse of Hobsbawm's critique of wages militancy was an endorsement of more radical non-wage strike demands by trade unionists, and the creation of alliances between trade unions and a range of social forces. As it has already been shown that strikers' wage demands can readily co-exist with more radical demands, whether pursued through trade union or political channels, we need to concentrate here on the argument about 'new social forces'. Campbell (1986), for instance, argued that the miners' strike was considerably enriched and strengthened by the support of women's groups. And both Brindle (1987) and Clay (1987) have suggested that the phenomenal growth and bargaining success of the RCN owes much to its advocacy of peaceful methods of persuasion as opposed to the traditional methods of the strike and the picket line which they regard as counter-productive because of their damaging effects on consumers and clients in particular and public opinion in general (as in the case of the teachers' dispute 1985-87).

The argument is often then extended to the conclusion that unions must actively seek out allies in struggle, both other workers and other social forces, and must do so by elaborating a range of social or political demands capable of mobilising such constituencies. During and after the 1984-85 miners' strike it was argued by Carter (1985), Reid (1985) and others that the NUM should have constructed a comprehensive critique of government energy and employment policies in order to mobilise a broad constituency behind their struggle and isolate the government. Likewise, during 1985 and 1986 the teachers were advised of the overwhelming importance of conducting ideological struggle on questions such as teaching standards, classroom size, educational resources etc., in order to effect a similar shift in the balance of forces by eroding the government's 'historic bloc' of support.

This line of argument and analysis does, however, contain a number of problems. Though it is often advanced as a *general* means for winning trade union struggles, it is more plausible to argue that the mobilisation of wider, public support is in fact only a particular strategy appropriate in very specific circumstances. As an adjunct to industrial action by public sector unions, faced with an employer, i.e. the State, sensitive to public opinion, it may be of some use. But the mobilisation of public support or opinion offers no obvious advantages to the majority of the workforce in the private sector, or to those groups whose consumers are difficult to organise. Even in the public sector, governments have a history of resisting the most well-organised and supported campaigns, from the bus workers in the 1960s (cf. Fuller, 1985) to the health workers in 1982 and the teachers in 1985-87.

Secondly, it is unclear exactly how class consciousness is supposed to develop in the course of such struggles. The implication of the argument is that the interaction between unions and other social forces will produce an escalation of class consciousness among trade unionists. Yet this is only one possible mechanism, and any number of other factors could be equally responsible for any observed radicalisation of strikers: a context of economic and political crisis; the scale of strike action (cf. Luxemburg, below); the levels and forms of participation by strikers (cf. Hartley et al., 1983 on the 1980 steel strike); the resistance and strategies of the strikers' opponents; or the ideological work of political leaderships. For these reasons, what is sometimes presented as a contemporary Gramscian or feminist critique of strikes and their impact on class consciousness contains serious weaknesses (only some of which, incidentally, can be found in Gramsci himself).

Luxemburg's mass strike theory

According to Luxemburg's argument, we would explain the growth of class consciousness during different periods of industrial unrest by considering the degree and form of state intervention and the levels of working-class mobilisation.

One result of the First World War, in almost all the belligerent countries, was a significant expansion of the State into economic and industrial life. The right to strike (where it existed) was curbed; labour was directed into particular branches of industry; collective agreements were suspended to allow the introduction of initially unskilled women workers into skilled engineering work; the State moved quickly to settle industrial disputes; and it became the major, and sometimes the only customer, for whole branches of industry, thus providing itself with considerable leverage (Geary, 1981, Chap.4). Troops were used on numerous occasions throughout this period to break strikes: notably the Glasgow rent and engineering strikes (1915), the railways strike (September 1918), Glasgow engineers (January 1919), Yorkshire miners (March 1919), Liverpool police (August 1919) and the railways again (September 1919) (Peak, 1984; Jeffery and Hennessy, 1983). In 1920 the government passed the Emergency Powers Act which provided the State with far-reaching powers of intervention, through the police, army and commissioners, in the event of industrial unrest. Similar actions were adopted by governments in Russia, Germany, Italy, Hungary and elsewhere as waves of strikes engulfed the warring countries from 1917 onwards.

But the function of troops varied both between and within countries, and in Britain their role was then in a transitional state. Traditionally troops had been used to restore and maintain public order through direct, physical assaults on strikers, picket-lines and demonstrations. But from the early years of this century their role has been more and more transformed into that of an alternative labour force, whilst their public order function has been effectively transferred to the police and to para-military police units (cf. Hain, 1986; Peak, 1984). After the mass picketing and flying pickets used so successfully in the 1972 miners' strike and the 1973 building strike, police forces throughout the country created Police Support Units, trained in crowd and riot control, and equipped with shields, helmets and truncheons. It was these forces which played such a prominent and violent role in the 1984-85 miners' strike (Geary, 1986).

States of Emergency were declared on five occasions during the 1968-74 strike wave—for the dock strike (August 1970), electricity strike (December 1970), miners' strike (March, 1972), dock strike (March 1972) and the miners' and power strikes (March 1974). In none of these cases, however, were troops actually used, though in the ensuing years they appeared five times—during the Ulster workers' strike (1974), the Glasgow refuse strike (1975), the air traffic control assistants' strike (1977), the firefighters' strike (1977) and the Clyde naval dockyard strike (1978) (Jeffery and Hennessy, 1983).

What provoked such extensive state intervention at the end of World War One was partly the sheer scale of the strikes. Though the numbers of strikes and strikers were fewer in 1915-22 than in the later strike waves, they resulted in far more days lost, as Table 5.11 shows.

Table 5.11 Strikers involved and days lost during three strike waves (annual averages)

	1915-22	*1968-74*	*1977-79*
Strikers involved (000s)	1075	1363	2272
% total labour force	5.9	5.9	9.4
Days lost (annual average in 000s)	23,023	11,703	16,340

Sources: Cronin, 1984, Table A.2; Bain and Price, 1983, Table 1.1; Bain, 1972, Table 4.12.

The high point of the 1968-74 wave was 1972 (the year of the miners' strike), when working days lost reached almost 24 millions. Otherwise days lost remained between 4.6 and 14.7 millions and averaged 11.7 millions per year. By contrast, the annual average for the period 1915-22 was *twice* that figure, at 23 millions, and reached an historic peak (apart from 1926) of 85 million working days lost in 1921.

It can also be argued that the deprivations of wartime and the dislocations attendant on the demobilisation of troops at the war's end contributed to a widespread economic, political and social crisis which severely strained the capacities and resources of ruling classes across Europe. The resort to repression of strikers was one expression of the ineffectiveness of traditional methods of rule based on institutionalised patterns of labour-capital cooperation.

The patterns of repressive State intervention, the scale of strike waves in these three periods, and the associated developments of class consciousness are all consistent with Luxemburg's model of strike politicisation and societal polarisation. Repressive intervention by the State is likely to engender a strong consciousness of corporate interests, a feeling that all workers share a common plight and a common enemy. Strikers *de facto* recognise conflict between themselves and their employers, but the recognition of fundamental antagonism is facilitated if workers feel that other political and ideological agencies—such as the State, press etc.—are acting at the behest of or on behalf of the employers. So long as they are seen as neutral, such agencies can be perceived by workers as means for resolving their dispute, with the State or its agencies representing a higher interest and an impartial means of dispute resolution. Once this perception is eroded by State *partiality*, workers may then feel more isolated and threatened, and consequently ever more hostile to their enemies. Jeffery and Hennessy (1983), writing of the Emergency Powers legislation in Britain, noted that the Lloyd George government was particularly anxious to stress its own neutrality, and to present its actions as being in the interests of 'the community' (p.65). The government during the later strike waves was Labour, and whilst its hostility to unions and strikes may help us understand its subsequent electoral fortunes, the decline of the Labour vote in 1970 and 1979 was not matched by any corresponding swing to the Left.

Is Luxemburg's theory still relevant?

Even if Luxemburg's argument is broadly compatible with the empirical evidence from Britain, there remains one outstanding problem. The defence of the radicalising potential of strike waves rests primarily on the 1915-22 period, to a lesser degree on the 1968-74 strike wave and not at all on the 1977-79 wave. It is interesting to observe that an American study of strike waves reached a similar conclusion, though it used far less systematic evidence. Brecher (1972) suggested that nineteenth-century strike waves had been far more unified and embraced wider patterns of solidarity than their twentieth-century counterparts. Likewise Davis (1986) argued that the post-World War One strike wave in America had failed to overcome deep-seated ethnic divisions and divisions between skilled and semi-skilled workers. And despite the scale of strike action throughout the capitalist world between 1968 and the mid-1970s, not one capitalist economy (with the remote exception of France) ever seemed to be in danger of passing into a crisis sufficiently deep to constitute a revolutionary situation.

This historical sequence raises an interesting possibility, alluded to in the critique of Luxemburg in Chapter 2. Might it be the case that waves of industrial unrest were associated with working-class radicalisation only during an historical period which has now passed? In the early years of this century many labour movements were effectively excluded from participation in industrial management (because of the underdevelopment of collective bargaining, joint consultation and industrial democracy) and from participation in State affairs because of the weakness of their political parties (cf. Geary, 1981). With the spread of institutionalised collective bargaining after World War Two, and the increased electoral success of workers' parties, it became fashionable to argue that the intensity and radicalism of large-scale industrial conflicts were a thing of the past. On this view, capitalist societies had successfully insulated industrial conflict from the political system, limiting the dysfunctional consequences of worker militancy (cf. Muller-Jentsch on West Germany, 1986; and Dahrendorf, 1959, more generally). Other observers pointed to a long-term decline in the size and relative weight of the industrial working class, and the growth of a large, less well-organised service sector. Allied to divisions within the workplace between 'core' and 'peripheral' workers, these processes constituted an historic segmentation and decline of the traditional working class, and with it the decline of the socialist project (cf. Gordon et al., 1982 on segmentation; and Gorz, 1982 on the working class more generally).

It would also be possible to invoke one of the several variants of the Stages theory of capitalist development to arrive at an equally gloomy prognosis about the contemporary relevance of Luxemburg's analysis of strike waves. Aglietta (1979), for instance, developed the notion of 'regimes of accumulation' to refer to the simultaneous epochal shifts in the capitalist labour process, modes of wage-earners' consumption and organisation of capitalist firms. Perhaps the transition from 'Taylorism' to 'Fordism' in the early part of this century was uniquely and sufficiently disruptive to precipitate strike waves and revolutionary situations across the globe, but the current transition to 'neo-Fordism' will be a more regulated and less painful adjustment (cf. also Piore and Sabel, 1984).

In reply to these points, it must be acknowledged that the permanent deradicalisation of workers and their struggles against capital cannot be precluded on theoretical or empirical grounds. On the other hand, as I shall try to demonstrate in analysing the state of the labour movement (Chapter 10), the 'deradicalisation thesis' cannot convincingly be supported by data on the decline or restructuring of the working class.

Beyond these preliminary remarks, Luxemburg's theory can be defended on three counts. First, it is possible to argue that the smaller *scale* of strikes and of State intervention between 1968 and 1974, and the greater stability of British capitalism compared to 1918-22, impeded class consciousness from developing in the way that Luxemburg envisaged. The model itself, on this argument, is basically sound, but the mass strikes of 1968-74 simply weren't massive enough.

The validity of this interpretation could be confirmed only by a future wave of strikes sufficient to elicit wide-ranging State repression and promote class polarisation. Some writers have been tempted to present the 1984-5 miners' strike in such a light, arguing that many workers were radicalised in the course of those stormy twelve months. But it is also true that many workers (including miners) became extremely antagonistic towards the NUM, and the strike level in Britain fell alarmingly in the twelve months after the strike (though other factors, principally the effects of the Trade Union Act (1984), may also have been responsible for the strike decline). But whatever the evidence suggests, the miners' strike did not, strictly speaking, conform to

Luxemburg's conception of a *mass* strike, since it remained a single industry strike; and therefore it has no strict relevance for a theory of mass strikes.

Secondly, we could *acknowledge* the smaller scale of strike action between 1968-74 compared to 1915-22, but maintain that under conditions of full parliamentary democracy and free elections, relative social stability and strong workers' parties, and institutionalised bargaining between unions and employers, strike waves (or mass strikes) *will* produce a radicalisation of workers, but that this will express itself through leftward pressure on the programmes and policies of the major workers' parties and the trade unions: it will not in the first instance take the form of support for insurrection, though whether it might ultimately do so is an open question. Under such conditions, mass strikes produce hostility to particular governments, not to the state apparatus of which they are a part. In the light of the evidence, which is ambiguous, complex and difficult to interpret, this proposition can however be no more than a hypothesis, but it is in my view considerably more plausible than the alternative scenario of mass strikes leading to insurrection.

Thirdly, since Luxemburg's theory requires the periodic occurrence of strike waves, then to demonstrate the probability of such events in the future is *ipso facto* to demonstrate one of the essential preconditions for working-class radicalisation. The major study of strike waves in Britain is by Cronin (1979), and he argued that

> six strike waves have occurred in England since 1880: 1889-92, 1910-13, 1918-21, 1926, 1957-62, and 1968-72. These beginning and end points are admittedly arbitrary and approximate . . . The period 1910 to 1926 could be considered one long wave, instead of three, or 1957-72 one instead of two (Cronin, 1979, p.48).

Theoretically, Cronin argued that strike waves were synchronised with Kondratiev's 'long waves' of economic development, 20-25 years of economic growth followed by 20-25 years of decline and so on in succession. Thus, the first great strike wave (1889-92) came at the end of the Great Depression, the next at the end of the Edwardian boom (1910-13, 1918-21). The 1968-74 strike wave occurred at the end of the post-war boom, but according to Cronin there should have been a strike wave at the end of the 1930s Depression (1979, pp.60-2). Looking at the statistics, however (Figure 5.2 above), there was certainly a

dramatic upsurge of strikes from 1934, though whether it constitutes a strike wave is a difficult question that can only be
answered with the aid of more precise criteria. Consistent
adherence to a Kondratiev 20-25 year long wave model would
lead one to say that strike waves occur at the *transition* between
economic boom and slump, viz. 1889-92 (end of slump), 1910-20
(end of boom), c. 1936-47 (end of slump), 1968-74 (end of boom)
(cf. also Gordon et al., 1982, p.9 and Screpanti, 1987 for similar
Kondratiev periodisations applied to the USA, Italy, Germany
and France). *If* this is correct, then Britain is due for another
wave of strikes as the economy moves out of the 1970s/80s
recession, which would be around the early 1990s on the simplest
interpretation of Kondratiev's 20-25 year wave model (see also
Screpanti, 1987). If this does occur, then Luxemburg's mass
strike theory may once more be tested.

Conclusions

This chapter set out to explore the relationship between strikes
and class consciousness, and in particular to test Hobsbawm's
argument that economistic militancy was unlikely to produce any
far-reaching advances in workers' class consciousness. In addition I wanted to consider the validity of the economistic defence
of wages militancy, and of Luxemburg's mass strike theory.

It is true that on some indicators of class consciousness,
particulary CP membership and Labour Party voting, the British
working class peaked in the 1940s and has declined since. But to
attribute these post-war trends to the rise of trade union militancy centred around sectional wage demands is almost certainly
wrong, for the advances in working-class consciousness registered
at the end of World War One coincided with a massive strike
wave that was overwhelmingly economistic in character. Likewise the advances in CP membership and Labour voting through
the 1930s and early 1940s went hand in hand with a rise in trade
union membership, strike frequency and wage struggles. Moreover, there were rather more advances in working class consciousness during the 1968-74 strike wave than Hobsbawm cared
to admit, particularly embodied in Labour Party and TUC
policy, in trade union membership and shop steward organisation, in far left political organisations, and in the attraction of
ideas about workers' control and industrial democracy. Above
all, the working class displayed a militant temper and a degree of

confidence in its own power that was truly impressive.

In general, then, the effects of economistic militancy on class consciousness are variable, and were most impressive in the strike wave of 1915-22, moderately impressive between 1968 and 1974 and extremely meagre in 1977-79, the last strike wave being an example of an almost purely economistic and defensive militancy. The variations in strike wave effects between historical periods *may* be associated with the degree to which other social forces have also been involved in struggles, as modern Gramscian Marxists suggest, though I haven't found the evidence very convincing.

What I have found convincing is Luxemburg's argument that it is the degree and forms of State intervention in 'mass strikes', as well as the scale of strike action, that have a crucial impact on workers' consciousness. The more massive the scale of strike action, the more likely it is that the State will be forced to intervene to restore industrial peace. And the more forcefully the State intervenes, the more likely it is to polarise society around the two major social classes and create the preconditions for an escalation of working-class political consciousness.

Now this scenario implies that in the midst of such struggles the sectionalism of the working class will somehow be overcome or transcended. Indeed, critics of Luxemburg would argue that it is the persistence and depth of working-class sectionalism that is likely to impede the process of radicalisation, and it is therefore to the problem of sectionalism that we now turn.

6

The Question of Sectionalism

Structural divisions in the working class have preoccupied social-ists from the earliest days of capitalism. For Marxists in particu-lar the belief that working-class unity was an essential precondi-tion for the transition to socialism has always had to confront the reality of divisions of one kind or another, whether based on skill, status, race, gender, region or nation.

The miners' strike of 1984-85 provided a graphic illustration of almost all of the divisions possible within the working class, and revealed the immense damage they can create for workers in struggle. A significant minority of miners voted *not* to strike in March 1984, a fact that was partly (and misleadingly) attributed to their relatively secure employment position. Divisions over strike tactics and strategy subsequently emerged between the left leadership of Scotland and South Wales on the one hand, and Yorkshire on the other. The wider trade union movement offered little concrete solidarity action in areas where it really mattered, and indeed some leaders of the trade union movement positively boasted of their complete unwillingness to engage in any form of sympathy action. Moving even further afield, the strike opened up a major rift between sections of the trade union movement and the leadership of the Labour Party, as the latter clearly found the strike embarrassing and distasteful. Encapsulated in the miners' strike was a working class deeply divided in its own ranks, despite the many gestures and acts of financial support and sympathy. So how have Marxists tried to explain these divisions?

Contemporary writers have tended to focus on two themes pursued by the classical Marxists: the division of workers into discrete groups, or sections, organised by trade; and the vertical division between trade union leaders and rank and file (examined in the next chapter, 7). Moreover each of these divisions can be interpreted in different ways, and feminists for instance have drawn attention to the occupational segregation which concentrates women in low-paid and poorly organised jobs, and to the dominance of men within the upper echelons of trade union hierarchies. The persistence of these divisions, it has been argued, constitutes a significant barrier to working-class unity and helps explain why class consciousness amongst British workers has 'failed' to reach the levels many have expected and hoped for, particularly during strike waves such as those of 1968-74, discussed earlier (Chapter 5).

In this chapter I want first of all to examine the concept of 'sectionalism' itself as an explanation of working-class action, and highlight some of the ambiguities in its usage. I shall then consider what relationship, if any, exists between the form of trade union organisation on the one hand and worker consciousness on the other, before moving on to consider the role and interests of women within the unions. Next I shall look at the relationship between militancy and sectional consciousness and examine in particular the claim that there has been a growth of 'sectionalism' in the British working class during the post-war period. And finally, I shall focus on the role of sectional action and consciousness in revolutionary situations, before arguing that the problem of labour sectionalism needs to be reformulated.

The Concept of Sectionalism

Recent histories of the British working class have devoted considerable attention to the phenomenon of sectionalism and its baleful influence. As Lane wrote:

> Sectionalism literally wrecked the several ambitious attempts at all-embracing unions in the 1830s . . . Sectionalism defeated the Triple Alliance in the 1920s almost a century later, and fifty years after that the attempts of the Union of Post Office Workers in 1971 and 1972 to get a united strategy among the unions in the public sector of employment did not even get a serious hearing (1974, pp.278-9).

Writing a few years later, Hobsbawm observed that '. . . we now see a growing division of workers into sections and groups, each pursuing its own economic interest irrespective of the rest' (1981, p.14). And Hyman, in a Marxist introduction to industrial relations, declared that 'the principal obstacle to a coherent [*sic*] radicalisation of the objectives of industrial struggle has already been much discussed: the sectionalism inherent in trade union action, (1975, p.177), a theme reiterated by Hinton (1983), Cliff (1985, pp.56-7), and with particular force by Selbourne (1985).

A related line of argument has been pursued by several German theorists who have drawn attention to the diversity of interests within trade unions, even in the large industrial unions of the German Federal Republic. According to them, workers' interests and priorities are shaped by their position in the labour market (degree of skill and mobility) and in the labour process (degree of centrality). Since there are frequent conflicts between these groups, over jobs and over wage priorities for instance, then trade unionism is inevitably plagued by profound internal structural competition, and broader, class-wide objectives and solidarity actions will be the exception rather than the rule (Erd and Scherrer, 1985; Offe and Wiesenthal, 1980).

Consistent with this theme is the argument of feminists that the working class is deeply divided on lines of gender. Skilled, male workers have been anxious to protect their pay differentials over unskilled (often women) workers, and have been hostile to the entry of women into their trades. The old Boilermakers Union contained only 100 women out of a total membership of 119,485 in 1982; there were fifteen women airline pilots in BALPA and 3,626 men; and seventeen female train drivers, compared to 22,257 men in ASLEF (figures for 1985 from *TUC Directory 1987.*) In addition, whilst men have been committed to maximising their earnings through overtime, bonuses, shiftworking and 'free collective bargaining', women have been more committed to reductions in working time and to legislative action to end low pay (Coote and Campbell, 1987; Boston, 1987).

American literature on working-class organisation has also placed considerable emphasis either on the debilitating consequences of ethnic and gender divisions (Davis, 1986), or on the impact of employer strategies in the labour process and labour markets. Gordon et al. (1982) have documented the division of jobs and terms and conditions of employment between different sections of the workforce, and used this to speculate about the different political priorities of these groups in pursuit of what they call 'class fraction' politics (cf. also Edwards, 1979). And with different analytical tools, Sabel (1982) has sought to delineate the different patterns of work career and work experience available in industry as a way of understanding the differing priorities and goals of sections of the workforce.

Other writers have been rather more cautious in reaching for the sectionalism label, for, as Cronin (1984, p.191) pointed out in connection with the 1968-74 strike wave, '. . . the militancy often took a sectional form, but this was largely determined by the structure of bargaining, and cannot be read simply as an outburst of sectionalism'. Some writers have mounted a rather more robust defence of 'sectionalism', arguing that even if sectional action has rarely generated 'macro-level' (i.e. political) class consciousness it has certainly caused enough problems to threaten 'the stability of the economic order' (Clements, 1977, p.322). And as if to underline the difficulty of the concept, and the confusions in this area, one of the original and most vociferous critics of trade union sectionalism conceded that he may have been wrong to assert it had grown at all in the post-war period (Hobsbawm, 1981, p.69).

It is not always clear exactly what the term sectionalism is meant to refer to. It has been variously used to denote working-class *organisation*, as in divisions between work groups or unions; working-class *action*, as in the post-war short unofficial strikes of the 1950s and 1960s; and working-class *consciousness* in which one's own group interests are placed above those of other groups. It has not always been made clear whether sectionalism denotes divisions between workgroups, between large aggregates of workers within unions, or between unions, and Lane (1974) is one of the few writers to have distinguished these different referents. Nor is it always made clear exactly what is the relationship between sectional organisation, action and consciousness. In Hobsbawm's discussion, sectional action appears to have been analysed simultaneously as a function, an expression, and a cause of sectional consciousness. Much of the discussion of sectional consciousness also assumes (explicitly or implicitly) that its presence necessarily inhibits higher levels of class consciousness, and that to demonstrate the pervasiveness of sectionalism is therefore *ipso facto* to portray the absence of anything socialists might recognise or appreciate as political class consciousness.

In order to try and resolve some of these issues let us look first at the evidence on the relationship between trade union organisation and worker consciousness.

The Organisation of Unions and the Consciousness of Workers

It is a truism that the British trade union movement still consists of a curious assortment of craft, occupational, quasi-industrial and general unions, despite a wave of recent (and projected) mergers in engineering, the civil service, post and telecommunications, metals and printing. Unions themselves are invariably divided into regions and branches, and often into trade or occupational groups as well as into workplace groups and sections. This untidy structure often corresponds to the structure of collective bargaining in Britain which itself is a complex web of arrangements and institutions at many different levels of economic activity (Clegg, 1976).

Of the classical Marxists it was Gramsci who analysed most closely the connection between the organisational forms of trade unions and the consciousness of their members, and who argued that organisation of workers by trade or craft necessarily produced in them a restricted, sectional form of class consciousness (see above Chapter 3 and cf. Flanders, 1970 for a similar, non-Marxist account). In other words, the consciousness of workers follows the contours of trade union organisation.

If we examine British data on trade union organisation, we find that the number of TUC unions has fallen from 186 in 1950 to 150 in 1970 and today stands at 85 (*TUC Reports*, various years). On this indicator, the sectionalism of the British trade union movement ought to have declined as its growing membership was concentrated in an ever shrinking number of unions.

But we can also examine the relationship between union organisation and worker consciousness using comparative data. One implication of the critique of sectional organisation is that where trade union structure is *less* fragmentary, there should be less sectional militancy and consciousness. And where there is less sectional consciousness there *might*, other things being equal, be found higher levels of political class consciousness amongst workers.

The three advanced capitalist countries which come closest to having a very small number of large industrial unions are West Germany, Austria and Luxembourg with 17, 16 and 14 trade unions respectively (see Table 6.1 below).

At the other end of the spectrum come the English-speaking countries—Australia, New Zealand, the USA and Ireland. The remaining countries of Scandinavia, Belgium and the Netherlands, France, Italy and Spain all have complex trade union movements, with numbers midway between the Germanic group and the English-speaking group.

There is however no obvious relationship between trade union structure, as defined here, and any other indicator of political class consciousness. Trade union density seems to relate most closely to a country's size: the smaller the country the higher the density. It is also difficult to find any connection between union structure and working-class politics. Europe's largest and electorally most successful Communist Parties are to be found in Italy, Portugal, Iceland, France, Finland and Greece, countries which vary considerably in trade union density, size and structure. The most successful socialist parties in the 1970s and 1980s were to be found in Austria and Sweden: each chalked up three election victories and secured on each occasion more than 50% of the vote, yet Austria has industrial unionism and one union federation, Sweden has a complex union structure with three federations (though the LO is admittedly the most influential).

It *is* true that the highly fragmented union movements of

Table 6.1 Trade unions and union federations in selected capitalist countries

	Number of unions	Trade union density 1980 (%)	Number of main union federations
Luxembourg	14	70	2
Austria	16	58	1
West Germany	17	33	1
Finland	28	75	1
Belgium	29	75	2
Switzerland	29	33-37	2
Netherlands	37	38	3
Norway	40	c.55	1
Denmark	40	79	1
Sweden	49	85	3
Italy	*	37	3
France	*	22	3
Australia	124	55	1
New Zealand	117	c.50	1
United States	105	25	1
Ireland	89	52	1

Sources: von Beyme, 1980, Table 1, p. 35; Therborn, 1984a, Table 2, p. 11.

Ireland and the USA coexist with exceptionally weak labour or socialist parties, but the similar fragmentation of unionism in Britain, Australia and New Zealand sits alongside mass labour parties that have enjoyed considerable, if mixed, electoral success. It is difficult then to discover in sectional trade union organisation (as defined here) any obvious, dramatic and negative impact on class consciousness in the other capitalist countries as measured by the strength and success of workers' political parties.

Still a Men's Movement?

Historically the trade union movement has in many respects been a male movement. Men have comprised the overwhelming majority of trade unionists, they have predominated in the large and powerful unions, and they have virtually monopolised positions of leadership (an issue examined in the next chapter). As a consequence, it has been argued that their particular interests have taken priority in the union world whilst the specific concerns of women have taken a back seat. And in particular historical periods there has been open gender conflict, as for instance when demobbed men at the end of the two World Wars insisted on returning to their old jobs, displacing the women who had occupied them in their absence.

But the past twenty years have witnessed rapid changes in the gender composition of the labour force and of the unions. Women now constitute over 40% of the employed workforce, and their participation rate is rising steadily towards 50% (Coote and Campbell, 1987, p.82). They also comprise a growing proportion of trade unionists, making up 21% of TUC membership in 1968 but approximately 32% in 1985 (Cockburn, 1987, p.6; *TUC Directory 1987*). Part of this growth is due to the increased numbers of women across a range of industries and the unions that recruit there, but it also reflects the concentration of women in occupations where union membership grew especially fast in the 1970s: COHSE (78% female), NUPE (67% female), NALGO (51% female).

To what degree has the growth of women members been reflected in union priorities, so that unions increasingly come to represent all of their members? By the mid-1980s, twenty-five unions had appointed equality or women's officers (e.g. USDAW, NUJ, ACTT) and forty had created women's/equality committees. Women-only courses have been established in a number of unions, and 'women's issues' given more prominence in union training courses. Several unions—e.g. USDAW, NUPE—set up working parties to examine the position and priorities of their women members, and quite a number of unions issued documents and guidelines on sexual harassment, in line with TUC policy and advice (see Cockburn, 1987, Chap.4; Boston, 1987, Chap.12). But Cockburn is perfectly right to argue that the 'bottom line' for women is whether these committees, officers, inquiries and documents are translated into union objectives for bargaining or political action (1987, p.12).

On that count there are some encouraging signs. Low pay has been an issue for women for many years, not surprisingly as they comprise the clear majority of low-paid workers in Britain, whatever definition is employed (cf. Pond, 1983). Unions have traditionally resisted the call to tackle this problem through legal intervention via a statutory minimum wage, preferring the method of collective bargaining which feminists and others have criticised as inadequate. But recently both the British and Scottish TUC and the Labour Party have finally swung round behind such a policy, after years of campaigning by advocates such as NUPE.

Shorter working time is another issue assigned priority by feminist writers (cf. Coote and Campbell, 1987, Chap.2), and the pressure of unemployment has pushed unions across Europe into a wave of disputes in order to cut working hours and help create jobs.

Unfortunately, evidence suggests that few extra jobs have been created in this way as employers have almost invariably insisted on shorter working time deals being self-financing, thus obviating the demand for extra labour (White, 1981). In Britain, the absence of effective controls on overtime working means that hours cut off the normal working week are likely to be converted into additional overtime rather than extra jobs. Nonetheless the issue of working time has at least been put on the bargaining agenda.

Other issues, such as equal opportunities, have been pursued with particular vigour by ASTMS. Sexual harassment cases have been taken up by a range of unions including the TGWU and the AUT. Paternity agreements have been signed by unions such as the NUJ, thereby challenging the idea that child care is solely a women's matter. Equal pay for work of equal value has been strongly pursued by TASS, APEX and USDAW amongst others.

These, and other advances, are very recent and it is still the case, as the GMB has pointed out, that women's issues are not receiving the priority they deserve. Issues such as sex bias in job evaluation schemes or sex discrimination in recruitment, training and promotion are still not assigned as much importance as some activists believe they merit (Cockburn, 1987). Nevertheless the moves being made by unions are in the right directions, and the continued growth of female employment provides unions with a powerful incentive to take women's issues more seriously than ever if they are to recruit and retain them within their ranks.

The Growth of Sectionalism in the Post-war Period: Sectional Militancy and Consciousness

To demonstrate the existence of sectional industrial action is not particularly difficult. Despite the re-emergence, around 1970, of the large, long, national official strike, the majority of strikes even today are small and short, lasting less than three days, and involving fewer than 500 workers (Edwards, 1983). Paradoxically, the emergence of large set-piece confrontations, often in the public sector, has served to underline the fragility of worker solidarity. Almost every large public sector strike in the 1980s has been bedevilled by non-support from sections of the unions and workers involved, notably during the steel (1980), civil service (1981), health (1982), miners' (1984-85) and teachers' (1985-86) strikes. Compounding these internal divisions has been an almost complete absence of effective solidarity action from other quarters, particularly damaging for the steel and miners' strikes, both of which were also undermined by domestic steel and coal stocks and by foreign imports (Hartley et al., 1983). Strikes by other public sector workers, in the 'winter of discontent', notably ambulance drivers and gravediggers, revealed for some commentators a rampant disregard by trade unionists of the public or consumer interest and led railway workers' leader Sid Weighell to liken some of his colleagues to 'pigs at a trough'.

Studies of the reference groups used by workers in draft pay claims provide further evidence, albeit indirect, of the narrow frames of reference used in evaluating employment situations and their rewards. Asked to say what sort of people were better off than themselves, 45% of a sample of Swedish workers mentioned businessmen, directors, managers, professionals and higher white-collar workers compared with only 20% of their British counterparts (Scase, 1977). In other words Swedish workers were twice as likely as their British counterparts to reveal an awareness of differences *between* social classes. Another study, comparing British and French manual workers' conceptions of inequality, found that French workers were also twice as likely to mention inequality between classes compared with their British counterparts, who focussed much more on inequalities between similar manual occupations (Gallie, 1983).

There is, in other words, no particular shortage of evidence revealing the existence of sectional action. But does such action produce a corresponding form of sectional consciousness? And has sectional consciousness become more prevalent throughout the post-war period? This is where the critique of sectionalism begins to run into difficulty, because much of the discussion has been conducted in such general terms that authors and critics have rarely stopped to consider carefully just what forms of action and consciousness constitute reasonably reliable and reasonably unambiguous indices.

Do all strikes by a section of workers, let us say a factory department, necessarily reflect only sectional consciousness? Surely not, for most people can think of strikes by small groups of workers which involved major questions of principle and which therefore reflected some higher level of consciousness. The refusal by a group of dockers to load military equipment for the Chilean junta in 1973; the refusal and subsequent strike of Dunne's workers in protest at handling South African fruit; a strike to secure the reinstatement of a victimised shop steward; a strike to protest at sexual harassment by a supervisor: all of these 'sectional' actions surely indicate more than just sectional consciousness. Perhaps we can say that wage strikes inevitably indicate sectional consciousness, that is the simple desire to advance the interests of a specific group irrespective of others. But again we can conceive of wage struggles conducted by a section of workers which can also benefit many other workers. The Ford sewing machinists' equal pay strike of 1969 would be one example, whilst the miners' strike of 1974 would be another. And just how large does a group have to be before its action ceases to attract the epithet 'sectional'? Is a strike by 70,000 Ford workers sectional? Or one million health workers? In one sense, any action short of a complete General Strike *could* be considered 'sectional', involving as it would only part of the working class, and probably causing inconvenience to those remaining at work. In the absence of any clear specification of just what constitutes sectionalism, the term is quite open to this sort of trivial usage.

In that case, then, perhaps it is only *some* sectional strikes which reflect such consciousness, but the problem then is to determine just what criteria a strike must have to qualify for inclusion on the list. Hobsbawm (1981) suggests it is pursuit of self-interest *at the expense of other workers and consumers* that provides the true hallmark of sectionalism. Obvious examples that then spring to mind would be strikes by social workers, health workers, teachers, and other groups dealing directly with the public. Therefore to examine the growth of sectionalism we can look at three types of dispute statistic. Firstly we can ask whether stoppages by service workers (i.e. those dealing with the public) have increased, absolutely or relatively, in the post-war period. Secondly, we can examine trends in the numbers of workers indirectly affected by stoppages. And thirdly, we can look directly at trends in the numbers of disputes between workers and between unions.

In order to assess stoppages by 'service' workers we need to define the category of 'service' worker. Let us take the industrial sectors of gas, water, electricity, railways, road passenger transport, communications, retail distribution, insurance and banking, professional and scientific services, miscellaneous services and public administration and defence as those which include the

Table 6.2 Strikes by service workers 1950-79

Year	Strikes per 1000 employees	Service sector strikes as % of all strikes
1950	0.01	7.2
1955	0.02	6.1
1960	0.02	8.7
1965	0.02	12.2
1966	0.02	12.7
1967	0.02	13.3
1968	0.04	23.2
1969	0.06	22.9
1970	0.07	20.8
1971	0.03	17.5
1972	0.03	14.5
1973	0.04	17.1
1974	0.05	20.0
1975	0.03	17.1
1979	0.03	18.8

Source: Calculated from data in Ballentine, 1986, Appendix.

overwhelming majority of workers dealing directly with the public (i.e. Industrial Orders XXI-XXVII inclusive), and whose industrial action would cause them inconvenience. Table 6.2 shows the numbers of strikes by such workers from 1950 to 1979, expressed in relation to the numbers of service sector employees, and as a percentage of all strikes in any given year.

The service sector workforce has grown throughout this period, from 9.1 millions to 13.4 millions, and in 1979 constituted 60% of the workforce compared to 45% in 1948. But the strike proneness of this category of employee, shown in the first column of Table 6.3, has increased at a faster rate since 1968. Even more significantly, the contribution of service workers ,to the total number of strikes has risen dramatically since 1960, at a rate well in excess of their employment growth. This first piece of evidence, then, appears to be consistent with Hobsbawm's assertion of a shift in the strike pattern towards groups of service workers whose actions are likely to hit their own consumers.

The number of workers indirectly affected by stoppages has fluctuated considerably over the years, showing no clear rela-

Table 6.3 Demarcation strikes[1] 1960-79

Year	Total number (or annual average)	Demarcation strikes as % of all strikes
1960-63	60	2.4
1964-67	63	2.8
1968	83	3.5
1969	80	2.6
1970	69	1.8
1971	57	2.6
1972	55	2.2
1973	166	5.8
1974	184	6.3
1975	142	6.2
1976	166	8.2
1977	189	6.7
1978	12	0.5
1979	135	6.5

Sources: Ministry of Labour *Gazette* and Department of Employment *Gazette*, various issues.

[1] Strikes to determine which of several groups of workers has the right to carry out certain jobs.

tionship to the number of strikes. But if we express the numbers indirectly involved in stoppages as a percentage of those directly involved, then a pattern does start to emerge. Throughout the 1950s this ratio only once rose above 25% (that was in 1952), but in the 1960s the pattern began to change. The numbers directly involved in strikes began to climb, but the numbers *in*directly involved climbed even faster, and in four years of the 1960s decade the indirect:direct percentage exceeded 25%. The same trend continued through the 1970s, with the ratio of indirect to direct workers involved in strikes exceeding 25% in seven out of those ten years (Ballentine, 1986, Appendix; Durcan et al., 1983).

Finally, we can chart the numbers of disputes between workers and between unions throughout the post-war period, and we find these data show a rising volume of inter-worker and inter-union conflict. Table 6.3 shows the number of recorded demarcation strikes between 1960 (this category of strike cause was first created in 1959) and 1979.

There is a fairly clear upward trend, especially prominent through the 1970s, and again this is consistent with the idea of a growing sectionalism in the working class as workers engage in battles to protect their own job territories against encroachments by other workers. Parallel to this trend was a growth in the number of cases handled by the TUC Disputes Committee, the body responsible for investigating and adjudicating disputes between affiliated unions. Between 1948 and 1967 the Committee received an average of 29 referrals a year; between 1968 and 1972 the figure had risen to 61; between 1973 and 1977 it rose to 81; and by 1978 it peaked at 130 cases, falling thereafter (Ballentine, 1986, p.71 and Appendix).

Although this evidence *could* be explained by the changes in attitude that Hobsbawm and others identify there are several other factors that also need to be taken into account.

Firstly, there was a substantial growth in the numbers of service sector workers throughout the post-war period both absolutely and as a proportion of the workforce. And the growing number of strikes by such workers, at least until 1967, largely reflected the simple growth in their numbers. As Table 6.3 showed, the number of strikes per 1000 service workers was almost unchanged until 1967 at an annual figure of 0.02. Only after 1967 did this group become significantly more strike prone.

A second factor that lay behind the strike proneness of service workers was the growth of their *ability* to strike, measured most clearly by their organisational resources. Union membership grew rapidly amongst these workers, especially from the late 1960s, and, with the exception of the teaching unions, their growth rates outstripped the rest of the trade union movement, as Table 6.4 shows.

Table 6.4 Membership of selected service sector trade unions 1949-76

	1949	1965	1976	% increase 1949-65	% increase 1965-76
NUPE	150250	248000	650530	65	162
COHSE	51319	68000	200455	33	195
NALGO	189261	349000	683011	84	96
NUT	184100	265000	289107	44	9
All trade unions	9318000	10325000	12386000	11	20

Sources: TUC *Congress Reports*; Department of Employment *Gazette.*

Thirdly, successive governments, from 1961 onwards, attempted to hold down public sector pay as part of their strategy for influencing pay settlements and labour costs in the private, manufacturing sector. It was hardly surprising that sooner or later there would be a rebellion by disadvantaged public sector employees, once they had the organisational resources to conduct successful strikes.

Finally, the structure of collective bargaining and union representation in the public sector began to shift from about 1970. Managerial efforts at rationalisation, involving the use of work study and job evaluation, in the context of incomes policies, stimulated a more or less simultaneous expansion of local collective bargaining and shop steward representation. Other things being equal, the expansion of collective bargaining units and the volume of bargaining in social services, education, hospitals and local government would be expected to result in a rising number of strikes, irrespective of any changes in worker attitudes, sectional or otherwise (cf. Clegg, 1976).

So some of the evidence designed to demonstrate the existence of sectional consciousness turns out to be ambiguous, since the growth of service sector strikes *could* indicate statistical changes in the composition of the labour force; growth of the *capacity* to embark on strikes; increased external pressure on living standards; increase in the volume of collective bargaining—as well as an increase in purely sectional militancy.

Similar arguments can be applied to the growing numbers of workers indirectly affected by stoppages. This trend *could* reflect an increasingly sectional outlook by workers, whose willingness to strike was unaffected by the consequences of their actions for fellow workers. But the same evidence could *also* indicate increased militancy by the employer. Strikes by small groups of workers were sometimes met with mass lay-offs of other groups as a way of forcing striking minorities back to work under pressure from their fellow-workers. Or the evidence could reflect the growing technical interdependence between production processes so that a strike by one group of workers would inevitably result in lay-offs elsewhere whatever striking workers felt about this.

But what about demarcation strikes, and inter-union disputes? Surely the trends here are clear and unmistakable, and point to growing sectional rivalry between groups of workers? This evidence does provide the strongest confirmation for the 'growth of sectionalism' thesis.

But before reaching the conclusion that sectional consciousness has indeed grown in the post-war period it is worth considering other evidence on strike patterns that suggests a rather different and more complex state of affairs. If the demarcation dispute is the epitome of sectional action (and possibly sectional consciousness), the sympathy strike might be thought of as its polar opposite, and indicative of a much higher level of *class* identity. We know that demarcation disputes became more common in the post-war period, so does this mean that sympathy strikes became *less* common?

The peak of sympathy strikes came during the big strike wave of 1968-74, during which the number of wage strikes reached a post-war high. Comparing these figures with those for demarcation strikes (Table 6.2, above) we can see that as the wave of sympathy strikes receded in 1973, so the upturn in demarcation strikes began, though it would be rash to try and read any direct connections into what could simply be coincidence. But on the face of it the upsurge of sympathy strikes during the late 1960s is hardly consistent with the picture of an increasingly sectional and divided labour movement.

What can we conclude, then, about the relationship between industrial action and sectional consciousness? The evidence, taken as a whole, is very mixed, and seems to fall into three categories. To begin with there is some data that points beyond

Table 6.5 Sympathy strikes 1952-79

Year	Number (or annual average)	Sympathy strikes as % of all strikes
1952-55	15	0.8
1956-59	24	1.0
1960-63	35	1.4
1964-67	20	0.9
1968	31	1.3
1969	67	2.2
1970	77	2.0
1971	37	1.7
1972	36	1.4
1973	39	1.4
1974	23	0.8
1975	20	0.9
1976	14	0.7
1977	20	0.7
1978	10	0.4
1979	13	0.6

Sources: Ministry of Labour *Gazette* and Department of Employment *Gazette*, various issues.

any reasonable doubt to a growth of sectional militancy and consciousness, notably in the figures for demarcation disputes. But there is a second category of widely-used evidence that turns out to be highly ambiguous in its meaning and difficult to interpret. The growth of service sector strike proneness, and the rise in the numbers of workers indirectly involved in strikes, could be the result of a number of factors, of which sectional consciousness is but one. And finally, there is evidence which appears flatly to contradict the thesis of growing sectionalism, namely the figures for the number of sympathy strikes.

The claim that there has been an unqualified growth of sectional class consciousness in the post-war period must therefore be considered not proven. More important, perhaps, the evidence on industrial action suggests that it is almost certainly much too simplistic to counterpose sectional consciousness against higher forms of class consciousness. This conclusion would also be consistent with the evidence and argument from the previous chapter, which suggested that 'economistic militancy' could express and produce quite different levels of class consciousness amongst workers according to circumstances. Luxemburg's mass strike theory was an important attempt to theorise the types of circumstances most conducive to such radicalisation. Perhaps the same point holds true for 'sectional' militancy, whose consequences for worker organisation and socialist advance may also vary between different situations. In order to examine whether this is the case we can look at revolutionary movements and situations, in Britain and Russia at the turn of the First World War, to see whether sectional militancy persists even under those conditions, and with what consequences.

Revolutions and Revolutionary Situations

Hinton's (1973) study of the first shop stewards' movement in Britain was concerned *inter alia* to explore how a revolutionary leadership emerged out of a traditional craft union, the ASE. How did this bastion of craft exclusiveness, and of sectionalism as it is normally defined, come to throw up revolutionary leaders and revolutionary doctrines? How was its sectionalism overcome? Hinton's answer suggests that it may not have been overcome at all:

> The craft tradition contained aspects of tenacious resistance to capitalist rationality, to the reduction of craft labour power to commodity status. When the craftsmen felt themselves pressed beyond endurance these aspirations, traditionally expressed in the defence of craft controls and of local autonomy, were forced to seek new modes of expression. The catalyst of war, the intolerable demands it placed on the attitudes and practices of skilled engineers, promoted an interaction between the doctrines of revolutionary syndicalism, industrial unionism and the craft tradition of local autonomy (Hinton, 1973, p.333; cf. also Sabel, 1982).

The craftsmen did not cease to be concerned with the traditional hallmarks of their status, nor did they evince any desire to open up the ranks of the ASE to more semi-skilled workers, dilutees or women, even though revolutionary industrial unionism was certainly one element within the ideology of the shop stewards' movement. It was arguably because they had gained so much within capitalism that the engineers had by the same token so much to lose, and were willing to fight to retain their position. In terms of ideology and consciousness there occurred what Hinton calls a 'fusion' of craft exclusiveness and revolutionary syndicalism, or as I would prefer to say, an articulation of two sets of ideological principles which proved in the context of war to be compatible.

The Russian revolution provides further evidence for this phenomenon of articulation of sectional and hegemonic consciousness and ideology rather than (or perhaps as well as) a straightforward suppression of the former. After the February revolution there was a tremendous and rapid growth of trade unionism, essentially along industrial lines, as the few craft unions which did exist, or came into existence, led a precarious and fragile existence or perished altogether. These trade unions engaged in collective bargaining with employers, and in late 1917 signed 25 collective agreements in Petrograd alone, covering all the city's major industries. Strikes were common, and their initial demands focused, often successfully, on wage rises, price controls and hours. The novelty of trade unionism in Russia, the extensive influence of revolutionaries, the chaos and dislocation of war, and the spate of factory closures and rundowns by employers virtually threw the trade unions into overtly political action from the first days of the Kerensky regime (Smith, 1983). These powerful radicalising forces did not however eliminate all traces of sectional consciousness, replacing it with pervasive hegemonic aspirations:

> Workers in Petrograd in 1917 did not necessarily identify spontaneously with that somewhat abstract entity the 'working class'. Their immediate loyalties were often more concrete, local collectivities, such as the workers in their workshop, factory or craft. It has been suggested that the strongest of these narrow forms of worker consciousness was loyalty to one's factory. This 'factory patriotism' was more common than . . . craft consciousness. *None of these narrower loyalties inhibited the development of a broader sense of belonging to a class of working people whose interests were antagonistic to those of the employers—at least not in the tumult of 1917* (my italics) (Smith, 1981, p.51).

Conclusions

The concept of sectionalism has frequently been used in an ill-defined and pejorative manner and it would therefore be valuable to distinguish between three different forms of the phenomenon. *Competitive* sectionalism refers to actions by one group of workers that are taken at the expense of another group. *Beneficial* sectionalism refers to actions by a group of workers that promote the interests of wider sections of workers. Finally *benign* sectionalism refers to actions by a group of workers that have no effects on others. From a Marxist standpoint it is only competitive sectionalism and its alleged growth in the post-war period that presents a problem. Much of the evidence used to support the thesis of a growth of sectional consciousness is highly ambiguous and difficult to interpret. It is true there are some good indices of sectional action which did rise through the 1960s and 1970s, in line with the idea that 'sectionalism' has become more pervasive amongst the British working class. But other indicators of higher levels of class consciousness, such as the numbers of sympathy strikes, and the numbers of political strikes and factory occupations, also rose throughout the same period.

These facts suggest that workers can and do manifest a variety of levels of class consciousness and they do not remain fixed for long periods at one 'level' awaiting a road-to-Damascus experience before their next ascent. In different contexts workers will display different levels of consciousness, and however displeasing this may be to intellectual devotees of order and simplicity it is a normal state of affairs in both peaceful and turbulent periods of history. It is also 'normal' for workers with grievances to try and resolve them close to their point of origin, which will often be in a particular workplace, or even a department within a workplace. No rational worker will try to promote class-wide action in order to resolve local or industrial problems when purely 'sectional' action will suffice. And given that many of the grievances workers have are local in origin and character, then 'sectional' action may be seen as a normal and pervasive feature of trade unionism.

This argument then helps us to recast the 'problem' of sectionalism in a different way. For revolutionaries the problem of trade union sectionalism is not its existence per se, but its lack of articulation with corporate and hegemonic aspirations. The problem is not so much how to overcome or suppress sectionalism, but how to articulate different levels of consciousness among different groups so that large numbers of people will come to see that their own sectional interests are compatible with, and indeed depend on, the promotion of socialism. As Gramsci said, the issue is to '... work to create the mass conditions in which all particular problems can be resolved as problems of the organic development of the communist revolution' (1920d, p.307).

The struggle for socialism will be doomed to failure if it tries to cut against the grain of working-class interests and aspirations (cf. also E.M. Wood, 1986). Sectional, economic interests should not be seen as the antithesis of socialist priorities but as the raw material out of which a desire for socialism must be created.

7

Trade Union Leadership and Collective Bargaining

In earlier chapters it was shown that whilst Marx had certainly been critical of contemporary trade union leaders, it was from Engels that we can date the truly modern critique of trade union bureaucracy. This critique was forcefully elaborated by Luxemburg and Lenin in the early part of the century, and later assumed its most intransigent and virulent expression in Trotsky's writings of the 1930s. The cautious and temperate behaviour of trade union leaders, ultimately if not immediately inspired by material interest, was further reinforced, in Gramsci's view, by their position as skilled, professional negotiators occupying a crucial niche in the emerging formal systems of labour-capital relations. From this classical Marxist tradition emerged the idea of revolutionary struggle on two fronts: 'outwards' against capital and its agents, 'inwards' against the trade union bureaucracy and other reformist leaders of working-class organisations.

Corresponding to these theoretical insights were a series of organisational innovations designed to transcend sectionalism, mobilise workers against their existing leaderships and prepare the unions for offensives against capital. Hence the emergence of industrial unionism and the amalgamation movement; of shop stewards and rank-and-file organisations such as the Minority Movement; and of the General Council of the TUC with its power to call a General Strike. These elements of Marxist theory and practice in the trade unions were lain down over sixty years ago and were commonplace among Marxists in the 1920s.

In the 1960s rapid union expansion under the shadow of

incomes policies, which were enforced with particular effect in the public sector, generated the discontent out of which revolutionaries began to mould classical rank-and-file movements modelled on those of the 1920s. In unions such as NALGO, NUT and CPSA these movements, often under the tutelage of the SWP and sometimes of the Militant Tendency, vigorously disseminated an orthodox classical analysis of trade union bureaucracy. At its peak in 1975 the SWP was able to convene a national conference of Rank and File Movements which attracted 800 delegates. Yet these movements, formed in the tide of labour militancy that surged across Britain from 1968 to 1974, declined just as rapidly. In his official obituary notice Callinicos (1982) charted the dramatic fall in circulation of all the rank-and-file newspapers throughout the 1970s. In March 1973 the SWP and its rank-and-file groups printed 68,500 copies of 16 different papers; nine years later there were just 11,300 copies of six papers. Despite this decline the SWP still has sufficient roots through the trade union movement to sustain and reproduce its ideas, many of which, in any case, have been picked up by a variety of more recent arrivals in union politics. Demands for the election of union officials were carried at CPSA conference in 1980, and have recently been debated at conferences of NALGO and the NCU. Inquiries have been conducted into the salaries of top union leaders in the UCW and the CPSA. That the election and remuneration of union officials has become an issue in several major British trade unions for the first time in many years is a tribute to the organised dissemination of orthodox classical Marxist ideas by small groups of revolutionaries and militants.

In this chapter I want to examine critically the claim that the trade union bureaucracy is inherently conservative, and that socialists must therefore endeavour to build rank-and-file organisations in opposition to it. I want to concentrate on trade union bureaucracy, not because the rank-and-file groups in many unions are less interesting, but simply because we lack good, detailed studies of such organisations. I shall begin with a brief exposition of the contemporary critiques of union bureaucracy before considering the nature of union bureaucracy and the ways in which it can be considered 'conservative'. I shall then look at the various explanations advanced for this alleged conservatism, and finally spend some time examining the nature of collective bargaining and the role of officials within the bargaining process.

The General Thesis of Bureaucratic Conservatism: Marxist Analyses of Union Bureaucracy

> If a plant is closed, the official who negotiates the redundancies will not get the sack. Constantly closeted with management, he comes to see negotiation, compromise, the reconciliation of capital and labour as the very stuff of trade unionism. Struggle appears as a disruption of the bargaining process, a nuisance and an inconvenience, which may threaten the accumulated funds of the union. Organization becomes an end in itself, threatening even the limited goal of improving the terms on which the worker is exploited (Callinicos, 1982, p.5).

This quote encapsulates three of the major themes normally used to illustrate the thesis of bureaucratic conservatism—the officials' willingness to compromise in negotiations, their hostility to strikes, and the importance assigned to preserving the union machine.

By contrast, 'rank-and-file' workers are said to have little interest in compromising on their demands, and can only pursue them effectively through industrial action despite the costs this imposes on the union. In other words critics of bureaucracy have discerned a fundamental divergence of interest between leaders and led, sometimes rephrased in the idea that workers assign priority to substantive interests—wages, conditions, job security etc.—whilst their leaders are more concerned with procedural issues such as the right to bargain, the acquisition of union facilities, the preservation of a strong bargaining relationship with management and the protection of the union as an organisation. Typically, some of the more polemical Trotskyist analyses have then proceeded to cite specific instances of disputes in which union leaders intervened either to prevent or call off industrial action, or to impose settlements unacceptable to sections of the rank and file—e.g. Ford's 1971, Pilkington's 1971, docks 1972, Grunwick 1977, BL toolroom strike 1977, BL Robinson dispute 1979, NHS 1982 (see Barker, 1971; Bell et al., 1977; Callinicos, 1982, 1983a; Cliff, 1975b, 1979; Deason, 1980; Thornett, 1983).

Some critics of bureaucracy have also attempted to demonstrate that the conservatism of union leadership is long-standing and is not simply the product of recent, specific developments. Typically this has been achieved by quoting the Webbs' account of the growth and consolidation of a stratum of industrially and politically conservative officials at the turn of the century (Callinicos, 1982, p.4, 1983a, p.27; Foot, 1977, pp.62-3; Hallas, 1977, p.11, 1980, pp.82-3; Pearce, 1959, p.107).

The obverse of bureaucratic conservatism is rank-and-file militancy, and many contemporary Marxists have echoed Trotsky's refrain that 'the masses wish to struggle'. This was frequently asserted, and with considerable justification, during the strike wave of 1968-74 (e.g. Cliff, 1970, p.196; 1975b, p.115), and throughout the rising tide of revolt against the Social Contract (e.g. Foot, 1977). The decline in strike frequency from 1979 produced more sanguine assessments of the strike proneness of workers, particularly amongst the theorists of the SWP who perceived a major 'downturn' in class struggle from around that time (e.g. Cliff, 1979; Callinicos, 1982; Beecham, 1984). Other writers have however adhered to the more orthodox Trotskyist position that the apparent unwillingness of workers to fight is principally the result of deficient leadership. A 'Handbook for Trade Union Militants', produced in 1984 by the RCP, declared that:

> Workers are always ready to use the strike weapon to enforce their will on employers. Trade union officials, however, are always reluctant to engage in strikes . . . While workers devote their energies to perfecting the strike weapon, officials pursue measures to safeguard agreements and procedures (Freeman, 1984, p.203; see also Thornett, 1983, p.6).

And the 1984-5 miners' strike was cited as proof that workers, in general, were willing to take on the employers provided they had militant and determined leaders such as Scargill.

Other Trotskyist writers have *never* been impressed with the idea that class struggles have been held back or derailed only by the treachery and deceit of reformist leaders. For these writers the militancy of the working class has been largely confined within the parameters of economism and reformism, and has represented no more than an attempt to wrest concessions from individual capitalists rather than challenge the whole capitalist system (cf. Banda, 1972). In this perspective it is the reformist ideology *common* to workers and union leaders that is stressed, not the differences between the groups (cf. Allen et al., 1978; Richards, 1975; Reed and Adamson, 1985).

But if the trade union bureaucracy *does* have a pronounced tendency towards 'conservatism', why is this the case? One line of argument, advanced by some contemporary Marxists and derived from Lenin and Trotsky, argues that the *social relations* of the union official generate almost irresistible pressures towards 'compromise' and conservatism. The material position of the official places him in a different world from the bulk of his membership, and his comfortable job, salary and lifestyle contrast starkly with the lower pay, hazardous and dissatisfying work and precarious living of the membership he represents. Typically many officials are appointed, rather than elected, but even the latter group are rarely subject to periodic or effective accountability. The official becomes isolated from the rank and file, and spends much of his time closeted in negotiations with employers or government ministers. This changed pattern of social relations begins to affect the outlook of the official, and he comes to have more understanding of, and sympathy for, his erstwhile opponents. Yet he also remains attached to his union and his members and the result of these conflicting pressures is to isolate the official as a mediating force *between* labour and capital, transforming him into a power-broker always in search of compromise. Finally, the officials realise that their own livelihoods depend on the viability of the union as an organisation, and, in a classic process of goal-displacement, the maintenance of the union, its agreements with the employers, and its accumulated funds all become ends in themselves, rather than means to other ends. Instead of mobilising workers in a struggle against capitalist exploitation, the 'bureaucracy' merely negotiates the *terms* of labour's exploitation (cf. Cliff, 1975b; Callinicos, 1982; Freeman, 1984; Stocking, 1978).

The implication of this analysis is that trade union officials will be overwhelmed by powerful social forces, irrespective of their own personal ideologies. Whether an official is 'left' or 'right' is less important, on this argument, than the basic fact that he is an official and as such acquires a set of interests different from and opposed to those of the rank and file (Nagliatti, 1974; Houston, 1984; Roddy and McHugh, 1985). This implication is often supported by showing that, in practice, 'left' and 'right' wing officials tend to act in the same way, as for instance during the 1926 General Strike (Callinicos, 1982, pp.15-17; Cliff, 1975b, pp.128-30; Hallas, 1979; Hallas and Harman, 1981; Cliff and Gluckstein, 1986).

Other Marxists and radicals have produced more subtle and nuanced analyses of trade union bureaucracy, which owe less to Lenin and Trotsky and rather more to Gramsci. Hyman (1975), for example, accepted that officials may well promote compromise settlements and intervene against strikes, but located these patterns of behaviour within a broader context. Both union

officials and shop stewards normally operate within the parameters of a set of bargaining institutions dominated by capital.
Their horizons, and those of their members, therefore reflect the
hegemony of capital, and they struggle, on the whole, for what
seems to them to be 'realistic'. Within these institutional and
ideological constraints the relationship between officials and
stewards is often one of interdependence, and as such entails
elements of *both* conflict *and* cooperation. Each relies on the other
for resources of various kinds, such as information, expertise and
membership support, and to abstract official—rank-and-file conflict from this relationship produces a one-sided and inadequate analysis. In any case, as Hyman has argued on several
occasions (e.g. 1979, 1987), the concept of 'rank and file' is itself
problematic and with the development of bureaucratic features in
workplace organisations (e.g. hierarchy, specialisation) the dividing line between bureaucracy and rank and file becomes
increasingly blurred.

The conservatism of union officials *may* be expressed therefore
in bargaining interventions or the termination of strikes, but it
also takes a more subtle and more pervasive form. The participation of officials in the routines of collective bargaining and other
industrial relations procedures helps to reproduce the working
relationship between labour and capital. And the conduct of
bargaining by expert, full-time negotiators demobilises the members by rendering the outcomes of bargaining dependent on the
negotiator's persuasive skills rather than the membership's willingness to act (Hyman, 1984a, pp.229-231). Allied to this analysis is a more specific argument against worker radicalism.
According to Muller-Jentsch (1985) unions prefer the low risk
strategy of bargaining to the high risk strategy of outright
confrontation for the simple reason that in most conditions any
benefits of confrontation would be rapidly nullified by a savage
employer's counter-offensive.

There is however a third and final strand of Marxist analysis
which offers a radically different account of union officialdom.
Offe and Wiesenthal (1980) begin their argument with the claim
that workers are not normally or inevitably 'collectivised' within
the capitalist labour process, but tend to be atomised and
divided. The first historical role of trade unions is to promote
collective organisation and identity amongst workers, and to
substitute collective for individual action. With the growth in its
power unions are increasingly able to win concessions simply by
threatening to strike, but for the threat to carry weight union

leaders must be able to 'mobilise discontent and then sit on it' (as C.W. Mills put it) and must be able to prevent strikes once agreements have been entered into. This process sets up tensions and internal conflicts whose effects unions try to minimise by securing external support for their bargaining role, from employers (through procedures and facilities) and from the State (through legislation or promises of non-intervention in industrial relations). At this stage in their development unions become increasingly prone to facets of opportunism: the preservation of organisation takes precedence over substantive goals; short-term objectives compatible with existing economic and political arrangements are pursued to the exclusion of longer-term ends; and there is a strong emphasis on quantitative rather than qualitative growth criteria—e.g. membership, revenue.

Sooner or later external sources of support are eroded as employers face profitability crises and are no longer able to afford 'cosy' relations with unions, and because changes in government alter the legal environment of unions. Once again therefore unions are forced to rely on their members, and to try and mobilise them in the struggle to defend both their procedural and substantive gains.

This account of the development and organisation of trade unionism draws attention to two important features of the role of full-time officials. Firstly, this role will vary between different historical periods, with the preservation of organisation and finance looming much larger during periods of extreme anti-unionism, e.g. early industrialisation or economic recession. Secondly, union officials will face a permanent tension between the need to mobilise members behind bargaining objectives, and the need to discipline members and ensure their support for bargaining agreements. A similar point has also been made by Lane (1974), who argues that union officials must keep a continuous balance between the requirements of employers and those of their members, whilst avoiding over-identification with either.

The feminist critique

Before looking at empirical evidence there is one recent approach to trade union organisation which should be highlighted. Feminist writers have often argued that the trade union movement is a 'male' movement, meaning that it pursues objectives such as pay differentials that are of more benefit to highly-paid men than to low-paid women, and that it is reluctant to pursue issues of specific concern to women such as creche facilities, or sexual harassment (cf. Coote and Campbell, 1987). One of the explanations offered for these priorities is that the key positions in unions are held by men, and this is even true in female-dominated unions such as COHSE and NUPE. In fact only three of the TUC's 85 affiliates have a woman General Secretary (Health Visitors, University Teachers and SOGAT). Union leaderships are therefore held to be unrepresentative on the dimension of gender, and the implication of the feminist argument is that even if the forces making for leadership conservatism were rolled back, then such leaderships would continue to be out of touch with their female rank and file.

Unions in Britain employ very few women officials, in total probably no more than 250 in 1986 (the number of ethnic minority officials was just 25) (Heery and Kelly, 1988). Amongst the big five unions which employ half of Britain's 3,000 officials, there were just 77 women, with the other main employers of women officials being COHSE (16), USDAW (12), and BIFU (9). Several smaller unions nevertheless have a high percentage of officials who are women: IRSF (5 women FTOs, 42% of their total), SCPS (6 women, 24%), UCW (3 women, 23%) (Heery and Kelly, 1988). During the 1980s there has been a modest increase in the numbers of women FTOs, a trend that has not been inhibited by the creation of women's officers as some critics of 'tokenism' had feared.

Before reviewing the evidence on leadership behaviour and its determinants, I shall first consider the conceptual issue of just what is meant by the term union bureaucracy.

What is the bureaucracy?

Despite the apparent simplicity of the term trade union 'bureaucracy' or 'leadership', the focus of many left-wing attacks is remarkably varied. Union General Secretaries or Presidents are frequently indicted, e.g. in Cliff (1970, p.173 ff.), but usually it is all full-time officials who come in for criticism. Sometimes— as in Cliff (1970, p.205), Cliff (1979, pp.32-4), Hyman (1979, p.57), Thornett (1983, p.7), or Beecham (1984, pp.103-4)—full-time convenors are also considered part of the bureaucracy, and Freeman (1984, pp. 213-6) appears to include union officers serving on any QUANGO, a category that embraces national executive members and local senior shop stewards.

Others have emphasised the complexity of the full-time convenor and senior-steward positions, noting similarities with the rank and file as well as with the paid officials of the union (Jefferys, 1979, pp. 35-6; Hyman, 1979; Callinicos, 1982, p.31). Arthur Scargill's leadership of the 1984-85 British miners' strike ought to have precipitated some reflection on the nature of bureaucracy since Scargill holds office on a salary of over £30,000 that puts him close to the top of the union officials' pay league. But several strike commentaries by erstwhile orthodox Marxists have fulsomely praised Scargill, whilst remaining totally silent on his 'bureaucratic' position (Reed and Adamson, 1985; WRP, 1985). By contrast, the SWP's strike chroniclers Callinicos and Simons (1985) differentiated Scargill from the truly bureaucratic Area NUM leaderships, apparently indicating that Scargill was a partial exception to their otherwise iron law of bureaucratic conservatism (pp.238-46), though *why* he was exceptional was never made clear. Others have given no definition at all, presumably on the grounds that the term bureaucracy is possessed of self-evident meaning (e.g. Clarke, 1977).

Rarely is the term 'bureaucracy' defined or its use justified on any theoretical grounds, and it is normally unclear which of several different definitions is actually being employed. Albrow (1970), for instance, listed seven modern usages of the term, at least three of which—'organisational inefficiency', 'rule by officials' and 'administration by officials'—could readily be accepted by critics of union leadership. The classical ideal-typical bureaucracy as defined by Max Weber has seven major components: clear hierarchy, clear job descriptions, appointment of officials, control through a unified disciplinary system, selection on the basis of professional qualifications, graded salaries and pensions, and a career structure. Many union officers have no clear job description at all; some are elected by members; rarely are they required to produce any professional qualification; and there is little opportunity for promotion. On four of these seven criteria, then, many unions are not 'bureaucratic' in the strict Weberian sense of the term (Kelly and Heery, in preparation).

But if sloppy definition were the only problem with the critiques of union bureaucracy, we might let it pass. Unfortunately, conceptual imprecision is characteristically compounded by questionable and dubious use of evidence in order to try and substantiate the general proposition of 'bureaucratic conservatism'.

Is the 'Bureaucracy' Conservative?

The principal difficulty in evaluating this proposition is that it is not always clear exactly what it means. 'Conservatism' has been defined in several quite different ways, and whilst some of these definitions are useful and testable, others are not. It has been argued that officials are more likely to favour compromises in disputes than the rank and file; that they are more likely to oppose strikes or to try and end them; that they are biassed in favour of constitutional and procedural action rather than direct, militant action; and that they are politically 'right-wing'.

We have already seen that what normally passes for evidence on these questions is the citation of selected, individual cases of 'conservative' officials confronting pro-strike rank-and-file workers. Commonly cited disputes include the 1971-2 engineering claim (Deason, 1975), the Pilkington's 1971 strike (Barker, 1972), the Grunwick 1977 recognition dispute (Freeman, 1984), the 1982 NHS dispute (Andrews, 1983; Callinicos, 1982; Freeman, 1984), the 1983 British Telecom privatisation dispute (Houston, 1984; Freeman, 1984), the 1984-5 miners' strike (Harman, 1985a, b; *Socialist Organiser*, 1985) and the 1985-6 Wapping print dispute (RCP, 1987). It is certainly true that in all of these disputes *some* of the rank and file were more militant, i.e. prepared to strike longer, than some of the trade union leaderships both national and local.

But this evidence *alone* is not sufficient for three reasons. The simple contraposition of rank-and-file militancy and leadership conservatism overlooks the fact that in at least four of the above strikes significant sections of the rank and file did not support the strikes and in three cases (NHS, Grunwick, miners) many workers actually crossed their own union's picket lines. Clearly conservatism, or hostility to striking, was not the exclusive preserve of the union leaderships. Secondly, critics of bureaucracy rarely mention situations where union leaders have campaigned for strikes and been rebuffed by the rank and file. BL stewards in 1980, the NUM leadership in 1982 (twice) and 1983, and the NUR leaders in 1985 and 1986 all had strike calls rejected by their members. Thirdly, a *general* argument about leaders and rank-and-file members cannot be proved by a handful of examples, particularly when these have been carefully chosen to suit an author's argument. General evidence, across a range of industries and unions, is required. Unfortunately the only published evidence comes from the Workplace Industrial

Relations Surveys of 1966, 1972 and 1973 and is therefore somewhat out of date. More seriously, the surveys provide evidence only on attitudes to industrial action, rather than behaviour; but they are interesting nonetheless (see Table 7.1 below).

Of the twelve questions asked (four questions in each of three years) stewards emerged as the most militant on eleven of them, thereby confirming the argument that union officials are less militant than the stewards. But what the data also show is that there was *no* difference in militancy between the officials and the members, both of whom were less militant than the stewards, at least on the definitions of militancy used in the surveys.

The other major source of evidence on the attitudes and behaviour of union officials is a study by the present author (Kelly and Heery, in preparation). Conducted between 1985 and 1987, and using interviews, observation and questionnaires, this was a major investigation of local union officials in the TGWU, GMB, AEU and ASTMS. Data were collected from 101 officers, and observations conducted in a range of establishments: public and private, manufacturing and service, large, medium and small.

We did encounter a minority of officers and situations in which FTOs argued for very modest objectives compared to stewards and members, and situations where they discouraged the pursuit of 'fringe' issues. We also encountered opposition to industrial action, and we heard modest objectives defended with arguments about the weak position of the employer and the need to restore competitiveness. But this was a minority, and the majority of officers in most situations acted very differently from the stereotypical image of the conservative bureaucrat. Frequently we found in pre-bargaining sessions a broad consensus between officials and stewards over the scale of objectives to be pursued, e.g. the size of a pay claim. Where differences did emerge, officials would usually argue their case with the stewards accompanying them on a bargaining committee. The outcomes of these debates seemed to vary with the strength of steward organisation: in larger, well-organised establishments with experienced stewards, it was often the official who gave way, and then continued negotiations on the stewards' position. In smaller establishments, or where steward organisation was weaker and the stewards less experienced, then the expertise of the official would often carry the day.

On the control of the bargaining agenda, it was common to

158

Table 7.1 Attitudes to industrial action (percentage agreeing)

	1966 Stewards	Members	FTOs
Workers are justified in withdrawing their labour or using other forms of pressure in breach of procedure . . .			
. . . if management has broken an agreement	77	74	62
. . . if management appears to be resorting to unreasonable delay in dealing with grievances	70	62	67
. . . if there is no other way of preventing management from discharging a workmate unfairly	78	69	73
. . . in any situation where they think that by acting in this way they can get what they want	23	27	11

	1972 Stewards	Members	FTOs
Workers are justified in withdrawing their labour or using other forms of pressure in breach of procedure . . .			
. . . if management has broken an agreement	74	65	63
. . . if management appears to be resorting to unreasonable delay in dealing with grievances	80	62	52
. . . if there is no other way of preventing management from discharging a workmate unfairly	80	63	77
. . . in any situation where they think that by acting in this way they can get what they want	25	25	10

	1973 Stewards	Members	FTOs
Workers are justified in withdrawing their labour or using other forms of pressure in breach of procedure. . .			
. . . if management has broken an agreement	76	67	65
. . . if management appears to be resorting to unreasonable delay in dealing with grievances	74	60	72
. . . if there is no other way of preventing management from discharging a workmate unfairly	80	66	75
. . . in any situation where they think that by acting in this way they can get what they want	24	22	13

Sources: McCarthy and Parker, 1968, Table 19; Parker 1974, Tables 131, 133, A5 Parker, 1975, Tables 110, 111, A71.

find broad agreement between stewards and officials on the range
of items to be included. There were also occasions when stewards
or members raised issues independently of the official, but in the
majority of cases these would be placed on the agenda and
pursued in negotiations. We also found situations where it was
the officials who played the pro-active role, pushing issues such as
equal opportunities or women's rights, and not infrequently
encountering either active resistance or indifference from the
stewards and members. Indeed women's and ethnic minority
rights and the recruitment of new members were the two issues
that FTOs were most frequently encouraged to pursue by their
superior officers (pay and job protection were the top two
priorities pushed by lay representatives).

Industrial action rarely occurred as an issue in the negotiations
we studied, but the attitudes of officials varied considerably. A
few were strongly opposed to industrial militancy, but the
majority adopted a much more pragmatic approach. Invariably
the question they asked when the issue arose was whether the
members would back it, or could be persuaded to back it. And
they used the knowledge possessed by the stewards to formulate
ideas about the employer's vulnerability and his likely response
to any action. The other issue that arose, particularly in multi-
union sites, was the reactions of other groups and the effects these
would have on the protagonists. Neither in interview nor in
meetings did we hear officials refer to the financial costs of a
dispute for the union. On the other hand some officials did
consider the effects of any action on the bargaining relationship
with the employer and weighed this in the balance along with
other factors.

Finally, it was noticeable that the systems of argument used by
officials invariably began with references to the aspirations and
needs of members, and to the problems (of morale, turnover,
recruitment etc.) which the employer would face unless their
demands were met. Only when no further headway seemed
possible did officials start to introduce the employer's view into
their own case, pointing out the mutual benefits that would
accrue from a particular settlement, rather than simply stressing
the workers' demands. But the use of such 'integrative' or
cooperative arguments seemed more often to be deployed out of
expediency than from any ideological conviction about a harmony of interests between labour and capital.

In general, then, the picture of the union official which
emerged from this research was one in which his (they were

almost all men) principal role was to service the collective
bargaining and grievance machinery of workplaces. In this role
he normally enjoyed the cooperation of stewards, and though
conflicts did occur over bargaining goals and tactics, it would be
simply wrong to portray this as a conflict between leadership
conservatism and rank-and-file militancy.

The other major point to be made about the theory of official
conservatism is that it is remarkably insensitive to historical
variation in trade union policies and actions. During the 1890s
many craft union leaders were deeply suspicious of the 'new
unionism' of the unskilled workers, and hostile to their demands
for working-class political representation independent of the
Liberals. Today such anti-Labour sentiment is almost unknown
amongst senior trade union leaders in the TUC. Again, contrast
the hostility to strikes of white-collar union leaders in the 1950s
with the attitude of their counterparts in the 1970s and 1980s.
Many officials in the teaching and health unions are now quite
willing to instigate and lead protracted campaigns of industrial
action. Or we might contrast the hostility to shop stewards of the
union leaders in the 1950s, men like Arthur Deakin (TGWU) or
Bill Carron (AEU), with the views of their counterparts in the
1970s—Jack Jones and Hugh Scanlon—who strongly encouraged
the devolution of power within their unions to workplace organisations of shop stewards.

Many of the officials currently employed by the TGWU,
GMBATU, NUPE, NALGO etc. belong to a generation that
came through the strike wave of 1968-74 and acquired their
industrial and political values in the heyday of the shop stewards
movement and the political struggles of the 1960s and 1970s.
These people, the products of a confident and militant working
class, were often quite different from many of their predecessors
who were socialised in the unemployment blackspots of the 1930s
and the Cold War of the 1940s. It seems quite unreasonable to
suppose that such differences in political socialisation can be
disregarded or downgraded in any explanation of the behaviour
of union officials, and yet this is precisely what many critics of
bureaucracy have chosen to do. The term 'trade union bureaucracy' has become an entirely ahistorical category of analysis.
The union 'bureaucrat' is a fixed and invariant type, always and
everywhere subject to the same eternal laws of bureaucratic
conduct and impervious to historical change. Yet the historical
changes in British union leaderships and union policies since the
1940s belie this caricature of the bureaucratic type, and are much

more consistent with Offe and Wiesenthal's (1980) claim that union objectives go through historical cycles.

It could still be argued that even the most militant officials remain confined within the limits of trade unionism and trade union consciousness, as defined by Lenin (see above, Chapter 2), and that their militancy stops short of a revolutionary challenge to capitalism because that would threaten their function as mediators between capital and labour, and jeopardise their own immediate job interests. In order to evaluate this component of the critique of bureaucracy we need to examine in detail the various explanations of officials' 'conservatism', before returning to look more clearly at 'revolutionary trade unionism' and its relationship to collective bargaining.

Explaining Leadership Behaviour

There is no consensus among critics of union bureaucracy in the tradition of Lenin and Trotsky as to why these leaders behave as they do, and it is customary to present a list of influences with little attempt to indicate either their inter-relations or their relative saliency. The various explanations can be grouped under four headings: material interests, power, social relations and social function. Most writers mention more than one of these factors, and a few mention all of them.

The material interests of the bureaucracy

One of the most common themes in critical analyses of trade union officials has been the relationship between the salaries of the officials and the wages of their members.

Data on top union leaders' salaries has been quoted in the past by critics such as Cliff (1970, pp.175-6; 1975b, pp.121-2) and Pearce (1959, p.108—who took his figures from Roberts, 1956), whilst other critics have simply noted that top union officials' salaries are well above those of the membership (Foot, 1977, p.62; Callinicos, 1983a, p.28; Nagliatti, 1974, p.9; Freeman, 1984). With salaries such as these (as well as other perks and fringe benefits worth as much as another 20% on top of basic salaries: Clegg et al., 1961), it is argued that union leaders no longer experience the deprivation and insecurity that drives rank-and-file workers to militancy: their radicalism (if it ever existed) is 'defused'. In most accounts 'material interests' have been defined

162

primarily though by no means exclusively in terms of pay, but
other perks and fringe benefits, such as an office environment,
expense accounts and subsidised cars and housing, have also
featured in the depiction of the 'social being' of the union official.
The same writers who attach explanatory significance to the pay
(and other perks) received by officials are, by the same token,
most likely to advocate paying officials 'the average wage of the
workers they represent' (Cliff, 1970, p.218, 1975b, p.157; Freeman, 1984, p.218; and Militant Tendency, 1980, p.24, 1981,
p.14).

It is well established that the most senior, national leaders of
trade unions—General Secretaries, Presidents and top National
Officers or Secretaries—receive a basic salary considerably above
the average earnings for the whole workforce, as the following
Table shows:

Table 7.2 Trade union General Secretaries' salaries 1987 (p.a.)

Fred Jarvis	NUT	£39,741
Clive Jenkins	ASTMS	£35,000
John Edmonds	GMB	£28,000
Ron Todd	TGWU	£26,000
Bill Jordan	AEU	£16,287
Average earnings	whole workforce	£10,500

Source: The Independent, 1 June 1987.

Other unions whose General Secretaries earn more than
£30,000 per annum include IPCS, NCU and the UCW (Kelly
and Heery, in preparation). On the other hand, the heads of some
small unions, such as the Wire Workers (5,142 members) and the
Northern Carpet Trades Union (830 members), earned as little
as £9,000 in 1986. Most union officials at all levels earn less than
their personnel management counterparts, although the lowest
paid personnel officers are probably worse off than junior trade
union officials. Comparison with members' earnings is difficult
because many unions organise a wide range of workers with very
different levels of pay and conditions. A single TGWU official
could be negotiating one day for £300-per-week tanker-drivers,
and the next day for female cleaners earning £65 per week.
Nevertheless it appears that the average salary received by the

officials in any given union almost invariably exceeds the average earnings for most if not all of its members. There are a few exceptions to this rule, notably in the printing industry, and there are probably manual occupations in oil refining or chemicals where the top paid workers earn more than their local union officials. But in general it is true that most union officials earn more than most, if not all, of the members they represent, and sometimes the gap is as much as 100% (Kelly and Heery, in preparation).

Nor is this situation peculiar to Britain, because what little evidence there is suggests that union officials throughout the capitalist world are generally paid considerably more than the members they represent. American and West German union officials appear to enjoy the highest earnings compared with their memberships, even though unions in both countries employ proportionately far more officials than their British counterparts (von Beyme, 1980, pp.103-10; Carew, 1976, Chap.6; Edelstein and Warner, 1979, pp.12-16).

Another important finding about officials' pay is that it is frequently linked to that of the members. Twenty-one unions base increases in officials' salaries on the rises obtained by the union's members, whilst eighteen unions link their official salary structure to the members' pay structure. (Almost all of these 39 unions organise fairly discrete occupational groups in which members' earnings can be determined fairly easily. By contrast, the general unions tend not to lay down precise criteria for fixing officials' salaries (Kelly and Heery, in preparation).) Thus even though officials frequently earn more than their members, there is often a link between the pay rises of the two groups so that an element of representativeness is built into the official's pay system.

As a general explanation of 'bureaucratic conservatism', this account *is* consistent with Marxist materialism, and indeed makes intuitive sense. After all, it seems plausible to argue that a social group which enjoys considerable material benefits will have rather less incentive to transform capitalism than workers who suffer insecurity, poor wages and subordination to authority.

But this materialist account does have two major problems. If pay, or more broadly material position, is a major part of the explanation of leadership conservatism, then the creation of a stratum of union officers earning the same as their members, *and* subject to periodic and frequent re-election (the major demands of the Militant Tendency and the SWP in the 1970s and 1980s), should have gone a considerable way to avoiding many of the problems experienced with full-time union officials. Such a group of officers *did* emerge in Britain from the 1960s, and by 1984 there were about 4,200 full-time union convenors, senior stewards or workplace representatives in British industry, paid the agreed rate for their nominal job, subject to re-election every year (or occasionally every two), and engaged full-time on union business (Millward and Stevens, 1986, p.84).

Did the removal of two of the alleged principal determinants of bureaucratic conservatism actually help to eliminate such behaviour? The consensus among many Marxist critics of bureaucracy is that it did not, and by the late 1970s it had become fashionable in some quarters to write of 'the bureaucratisation of the rank and file', a reference to the senior stewards and convenors in large enterprises (cf. Hyman's writings—1979, p.58, 1980, p.74, 1983, 1984a, 1985; as well as Cliff, 1979; Callinicos, 1982; Beecham, 1984; Hallas, 1980). Steward organisation, it was suggested, had increasingly come to resemble the apparatus of the union outside the plant, with its full-time convenors, internal hierarchy, remoteness from the rank and file, offices and secretarial facilities, and disciplinary powers over individual stewards. The resemblance in organisation was thought to mirror a resemblance in ideology and both Beecham (1984) and Hyman (1979) have argued that this internal cadre of full-time convenors and stewards played a critical role in winning support for the 1974-79 Social Contract and dampening down opposition to the cuts in living standards that accompanied it.

Even if it is conceded that convenors *did* play this role, and that they were critical in ensuring the success of the Social Contract (and both propositions are highly contentious—see England, 1981), how do their material interests help us understand their behaviour? Proponents of classical Marxist materialism have seemed unable to make up their minds: some have persisted in the belief that workplace officials *did* earn more than their members, others have denied this, and some have argued it was the stability, not the higher level of earnings that was critical (Cliff, 1979; Jefferys, 1979; Callinicos, 1982). Others again have advanced general claims about the 'corruption' induced by material privileges but have made no reference to such privileges in their detailed analyses of particular officials (Freeman, 1984, 1985). But the materialist account cannot be rescued by shifting its focus to earnings stability and away from earnings level. Many convenors and senior stewards received the average earnings for their work group—which means that their weekly earnings fluctuated in the same way as their members (cf. Thompson and Bannon, 1985, p.94). In short, if it was true that the full-time convenors and senior stewards who rose to prominence in the 1970s often behaved in the same way as the paid officials of the unions, then their behaviour cannot be explained as a product of material interests alone, such as high salaries.

But there is a second reason for disputing the relative privilege–conservatism argument. Historically, the most class conscious and militant sections of the working class have often been those whose earnings, job security and status placed them in a position of considerable privilege relative to many of their fellow workers. As Geary has observed, 'the kinds of workers who formed the rank and file of organised protest in the early days of the Industrial Revolution were almost invariably skilled and rarely worked in large factories' (1981, p.70). And in a survey of the social base of the socialist parties at the end of the nineteenth century, he noted:

> In France most socialist groups recruited predominantly from skilled workers in the construction industry and from metal-, wood- and leather-work. In Italy the PSI drew its major support from small-scale artisan production in the textile and metal trades . . . The great majority of [the German SPD's membership] were skilled men working in small or medium-sized concerns . . . In Spain too the printers constituted the backbone of the PSOE in its early days. The Social Democratic Party in Russia began life as a movement of skilled workers . . . (1981, p.95; cf. also Polan, 1984, p.180).

In Britain the First World War shop stewards' movement was composed almost entirely of skilled engineering workers, and it was these, along with comparatively well-paid miners and railway men, who formed the backbone of the Communist Party and the National Minority Movement for many years after the War (MacIntyre, 1986, p.31).

Yet we also know that many of the nineteenth-century craft unions, observed by Marx and Engels, *were* politically conservative, so how are all these findings to be reconciled? According to Sabel,

> to debate whether the craftsman is a labour aristocrat or a revolutionary misses the point. He resembles both in turn because he is neither. His strategy of self-defence shapes his view of his work, his relations to managers and other work groups, and his jokes; but it does not unambiguously determine his political views (1982, p.179).

Group interests can be defended conservatively, by excluding
others who threaten those interests (as in the craft union exclusion of women), or progressively, by including and allying with
other groups and social forces. It is not simply material *interests*
that determine consciousness, as critics of union bureaucracy
sometimes suggest (Callinicos, 1982, p.23; 1983a, p.28; 1983b,
p.98), but material *practices*.

For Marx ideas were formed in the continuous *dialectic* between
an objectively given and determining material world and the
material practices entailed in the production, reproduction and
transformation of that world (see Larrain, 1983). Practice did not
occur in a vacuum, but equally ideas were not stamped into
people's minds by material reality irrespective of their practice.
In the hands of Callinicos and others this dialectic has been
wrenched apart and its elements assigned respectively to different
social groups. Workers' ideas are actively determined through
practice, understood as *struggle*; but the ideas of union officials are
passively determined by material interests such as relatively high
salaries. Absent from this bowdlerised Marxism are workers'
material interests in high wages under capitalism, an omission
which leads to a characteristic neglect of the conservative social
forces acting on workers. This in turn generates a systematic
over-assessment of the radicalising impact of individual strikes
(see Chapter 5). The same line of argument has nothing to say
about the impact of struggle on the union officials who initiate,
organise or lead disputes. This omission underestimates the
degree to which struggle can radicalise union officials and
thereby produces an equivalent overestimation of leadership
conservatism. Both errors stem from a common source, the
destruction of Marx's dialectical understanding of the formation
of consciousness and its transposition into crude and one-sided
emphases on material determination and material practice respectively.

Power and accountability

A second theme commonly emphasised in critiques of union
bureaucracy is the power wielded by officials either as part of the
union's constitution or informally on the basis of their expertise.
Indeed for some critics the power of the union officer's post is
considered to be one of the most important advantages of the job
and to form part of the material interests that officials so
assiduously defend. Cliff (1970, 1971, 1975b), Foot (1977),

Engineers Charter (1980), Freeman (1984), Callinicos (1983a) and the Militant Tendency (1980, 1981) have all noted the tendency for union officials to be appointed, rather than elected, and almost all have called for election and re-election. The insistence on re-election is particularly important as the majority of union General Secretaries (or equivalents) already face election, either by the whole membership (in 51 unions) or at conference (in 14 unions), but in only 22 unions do they face re-election (Undy and Martin, 1984, Tables 2.1, 2.3, 2.12, 2.14).

For other full-time officers, even fewer unions elect or re-elect, and EC appointment is the dominant method, being used by many of the unions with the largest corps of officers—TGWU, GMBATU, NALGO, NUPE, ASTMS. In total approximately 2400 of Britain's 3000 full-time paid union officials are appointed (Kelly and Heery, in preparation).

There can be little doubt that on democratic grounds alone union officials ought to be subject to election and periodic re-election. The right to vote in free elections for those holding positions of power has long been fought for in the labour and trade union movement, and the classical defences of appointment rather than election are as weak now as they were when first advanced against universal suffrage in the last century. It is sometimes claimed that the job of the union official is so complex and demanding that it requires qualities which can only be explored and detected by a small select panel of interviewers. Exactly the same defence could be made for the appointment of MPs, whose job is also highly complex and often requires specialist knowledge. It is also claimed that elected officials would have to spend their time campaigning, instead of getting on with their job, and that an official unfortunate enough to be turned out of office would find it hard to obtain fresh employment. The 'campaigning pressure' argument would again apply with equal force to MPs and if we reject it in their case we should not invoke it in the service of union officials. Would unsuccessful union candidates subsequently experience difficulty in finding employment? There is no reliable evidence on this question, but if this is to be the last and the only line of defence against election, it is a flimsy counterweight to set against the overwhelming pressure of the democratic rights of union members.

But the argument about election of officials turns not only on its desirability in principle, but on its effects in practice. On this score what has to be shown is that there are significant differences in the behaviour of elected as against appointed officials, and more specifically that the existence, or introduction, of elections provides effective rank-and-file control over the officials and helps to ensure their industrial and/or political militancy. Unfortunately we simply do not have the evidence to compare officials under different selection arrangements, and for the moment all we can do is compare the unions in which they wield power.

If a union's leading officials do in fact occupy a crucial and powerful position in its decision-making process and if they use this power to thwart militant policies and actions, then on *major* policy issues, such as the 1970s Social Contract, it should be possible to discern their influence. Unions with an entrenched hierarchy of appointed officials ought to be more 'conservative' than those whose officials are elected and subject to *some* rank-and-file control. There may, of course, be exceptions to this rule but these should be rare, or else be explicable in terms of countervailing rank-and-file pressure exercised through organised factions or caucuses.

The left policy of opposition to the Social Contract was maintained by a curious assortment of unions. It was argued (in 1975) by the elected officials of the AUEW(E) and the FBU, as well as by the appointed officials of TASS, NUPE, ASTMS, CPSA and the SCPS. With the exception of the CPSA, none of the anti-Social Contract unions of 1975 had significant rank-and-file or Broad Left groups whose pressure could explain the militant stance of their leaders. Moreover, the white-collar union TASS—the only section of the AUEW which appointed its officials—has been the most consistent and vociferous opponent of incomes policies for many years and its General Secretary, former Communist Party member Ken Gill, has regularly moved motions at Congress rejecting wage controls.

Is there any evidence to support the thesis that in general left-wing and/or militant candidates will be favoured by electoral systems, whilst right-wing and/or moderate candidates will be more likely to emerge under systems of appointment? Secret postal ballots to elect union General Secretaries or Presidents in the 1970s and 1980s have produced Bill Jordan, Gavin Laird, Terry Duffy (AUEW), Frank Chapple and Eric Hammond (EETPU) on the right, but Joe Marino (Bakers Union), Ben Rubner (Furniture Workers), and Jim Slater (NUS) on the left, suggesting there is no obvious connection between electoral procedure and the political or industrial militancy of the successful candidate. Secret workplace or branch ballots in the early 1980s produced Arthur Scargill (NUM), Jimmy Knapp (NUR),

Ron Todd (TGWU) and John MacCreadie (CPSA) on the left, but Albert Williams (UCATT), David Williams (COHSE), Alistair Graham, John Ellis (CPSA), John Golding (NCU) and Alan Tuffin (UCW) who generally line up with the centre-right on union policy. Meanwhile, recent appointees have revealed a similar political spread, with Rodney Bickerstaffe (NUPE) on the left as well as three more moderate candidates: John Daly (NALGO), Diana Warwick (AUT) and Roy Evans (ISTC). It is certainly true that the *introduction* of elections for officials has almost invariably been the result of left agitation (as in CPSA) and the target of right opposition. But it is difficult to conclude from any of this evidence that workplace elections work to the advantage of the left (or of militancy) whilst appointment or postal ballots work to the advantage of the right and/or the 'moderates'.

The complexity of this situation perhaps explains the emphasis in some writings on re-election or rights of recall as means to ensure that officials once elected do not 'backslide' (cf. Militant Tendency, 1980, 1981). But would such procedural rights actually place power in the hands of the rank and file? It is here that we arrive at the central weakness of the electoral argument, which is its theory of union power. The *implication* of the argument about appointment vs. election and recall is that the power of the official derives from a constitutional defect, from the absence of any formal provision for popular control over leaders and their behaviour. Yet there are strong grounds for thinking that the power of the officials also rests on their own expertise and sometimes on their popularity with rank-and-file members.

What expertise do union officials possess? In many unions it is still the practice to appoint, or have running in elections, branch officers or shop stewards with good records of organising and negotiating—experience that always equips them well for most of an FTO's workload, but does not specifically train them for tasks such as office administration. Because of this fact, there is now considerably *more* training for officials than there used to be, and the TUC has recently expanded its short courses for FTOs. In white-collar unions, which tend to appoint rather than elect, expertise is more highly prized and unions look for a combination of experience and formal qualifications (Kelly and Heery, in preparation). Many of the more recently appointed officials will now possess knowledge of law, economics, perhaps accounting, in other words they will have a general knowledge of several industries and not just particular experiences of one (cf. Gramsci,

Chapter 3). As the problems faced by local workplace representatives in a time of recession become more intractable or more remote in their origins, the dependence of such reps on local or national full-time officials is likely to increase.

The same effect will occur if the law comes to play a greater role in industrial relations, or if solidarity between enterprises or unions is required in particular disputes. Combine committees or even trades councils could organise such links and solidarity action, but full-time officials will also almost inevitably come to play a crucial role. Indeed full-time officials will almost certainly have more or less ready access to a network of union contacts that cuts across a single union and across the geographical boundaries that restrict local branch officers and stewards (Kelly and Heery, in preparation). The greater expertise, information and contacts of the union officials as compared with many rank-and-file activists will often enable them to wield considerable influence over those activists despite the formal institutions of election and accountability.

Nor should rank-and-file loyalty to union officials be underestimated, as Michels pointed out many years ago. The results of union re-elections have repeatedly shown that members will very rarely vote an incumbent official out of office (Kelly, 1984). One of the reasons for this fact is that local union officials and shop stewards frequently work very closely together, and the relationship between them is cooperative and interdependent (Boraston et al., 1975; Batstone et al., 1977; Kelly and Heery, in preparation). Detailed empirical research suggests that such official–steward cooperation is not confined to a single union or industry, but is commonplace amongst the large general unions such as the TGWU, GMB and ASTMS which cover a range of workers, workplaces and industries. Whilst an older generation of officials was often hostile to workplace organisation, and to industrial militancy, the officials who now predominate in Britain's unions are very different. Most of them have been shop stewards and convenors themselves and are less likely to share the hostility to stewards and to militancy of their predecessors (Kelly and Heery, in preparation). Therefore to analyse the power of union officials in purely constitutional terms, overlooking power based on expertise and membership loyalty, is theoretically inadequate. As a result the policy prescription—election and re-election of all officials—may go *some* way to eroding officials' power, but it leaves other bases of power quite untouched. Without radical changes in the abilities and expertise of

stewards and branch officers, and without a dramatic extension
of their networks of contacts (e.g. through Broad Left, rank-and-
file groups, combine committees), officials will not only continue
to wield considerable power inside unions but will also continue
to win elections on a variety of political/industrial slates—right,
centre and left.

Isolation from the rank and file

A further important charge in many of the critical analyses of
union leadership is that leaders are isolated from the rank and file
and that this affects their attitudes and behaviour. On the one
hand full-time union officials are said to have relatively little
day-to-day contact with rank-and-file workers, leading them to
lose touch with their opinions and with their problems and
interests (Cliff, 1970; Callinicos, 1982, 1983a; Pearce, 1959). On
the other hand their own work brings them into frequent contact
with employers (Callinicos, 1982; Beecham, 1984) and with
various branches of the state (Cliff, 1970, 1971; Jefferys, 1979,
Freeman, 1984), whose subtle influences they are said gradually
and imperceptibly to absorb. The same argument has sometimes
been applied to full-time union representatives at the workplace
(Cliff, 1970; Callinicos, 1982; Hyman, 1979, 1980), and has
sometimes been presented through the concept of 'incorporation'
(see Edwards and Heery, 1986 for a review and critique; see
Chapter 8 below).

It has been argued that the widening scope of collective
bargaining and the rapid expansion of joint consultative committees from the mid-1970s took convenors and senior stewards away
from their members and locked them into a hierarchy of committees which held discussions on managements terms:

> The result was to strengthen management ideology—the need for
> profitability, viability, greater rates of exploitation—hand-in-hand
> with the strengthening of the 'national interest' ideology peddled by
> the Labour government and the union bureaucrats, both right and
> left (Beecham, 1984, p.104).

In a number of well-publicised cases, such as BL cars and British
Steel, stewards probably did spend an unusual and unprecedented amount of time in consultative and participative committees, but it seems unlikely that this was universally true. A
study by Partridge (1978) of stewards in a small company

suggested that almost half the time on union duties was spent in meetings with fellow stewards (42%), with management meetings consuming just 15% of time, and meetings with workers 39%. These figures do not indicate isolation from the rank and file, nor do they support the idea of stewards being perpetually wined and dined by employers or constantly locked in discussions on profitability and the survival of the firm. Other case studies also suggest that in strong workplace organisations stewards are likely to spend a considerable part of their time with other stewards (Batstone et al, 1977; Beynon, 1984). A more recent study suggested that it was not so much the frequency of steward–worker contact that changed in the 1970s as its form, with a shift away from collective action and meetings to individual grievance processing, a form of contact that arguably both reflected and intensified a decline in workplace collectivist ideology (Schuller and Robertson, 1983).

It is not clear from any of these accounts, or from studies of 'worker directors' (discussed more fully in the next chapter), that participation in managerial committees effectively promotes managerial ideology, though this is undoubtedly what management intends and hopes for. Detailed study of such committees provides little support for this argument, and it appears more likely that acceptance of management ideology leads to participation, rather than the other way round (see Cressey and MacInnes, 1985, and Chapter 8 below).

Finally, several critics have identified the growth of the 'check-off' (automatic deduction of union dues at source) as a factor contributing to the isolation of senior and regular stewards from their members. As Freeman (1984) rather nostalgically noted,

> The payment of small sums to the union representative ensured regular contact between shop stewards and rank and file members. The steward was obliged to account for his stewardship and to canvass support for union objectives. The worker renewed his commitment to the union (p.85).

In some cases it was at the union branch that dues were collected, and the spread of check-off has also been linked to the alleged decline in branch life and attendance (as well as to the spread of the closed shop).

Some of these arguments raise much wider questions of managerial and State policy and will therefore be dealt with in later chapters. For the moment it is important to bring out two central assumptions that pervade much of the preceding argument. If the isolation of full-time convenors and full-time officers from the rank and file is to explain 'bureaucratic conservatism' then it has to be shown that in general rank-and-file members are more militant than their full-time union representatives, and that the alleged conservatism of the full-timers either derives from or is substantially reinforced by their contacts with employers and the State. The first point is often assumed by Marxist critics of bureaucracy, as I noted earlier in this chapter, but the kind of evidence typically cited rarely *proves* the argument (see above, Table 7.1). Specific instances of rank-and-file militancy can be recounted ad infinitum, but so too can examples of rank-and-file conservatism, such as the opposition of CPSA and NALGO members to financial support for striking miners in 1985.

Furthermore, what evidence there is on the political attitudes of shop stewards and trade union officials suggests that they are far more active in Labour and left-wing politics than their members, more likely to belong to left political parties (Labour, CP, SWP etc.) and single-issue campaigns, and more critical than their members of media coverage of politics and industrial relations (Blumler and Ewbank, 1970). Insofar as we can talk of a dominant political culture amongst union officials and shop stewards, it is overwhelmingly Labourist (Kelly and Heery, in preparation). Contrast this with the fact that in 1983 only 39% of trade unionists voted Labour, whilst in 1987 less than half did so (Kellner, 1987).

The bargaining function and the maintenance of organisation

The fourth factor often addressed in accounts of trade union leadership is the official's bargaining function. Hyman (1984a) put this view clearly:

> Collective bargaining undertaken by 'specialist' negotiators *on behalf* of the broader membership consolidates a representative hierarchy functionally oriented towards accommodation and compromise with capital and its agents; committed to what has been called an 'industrial legality' which may permit some improvement in workers' conditions yet simultaneously endorses the legitimacy and security of the employer. Representation becomes detached from mobilisation; the preservation of the bargaining relationship with the employer bespeaks a containment of 'unofficial' exercises in class struggle (1984a, pp.229-30).

And Freeman put the same point more directly when he declared that 'workers enter disputes with their employers aiming only for *victory*. Union officials, however, are always inclined to put off confrontation by going for *compromise*' (italics in original, 1984, p.203). More generally, Selbourne has argued (in a way very reminiscent of Gramsci) that

> In the political culture of the market, the trade unions are above all the brokers of the private interests of labour, the producing class, and not the opponents of the capitalist system. Brokerage is their social and economic function: they could not avoid it even if they chose; and they do not choose to (1985, p.158).

Collective bargaining, then, serves to reconcile the interests of labour and capital insofar as that is possible, and the officials responsible for negotiations therefore come to see the preservation of bargaining arrangements, good relations with the employer, and union organisation as ends in themselves, in a process of goal displacement carefully analysed by Offe et al. (see above, and also Callinicos, 1982, 1983a; Hyman, 1975, Chap.3, 1979; Nagliatti, 1974). In general this orientation on the part of officials is thought to generate antagonism towards strikes, though such accounts do not preclude the possibility that union officials may seek to lead strike movements in order to head off and isolate independent, rank-and-file leadership (Hallas, 1977; Montague, 1979; Real Steel News, 1980; International Marxist Group, 1980).

This critique raises a number of questions about collective bargaining and the role of union officials. Do union officials have organisational interests to defend? Would strikes threaten those interests or strengthen them? Are union officials invariably wedded to 'procedure'? And more generally what are the costs and benefits for workers of institutionalised collective bargaining and the alternatives to such bargaining?

Union funds and organisation

Let us begin with strike pay, and consider whether union officials may have some incentive to withhold official backing from strikes in order to conserve the union finances that pay their salaries. In 1971 60% of British trade unionists could obtain strike pay of between £5 and £6 per week, in 1977 87% of TUC members were entitled to dispute benefit (Taylor, 1980), and in 1983 at least

83% of TUC members were in unions which gave strike pay (TUC, 1985). In some unions the payment of such benefit is discretionary and in several recent large strikes has been withheld (steel, 1980, and miners 1984-5). This however had less to do with 'bureaucratic conservatism' than with real fears about the costs of large-scale action. If the NUM had acted on the government assumption that all strikers received £15 per week strike pay and actually paid this money to an average 100,000 strikers for one year (1984-5), the total cost would have been £78 millions, six times its annual subscription income, four times its total investments and twice the size of its total assets. This is not to defend leadership hostility to strikes, or to place the 'survival of the organisation' above all other objectives, but to make the simple point that so long as large strikes are expensive and British trade unions poor, then the conservation of finance and organisation must be a major consideration in official attitudes to strikes.

But suppose that union officials were to support strikes more vigorously. Would this necessarily damage union organisation and with it their own job security? There are several reasons for thinking it might not. To begin with, the majority of strikes in Britain since 1945 have been unofficial, and the highest percentage of official strikes was recorded in 1971 at just 7.2%. That figure represented 74.2% of striker days for the year, underlining the association between size, duration and official status. Many unofficial strikes are short and small and receive no official backing either because they are over by the time the union can be notified or because they are too short to qualify for strike pay. Throughout the 1960s between two-thirds and three-quarters of all recorded strikes were over within three days (Edwards, 1983, p.211; Durcan et al., 1983, p.188).

If *all* recorded strikes were to be made official and strikers to receive immediate £15 per week strike pay, what would be the cost to unions? In the 'quiet' year of 1981, with just 1338 strikes and 4,266,000 'days lost', the total cost would have been £12.8m. In fact unions actually paid out £9.1m so the difference is not substantial. In 1980, with 11,964,000 days lost (a high figure exceeded only eleven times this century), the cost of paying £15 per week to all strikers, official or unofficial, would have been £35.9m: unions actually spent just £9.1m, a difference of almost £27m, or 10% of total union expenditure for the year. On the assumption that *all* strikes were made official and all those involved given £15 per week strike pay, then the extra cost to the unions *as a whole* based on figures for 1981 and 1980 as years of low and high militancy would be between 1% and 10% of their normal annual expenditure. The lower figure could easily be accommodated with no damage to the officials' position, but what about the upper figure? In this case would officials' positions be threatened as union funds were depleted?

In 1971 the postal workers (then the UPW) struck for almost seven weeks and by the end of the strike the union had spent £1.2m in hardship money. As the union stood on the brink of bankruptcy it did not sack or lay off any of its officials but instead raised subscriptions by 25%, borrowed heavily from other unions and cut back on education spending. Nor is there reason to think the UPW's response was unusual. Compared to their continental counterparts British unions have a very low ratio of full-time officials to members and so there is often little scope for any cutbacks even under financial duress (cf. Carew, 1976, Chap.6).

Evidence on the behaviour of unions in recession suggests that falling membership income can be offset by increasing subscriptions, so the financial base of many unions is more flexible than is sometimes thought. The same evidence shows that the number of officials has declined at a much slower rate than the membership since 1979 (Kelly and Heery, in preparation; Willman and Morris, 1987).

Another response of unions has been to make further cuts in their already rapidly dwindling welfare benefits to members, as the following table shows:

Table 7.3 British trade union expenditure 1960-85 (subdivisions and percentages of total)

	Working expenses (i.e. administration)	Dispute benefit	Other benefits
1960-64	68.8	1.9	26.7
1965-69	69.1	2.6	26.3
1970[1]	67.3	7.1	22.5
1975-79	74.3	3.8	16.1
1980-84	75.2	3.1	12.9

Sources: Registrar of Friendly Societies Annual Reports; Certification Officer's Reports 1976-85.

1. Figures are unavailable for 1971-4 inclusive because of union non-registration under the Industrial Relations Act.

Only when unions have faced strong member resistance to benefit cuts, as in the AEU, have they been forced to respond to a big decline in their membership by laying off officials.

Overall, then, it is difficult to establish that officials have a strong and clear-cut interest in opposing strikes in order to protect union funds. The vast majority of strikes are unofficial because they are short and quickly settled, and do not qualify for dispute benefit. But a rising volume of dispute expenditure need have no impact on the position of union officials because (a) dispute pay is a very small percentage of total union expenditure even during periods of high levels of militancy (see Table 7.3), (b) many unions can often make savings elsewhere, e.g. education, welfare benefits etc. and (c) income can often be increased to offset strike costs either through membership growth and/or through raising subscriptions. In any case Marxists have often argued that militant policies would help to attract into unions workers who were low-paid, part-time or otherwise disadvantaged, thereby increasing union revenues and providing potential for even more officials to be employed. Indeed there is a close statistical association between rising strike frequency and growth of union membership, particularly during the strike waves of 1889-91, 1910-14, 1916-20, 1939-45, and 1968-74 (Cronin, 1979). And anecdotal evidence on particular unions and strikes is consistent with this picture (Undy et al., 1981, pp.155, 162).

Even if official hostility to strikes could be demonstrated this would not necessarily indicate the operation of bureaucratic self-interest or goal displacement. It might simply be the case that officials genuinely believed a dispute was unwinnable or that no further gain was to be made in negotiations, and that to finance a strike would merely be wasting money. Indeed questionnaire data from a recent survey of local union officials suggests that their support for strikes depends largely on the perceived degree of membership support, and the prospects of victory, with financial considerations coming much lower down their rank order of criteria (Kelly and Heery, in preparation).

An addiction to procedure?

Are union officials wedded to procedure, and hostile to attempts at short-circuiting the normal machinery of bargaining? Again there are anecdotal and individual cases of national officials ordering their members back to work whilst procedure is exhausted or negotiations resume, but *systematic* evidence is hard to

178

come by. What little evidence is available suggests if anything that union officials have *less* belief in procedures than either stewards or rank-and-file members. In three Workplace Industrial Relations Surveys conducted in Britain, samples of these three groups were asked to say whether 'going through procedure' got better results than 'taking industrial action' and union officials emerged as having the least faith in procedures.

Table 7.4 Proportions of union members and officers who believe procedures produce better results than industrial action

	Rank and file union members	Shop stewards	Full-time union officers
1966[1]	82%	62%	43%
1972	72%	70%	46%
1973	71%	62%	38%

Sources: McCarthy and Parker, 1968, para 161; Parker, 1975, Tables 108, 109 A70.

1. These data are not strictly comparable with 1972 and 1973 as respondents were asked whether they could obtain results that were 'as good', not better.

Of course the meaning of these figures can be disputed since they refer to attitudes not behaviour, and they were collected from local not national officials. In any case, the fact that officials may be sceptical about the relative efficacy of procedures does not of itself imply they are doubtful about their desirability or legitimacy. But *if* we take these figures at face value then they appear to be inconsistent with the critiques of official conservatism.

Bureaucratic Conservatism Reconsidered: Collective Bargaining, Class Consciousness and Leadership

What lies at the heart of the many critiques of collective bargaining is the view that negotiating procedures are designed to accommodate the interests of labour and capital and are operated as such by union officials whose political horizons rarely, if ever, extend beyond the next bargaining round or dispute. In the course of their careers, if not before, they come to regard negotiation as 'the very stuff of trade unionism', highly dependent on the personal skills of bargainers, and see industrial action as playing a strictly subordinate if not marginal role (Callinicos, 1982, 1983a; Nagliatti 1974; Pearce, 1959). A recent pamphlet from the Revolutionary Communist Party sharply criticised the militant leadership of the NUM for '. . . seem[ing] to believe that victory depended on convincing MacGregor and the other coal board bosses of the intellectual superiority of the NUM's case in negotiations . . . Pickets were important only as a lever on negotiations' (Freeman, 1985, p.21).

Collective bargaining, in this view, is a regulatory not a subversive institution (cf. Selbourne, 1985) and its achievements do not reflect workers' needs and aspirations in general, but only those acceptable to capital. Since the interests of workers and their employers are fundamentally opposed, then any *agreement* reached between union and management negotiators must to a degree be at the expense of workers. The logic of this position is for critics to treat negotiations with considerable scepticism, if not outright hostility, in a way that is reminiscent of the classical Marxism of Lenin, Trotsky and Gramsci, and of British syndicalism. In the words of the 1921 Programme of Action proposed by the Comintern for the newly-formed Red International of Labour Unions (RILU),

> The collective agreement is nothing more than an armistice. The owners always violate these agreements at the earliest opportunity. This religious attitude towards collective agreements is evidence that bourgeois ideology is firmly rooted in the minds of the leaders of the working class. Revolutionary trade unions must not reject collective agreements, but they must understand that their value is limited, and must be prepared to break the agreements when this benefits the working class (Communist International, (Third) 1980, p.272).

If the conditions for struggle are ripe and if workers are willing to fight, but still lose or compromise, then it seems obvious to many militants that the fault lies with their leaders and negotiators (cf. on recent leadership 'sell-outs': WRP, 1985; IMG, 1980; Andrews, 1983).

This 'model' of collective bargaining rests in fact on three assumptions which are not commonly made explicit and which therefore deserve closer scrutiny: first, that the alternative to compromise settlements negotiated by officials is a fight until victory; second, that the possibility of victory depends on the leadership and organisation of labour's resources; third, that even if victory in strike situations is not always possible then it is better to go down fighting than to compromise.

The validity of some of these assumptions can be considered by looking at strike statistics before, during and after the strike waves of 1910-14 and 1918-22.

Table 7.5 Percentages of strikes ending in compromise, or employers' or workers' victories, 1906-24

Year	Number of strikes	Workers' victories %	Compromises %	Employers' victories %
1906	486	32	31	37
1907	601	32	27	41
1908	399	21	36	43
1909	436	19	35	46
1910	531	26	37	37
1911	903	25	43	32
1912	857	28	42	30
1913	1497	29	46	25
1914	975	25	42	33
1915	672	23	40	37
1916	532	23	51	26
1917	730	31	47	22
1918	1165	30	47	23
1919	1352	25	52	23
1920	1607	24	44	32
1921	763	20	39	41
1922	576	19	42	39
1923	628	30	41	29
1924	710	23	44	33

Source: Calculated from Cronin, 1979, Table B.5.

What these figures show is that during the most sustained periods of labour militancy ever witnessed in Britain, the employers' 'win rate' in strikes fell dramatically to only a quarter in 1913 and even less at the end of the First World War. Under the prevailing conditions direct action seemed to bear fruit. But what also happened was that the proportion of negotiated compromises rose simultaneously, peaking in 1913 at 46%, and in 1919 at 52% of all strikes. Workers therefore defeated capitalists in *two* ways: by securing a higher proportion of outright victories; and by forcing compromise settlements where the employers would previously (we presume) have won. Under *these* conditions, 'compromise' *was* victory of a sort, *not* because timid union leaders said so, but because the real alternative in previous years had been victory for the employer. What is also worth noticing is that in the midst of labour's most significant industrial and political advances in this country, between 1916 and the early 1920s, employers were *still* winning 1 in 4 strikes. Even under these extremely favourable conditions for workers' struggle, some workers were still defeated.

One explanation for these facts is that capitalists faced with a well-organised strike are *not* ultimately obliged to concede. They may be able to sit out a long strike if markets are slack; if they can obtain adequate profit from other branches of their organisation; or if the strike-bound plant is itself unprofitable. They may be able to make up lost production in plants elsewhere in the UK or overseas. They may be able to dismiss their workforce and replace it with scab labour. They may even close down a strike-bound plant and relocate permanently elsewhere (cf. Offe and Wiesenthal, 1980, on the mobility of capital).

Conceding labour's demands will often be just one of the options available to capital, a fact which makes clear why victory is *not* always possible. The outcome of a strike depends not only on labour's organisation, leadership and resources but on those of its opponents as well. It is the *balance* of resources between the sides, not the absolute level of labour's arsenal, that decides the outcome of struggles (cf. Mayhew, 1979).

Even if all of these arguments were accepted it could still be asserted that 'struggle' is a valuable political process irrespective of its substantive outcome, and that it is better to fight than to compromise (Harman, 1985a; Cliff, 1975b; Callinicos, 1983a). The effects of strikes and strike waves have already been considered and the points made earlier (Chapter 5) will not be repeated. But evidence does suggest that a strike *defeat* can have crippling consequences for workers, as the miners discovered in 1926 and 1985. Unless you believe that victory is always possible with determined leadership (and some people seem to: Pirani, 1985; Freeman, 1984, p.171) then the possibility of defeat must at least be considered, and strikes should therefore be approached strategically: 'Another principle of strike strategy is that there is a time when the members simply do not want to strike, a time to fight against a strike, a time to argue for acceptance of an offer and a time to call for a return to work' (McIlroy, 1984, p.10).

Merely labelling these actions as betrayals is unhelpful and invariably superficial, as Engels observed many years ago:

> When you inquire into the causes of counter-revolutionary successes, there you are met on every hand with the ready reply that it was Mr This or Citizen That who 'betrayed the people'. Which reply may be very true or not, according to circumstances, but under no circumstances does it explain anything—not even how it came to pass that the 'people' allowed themselves to be thus betrayed. And what poor chance stands a political party whose entire stock-in-trade consists in the knowledge of the solitary fact that Citizen So-and-So is not to be trusted (Engels, 1852, p.6).

Conclusions

Much of this chapter has criticised a contemporary and significant analysis of trade union leadership whose origins can be traced back to a series of classical Marxist arguments: Marx and Engels' caustic attacks on the leaders of the labour aristocrats; Lenin's exposition of the material basis of reformism; Trotsky's designation of trade union officials as a sociologically discrete and powerful group locked into policies of compromise and collaboration by the weight of their social milieu and by their own material interests. I have also considered the critique of collective bargaining as a form of institutionalisation to which union officials are thought to be particularly committed.

I have argued that, *in general*, there is no convincing evidence that union officials, on the whole, are more 'conservative' than their memberships. Much of the evidence designed to support the thesis of 'official conservatism' is ad hoc, unsystematic and anecdotal, and for all these reasons is unreliable. Clearly there are 'conservative' officials and militant workers, but there are also militant officials and conservative workers, and the precise balance between these groups is likely to vary with circumstances. It seems reasonable to suggest, for instance, that senior union officials in Britain were considerably more conservative in the 1950s, i.e. they were more hostile to strikes, more anti-communist, and deeply opposed to shop steward organisation.

Some of the explanations of official 'conservatism' turn out to be generally unconvincing and inadequate in the light of empirical evidence: the relationship between material privilege and consciousness is far more complex than the critics of union bureaucracy are prepared to admit. Consequently, it is naive to imagine that reductions in the salaries of union officials would have any dramatic effect on their attitudes and behaviour, though it would certainly cut down on trade union expenditure. It is hard to discover any systematic differences in the politics of elected as compared with appointed officials, and it is equally difficult to discover any major differences between the policies of unions controlled by elected and by appointed officials. 'Left' policies are just as likely to emerge from appointed and unaccountable officials as from elected officials. Lay union representatives who are 'isolated' from the membership appear to spend most of their time in meetings with fellow stewards and union officials, and not closeted away with employers as their critics imagine.

Finally, the idea that increased union expenditure on strikes would jeopardise the jobs of union officials is not supported by empirical evidence.

Full-time officials are deeply involved in collective bargaining and will continue to be so for the foreseeable future. It is true that collective bargaining has a conservative side to it, reproducing the legitimacy of two parties in industry and their more or less peaceful co-existence. Yet under most conditions this is the most that is possible for workers and the most that many of them want and expect. Such 'cooperative' trade unionism does bring rewards for workers in the form of employer concessions over wages and benefits, particularly for core groups during recession (see also Chapter 10 below). But there are circumstances in which worker mobilisation rises rapidly, where periodic strike waves throw the balance of power and the orderliness of industrial relations into flux. As workers' confidence increases and their horizons expand, the role of union leadership becomes critical in retarding or advancing such struggles. All the evidence reviewed in this chapter suggests that union officials are much more likely to be advancing such struggles and promoting radical demands than they have been in the past.

8

Trade Unions and Industrial Democracy

The three previous chapters have examined different components of one distinctive trade union strategy for raising workers' class consciousness and advancing towards socialism. Its hallmarks are the aggressive pursuit of economic militancy, coupled with struggles against sectionalism and against bureaucracy in the trade union movement. But as I noted in Chapter 4, the classical Marxists indicated a second major road for trade union advance, and it is this which forms the subject matter of the present and succeeding chapters.

This strategy begins with elements of both Lenin's and Gramsci's critique of trade union economic struggle, and asserts that through wages (or economic) militancy alone, trade unions will not develop the class consciousness of their members or inspire them with the vision and confidence to struggle for a socialist society. What is required instead is a much more far-reaching challenge to capitalist power and prerogatives. In addition to bargaining and struggling over terms and conditions of employment, unions should also seek to challenge the priorities of capitalist production and assert their own needs and interests over and against the requirements of profitability. Through struggles over 'industrial democracy' or 'workers' control' unions could then begin to challenge capitalist power within enterprises, and to develop new skills and a new-found confidence in their ability to control the economic decisions that affect their lives. Workers could perhaps begin to glimpse in embryonic form the possibilities of a truly democratic industry as opposed to the thinly-disguised authoritarianism under which they now labour.

This strategy of 'encroaching control' over capital was put to the test in a number of advanced capitalist countries in the 1970s and 1980s. The significance of those experiences remains as contentious today as it was then. In Britain, there were three major experiments in worker cooperatives, sponsored and partly-funded by the Department of Trade and Industry, and designed to save the jobs of hundreds of workers in ailing capitalist enterprises. There was the involvement by British Leyland shop stewards in the company's participation scheme, designed to restore BL's competitive position with trade union collaboration. There was the attempt by Lucas shop stewards to counter their employer's redundancy proposals with an alternative corporate plan of their own which argued for the production of socially useful goods and the retention of jobs, an initiative that was imitated under the auspices of the Greater London Council and Greater London Enterprise Board in the 1980s. Finally there were experiments in 'worker participation', taking different forms in different countries, but including worker directors, 'autonomous' work groups and quality circles.

Some socialists regarded these initiatives as courageous and pathbreaking attempts to challenge capitalist production criteria, and were undeterred in their advocacy by the failure of the intiatives to achieve their stated aims. Others responded quite differently and discerned in these proposals and their fate a vindication of their claim that 'encroaching control' over capital was a delusion. On this line of argument trade unionists could only lose out by involving themselves in the running of capitalist enterprises. They would inevitably become 'incorporated' and would cease to represent the interests of their members and to mobilise them in struggle. Once the independent, militant and oppositional role of the union was compromised, only the employer would benefit.

These are the issues I propose to examine in this chapter. To what extent can trade unions advance the interests and consciousness of their members by effectively challenging capitalist power and priorities at the level of the enterprise? Or will such challenges inevitably succumb to the pressure of market forces and result in the 'incorporation' of trade unions?

Many of the industrial democracy debates in the labour movements of the world took place in the 1970s, and since 1979 it has to be said that we have heard very little about industrial democracy, let alone workers' control. But it would be an extraordinary error of judgement to think that the issues raised in these debates have been buried in the mounds of recession. The same issues which stimulated trade union interest in the 1960s and 1970s—job insecurity, remoteness of managerial decisions, multinational power—are no less pressing in the 1980s, even if the overt level of union interest in industrial democracy has waned. But in any case the *formal* policies of both the British TUC and the Labour Party remain committed to some form of industrial democracy (TUC-Labour Party Liaison Committee, 1982, 1983, 1987), whilst the SDP-Liberal Alliance has been obliged to come up with some weak and diluted proposals for worker participation. Finally, the 1984-5 miners' strike graphic-ally illustrated the divisions in the British labour movement between those committed to economic militancy and confronta-tion with capital and the State, and those who believe in the prospects of a less confrontational, more gradualist strategy of encroaching control.

Industrial Democracy as Incorporation

There is no single definitive version of the argument that modern schemes of industrial democracy will serve to 'incorporate' trade unions into the management of capitalism and thereby damage their independent capacity to mobilise workers in struggle against the employer and the capitalist state. Various forms of this argument have been presented by Marxist intellectuals such as Clarke, David Coates, Panitch and Hyman; by trade union leaders such as Arthur Scargill; and by political organisations such as the CPGB, SWP, Workers' Power and the SPGB. Heavily qualified versions of the argument can be found in Terry (1983) and Ramsay (1983). Proponents of an incorporation argument differ over the definition of the term itself, the results obtained, the agencies responsible and the mechanisms of its operation.

Strictly speaking, the term 'incorporation theory' denotes a field of many, overlapping arguments rather than a single set of agreed propositions. In relation to worker director schemes and to participation schemes such as that at BL, 'incorporation' was thought to be evidenced in a reduction in strike frequency (Beecham 1981; Freeman, 1984; Callinicos, 1982), a reduction in workers' living standards (Beecham, 1984), union acceptance of rationalisation (Thornett, 1983), entry of profitability as a trade union bargaining criterion (Panitch, 1981), and the inability of the union to represent workers' interests (Scargill and Kahn, 1980). Occasionally the same factors have appeared as both the mechanisms by which 'incorporation' operates and the outcomes of the process—e.g. isolation of union representatives from the rank and file (cf. Hyman, 1984a, pp.227-8). Whilst most writers have stressed the role of employers as the major agency of incorporation, some regard the State as more central, e.g. Panitch (1981). The organisational forms through which incorporation is thought to have been achieved include collective bargaining arrangements (Hyman, 1984a; Cliff, 1979; Freeman, 1984; Terry, 1983), worker directors and joint consultative committees (Beecham, 1984; Jefferys, 1981; Freeman, 1984; Panitch, 1981), and tripartite or bipartite national bodies such as the NEDC (Freeman, 1984), though there is no single view as to which, if any, of these forms should be considered crucial.

The mechanisms by which the various forms of incorporation, variously defined, achieve their varying results are even more numerous. The main ones cited have been isolation of trade union representatives from their members; check-off and the closed shop; integration of shop stewards into formal union structures; workplace trade union hierarchy; union dependency on management for facilities; elevation of collective bargaining to company level; formalisation of union-management links; managerial control of committee agendas; perks and benefits of union office; absence of accountability of union leaders to the membership; pro-'business' ideology of union leaders; reformist consciousness of the working class; workers' loyalty to the Labour Party; content of union representatives' training; impact of political and economic climate; State provision of legal 'rights'; socialisation of union representatives on management dominated committees; lack of training of worker representatives in accounting etc.; consensus form of managerial decision-making; union minority status on strategic joint committees; union lack of information; union lack of experience and expertise (see Cliff, 1970, 1979; Beecham, 1984; Callinicos, 1982; Terry, 1983; Hyman, 1979, 1980, 1984a; Freeman, 1984; Thornett, 1983; Workers' Power, 1984; Panitch, 1981; Jefferys, 1981; Clarke, 1977; Coates, 1980). The purpose of presenting this list of 22 points is only to show that the 'theory of incorporation' has taken on board an enormous variety of developments in industrial relations whose collective implications for union practice are often contradictory and inconsistent. Some of these mechanisms have already been examined (Chapter 7) and their effects on the behaviour of union leaders found to be very weak. The isolation of workplace representatives or officials from their rank-and-file members, and their possession of power and material perks, were found to be inadequate explanations for any observed 'conservatism' or incorporation on their part.

Perhaps the key theme in 'incorporation theory' is the idea that unions and workers should not become involved in the management of capitalist enterprises, but should adopt an independent militant stance towards the employer. The 'joint management' of enterprises is opposed because it would legitimate capitalist business enterprise and its objectives, and it would make no fundamental difference to workers' interests. With or without 'industrial democracy' workers will be exploited by capital and will remain subject to the whims and vagaries of market forces. So powerful and compelling are these forces that no single firm can evade their logic.

In other words what is central to incorporation theory is a set of assumptions about the connections between the capitalist firm and its economic and political environment. On this issue incorporation theory splits into two quite distinct branches. The *weak* form of the theory asserts that the market constrains but does not exclusively determine the behaviour of the capitalist enterprise. The autocratic character of enterprises, and their exclusion of trade union influence, are not therefore necessary or inevitable products of 'the logic of capitalism' but are derived from historically specific and archaic structures of control. Reform of these structures *may* serve to 'incorporate' trade unions but since enterprises have a degree of latitude in their relations with the market this is not an inevitable result and can be minimised by careful organisational design. Since this analysis typically influences strategies of encroaching control or extended collective bargaining it will be considered more fully later on.

The *strong* form of incorporation theory rests on a quite different view of the relation between enterprise and environment and comprises seven basic assumptions:

a) the capitalist firm is a profit-maximising unit
b) the behaviour of firms is very closely regulated by markets
c) the individual firm is an integral component of an economic *system*
d) two economic systems, or modes of production, cannot coexist within a single nation state for any substantial period of time

e) the interests of capital and labour within the firm are fundamentally antagonistic

f) the power of capital is generally greater than that of labour

g) workers' major economic interest lies in the abolition of exploitation, not in its amelioration

What is the argument in full? According to the classical Marxist view, as presented in the first volume of *Capital*, the capitalist firm is an economic unit whose primary purpose, indeed *raison d'être*, is the accumulation of capital, that is the creation of profit on capital invested. Firms compete in both product and labour markets and endeavour to pay as little as possible for labour power, to extract as much effort from workers as they can within physical, social and political limits, and to sell their goods at the highest price possible consistent with continued accumulation.

These characteristics of firms are not dependent on the individual character or beliefs of particular capitalists, but are ruthlessly imposed on them by the market. If one firm raises its labour productivity with new machinery, and cuts the selling price of its product, then other firms must follow suit or go out of business: that is the only choice they face. This assumption, critical to strong incorporation theory, has been articulated in numerous publications, and it is intimately connected with the idea that a capitalist economy is a system of interlocking enterprises regulated by economic laws. According to Hyman (1974, p.252), in his review of the Institute of Workers' Control,

'Socialism in one industry' is an illusion because industry is a component of an environing *political economy*, a structure of political and economic domination. Whatever control structures are attained on a local or sectional level are subject to virtually irresistible pressures to accommodate 'realistically' to the coercive demands of market forces or government requirements (italics in original).

And the logic of this *systemic* view of capitalism has been clearly enunciated by Armstrong et al. (1984), Mandel (1973), Panitch (1978), and by Clarke: *'reform of the authority relations of the factory is impotent in the absence of structural reform of the production relations of society'* (Clarke, 1977, p.365, italics in original).

This position, in turn, leads to the denunciation of worker cooperatives on the grounds that 'you cannot build islands of socialism in a sea of capitalism' (*Socialist Worker*, 20/7/74, quoted

190

in Coates, 1976, p.17; see also Scargill, 1978). Proponents of strong incorporation theory disagree on the possibilities for co-existence between capitalist and socialist modes of production. Arthur Scargill (1978) and the SWP appear to envisage the transition from capitalism to socialism as a more or less rapid period of general strike-cum-insurrection (see Callinicos, 1983a). Mandel (1973), by contrast, has argued that a prolonged period of 'dual power' is feasible during which there could be competing modes of production.

The antagonistic interests of labour and capital are also thought to render 'industrial democracy' utopian. In their continual drive to maximise profits, capitalists endeavour to lower labour's cost whilst increasing its productivity. Since workers are alienated or estranged from the means of production and enjoy no rights in the disposal of the products of their labour, they are assumed to have no interest in production other than that of maximising their own wages whilst minimising the effort expended to obtain them. The relation between capital and labour is therefore one of antagonism and capitalists continually strive to exert real control over the labour process in order to maximise labour's exploitation. This is held to be particularly true during economic recession, when '. . . putting workers on management boards would involve them in agreeing to attacks on their own jobs, pay and conditions in the interests of capitalist viability' (Glyn and Harrison, 1980, p.161; see also Glyn 1978).

It is also assumed that in a capitalist economy the power of capital will generally exceed the power of organised labour. Workers will of course secure victories in struggles over a wide range of issues—wages, hours, grading, victimisation and so on—but at the end of each particular struggle, capital is still in command, and capitalist firms remain locked within a capitalist system driven by the desire for profit. Furthermore capital can often claw back concessions more easily than workers: wage rises, for instance, can be nullified by price rises or redundancy (cf Mandel, 1973). The significance of this model of power disparity is that it both permits and makes intelligible discussion based on the *intentions* of capitalists in introducing schemes for industrial democracy. For if the power of capital generally does exceed that of labour then the intentions of capital are likely to constitute a reliable guide to the probable outcomes of such schemes (Clarke 1977, Panitch, 1978, and Mandel, 1973).

There is one final and very important assumption to be added to those dealt with already, and that concerns workers' interests

In the classical theory of the firm, as we saw in Chapter 1, Marx argued that whilst workers could obviously be said to possess a variety of interests—in a safe workplace, in shorter hours and so on—they were the bearers of one over-riding interest, namely the abolition of capitalist exploitation *tout court*. Marx was at pains to insist on this point because the specific problems that workers were aware of, and fought, such as speed-up, sacking, accidents at work and the like, could all be traced back to the antagonism between labour and capital founded on the latter's exploitation of the former. It followed that workers' specific interests could 'ultimately' be satisfied only through the abolition of class exploitation.

For all of these reasons the theorists of incorporation regard schemes of 'industrial democracy' as inevitably doomed to disappoint their proponents. The meagre fruits of incorporation have not been highly visible in Britain, however, because schemes of 'industrial democracy' have not taken off to anywhere near the same extent as in West Germany or Sweden. This explains why the short-lived 'participation scheme' at BL aroused such interest amongst Marxists, and why it was taken as a paradigm case. Thornett summed up the experience like this:

> Perhaps the most insidious damage to the stewards' movement was the political corruption introduced in the period of 'participation' . . . By sucking a whole layer of convenors, shop stewards and union officials into a framework of collaboration with management, this set-up struck a major blow at the independence of the shop stewards' movement from the bureaucrats and the management (Thornett, 1983, pp. 5-6).

A similar account can be found in Lyddon (1977).

The alternatives to 'incorporation'

There are two main alternative strategies on offer: militant, rank-and-file trade union action, as advocated by Scargill and Kahn (1980) (see also Scargill, 1975), and in a slightly different way by the SWP and the RCP; and revolutionary, political trade unionism that will fight for workers' control of production in a fully socialist economy. In practice the difference between these positions is more easily stated than observed but the two following quotations are illustrative:

> We have to take a stand in defence of our jobs and living standards, whether in the private sector or the public sector. How the employers organise their industries, and services is their problem—not ours. We simply have to insist that our livelihoods are guaranteed. The only way we can guarantee our survival is by fighting—and the harder we fight, the more they will be forced to concede (Freeman, 1984, p.266).

> Thus ongoing workers' struggles for obtaining sufficient power on the factory floor to refuse speed-ups, arbitrary redefinitions of work rules, skills and rates, etc., must be treated as more than a negation of capitalist authority structures. They must be practically connected with a revolutionary affirmation of workers' power. Today's struggles against the authoritarian factory system must become one moment in the broader assertion of the capability of workers to take control of the process of production and to organise the working process as *they* think best (Panitch, 1978, p.44).

The strategy of industrial militancy espoused in particular by the SWP has sometimes, though not always, gone hand in hand with a defence of job controls (rather than 'workers' control') on the grounds that they have been constructed 'from below' by independent shop steward organisations through conflict with employers. But critical to the defence of industrial militancy has been the over-riding desire to preserve the *ideological* and *organisational* independence of the unions since, in line with Trotsky's 1930s writings (see Chapter 2 above), the independence of trade unions is regarded as the main focus of ruling class attacks and the main bulwark of workers' defences against them. Moreover, any participation in the running of capitalism has been considered a debilitating admission of responsibility for the crisis of capitalism and inimical to any desire for its overthrow (cf. Parker, 1975; Bullock and Yaffe, 1975).

The industrial militants' strategy has been denounced by proponents of revolutionary trade unionism on three grounds: that it concedes, in practice, managerial prerogative over the labour process; that without a political challenge to capital and the State it will prove ineffective in periods of recession; and that it lacks any obvious strategy for translating economic into political struggle (hence the frequently heard charges of economism and syndicalism) (see Workers Power 1978, 1984; Mandel, 1973; von Beyme, 1980). The proponents of revolutionary trade unionism appear for their part to believe in an immediate and continuous struggle to restrict managerial prerogative through 'workers' control'. Precisely what this entails in practice, or how it differs from 'extended collective bargaining', is not always clear; nor is it always clear how it differs from the strategies of the SWP and RCP and the views of Glyn (1978) and Scargill (1978), all of whom profess to believe in workers' control only as an 'ultimate' achievement within the context of a fully-planned socialist economy.

A Critical Appraisal

The nature of the capitalist firm

In examining the strong form of the incorporation argument I propose to focus initially on the underlying assumptions before then looking at specific examples of 'industrial democracy'. The ideas that capitalist firms set out to maximise profits, and that profitability is the principal measure of their success, are perfectly acceptable as broad generalisations. Nevertheless capitalist firms do pursue a range of other goals, such as raising their market share, achieving industrial peace or diversifying their product range, particularly if their rate of profit is high. Indeed a considerable body of evidence suggests that senior managers may be more accurately described as profit-optimisers, or satisficers, rather than maximisers; and Japanese managers have long been criticised within Japan for their relentless pursuit of overseas market shares even to the detriment of profit rates (cf. H.A. Simon, 1976).

Even where profitability is the firm's major goal, or the criterion for judging other goals, firms will operate within an acceptable profitability range, and may have discretion as to the time-scale over which profit targets are to be met. Consequently firms may enjoy some degree of choice as to the precise nature of their goals and, more importantly, the means for their achievement (Tomlinson, 1982). What follows is that workers *may* be able to intervene at the level of the enterprise—if not to alter the firm's goals (e.g. to depress the rate of profit, or raise wages) then to influence the means for achieving them (e.g. redirecting investment to areas of high unemployment, creating flexible work groups instead of Fordist assembly lines). However, the *scope* for such influence should not be overstated, and the incorporation theorists are right to stress the constraints on capitalist firms and on the possibilities of effective union influence.

Secondly, incorporation theorists have frequently assumed that capitalists are rational economic agents and therefore the best judges of a firm's interests. *If* this assumption were correct, there would be no point in workers participating in decisions since capitalists would have responded to market pressures and made the 'best' decisions already. But there are issues and contexts where the assumption may be false. Nichols (1986), for instance, has argued that Britain's comparatively poor manufacturing productivity owes a considerable amount to the poor technical competence and quality of British management, and their reluctance to train either themselves or their workforces. Eccles' (1981) study of the Fisher-Bendix cooperative maintained that the firm was run down under its former owners largely as a result of their own incompetence in responding to market openings. The steel union ISTC (1980) produced a study of the British Steel Corporation which revealed a catalogue of managerial investment and operational blunders that compounded workers' problems in a deteriorating market. And finally the Greater London Enterprise Board was involved between 1981 and 1986 in restructuring almost 200 small firms, many of which were managed abysmally (Mackintosh and Wainwright, 1987, Chap.6).

If there is significant managerial incompetence, and *if* there are different ways of achieving a given profit target which have differential effects on workers, then it follows that there is *some* purpose in workers trying to influence some managerial decisions. The problem with the incorporation argument, at least in Britain, is that it portrays an extraordinarily flattering and uniform picture of the way capitalist firms actually work, a picture that bears more resemblance to the fictive abstractions of bourgeois economic theory—perfect competition and the like— than to the reality of the modern firm.

It is therefore not wholly true to say that 'competition makes the immanent laws of capitalist production to be felt by each individual capitalist, as external coercive laws' (Marx, *Capital Vol. 1*, quoted in Clarke, 1977, p.365). Similar firms in local labour markets pay an enormous range of rates for the same job and operate at widely differing profit levels. Again, this is not to suggest that market forces are irrelevant—far from it—but only to point out that capitalist firms *vary* in their responses to markets, and that unions may be able to exploit this fact.

Nor is it sensible to argue that the systemic character of capitalism precludes any breach in the domination of enterprises by the market. In Britain the National Health Service, for all its inequalities, under-resourcing and lack of democracy, *is* an island of socialism in a sea of capitalism! It is an enterprise which supplies use values, not exchange values, largely, though not entirely, on the basis of need. Health care is not 'sold' in Britain, as it is in America, a point that underlines the significance of its achievement. This and other services represent, in the words of Claus Offe (1982), the front line of a process of 'decommodification' in which various types of goods or service are removed from the direct sway of commodity production and exchange. It remains unclear how far this process can go and to what extent forms of social ownership could penetrate the profitable sections of industry and commerce, and not remain confined to 'social services', or to 'natural monopolies' such as water and energy. But the variation in the size of the 'decommodified sector' between nation-states, and over time, suggests that the slogan 'no islands of socialism in a sea of capitalism' underestimates the degree to which competing modes of production actually do coexist.

Finally, the incorporation argument rests on the view that since workers' primary interest lies in the abolition of their own exploitation, and since 'industrial democracy' will not achieve this, then they can have no interest in 'industrial democracy'. Whilst the *basic* relationship between capital and labour is antagonistic, resting as it does on exploitation, the full relationship is more complex.

Labour is dependent on capital, a fact that follows from its not owning the means of production, and which is reinforced by the organisational forms of capital and labour. Whilst capital can be converted into land, bank money, or commodities such as paintings and still produce income without a direct dependency on labour, workers cannot reproduce themselves except through their relation with capital:

> Because of this asymmetrical dependency relationship, the collectivity of all workers must be, paradoxically, more concerned with the well-being and the prosperity of capitalists than, inversely, the latter is concerned with the well-being of the working class (Offe and Wiesenthal, 1980, p.76; also Kitching, 1983, p.108 ff; Cressey and MacInnes, 1980, p.15).

In the highly competitive and declining furniture industry, GLEB encountered numerous firms where capitalist strategy consisted of little more than cost-cutting and profit-taking: it was the workers who were concerned about lack of investment, poor product design and ineffective marketing, because their jobs were at stake (MacKintosh and Wainwright, 1987, Chap.8).

The power of capital

The assertion that 'industrial democracy' is precluded by capital's power advantage over labour is not, on the face of it, consistent with the strategic thrust of incorporation theory towards confrontation with capital. For if labour is unable, because of the all-pervading power of competition and the market, to impose its will and its priorities on capital through worker directors in the board room or extended collective bargaining, why should 'shopfloor action' be any *more* effective? If the logic of the market dictates capital's refusal, let us say, to invest in a depressed region, why should capitalists change their minds when confronted with militant action?

One answer might simply be that such action imposes significant costs to capital instead of merely wasting their time with well-researched reports in board room meetings. But the strike weapon does have its limits: capitalists mày be keen to avoid a six-week strike if the alternative is only to concede an extra 2% on a pay claim, but they may be equally keen to resist if the alternative is to invest in Scotland instead of France and lose millions of pounds in potential profits, particularly under conditions of economic recession. The UCS workers, for instance, were able to compel the British government to save thousands of shipyard jobs after their work-in of 1971. But in the throes of the chronic over-capacity of the 1980s, the British shipbuiliding industry has been decimated. In other industries, such as steel and mining, the strategy of fighting closures through industrial action has been notably unsuccessful, not only in Britain, but in other countries such as France and the USA. Some sections of capital, however, are more vulnerable than others: firms producing exclusively for the British market or the British State are more susceptible to State pressure than multinational firms.

Before incorporation . . .

The incorporation argument also suggests, if only by implication, that in some bygone era—before the days of industrial democracy, corporatism, productivity bargaining or the many other mechanisms of 'incorporation'—there were more struggles against the employer, greater resistance to State and union officials' intervention in bargaining, faster movements in real earnings, closer links between stewards and members, and less willingness on the part of workers to accept employers' arguments for rationalisation. In many ways the shop steward organisations of the engineering industry or the car industry were the models for this type of 'unincorporated' and independent workplace organisation.

Various writers have exposed some of the weaknesses of this type of argument (Batstone, 1984 in particular): its excessive reliance on a selected sample of steward organisations; its refusal to take seriously the Donovan Commission finding that 75% of shop stewards were regarded as 'fairly' or 'very' helpful by management as early as 1966 (Royal Commission, 1968); the facts that steward hierarchy, union facilities and strong bargaining relationships were well established in many large engineering plants during the hey-day of the short unofficial stoppages, that union acquiescence to incomes policies was not simply a product of the 1970s because unions had acquiesced in similar policies during 1968, 1966, 1965, 1950, 1949 and 1948 (perhaps 'incorporation' goes back to the 1940s . . . or earlier?), and that real wages rose faster during the 1970s as a whole (as incorporation of stewards supposedly became more widespread) than during the 1960s.

The principal difficulty of this view, however, is that it tries to plot the trajectory of shop steward policies, ideology and action by recording the changes in workplace organisations and institutions. From the growth of shop steward hierarchy, we can, so it is claimed, infer the emergence of a bureaucratic, conservative lay elite exercising discipline and control over rank-and-file insurgency. From the growth of joint consultative committees we can infer the emergence of an ideological current sympathetic to capitalist restructuring and rationalisation, and of stewards willing to be consulted by management about such issues (cf. Beecham, 1984).

Now in particular cases it may be that new institutional arrangements do produce these outcomes and *do* 'incorporate' shop stewards. But why should this be thought inevitable, rather than purely contingent on local circumstances? Why couldn't shop steward hierarchy be used to transcend sectionalism, and unify disparate workgroups in a coherent challenge to the employer, as happened at Massey Ferguson (Batstone et al., 1977)? Why couldn't joint consultative committees be used by workers simply to gather information needed for collective bargaining, without otherwise affecting their involvement in capitalist restructuring (see Cressey and MacInnes, 1985, for examples)? The theoretical error here is to believe that from a given set of institutional arrangements you can simply 'read off' the behaviour of trade unionists and employers and the outcomes for workers. Empirical evidence shows that any given set of institutions at the workplace can generate a variety of outcomes.

Incorporation in practice

The assumptions underlying the incorporation argument are not wrong *in toto*; but they comprise only partial characterisations of the labour-capital relation and the structure and dynamics of capitalist enterprises, and they underplay the variability between firms in their market position and power. This is not to say that 'incorporation' is a myth but that it occurs under certain specific conditions.

From 1975 until 1977 BL (the former British Leyland cars) convenors and senior stewards were involved in the participation exercise that was jointly designed to review the whole spectrum of company performance. One story goes that the more the stewards participated, the more they became detached from and unable to represent their members. Their growing sympathy with management, induced by 'cosy boardroom chats', led them into collaboration with speed-up, rationalisation, and State incomes policies, and was responsible for their opposition to actions such as the 1977 tool room strike, because of its damaging effect on production.

However, it was not the case that BL stewards backed productivity drives *because* they were locked in participation; rather, they decided to participate in order to promote production, a policy on which the influential CP stewards, such as Robinson and Adams, had agreed some time previously. The CP programme and National Congresses of the CP were agreed on the necessity to increase the output of British industry as a way of protecting jobs in the face of a rising tide of imports. Government threats to cut back much-needed finance were taken seriously. Management statements that the cars market was entering a downward slide, with all that implied for output and employment, were also taken seriously because they happened to be true. At the end of the day it was the parlous finances and the declining product market of BL that pushed the stewards into last-ditch efforts to 'participate' in management decision-making, and to offer concessions to management on working practices. And it has been similar product market pressures, not the seductive charms of 'cosy boardroom chats', that have resulted in widespread 'collaboration' by unions across the whole of British industry (see Chapter 10 below). BL just happened to be in the forefront of a long queue of firms entering recession and all the evidence from other industries suggests that its unions would have responded the way they did with or without participation.

Evidence from other countries shows a similar trend, with workers in the declining steel and docks industries of America agreeing to participate in extensive programmes of rationalisation and job loss. Again it was product market pressures and technological changes which led workers to cooperate in such programmes and try to extract what concessions they could (Kochan et al., 1986; Peterson and Tracy, 1985). Likewise it was the rising volume of imports and the competitive pressure of Japan that led the American UAW into an extensive (and, some would argue, an excessively generous) programme of concessions to General Motors (Piore and Sabel, 1984).

The experience of those workers who *have* fought closures and redundancies—at Speke, Dunlop, BSC, the Coal Board, and elsewhere—is generally, though not universally, depressing: virtually all have gone down to defeat, whether their unions were led by the 'left' (NUM, 1984-85 strike) or the 'right' (COHSE and others, 1982 NHS dispute). Indeed it is surprising that any Marxists are surprised at this fact. For if the power of capital and the State, and the coercive power of the market, is as great as we are led to believe, what result other than defeat would be expected in the midst of recession?

Conclusion

Despite its many problems, the incorporation argument does possess three important and distinctive strengths, and these are its grasp of capitalist *power*, its insistence on the fundamental antagonism between labour and capital and its appreciation of the constraints on capitalist firms. To those who would advocate the extension of collective bargaining or the statutory creation of worker directors in order to influence capitalist decision-making, the incorporation theorist would pose one crucial question: why should capital negotiate and reach agreements with labour on its business strategy if it has the power to refuse? What effective sanctions can labour deploy against the multinationals who won't disclose information, the firms who engage in purely token consultation, the board of directors, as at Lucas Aerospace, who refuse to discuss a workers' plan, or the management of United Biscuits who discuss such a plan only to reject it (for details of these cases see Gilhespy et al., 1986, pp.46-8)?

Under specific conditions there are some sanctions labour and/or the State *could* deploy, though with what effect is unclear, and the refusal of incorporation theorists to recognise this fact is one of their weaknesses, as is their reluctance to recognise the interests of labour in capital's viability, or of capital in labour's consent.

Extended Collective Bargaining

The British TUC has long supported the extension of collective bargaining to embrace the major components of business strategy, as have several prominent Marxist individuals and organisations. Several European union federations have pursued a similar strategy, in Italy, Sweden and Norway (see the essays in Goldthorpe, 1984), but the American labour movement has until recently been sceptical about or disinterested in such initiatives, concentrating its efforts on workplace collective bargaining (Kochan et al., 1986, Chap.7; Wheeler,1987). The British Communist Party had long been an advocate of 'free collective bargaining' and its opposition to any entanglement in State corridors of power was maintained in its insistence that collective bargaining, not worker directors, was the road the union movement had to travel (cf. also Aaronovitch, 1981). The Institute for Workers' Control had always favoured a strategy of 'encroaching control' over managerial prerogative and in the 1970s steadfastly opposed the 'incorporation school' and its associated strategies. And despite the continual if diluted presence of worker directors in 1980s labour movement documents, the extension of collective bargaining remains central to TUC thinking within a context of economic regulation through planning agreements and investment controls. What, then, is the argument and the evidence for 'the extension of collective bargaining' as a route to industrial democracy?

The term itself is hardly free of ambiguity: some advocates of incorporation theory would favour militant struggles to veto or control the outcomes of bargaining over capitalist decision-

making, whilst some advocates of worker directors would regard
the boardroom merely as a new level, or tier, of collective
bargaining (Hirst, 1981). What is distinctive about the strong
'extension of collective bargaining' position is a desire to stay free
of the boardroom whilst avoiding the pitfalls of 'militant absen-
tionism'. In its evidence to the Bullock Committee of Inquiry, the
Communist Party declared that:

> There has been an extension of industrial democracy over the last 100
> years in that the questions subject to some form of negotiation
> between the two sides of industry, management and labour, have
> been increased. . . . Bit by bit collective bargaining has been able to
> encroach on new areas, bringing what was hitherto regarded as
> managerial right under some sort of control . . . Fundamental to all
> these advances has been the determination of workers and their trade
> unions to insist, frequently with great tenacity and great hardship, on
> their right to be heard (CPGB, 1976, paras 2, 3).

Collective bargaining was the traditional method of British
trade unionism which had worked in the past and which allowed
the trade unions to remain independent of management by not
involving them in standing committees whose terms of reference
could conflict with trade union objectives and structures (TUC-
LPLC, 1982). Scargill and Kahn (1980), for instance, illustrated
this problem with the case of the miner dismissed by a joint
union-management disciplinary panel. Since the union had participated in the original decision, its officers felt unable to 'turn
around' and oppose it through the NUM lodge. In Scargill's view
their independence had been compromised (see also Ogden,
1982).

A further objection to such joint union-management committees was that they enshrined the principle of 'responsibility
without power' (Coates and Topham, 1974). By limiting the
capacity of unions to report back to their members, they secured
maximum union support for decisions whilst minimising their
power of opposition. In collective bargaining, unions are not
obliged to accept joint responsibility for agreements in the way
that company boards are, but can register a 'failure to agree' or
go into dispute. It has also been argued that the institution of
collective bargaining embodies the idea of 'conflicting interests',
notwithstanding the fact that agreements are ultimately reached.
The consensual form of decision-making, common on company
boards, conflicts with traditional trade union practice, and, more
importantly, embodies the idea that in industry there is one team,

not two sides (Ogden, 1982). It has also been maintained that less inequality prevails in collective bargaining than in company boardrooms, because trade unions can choose which issues appear on the bargaining agenda, something they cannot do in the boardroom (Ogden, 1982). Finally, it has been argued that the extension of bargaining can, and almost certainly will, be based on mobilisation of workers in struggle, a process inhibited by the responsibilities of board representation (Ogden, 1982; Hyman, 1974; Scargill and Kahn, 1980; Aaronovitch, 1981).

There is no single view of the capitalist firm and its dynamics behind this strategy, though proponents of extended bargaining place less emphasis on market constraints than do the incorporation theorists. In this sense they are closer to an 'organisational politics' rather than a classical economic view of the firm. Much of their argument has been rehearsed in the critique of incorporation theory and need only be repeated briefly here. Since capital and labour are interdependent, as well as antagonistic forces, they have some interest in seeking ways of reaching agreement on contentious issues. This is feasible for labour, it is held, because capital's power is not absolute, and because the decision-making of firms is a political process in which unions can usefully intervene, as they have in the past, to argue for and ideally impose their priorities (see Burawoy, 1979; Cressey and MacInnes, 1980; Tomlinson, 1982; Hodgson, 1984; LCC, 1981; Hughes, 1981; Wainwright and Elliott, 1982; Rustin, 1985).

This 'political' model of the firm has often gone hand-in-hand with a non-insurrectionary view of the transition to socialism. In their reply to Hyman's (1974) critique of the IWC, Barratt Brown and his colleagues (1975) stated that '. . . we see the possibility of the disintegration of [capitalism's] baneful power-structure by encroaching control from within' (p.302). They readily accepted that such a process *may* lead to an unstable, even revolutionary situation of dual power (as did Cooley, 1980), but that remains an open question. They clearly opposed the view that 'nothing can be done' to wrest power from capital before 'the Revolution' and rejected the thesis that capitalism was such a highly integrated system that it could not be transformed from within but only shattered 'from without'. Industrial democracy, then, was not only a definable end-state (workers' control, or workers self-management) but a 'process of limitation, and ultimately of annulment, of blind market powers' (Coates, 1976, p.19; see also Tornquist, 1973).

Writers within this tradition have also stressed the role of State intervention as the essential context within which extended collective bargaining will take place. The role of the State has been variously described as: expanding demand, output and employment (Hughes, 1981; Aaronovitch, 1981); protecting union bargaining rights and freedoms (TUC Labour-Party Liaison Committee, 1982, 1983, 1985, 1986); providing resources to strengthen labour and, if necessary, weaken capital (Hughes, 1981); curbing or rolling back the domain of market regulation (Aaronovitch, 1981; Tomlinson, 1982, Gilhepsy et al., 1986). Indeed some proponents of extended collective bargaining, e.g. Ogden (1982), would readily accept that without an appropriate political and economic context, the scope of collective bargaining will undergo very little extension, and workers' involvement in decision-making may take place largely on management's terms according to the incorporation scenario.

Some of the evidence from Britain and elsewhere on the extension of collective bargaining is impressive. There is considerable anecdotal or case study evidence on the spread of job controls and mutuality clauses in certain British industries in the 1970s (Hyman and Elger, 1981; Kilpatrick and Lawson, 1980). More systematic evidence was produced by Storey (1980), who studied industries not normally thought of as centres of strong workplace organisation: textiles, brewing, artificial fibres, and public transport (as well as engineering). He found that between 1971 and 1978 there was a small though significant increase in the spread of joint regulation through collective bargaining. On 18 out of 25 issues, from rest periods to investment plans, there was an average increase of 6.8% in the number of local establishments where these matters were settled by negotiation (Storey, 1980, p.129). On some issues more dramatic shifts were reported in the frontier of control: manning, an increase of 11%, from 55% to 66% of establishments negotiating with unions; job content, an increase of 9% (49% to 58%); level of output or service, an increase of 13% (16% to 29%). The document *Economic Planning and Industrial Democracy* (TUC-LP Liaison Committee, 1982) expressed a similar view when it said:

Collective bargaining has evolved—and is evolving—to meet new needs and circumstances. New areas continuously arise where collective bargaining can be used to extend joint control into the administration and the execution of corporate policies within the enterprises. One such area is bargaining over the introduction of new technology (paras. 130, 131; see also Ogden, 1982).

In America unions in manufacturing industry have for many years negotiated extremely detailed contracts, with work rules governing issues such as job mobility, promotions, seniority and grading (Kochan et al., 1986, Chap.2).

Since then, the impact of recession has produced a reversal in the scope of collective bargaining in a large number of establishments, though it is too early to say whether this is a purely temporary phenomenon (Millward and Stevens, 1986, pp.248-53). In the particular area of new technology evidence suggests that consultation with unions occurs in only 50% of firms, whilst negotiation takes place in only 10% (Daniel, 1987). Some white-collar unions have signed specific agreements with employers, covering issues such as training, health and safety, and job regrading, but few of these agreements have prevented loss of jobs, and the 'negotiation' which takes place may be more apparent than real (Williams and Steward, 1985; Daniel, 1987). In American industry some employers have pushed hard to recover areas of control from workers, through union 'give-backs' in collective bargaining. Others have gone further, making dramatic inroads into collective agreements and insisting on high levels of worker flexibility, inter-job mobility and payment linked to skills rather than job performance (Kochan et al., 1986; Piore and Sabel, 1984).

Proponents of extended collective bargaining also drew support from the Lucas Aerospace initiative in the 1970s (Wainwright and Elliott, 1982). Faced with a major programme of redundancies, Lucas stewards responded with a rival corporate strategy, a Workers' Plan, designed to protect jobs through the production of non-military, socially useful products. Although Lucas management successfully refused to negotiate their business strategy with the trade unions, the idea of a Workers' Plan aroused considerable interest in trade union circles, even though it was emulated only infrequently.

There have also been attempts by a number of unions (mostly outside Britain) to bargain over the content of jobs and the organisation of work. American trade unions have often pursued such intitiatives through specially-created joint labour-management committees, frequently set up in the shadow of plant run-downs, industrial decline and intensified market competition. Some of the Italian unions explicitly promulgated demands during the late 1960s for the abolition of assembly-line work with its 'Taylorist' division of labour. The Swedish federation, LO, embodied demands for work redesign in its 1971

Programme for Industrial Democracy (see Kelly, 1982b, 1985).

A Critical Evaluation

There are four obvious strengths in the proposals to extend collective bargaining over a much wider area of decision-making. They appear, on the surface, less vulnerable to processes of incorporation and dilution; they involve, usually explicitly, attempts to mobilise workers and involve them however indirectly in the bargaining process; they build on the traditions of British and American trade unionism and to that extent are more readily absorbed into union thinking than ideas of worker directors; and finally they appear consistent with the long-run trend for unilateral employer regulation to give way to joint regulation through collective bargaining.

The evolution of collective bargaining

The implication of these arguments is that because wages, hours, job content and so on have previously been brought under joint regulation, then the 'frontier of control' will continually move onwards, shifting the boundary between unilateral and joint regulation. The question we must ask, however, is why should companies bargain with unions over their investment plans, for instance, and what sanctions will unions be able to deploy if they refuse (cf. GMWU, 1976)?

The oft-cited case of the Lucas Aerospace shop stewards' combine provides an interesting lesson. The combine endeavoured to bargain with the company over its product range, insisting that 'socially useful products' should be manufactured in order to stave off proposed redundancies. The workers' plan was superbly researched by a dedicated and highly skilled group of stewards: they were well-organised, well-supported, articulate and enjoyed good political and media contacts. The Lucas plan has been quoted approvingly by the Labour Party and the TUC, it has provided the model for other groups of workers (of which more shortly), it has featured as the subject of a book, and its fame has spread throughout the world (Wainwright and Elliott, 1982; Kitching, 1983; Rustin, 1985). Yet amidst the enthusiasm for the Corporate Plan, one important point is sometimes forgotten: Lucas corporate management refused to negotiate. It is true that the Lucas managers took a particularly tough attitude to the combine, and felt their own authority as managers was being called into question by its activities. But experiences in other capitalist countries suggests Lucas is unlikely to be an isolated case.

In the early 1970s the major Italian trade union federations gradually endeavoured to shift the focus of their company and industry level bargaining from an exclusive emphasis on wages and benefits, towards joint control of resource allocation such as investment plans. Before the oil crisis of 1973-4 a number of unions achieved limited agreements in companies such as FIAT, Alfa-Romeo and Zanussi. Unions traded concessions on worker mobility, effort levels and short-time working in exchange for understandings and proposals to maintain employment and direct new investment into Italy's depressed southern regions (see Treu, 1983; Lange et al., 1982). By the end of the decade few agreements had been signed; of those that had been signed many provided unions only with rights of consultation, preserving the employer's prerogative; and the actual total investment re-directed into the south was minimal (Regini, 1984).

It seems that the greatest advances in bargaining on workers' plans have been made where local authorities (L.A.s) or L.A. funded bodies such as technology networks have contributed financial and other resources to exercise leverage over State dependent firms (MacKintosh and Wainwright, 1987). Unions alone have found it difficult to force employers to bargain over such plans.

Regulating capital

Whilst it is easy to appreciate labour's interest in extended collective bargaining, it is not obvious why capitalists should want to comply. Writers within this approach have proposed statutory rights for workers and/or have considered economic levers that could be deployed to shift the cost-benefit calculations of firms. However, both sets of proposals contain serious problems. The problem with any system of statutory rights to representation, apart from the technical difficulties of framing such legislation, is the sanctions to be imposed for non-compliance. It seems reasonable to presume that many firms would prefer to pay a meagre fine (as they do under the Health and Safety Act (1976)) for non-compliance than allow well-informed worker representation in the highest chambers of corporate decision-making. The obvious solution, which is to raise dramatically the penalties for breach of the law, runs into a second problem. For if the firm in question is relatively independent of the nation-state (for markets or other resources) and relatively mobile, it may decide to run down or even close its British operation rather than continue under a hostile political/industrial regime. The probability of its acting this way would be enhanced in a period of economic recession when other governments would be offering a wide range of inducements and incentives for firms to invest in their respective countries.

The problem of capital's power takes on particular force in the USA, home to more multinational corporations than any other country in the world, and in Britain, an economy more heavily dependent on multinational corporations than any other in Western Europe:

> The British economy has an unusually high proportion of multi-national corporations, and the 1960s and 1970s saw a considerable expansion both of such foreign capital in Britain and of British firms with operations abroad. . . . If we add together the foreign capital operating in Britain and the overseas capital of British firms to indicate the significance of multinational capital as a whole, it was between 27 per cent and 32 per cent of the UK's gross national production in the years from 1962 to 1978 (Harris, 1985, pp. 11-12).

Britain's dominating position in the multinational league is shown by its share of international MNC employment. British firms alone employed 17.3% of the world's overseas multinational employees in 1973, almost 50% more than West Germany, over twice as many as France and five times as many as Italy (Enderwick, 1985, p.46).

The nature of bargaining

Some of the proponents of 'extended collective bargaining' fail to make it clear, finally, exactly how the process would differ significantly from the institution of worker directors. The similarities, after all, are striking. Unions would be setting out to investigate and discuss issues such as investment plans. They would need to gather information similar to that supplied to worker directors. They would presumably present their own proposals, as worker directors have often done in Britain (cf. Batstone et al., 1983; Brannen et al., 1976), and views would be exchanged in an attempt to reach an agreement.

A study of the Post Office worker-director scheme which ran from 1978 until 1980 illustrates the fact that even on the corporation's Main Board unions did in fact 'negotiate' with their management counterparts. They prepared their own positions, presented their cases, questioned management and frequently declined to accept responsibility for majority decisions (Batstone et al., 1983). The study suggests that the problem of worker representation in corporate decision-making is not primarily a problem of institutional setting (boardroom vs. bargaining committee). Workers can and do bargain in the boardroom, and conversely they can collaborate on bargaining committees. The major problem faced by worker representatives is the often antagonistic relationship between their interests and those of the employers, and their limited capacity to impose their will on the employer in cases of conflict.

Conclusions

The 'extended collective bargaining' strategy may well keep unions clear of the worst forms of 'incorporation' in company boardrooms. But the strategy is naive in its apparent belief that excessive labour cooperation with capital is a virus to which collective bargaining is resistant in a way that boardroom discussions are not. It is equally naive to imagine that the forward march of collective bargaining has hitherto been so far-reaching that we can easily contemplate its continued, evolutionary extension into further areas of corporate decision-making (cf. Topham, 1983). Proponents of 'extended collective bargaining' have not devoted sufficient attention to the idea that bargaining over investment and other business policy issues is *qualitatively* different from bargaining over wages, and requires new resources for labour, as well as entailing new costs such as plant relocation and disinvestment (see Lane, 1986).

'Extended collective bargaining' was an attractive option in Britain because it represented a middle course between the extremes of aggressive non-participation and 'boardroom discussions'. It also enjoyed considerable support because it represented the least radical break with traditional labour movement methods, a factor bound to appeal to a movement not renowned for its political radicalism.

Workers in the Boardroom

The Bullock Report

The Bullock Committee of Inquiry set up in 1975 was an integral part of the 'trade union' element of the Social Contract, whose other components were the repeal of the Tory Industrial Relations Act of 1971, and the enactment of positive individual and collective rights. The TGWU General Secretary Jack Jones played a major role in persuading his senior colleagues of the potential benefits of industrial democracy, and of the desirability of worker directors in the private sector.

The main proposals of the Bullock Report were as follows:

i) workers should have the right to elect directors onto the boards of companies with 2,000 or more employees

ii) these directors should be elected onto a single tier Main Board, not onto the upper level of a two-tier board structure as in West Germany

iii) the number of worker directors should equal the number elected by shareholders

iv) these two groups should agree on a smaller, third group of independents (the $2x + y$ formula)

v) boards should be obliged by law to take account of workers' as well as shareholders' interests

vi) worker directors should normally be trade unionists and be elected only by trade union members

vii) the right to elect worker directors should apply in all companies with 2,000 or more employees and should be triggered by workers' request.

The Bullock Report was effectively killed off by concerted employer hostility in the context of deep divisions among trade unions. Whilst several unions welcomed the concept of worker directors and gave evidence to Bullock in their favour, e.g. APEX (n.d.), other unions regarded Bullock as a serious dilution of the TUC's original proposal for parity of worker and shareholder directors, e.g. GMWU (1976), and others submitted evidence that was deeply hostile to the whole endeavour, e.g. EETPU (1976) and AUEW (1976) (see also TUC, 1979). The Labour government, already clinging to power only through its pact with the Liberals, issued a White Paper in 1978 that diluted Bullock's proposals yet again by reducing the proportion of trade union representatives on company boards to one-third, modifying the proposed single-tier board structure and stretching out the triggering process for establishing worker directors. The proposed Bill never appeared: Labour was defeated in the General Election of May 1979 and the Conservative victory seemed to mark the end of the 'industrial democracy' debate.

Recent developments

It would be more accurate, however, to say the debate went into cold storage, and before examining Marxist responses it is worth establishing just why industrial democracy is once more becoming an issue and whether this renaissance is to be just another short-lived fad that will fade away in a few years.

One source of pressure that will certainly not disappear is the EEC, which had two directives in draft form until they were temporarily shelved in 1986. Nevertheless, it is likely that they will acquire legal status sooner or later. Both were concerned with the extension of workers' rights in large enterprises. Predictably, they have met vehement opposition from the Thatcher government and the CBI, and attracted strong, if low-key support from the TUC. The older and revamped Fifth Directive would require companies with 1,000 employees or more to provide the facility for one-third to one-half worker directors on a unitary or a two-tier board, either through election or co-option. Alternatively, companies would be able to establish a new body, such as an employee company council with consultation and information rights, or negotiate the introduction of some equivalent mechanism. The Vredeling proposal would require similarly sized companies to provide information to workers on a wide range of subjects, and would oblige them to 'consult' employees on all decisions with 'serious consequences' for them (see IDS, 1984, for text and commentary). Even if these directives come to nothing, similar discussions taking place within the EEC on the regulation of multinationals *are* likely to persist, given the significance of MNCs within the employment, investment, production and trading patterns of EEC member countries.

This second and much longer-term pressure is being supplemented by the inevitable revival in Britain of a new 'social contract' at the centre of which is a series of interconnected measures for planned economic growth and industrial democracy. The latest form of these proposals—the 1987 document *Work to Win*—was based on the statement *Economic Planning and Indust-*

rial Democracy adopted at the 1982 TUC Congress. There was virtually no debate on the 1982 document either at that or subsequent congresses, a fact which will render its implementation extremely problematic. Both documents (but particularly the earlier one) propose to extend workers' rights within a series of national and regional planning agreements covering investment, production, pricing etc. Workers would have rights to information disclosure on 'the financial position of the enterprise as a whole, . . . investment plans, . . . performance, output, productivity and sales, . . . pay and benefits . . . ' (TUC-Labour Party Liaison Committee, 1982, para. 137). There would also be an obligation on employers to consult workers 'on decisions affecting the operation of the enterprise', and to discuss seriously workers' alternative proposals (para. 139). The document also envisaged extended collective bargaining through a 'Joint Union Committee' (para. 141), but its belief in the inherent limitations of collective bargaining was reflected in strong support for worker representation on company boards (para 146). In short, the document canvassed four main approaches to augmenting workers' rights—information disclosure, consultation, extended collective bargaining, worker directors—without specifying their relative significance or impact (for a critique, see Kelly 1987c).

Even in America, where the trade unions have traditionally been hostile to boardroom representation, a number of experiments in this field have recently been started. In the face of corporate decisions to run down production, close facilities and relocate to the Southern States or overseas, a number of union leaders and officials have begun to rethink their traditional opposition to boardroom involvement (Kochan et al., 1986, Chap.7).

The trade union defence of worker directors (supported by intellectuals such as Crouch, 1983) ran as follows: in the post-war era trade union power had been augmented by full employment, as well as by permissive legislation and managerial policies. But this trend concealed a deeper and more worrying development whose long-term effect would be to erode union power. For as trade union organisation and collective bargaining became progressively decentralised, devolving power onto union stewards, corporate decision-making was becoming progressively more centralised in the headquarters of the large, often multinational, corporations that were coming to dominate many sectors of British industry. Since there was little unions could do to influence the levels and structures of corporate decision-making, it seemed that union structures and representation would have to follow that of the large companies.

The incentive for unions to move in this direction became clearer in the wake of the British company merger wave in the late 1960s and the rise in unemployment from about the same period. The incomes and security of union members were being adversely affected more and more (so it seemed) by decisions taken well beyond the reach of workplace or even corporate bargaining. Unions were being forced increasingly to react to decisions on plant closures and redundancies long after they had been taken. One successful response was to press for statutory rights to information disclosure; the second and largely unsuccessful response was to insist on being involved from the earliest stages in the full range of corporate decisions that directly or indirectly impinged on the terms and conditions of employees (Jones, 1970).

The TGWU (1978) response to Bullock and to the ensuing Government White Paper emphasised the democratic right of workers to participate in decisions but also supported Jack Jones' view that such participation would contribute to economic efficiency. Collective bargaining was described as 'reactive' and therefore limited in its capacity: unions had to find new ways of influencing corporate decisions. Parity representation was essential and minority representation was strongly criticised:

> Minority representation will not facilitate any shift in the existing power relationships. Indeed it would virtually guarantee the out flanking of the worker representatives by informal meetings of the shareholders' directors deciding policy in advance of board meetings, and by the likely practice of delegating matters to subcommittees . . . *Responsibility without power is a disastrous recipe for any system of representation* (TGWU, 1978, p.8).

Both the TUC and the TGWU also believed it essential that worker directors should be fully trained for their new roles, and that facilities should be available for regular report-backs to union members. This would prevent worker directors from losing touch with their constituents and would enable their knowledge and experience to be fed into the normal channels of collective bargaining (TGWU, 1978; TUC, 1979).

The radical defence of worker directors

The starting point for radical support of worker directors was the upheaval in Marxist theory in the 1960s and 1970s, inspired by Althusser and Poulantzas. According to Althusser (1979a), the political and ideological 'levels' of society were not wholly determined by economic foundations, but enjoyed a degree of 'relative autonomy'; they were determined only in 'the final instance' (to paraphrase Engels). The concept of relative autonomy enjoyed a considerable vogue in the 1970s but was fiercely attacked by a group of British writers (Cutler, Hindess, Hirst and Hussain, 1977, 1978). They agreed with Althusser that the economy did not 'determine' the superstructure of society in a simple or direct fashion, and that Marx's historical materialism (as outlined schematically in the 1859 'Preface') could not be accepted *tout court*. But they departed from Althusser by insisting that his concept of 'relative autonomy' was theoretically incoherent because there was no way of deciding just what degree of autonomy was ever enjoyed by different 'levels' in society. They argued that Marxists had either to accept what I have called 'simple economic determination' (which they held to be untenable), or to abandon the privileged status of the economy altogether, and grant full autonomy to the political and ideological 'levels'.

In terms of understanding and intervening in the arena of 'industrial democracy', this critique of classical Marxism threw up two key propositions. The first was that the organisational properties of firms—forms of work organisation, modes of decision-making, etc.—were not epiphenomena which passively reflected economic forces: they were determined by a series of factors—political, social, cultural, ideological and economic—whose relative impact varied from one situation to another. Secondly, because the structure and actions of firms were not 'necessary effects of economic laws' but the contingent products of struggles and managerial class calculations, it was therefore possible for workers to change them.

> To Marx's conception of homogeneous, despotic enterprises with given forms of calculation and analysed best in terms of a labour process, has been counterposed a notion of the enterprise which denotes a set of heterogeneous practices which have mutual interdependencies . . . but no given unity, which have varying conditions of existence and tend towards no one particular end. Conceived in this way the enterprise can be seen as the site for a multiplicity of interventions by socialists, because all the different practices of the enterprise can be challenged in some degree separately. By contrast the orthodox Marxist position tends to imply that because the

enterprise has an 'essential' character one either fights that
essence . . . or engages in what must be seen as necessarily unimpor-
tant battles because they concern only peripheral issues (Tomlinson,
1982, p.26).

The Bullock Report and the ensuing debate over worker directors
and industrial democracy was considered by such theorists to
have been a wasted opportunity, squandered by the left because
of outmoded and untenable theoretical conceptions and political
practices. Hirst (1981) pointed out ironically that some inkling of
the possibilities for labour in this debate could have been gleaned
from the strident tones in which Bullock was denounced by the
main employers' federation, the CBI. Even the most vulgar of
Marxists might have been tempted by the idea that what was bad
for capital must *ipso facto* be good for labour. Moreover, whatever
the views of employers, Tomlinson (1982) argued that there was
no a priori reason why the institution of worker directors should
benefit capital since 'in Marxist terms the class struggle decides
who wins' (p.39). Some writers discerned even more radical
horizons opening out in the wake of Bullock, in which unions had
the opportunity to take responsibility for production . . . and
develop working-class power and responsibility (Ernest Bevin
Society, 1984, p.13), or even to 'move decisively into the position
of a ruling class' (British and Irish Communist Organisation,
1984, p.9).

Hodgson's 'Democratic Economy'

The most recent significant contribution to this discussion has
been produced by Geoff Hodgson and the interest aroused by his
book, *The Democratic Economy*, as well as its wide-ranging coverage
of issues, compels a closer examination.

Hodgson defines worker participation very broadly as 'the
ability of workers to directly influence or form the management
and work process in an enterprise' (1984, p.131)—a definition
which covers, but is not confined to, worker directors. He begins
by noting that a considerable body of evidence, particularly from
industrial psychology, suggests that workers seek more from
employment than high wages and minimum effort: they also want
interesting and challenging jobs which permit the exercise of
some element of control. He cites with obvious approval the
conclusion reached by Blumberg in 1968 that when jobs were
redesigned so as to provide such control the almost invariable

result was an increase in worker satisfaction and productivity. Beyond these tangible achievements worker participation also provided both employers and workers with better flows of information, and thereby contributed to improved decision-making (pp.132-3).

Why then have employers persisted in their defence of hierarchical and non-participative forms of organisation if these are, as Hodgson maintains, inimical to improvements in economic efficiency? The answer he gives is that managers have gained personally from the 'higher salaries, status and prestige' associated with positions of dominance. Therefore a strategy of increased worker participation in decision-making would simultaneously increase productivity and worker satisfaction, *and* constitute a shift in the balance of power towards labour as hierarchy was eroded. To those who maintain that such participation is a form of class collaboration, he responds that in a general sense the institution of trade unionism constitutes collaboration, if only by virtue of its contribution to order and efficiency. In any case, following Tomlinson (1982), he suggests that there is no a priori reason to assume that in a participation forum, the only outcome would be labour's incorporation.

A critical evaluation

Against the ideas of 'necessity' and 'inevitability', Cutler, Hodgson and others have counterposed a contingent universe in which the limits of what is possible are difficult to establish and likely to remain so. Tomlinson argues for a 'theoretical iconoclasm' (1982, p.146), Hirst maintains that there are 'no *essential* limits to the form and content of trade union struggle' (1981, p.67) and Hodgson (1984) notes that 'each firm has its own strategy . . .' (p.143).

As a critique of some of the more dogmatic forms of essentialist Marxism this type of work is valuable, because it throws up a series of specific problems and issues that cannot easily be accounted for with the concepts of classical Marxism. But this is where the problems begin, for once the job of demolition is over, what concepts are to replace the ruins? On this point the confidence of our critical theorists begins to evaporate, as they face up to the difficult task of transcending the trivial observation that the behaviour of enterprises and economic agents is 'complex' and 'determined by many factors', or that the outcome of a particular scheme of industrial democracy cannot be determined a priori. Their efforts to be more concrete have been extremely disappointing: Hirst's (1981) analysis of 'the organisational limitations of British trade unions' promised much but turned out to be a familiar run through the well-known favourites—their focus on collective bargaining, the limitations of strikes, the problems of sectional organisation, and the weakness of inter-union links. It is almost certainly true that the 'incorporation' of worker directors is neither 'necessary' nor 'inevitable', but this bold proclamation leaves us with no guidance whatever as to the *probability* of incorporation under specific conditions.

Unfortunately the evidence available on the possible achievements of worker directors is not encouraging, and the review by Batstone and Davies (1976), commissioned by the Bullock Inquiry, concluded that European experience suggested worker directors had little effect, one way or the other, on company performance and decision-making. More recent reviews of experience in the past ten years, particularly in Europe, have reached the same conclusion. Whilst worker directors have sometimes increased the flow of information to union representatives, they have provided no discernible influence on corporate decision-making (Brannen, 1983; Bean, 1985, Chap.7). The few American experiences of union involvement in strategic business decisions have produced equally meagre results (Kochan et al., 1986, Chap.7). Studies of the relatively few worker-director experiments in Britain have reached the same sort of conclusion. In BSC, the Post Office and a handful of private companies, worker directors made some impact on specifically industrial relations issues such as the levels of redundancy payment, but exerted virtually no influence over the wider range of business policy decisions that normally predominate in boardroom discussions (Brannen, 1983).

It is true that some of the early 1970s schemes had specific organisational deficiencies, from a trade union viewpoint. The first group of BSC worker directors constituted a minority on divisional, not main, boards; they were obliged to relinquish their union positions; they were appointed by the Secretary of State; they were obliged to respect the canons of business confidentiality; and they did not enjoy adequate report-back facilities (Brannen et al., 1976). Similiar problems were found in the handful of private sector schemes studied between 1976 and 1979 (Towers et al., 1987). All these problems were corrected in the Post Office scheme, which was a model, Bullock-style exercise, with elected and experienced union representatives sitting on the Main Board in equal number to the management representatives, and with a third group of nominal 'independents' (Batstone et al., 1983). The observers of the Post Office scheme reached the conclusion that despite its organisational advantages over earlier practices, the PO worker directors were still unable to affect significantly any major item of business policy. Unlike the rather supine and deferential nominees in BSC, these worker directors were not intimidated or overawed by the Boardroom ethos and were never successfully socialised into management's ways of thinking. Their training was considered adequate and they maintained close links with the decision-making structures of their respective unions. Their ineffectiveness could not therefore be explained by specific organisational problems or processes *except* for their minority status on the Board against the management-independents 'bloc'.

If this one remaining defect were remedied and full parity representation established, would worker directors then be able to make a significant impression on corporate power? One of the authors of the BSC study thought not:

> The paradox of boardroom participation is that if worker representatives are strong enough and willing to put forward competing rationalities they are likely to create conflict in the boardroom, and ensure that the real centres of decision-making move elsewhere, thus rendering themselves impotent in the director role; but if they adopt the director role then their *raison d'être*, from the perspective of the workforce, disappears (Brannen, 1983, p.114).

Worker directors face two sets of constraints in trying to influence corporate decisions: organisational and environmental. The former comprise matters such as the board structure, the links between worker directors and their unions, inequalities of expertise, control over agendas and other aspects of organisational structure and process. These are in principle remediable as they are within the control of company boards, and in schemes such as the Post Office experiment these types of constraint were largely, though by no means entirely, overcome.

However, even advanced schemes of worker directors would still have to confront the environmental constraints on firms arising from markets and politics. If large corporations are to continue in competitive product markets then they will have to ensure that their labour productivity, unit costs, product quality and other salient dimensions of competitiveness are kept broadly in line with their rivals. In the car industry, for instance, BL is virtually compelled to displace labour with robots if it wants to retain an adequate share of the British, let alone foreign, markets in competition with Japanese firms. Worker directors could conceivably negotiate improved severance terms for workers losing their jobs, stretch out the process of displacement, press for retraining and job search programmes, and try to encourage local investment by BL to absorb displaced labour. But in the face of market competition over unit costs it is hard to see how they could halt labour displacement as such.

This constraint helps us understand one of the basic dilemmas of 'workers in the boardroom', or for that matter of extended collective bargaining. To obstruct the pursuit of competitiveness with proposals for job protection will ultimately damage a firm's viability and threaten job security, but to cooperate with the requirements of competition may damage the union's viability in the eyes of its members. It is not necessary to maintain that the interests of labour and capital are wholly antagonistic, as do Glyn and Harrison (1980), to appreciate that the areas of cooperation can easily be swamped by the issues that divide the parties.

In this respect Hodgson's proposals for a *Democratic Economy* are open to serious doubt. He claims that experiments in worker participation have shown overwhelmingly that worker satisfaction and productivity have been improved, which, if true, would provide a significant basis for labour-capital cooperation. But more detailed and critical studies of exercises in job redesign have produced rather different and less comforting results. Kelly (1982a, 1985) reviewed over 200 cases of job redesign for manual and non-manual workers, conducted in both public and private sector firms in ten countries between 1950 and 1980. This comprehensive review showed that labour productivity did indeed increase in almost every case of redesign and reorganisation of work, generally by between 10% and 20%. The evidence on job satisfaction was more mixed with cases showing a variety of outcomes: long-term increases, short-term gains, no change, even long-term deterioration in a few cases. More significantly, the results showed that in two-thirds of these cases some workers lost their jobs: over the 200 cases, for every 80 jobs 'redesigned', 20 were lost. The same study also showed that the intensity of labour (rate of effort expenditure) was significantly increased in many cases, though on two-thirds of all occasions workers did receive compensatory pay rises. The precise pattern of outcomes varied between national contexts, with the most favourable conditions and significant gains for labour obtained under a combination of full employment and left governments committed to a wider democratisation of industry through the augmentation of trade union power. Hodgson's arguments would become more pertinent under these conditions but even then there is no advantage in trying to present worker participation as a panacea for a range of disparate economic and political problems without highlighting its costs as well as its benefits.

Conclusions

This chapter has examined three approaches to industrial democracy that have been argued for by contemporary Marxists: incorporation theory which advocates militant, independent trade union struggle and refuses to countenance trade union involvement in the management of capitalist enterprises; the extension of collective bargaining to cover major aspects of corporate business strategy; and the election of worker directors onto the boards of companies.

Capitalist enterprises, it was established, do possess considerably more latitude in their business strategies than most incorporation theorists have been willing to concede. There can be different ways of remaining competitive, and workers may have definite preferences amongst them which it would make sense for them to try and impose on their employers. Nevertheless, it is also true that competitive pressures will, in some way or other, damage some of the interests of workers whatever their other advantages. As firms strive to become more competitive and to provide more stable and secure employment for workers, they are also likely to be intensifying work and displacing labour with machinery. In a context of high or rising unemployment the displacement of labour should be seen as a major cost for workers and the site of a major difference of interest from the employer.

The central problem for labour with schemes of industrial democracy is that they provide no resources or sanctions that can be used to impose workers' priorities over and against those of capital in situations of conflict. There are simply no grounds for thinking that a rational employer will agree to a set of labour demands that he believes inimical to his own interests. In practice therefore worker–director schemes, or attempts to extend the scope of collective bargaining, have proved poor vehicles for asserting workers' priorities within capitalist enterprises. Several worker–director schemes have suffered from obvious design faults, such as inadequate training or accountability of workers' representatives, and some writers have emphasised these failings. But even the well-designed schemes, such as those in the Post Office, have proved disappointing, a fact that suggests the problems of industrial democracy do not lie primarily in poor organisational or institutional design. It is more plausible to argue that they lie in the market constraints on capitalist firms, and in the limited resources that trade unions alone can mobilise within a firm. Consequently, any major advance in industrial democracy will require the mobilisation of extra-organisational resources by labour. The principle resource in that camp is the State, and it is therefore to Marxist theories of the capitalist State that we now turn.

9

Trade Unions and the Capitalist State

The previous chapter established the fact that a radical and general extension of workers' power against capital could not be secured by trade union action alone. Neither militant direct action, extended collective bargaining nor worker directors are sufficient in themselves to extend and consolidate workers' power. This is because of the retaliatory and evasive actions open to capital. Capital has the advantages of mobility, greater resistance power and transformability (into money, land etc.), by contrast with the limitations of labour's sectional organisation and the relative immobility of individual workers. There are, of course, exceptions to this general state of inequality, and under certain conditions labour's resources alone will be sufficient to underwrite a considerable incursion into the rights and powers of capital. In general, however, any advance of labour against capital within the enterprise will require additional resources if the shift in the balance of power is to be more than temporary.

The most obvious resource that might be available to organised labour is the State, by which I mean not only parliament, but the other institutions which also comprise the State, such as the civil service and judiciary. Trade union access to the State may be secured either through some form of bipartite or tripartite negotiations with government and employers, or through the medium of a working-class political party. In addition, unions may be able to influence state policies through the intended or unintended effects of their actions, such as strikes or wage demands.

The idea that organised labour can make any effective use of

221

the State runs counter to a very powerful tradition of Marxist theory, most notably associated with Lenin, and expressed in the idea that the State is a capitalist institution which can only serve to benefit capitalist interests. In Britain this idea has often taken a particularly virulent, 'ultra-left' form, and issued in a complete dismissal of parliament and parliamentary democracy by far left political groups such as the Workers' Revolutionary Party (WRP) which believes quite simply that 'Parliament decides nothing . . .' (WRP, 1985, pp.10 ff; and for the SWP cf. Callinicos, 1983b, p.22). For the RCP, the state is a trap to be avoided at all costs:

> The British left is under the illusion that it can use certain parts of the bourgeois state to its own advantage. But a state machine that oppresses with one hand cannot fight oppression with another . . . The struggle against capitalism will advance through the development of a broad anti-state outlook among workers . . . (RCP, 1984, pp.41, 42).

In the present chapter, I intend to review three Marxist theories of the capitalist State. In each case I shall consider their implications for organised labour's use of the State either directly or indirectly (via political parties) as a component of a trade union strategy for socialism. The first theory can be traced back to Marx and Lenin and is generally described as the 'instrumentalist theory' because of its core idea that the capitalist State is, and can only be, an instrument in the hands of the ruling class. As we shall see, this theory can generate a variety of political practices: electoral abstention and use of parliament for propaganda purposes only, as well as democratisation of the state apparatus. Critics of instrumentalism have begun from the idea (also present in Marx) that the State does in fact enjoy a degree of 'relative autonomy' from the capitalist economy. Some have then proceeded to argue that this autonomy helps the State to reproduce capitalism even more effectively and allows few, if any, political opportunities for organised labour: the State obeys 'the logic of capital'. But others have advanced a third approach which says that the State's autonomy is not necessarily functional for capital, and that it can also permit labour to exercise its voice within the corridors of power. Organised labour can therefore contest the priorities of capital so that the State becomes an 'arena of struggle'. These competing theoretical perspectives have been argued out primarily amongst Marxist intellectuals, but their significance for labour movement and trade union politics is impossible to overstate. Two examples will illustrate the point.

At the time of writing (1987) the Trades Union Congress has, for all practical purposes, agreed to a new 'Social Contract' with the next Labour government (see Kelly, 1987c). The term itself is never used (because of the odium still attached to the 1970s experiment) and some commentators seem to believe that the unions are still wholeheartedly committed to 'free collective bargaining'. In fact, the TUC has agreed to discuss macro-economic policy at regular intervals with the next Labour government and pay 'would unavoidably be on the agenda'. The union-party strategy places top priority on job creation, a fact which means some diversion of public funds from potential pay rises, and constitutes the context in which 'free collective bargaining' will operate. The government will be looking for a measure of pay restraint; the unions for job creation as well as new legal rights. Those who believe the capitalist State cannot be made to serve labour's interests in this manner will, quite logically, oppose such a strategy root-and-branch and will, as in the 1970s, persuade and encourage other workers to do likewise. These arguments will not be conducted in terms of rival theories of the capitalist State, but such theoretical disputes are no less signifi-cant for being obscured.

Secondly, the Swedish labour movement's attempt to establish labour ownership of capital through wage-earner funds financed out of company profits will become an increasing focus of attention as they try to assert more influence over the Swedish economy. This top level agreement between union and party leaderships, the use of the State apparatus, and the inevitable compromises made with capital, have all attracted criticism both here and in Sweden (cf. Pontusson, 1987). For some Marxists the idea of a beneficial 'political exchange' between organised labour and the State is a dangerous illusion, and they would regard the Swedish labour leaders as the most consummate reformists and practitioners of class collaboration. Others would take a different view, based on the idea that the capitalist State *can* be used by labour to promote its interests. So let us look in turn at the three theoretical positions identified earlier, at the arguments and evidence adduced in their support, at their implications for labour movement policies, and at their problems.*

* Certain writers, such as Miliband, Offe and Poulantzas, appear under more than one of the three theoretical positions I have outlined. This is either because their positions have changed over time or because one and the same work combines different theoretical positions.

The Leninist Theory of the Capitalist State

Lenin's theory of the State was expounded principally (but not exclusively) in *The State and Revolution*, a pamphlet he wrote in 1917 against the type of view expressed by Kautsky, who had argued that 'it is beginning to become clear that a genuine parliamentary regime can be as much an instrument of the dictatorship of the proletariat as an instrument of the dictatorship of the bourgeoisie' (quoted in Salvadori, 1979, p.37). For Lenin, the most distinctive feature of the capitalist State was its class monopoly of the legitimate use of violence. The State consisted of 'special bodies of armed men with prisons etc. at their disposal' which alone, of all the public bodies, was 'allowed' to use force. This force was not put to work, argued Lenin, in the service of a general interest, or the public good, but was used to defend the specific interests of the ruling class. Quoting extensively from Engels' observations on the concomitant rise of class society and the State, Lenin offered a definition of the State as a machine for the suppression of one class by another. The capitalist State was wielded exclusively by the ruling class; it was an instrument of that class.

Lenin acknowledged the spread of parliaments throughout the capitalist world but declared that these bodies wielded no real power at all, since political power rested on the ownership and control of the means of production. Parliaments did however delude certain sections of the labour movement into thinking that the capitalist State could be transformed from within, that it could be wrested, step by step, from the hands of the ruling class. Behind this illusion of parliamentary democracy lay the reality of bourgeois dictatorship against which socialists ought to counter-pose, and struggle for, proletarian dictatorship. This struggle could only be a revolutionary struggle, a frontal assault on the State apparatus by the revolutionary party and its allies. Whilst socialists contested parliamentary elections (unless the revolu-tionary tide had swept aside such institutions), they did so in order to obtain access to a public platform from which to disseminate anti-capitalist propaganda, and in order to build up the party's membership and organisation ready for the time when, along with its allies, it could 'smash' the state machine.

The two central elements of the Leninist theory of the State are that *in essence* it is an apparatus of class coercion, and that parliament is an institution wielding little or no real power. The British miners' strike has lent dramatic force to the first of these propositions, providing for many Marxists a clear view of the 'true' face of the State. Several publications of the left gave detailed lists of police deployments, numbers of miners arrested, charges and convictions (Socialist Organiser, 1985; Reed and Adamson, 1985), and suggested that facts such as these showed 'the vicious class character of the British imperialist state . . . its police, courts and prisons' (Reed and Adamson, 1985, p.9) or 'brought home to the whole working class the class nature and repressive role of the capitalist state' (WRP, 1985, p.10; see also Harman, 1985a, p.7; Callinicos and Simons, 1985, pp.248-51). The strike has also generated renewed interest in the history of State intervention against strikers, a recent study showing that troops were deployed in 36 industrial disputes between 1945 and 1983 (Peak, 1984, and also Geary, 1986; Hain, 1986). In the wider political arena, the military coup in Chile which crushed Allende's socialist government in 1973 has been frequently cited as a dire warning of the ruthless and coercive nature of the capitalist State.

Lenin's second thesis implied that it was impossible for the working class to use parliament for its own ends (as Kautsky had advocated). It is certainly the case that '. . . in the course of three quarters of a century, the Kautskyan road has not achieved socialism anywhere, and in many cases it has led to catastrophe for the working class and people' (Claudin, 1977, p.65; see also Mandel, 1978, Chap. 10). The achievements of social democratic parties which have worked within the capitalist state have indeed been modest. In the inter-war period 'with the exception of the French armament industry in 1936, not a single company was nationalised in Western Europe by a social democratic government . . .' (Przeworski, 1980, pp.47-8). In the post-war period social democratic parties have ruled for many years in Sweden and Austria and enjoyed more recent electoral success in Britain and West Germany (1960s-70s) and in France, Spain and Greece, yet the number of companies nationalised has been very small.

One of the most recent indictments of social democracy has been provided by Mitterand's government in France. By 1982, this had nationalised large numbers of firms in the metals, chemicals, fibres, glass, armaments, electrical engineering and aircraft industries. The proportion of employees in nationalised industries rose (as a proportion of total employment) from 11% to 22%, and almost half the workers in firms with over 2,000 employees are now in the nationalised sector (Armstrong et al.,

1984, Tables 19.1, 19.2). Yet the process of restructuring in these industries has shaken out labour at a time when labour demand and State spending have been insufficient to absorb those displaced. The steady growth in unemployment has gone hand-in-hand with a slow, rightward drift in economic policy, sadly reminiscent of the 1974-79 British Labour government (for other countries, see articles in Miliband et al., 1986; and more generally, Panitch, 1986).

There is also the still more recent example of the hotly debated wage-earner funds in Sweden. This proposal to transfer a percentage of company profits into a labour-controlled investment fund was bitterly opposed by big business and the political right, and this led eventually to the dilution of the proposals and their enactment in a much weakened, smaller-scale and less radical form (Pontusson, 1987; Hammarstrom, 1987).

This type of evidence does not in itself prove the Leninist case. It shows that the capitalist state *has* been used to promote some of the interests of sections of capital against some of the interests (such as short-term job security) of some workers, but it does not in itself show that such outcomes are inevitable or that they are the only possible outcomes of state action. What are the grounds then on which the State is held to be inevitably and necessarily pro-capitalist?

The mechanisms of ruling-class State domination

Writings within this theoretical tradition have between them advanced seven reasons in support of the proposition that the State inevitably acts solely to benefit capital: the interweaving of economic and political power; the composition of state personnel; the access to the State of business elites; the power of capital in the labour process; the constraints of the world capitalist system; the limitations of social-democratic ideology; and the nature of parliament.

The idea of an *interweaving of economic and political power* is an expression of Marx's materialist argument that on the economic foundations of society there arises a legal, political and ideological superstructure. The State, as part of this superstructure, is 'determined' by the economy; more specifically, the class which rules in the economy rules the State. Hence the oft-quoted idea that the State is 'nothing but the concentrated power of capital' (Callinicos and Simons, 1985, p.251) or the 'concentrated power of the capitalist class' (RCP, 1984, p.36).

Far more attention has been devoted by Marxists to the idea that the policies of the State directly reflect and express the *social backgrounds, interests and attitudes of its leading personnel*. In his seminal work *The State in Capitalist Society* (1969), Ralph Miliband devoted considerable attention to these questions and demonstrated the predominance in the upper echelons of the State of public school, Oxbridge educated white men from wealthy backgrounds who retained both formally and informally many links with businessmen—through directorships, shareholdings, social clubs and residential areas—and who shared a common outlook in favour of capitalism and the principles of accumulation for profit and market regulation (see also Miliband, 1977). The conservatism of the judiciary has been a frequent topic of discussion amongst trade unionists and the focus of some academic research (Griffith, 1985), and the reactionary role of figures such as Lord Denning is by now notorious. The impact of the state elite has been repeatedly documented in studies of Labour governments whose leaders have

> . . . underestimated the extent to which the close connections between the civil service and the senior managerial hierarchies of private business reduce the availability of the civil service for use in programmes that seriously challenge the social power and class prerogatives of these well-organised and class conscious groups (Coates, 1975, p.148).

This quotation captures nicely the link between the conservative attitudes of state personnel and their *connections with businessmen*, each reinforcing the other over many years of contact (cf. also Coates, 1980; Taafe, 1983, pp. 26-7; Callinicos, 1983a, p.22).

However, as Coates argued in a later work,

> The character of private elites in British society, important as it is as a constraint on Labour governments, is not the main problem which faces the Left in Britain today . . . It is not the class structure alone which constrains Labour radicalism, but the impact through that class structure of the *capitalist* economy on which it is built (Coates, 1980, p.159; and see also Colletti, 1977, and Poulantzas, 1972 for similar views).

Within this economy capital can exercise its power over labour, through its *control of the labour process*. Collectively, individual capitalists can influence the level of unemployment through decisions on the level, form and location of investment. Programmes of heavy capital investment, high in labour-saving potential; investment in overseas facilities; and relocation of plant out of high unemployment areas (typically union-organised and Labour voting)—these can all have dramatic consequences for a Labour government pledged to reduce unemployment. There is no suggestion that such economic decisions are taken purely on political grounds (though parts of the City of London and *some* capitalists may act this way) but only that such decisions have, as a by-product, negative consequences for Labour.

More serious still than the decisions of individual capitalists are the *systemic criteria and constraints* within which they are taken: Coates (1975, 1980) has argued forcefully and at length that so long as a Labour government operates within a world capitalist system it will be forced to comply with the requirements of competitiveness and profitability if it wants to sustain any significant economic growth. He summed up his own position clearly and graphically as follows:

> The situation of a Labour government is very like that of a stone dropped into a pool—surrounded by an ever-widening set of ripples. If the innermost set of constraints (ripples) are parliamentary, and the next the civil service, followed by the institutions of private capital, then the ultimate ripple-circle of constraints is set by the competitive processes of the world market through which capital is accumulated and realised (Coates, 1980, p.264).

Mandel (1978) put it more bluntly:

> Capitalist relations of production . . . cannot be modified gradually, piece by piece. Either they function on the basis of their own logic or they do not function at all. They cannot function halfway, just as a woman cannot be a little bit pregnant. The concept of a 'mixed economy' is a delusion . . . (p.114).

The numerous structural constraints on Labour governments would seem to render superfluous any recourse to *social-democratic ideology* as a factor in the explanation of government performance, yet left analysts have dwelt at length on this very subject. The idea of 'parliamentarism' was a key concept in Miliband's classic study of *Parliamentary Socialism* (1973) whilst Coates (1975, 1980) and Panitch (1976) have both argued that social democratic parties such as Labour invariably adapt their programmes so they can be implemented within the confines of a capitalist State and economy: hence the characteristic differences between the radicalism of electoral programmes—designed to mobilise working-class support—and the conservatism of government policies—designed to avoid capitalist reaction.

The critique of social democracy intersects with the critique of '*parliamentarism*' since it is the latter which largely informs the former. After all, if the State is no more than 'the condensed power of capital' how can parliament alter this fact? The extreme view that 'parliament decides nothing' is often allied to the Leninist critique of 'bourgeois democracy' as a fraud in which the illusions of universal suffrage and equal rights conceal the reality of class power. The significance of party competition is downplayed by describing the underlying attachments of political parties to capitalism and to constitutionalism (cf. Miliband, 1973), and the significance of voting is mocked by computing the minute quantity of her or his lifetime spent by the average citizen in a polling booth (cf. Hyman, 1975, p.123).

Theoretical critique and political logics

Marxists are agreed that the State *is* an instrument of coercion, and that it tends to reproduce capitalism. We are not arguing therefore about what the capitalist State normally does; nor are we concerned here with non-Marxist theories of the State. The argument amongst Marxists turns on the theoretical question of *how* the actions of the State are produced and determined, and hence on the political question of how state power is to be challenged.

The instrumentalist theory of the State has been criticised elsewhere (Dunleavy and O'Leary, 1987; Jessop, 1982; Held, 1983) on a variety of grounds and from many different perspectives. Since I am concerned here only with the State and the labour movement, I will summarise these criticisms very briefly:

i) instrumentalist theory cannot easily explain why industrial capitalism is reproduced when another class, say the aristocracy, controls the state apparatus

ii) the theory assumes the unity of state institutions for capital, and against labour, and either cannot account for disputes and divisions within the State (e.g. between parliament and judiciary in relation to trade union rights), or regards them as a secondary phenomenon

iii) the theory assumes that capital in general has a single interest or set of interests that can easily be determined, and

consequently underplays differences between capitals—e.g. between foreign and domestic, industrial and financial, large and small, national and multinational
iv) the theory elevates workers' interest in eliminating their exploitation to a position of pre-eminence but neglects any interests short of this, especially those interests shared with capital
v) the theory is weak on the mechanisms by which capital's interests come to dominate State policy formation, and tends to view the State as little more than a 'cash register', or cipher, automatically ringing up appropriate policies
vi) it is not clear from the theory why, from time to time, the State acts against the professed wishes of some capitalists, e.g. mining capitalists who opposed the nationalisation of the mines or the many capitalists who opposed the introduction of compulsory training programmes for skilled workers
vii) the theory cannot easily explain why workers have been able to use the capitalist State to push through policies and reforms geared to their interests, particularly in the area of social policy.

So far as trade unions are concerned the instrumentalist theory as a whole is important for its identification of two sets of obstacles to socialist or radical trade union policies: externally, the economic laws of capitalism and internally the organisation of the political machinery of the State. The assignment of theoretical primacy to either of these sets of obstacles generates two characteristic, and different, political logics.

The implications of 'instrumentalism': economic limits to reform

The classical Trotskyist view of an interlocking, world system of economic and political power strongly implies that a small change in one part of the system (say, the politics of the judiciary) will be neutralised by a change elsewhere. It is the same logic that damns worker cooperatives because you cannot have 'islands of socialism' in a sea of capitalism. Either the whole system is changed or there is no change at all. In the case of the state this logic is taken by some Marxists to imply, in Lenin's immortal phrase, that the State machine must be 'smashed' and replaced by a State power different in type to capitalism, with its divisions between executive, legislature and judiciary (cf. Callinicos, 1983a; RCP, 1984). What is meant by this idea is that the entire economy is regulated by 'the law of value', so that socialist and capitalist production cannot co-exist within its boundaries, and any temporary reforms will be neutralised by the self-regulating mechanisms of capitalism. Yet the history of capitalism, even in Britain, is replete with examples which contradict these propositions. The National Health Service, for all its imperfections, delivers health care to the mass of the population according to criteria of need, not wealth, and those who emphasise its limitations and shortcomings to prove the limits or impossibility of radical reforms should study the grossly inferior and truly capitalist health service in the USA.

Several Marxists have tried to advance a rather more sophisticated account of reforms within capitalism and the interests they serve whilst remaining loyal to the instrumentalist tradition. Writers such as Coates, Hyman and Panitch have acknowledged the existence of a series of pro-working class or social-democratic reforms, such as universal suffrage, and legal rights for unions, but have argued that these were functional for capital and that this fact, not working-class pressure, explains their genesis. Every advanced capitalist country now has a 'welfare state' of some description and it has been shown that the creation of public health care or public housing often coincided with bourgeois concern about the health of factory workers or army recruits. However, these facts do not prove that the welfare state was introduced *solely* to serve capital's interests. As Stephens (1979) and others have shown, the timing, the quality and the form of welfare provision are significantly associated with working-class organisation: the stronger the labour movement, the more extensive the welfare state in its scope and level of provision.

Another line of defence of the 'limits of reform' thesis is based on a distinction between system-maintaining and system-destructive reforms. It is argued that whilst the former can feasibly be 'granted' or extracted from a capitalist State, the latter cannot. The notion of some outer limit of reform is intuitively appealing, and widely used amongst Marxists, but the perennial difficulty has been to pin down exactly where this limit lies. A good critical history of Marxism could be written solely about the reforms that were declared at the time to be 'impossible', 'unrealisable' or 'incompatible' with capitalism, and which nevertheless came to fruition without any of the crises prophesied by Marxists. Over the years Marxists have repeatedly and severely underestimated the adaptive capacity of the capitalist economy, its ability to absorb what seemed like radical threats to its very survival and carry on bruised and battered but basically intact. Other Marxists have completely trivialised the distinction between types of reform by professing disinterest in anything short of revolution, and refusing to discriminate more finely between, say, different types of legal intervention in industrial relations (rights vs. immunities, for instance). Nonetheless, the fact that a distinction between system-maintaining and system-transforming reforms has frequently been abused is not sufficient grounds for its rejection.

A final instrumentalist response to reforms has been to attribute them to working-class struggle outside parliament. Hyman (1975) and Panitch (1976, 1981) have both noted the tendency of British incomes policies to be destroyed by bouts of working-class unrest and industrial action, in 1969, 1974 and 1979. But this reasonable argument has a serious consequence, for if the State is obliged to take notice of working-class action and abandon a policy deemed to be in capital's interests, then it is difficult to see how the State can be considered an 'instrument' of capital in any meaningful sense of that word.

The implications of instrumentalism: the political limits to reform

While some Marxists have concluded from 'instrumentalism' that the scope for reforms within capitalism is so limited that there is no point in 'participating' in the capitalist State, a second strand of Marxist theory has drawn entirely opposed political conclusions from the same Leninist premises. The Militant Tendency (see Taafe, 1986; Taafe et al., 1983) have asserted the capitalist nature of the State, its domination by bourgeois civil servants and judges, and the willingness of the capitalists to use its coercive apparatus to crush socialism—as they did in Chile. However, these arguments are made to yield distinctly non-Leninist conclusions by being extended from the state elites to the whole of the state apparatus. If the judges and civil servants are reactionary by virtue of their bourgeois background then by the same logic the mass of lower-grade, low-paid State employees should be socialists because of their working-class background. Equally, the mass of working-class soldiers could be detached from their bourgeois officer leaderships by the creation of soldiers' trade unions with full rights. With the backing of the organised labour movement outside parliament, which constitutes the vast majority of the population, socialist policies could be forced through parliament despite capitalist resistance (cf. also

Socialist Organiser 1985, p.41). A socialist parliamentary majority, reform of the state apparatus and support from a united and
organised working class: these proposals together constitute
neither a Trotskyist nor a Leninist programme but a Kautskyan
'peaceful road to socialism', a fact that 'Trotskyists' such as Taafe
and his colleagues have never acknowledged (cf. Salvadori, 1979;
Kautsky, 1983; Hindess, 1983).

This type of political strategy has the advantage of being much
closer to the mainstream of contemporary labour movement
politics than the insurrectionary scenarios of some of the Leninist
revolutionary groups, and although critics would argue that the
'parliamentary road to socialism' has failed to produce socialism
anywhere, there is an obvious rejoinder. In the British context it
could be argued that no Labour government has ever seriously
embarked on such a project and so its feasibility has never
actually been tested. It is true that the 1945 Labour government
moved some way down a socialist road, as it was then understood, through the creation of the modern welfare state and
through its programme of nationalisation of basic industries. But
the fact that Labour made no further encroachments on the role
of capital, either in the State or the economy, owed as much to the
loss of direction of the party leadership as to capitalist hostility, a
point acknowledged by the party's most intransigent critics
(Coates, 1975; Miliband, 1973).

What role do trade unions play in this type of political strategy?
In Andrew Glyn's writings trade unions are seen as having
played a significant role in depressing the manufacturing rate of
profit through class struggle (cf. Glyn and Sutcliffe, 1972), but
their considerable power to erode capitalism is rarely translated
into any constructive role in its elimination. The strategic
chapters in Glyn (1978) and Glyn and Harrison (1980) have
nothing to say about trade unions except that they will take
one-third of the seats on the boards of all nationalised companies.

Conclusions

It is fashionable to reject instrumentalist theory as empirically
and theoretically inadequate, but whilst many formulations of the
theory are unsatisfactory it does have several very important
strengths. It asserts that beyond a certain point labour movements will be prevented from making effective use of the State by
both external and internal constraints. Whilst it has always

proved difficult to specify the limits of labour-inspired State-managed reforms, instrumentalist theory has identified a series of mechanisms which will inevitably constrain even the most powerful, well-organised and well-intentioned socialist leaderships. The tightness of these constraints, the degree to which they can be effectively challenged and the costs of such a challenge are all issues on which there is disagreement. Historically, theorists in this tradition have overestimated the constraints on socialist administrations. They have also advanced propositions about the interests of labour and capital which are too simple and undifferentiated, permitting no significant scope for intra-class conflicts of interest and inter-class mutuality of interests. Nor do they make it clear how it is that organised labour movements have been able to use the State (an instrument of capitalist rule) for their own ends, often in conflict with sections of capital. Indeed the responsiveness of capitalist states to working-class pressure suggests that even if the State does normally function as an instrument of the capitalist class, it can also be made to function in workers' interests. This view would have been anathema to the arch-instrumentalist V.I. Lenin, but perfectly acceptable to his theoretical and political enemy, Karl Kautsky (see Chapter 4 above).

The Relative Autonomy of the State: the Capital-Logic Theory of the State

The many problems, both theoretical and political, of the instrumentalist theory of the State have led numerous Marxists to argue that the capitalist State cannot be seen as the simple instrument of the ruling class. Many now accept that the periodic actions of the State against sections of the capitalist class point to its enjoying a degree of real autonomy from capital. In the words of Miliband (1977), whilst the state may act on *behalf* of capital, it does not act at its *behest*. But the admission of 'relative autonomy' immediately raises a problem: for if the autonomy of the State is real (however relative), then why and how does it reproduce capitalism? If its autonomy is real, perhaps the State could be used for other, non-capitalist objectives? Marxists have divided in their answer to this question, and our second group of theorists, generally known as the capital-logic school, has argued that the 'relative' autonomy of the State is both necessary and functional for capital, and does not provide an opening for its use by socialists. What these writers wished to avoid was an older liberal-pluralist view of the State as a class-neutral institution, mediating between the social forces in society but with no particular bias of its own (what Dunleavy and O'Leary call the 'weathervane' and neutrality models of the state, 1987, Chap.2). The continued existence and dynamism of capitalism, and the accelerating growth of State intervention, have suggested the State *does* play a major role in the reproduction of capitalism, but how is this to be understood?

These theorists have argued that, contrary to Adam Smith, there is no hidden hand guiding the economy: the individual capitalist's pursuit of his own self-interest has not necessarily led to a result that was in his long-term interests, or in the interests of capital as a whole. In the nineteenth century, for instance, industrial capitalists often behaved as if the supply of labour was effectively infinite, and compelled their employees to remain at work for fourteen or fifteen hours per day, six or seven days per week, often in dirty, dangerous, noisy and unhygienic conditions. The individual capitalist, argued Marx, thought it perfectly rational to drive his labour force to exhaustion, believing that he could simply poach fresh workers from other firms or from the labour market. Training policy provides a twentieth-century example: individual capitalists often refused to bear the costs of training workers because it was cheaper to let other firms bear the costs, and then poach skilled workers by bidding up wages. In both cases what was rational for an individual capitalist was irrational for the class as a whole, producing in the first case a physically-weakened and sick labour force increasingly unable and unwilling to tolerate high levels of work intensity, and in the second a general shortage of skilled workers as more and more firms chased a shrinking number of trained employees. In other words capitalists were faced with the problem of having to organise collective action in the face of powerful incentives to 'free-ride' (cf. Olson, 1965).

How could capitalists respond to these problems? They could form associations or cartels to regulate such behaviour but the original German capital-logic theorists appeared to assume that the force of competition would always provide an incentive for some firms to break ranks for short-term gain, thus destroying the association (see Jessop, 1982, Chap.3, and Offe, 1975). Since capitalism continues functioning despite these problems there must be some agency or mechanism to promote the general or collective interests of capital. That agency, they said, was the

State. The State is dependent, directly or indirectly, on the continued process of capital accumulation for its own revenues and hence has an interest in accumulation. The functionaries of the State have a similar interest, since their own livelihoods, status and power depend likewise on the continual flow of revenue from a growing economy. This dependency, coupled with the political conservatism of its leading functionaries (as noted by instrumentalist theory, above), provides the State with an in-built bias in favour of capitalism. But in order to perform the function of general or collective capitalist the State must be able to act against the interests of specific sections of capital. It must for example be able to impose training programmes on capitalist firms in order to ensure an adequate supply of skilled labour. In order to perform this function the State *must* therefore enjoy a degree of relative autonomy from capital, and must not be the mere instrument of particular sections of capital (cf. Offe, 1975).

According to these writers, the State does enjoy such relative autonomy because of the structure of capitalism itself, in particular the separation between the spheres of economics and politics. Means of production are privately owned and economic power is wielded by their owners, not least in their relations with labour. Formally speaking this economic power enjoys no direct translation into political power: in a parliamentary democracy all citizens have a single vote, whether capitalist or worker. On the other hand, the State (according to this argument) is a qualitatively different type of institution, owning no means of production itself, and hence wielding little economic power, but being the repository of political power through parliament and the monopoly of legitimate violence. The separation of economics and politics within capitalism provides the real foundation for State autonomy; the dependency of the State on revenues from capital accumulation makes that autonomy strictly relative. Characteristically writers in this tradition have then proceeded to list a variety of State policies designed to maintain the general interests of capital, some of which have been opposed by sections of capital. The Factory Acts, and other employment and labour market legislation; maintenance of full employment (until recently); value of the currency; external and internal defence and legal order; provision of skilled and healthy workers; the general conditions for both accumulation and legitimation (Offe, 1982); regulation of the labour-capital conflict; defence of national capital against foreign competition (Jessop, 1982, Chap.3).

Theoretical critique and political logic

We know that capitalist states have in practice performed (and continue to perform) many of these functions, and more besides. It is also true that this theory of the State is a definite advance over instrumentalist theory because of its attempt to explain periodic State policies that conflict with particular interests or sections of capital. Yet the capital-logic theory is nonetheless flawed, and so too are the politics associated with it.

The root problem with the theory is that it *assumes* State policy is functional for capital, but never proves it. More to the point it has no concept of *dysfunctional* policies, or of *contradictions* between policies. Let us take British industrial relations legislation as an example of the former. The government of Edward Heath (1970-74) was convinced of the economic damage wrought by trade union power and militancy, and proceeded with a wide-ranging set of legislative controls over trade union behaviour, in the 1971 Industrial Relations Act. The Act was clearly *intended* to be functional for capital, but did it *succeed* in its intention? It generated a wave of political strikes; helped unite the trade union movement; helped push the Labour Party leftwards; made almost no impact on collective agreements; left the closed shop virtually intact; and (for a period) discredited the law (Weekes et al., 1975). What was 'functional' for capital in any of that?

The failure of capital-logic theory to analyse unintended and dysfunctional effects of this type makes the theory both one-dimensional and unMarxist in its depiction of a rational and omniscient state calmly overseeing the general interests of capitalism without crises or contradictions. Indeed the term theory is misleading, for the capital logic approach *asserts* that State policy is functional for capital, but doesn't prove it. Facts are simply wheeled out to 'illustrate' the truth of the 'theory' but facts that don't fit are 'explained away' as accidental, irrelevant, or otherwise exceptional.

Panitch on trade unions and the capitalist state

The most recent attempt to apply a variant of the capital-logic approach to trade union-State relations is the work of Panitch, and his arguments therefore merit detailed scrutiny. In his article 'Trade Unions and the Capitalist State' (1981), he set out to achieve a number of objectives, one of which was to demonstrate that 'corporatism must be seen as a system of state-structured class collaboration' (1981, p.42; see also Beilharz, 1986, for a similar analysis of the Australian Accord). Panitch accepted that 'the capitalist state' enjoys a degree of relative autonomy from the ruling class, that it responds to working-class pressure (within limits), and that consequently State policies vis-a-vis trade unions will vary both between countries and between time periods. He identified the major determinants of this variation as the level of unemployment, State commitment to full employment, and the political strength of the organised working class (p.30). Full employment, maintained by the State, considerably strengthened working-class bargaining power after the War and allowed workers to restrict rises in the rate of exploitation. The response of the State, particularly when there was a social-democratic government committed to economic growth, was to integrate unions into the State via the mechanism of incomes policies, as in Britain, Austria, Holland, Norway and Sweden.

The initial effects of such involvement were threefold: it encouraged the centralisation of power within trade unions; it introduced 'capitalist growth criteria within the formulation of union wage policy' (p.33); and it precipitated a rank-and-file revolt. This last consequence in turn precipitated a coercive reaction from capitalist states, manifested in anti-union and anti-strike legislation. The failure of coercion led to new efforts by the State to revive corporatism, and union federations generally agreed though only after exacting a higher price. As it turned out, however, this higher price was more illusory than substantial. On this important point, it is worth quoting Panitch at some length:

> The State . . . set about, partly in response to the new demands coming from the unions themselves, to integrate lower levels of the movement—right down to the shop floor—more effectively. This took the form of progressive legislation and state-fostered managerial practices designed to facilitate union recognition in unorganised sectors and extend union membership in organised sectors; to foster workers' participation schemes in company boards and works councils (this time under the direct aegis of the unions); to institutionalise local-level bargaining and shop-steward committees; and to provide a legal framework for qualitative issues (e.g., health and safety) unfair dismissals and redundancy . . . These reforms were progessive but they further enmeshed the trade unions in the legal apparatus of the state . . . (p.37).

As a result real wages and strike frequency fell in several

European countries in the mid-1970s (pp. 37-8). These experiences led Panitch to conclude, against certain Eurocommunist Marxists to be considered shortly, that 'only class collaboration, not class struggle, can be practised in the corporatist "heart" of the state apparatus' (p.38). As in other publications Panitch presented a powerful, well-argued and carefully-documented case, yet for all its strengths his analysis is flawed.

Firstly, while he was at pains to try and show that corporatism was 'a form of capitalist domination' and of 'class collaboration' ana that corporatist structures '*necessarily*' (my emphasis) played these roles, he actually demonstrated no such conclusion. What he showed was that the British, Swedish and German labour movements achieved some modest reforms at a rather heavy price under specific political and economic conditions. But no inference can be drawn from these results as to what *could* have been achieved. Panitch *assumes*, though he never proves, that labour extracted as much as it could, but he never entertains the possibility that under different economic and political conditions, different political forces could have obtained far more substantial concessions from capital. He assumes, in other words, that the observed outcomes of 1970s corporatism were the only outcomes possible, an assumption which is neither argued nor demonstrated.

Secondly he assumes, though again he provides little evidence, that independent trade union organisation and action would have produced benefits for the working class greater than those obtained under corporatist arrangements. Now in order to effect such a comparison, which is surely central to Panitch's argument, we need some specification of the interests or benefits most salient for the working class. Panitch provides no such specification, but it can easily be inferred from his argument (and from previous publications) that he regards the level of real wage increase and the level of strikes—but not the level of employment—as the best indicators of the achievement of working-class interests. Data collated by Cameron (1984) on the level of strikes, money wage rises and unemployment in the OECD countries between 1950 and 1980 partly confirm Panitch's argument; but there is an important sting in the tail. Countries with the least developed and most unstable corporatist arrangements, such as Britain, Ireland and Italy, were also the countries with the highest wage increases and the highest strike frequencies over the period as a whole, but they were also the countries with the highest levels of unemployment. In the countries with more developed corporatist arrangements, the level of unemployment was consistently and significantly lower than in those with weaker (or absent) forms of corporatism. The effects of corporatism will thus be assessed in opposite fashion depending on whether you assign primacy to workers' interests in average real wage rises (corporatism is against workers' interests) or to the level of employment (corporatism promotes workers' interests). Panitch clearly opts for the former but he provides no rationale for doing so.

Thirdly, Panitch is quite dismissive of the legal rights secured during the years of corporatism, an attitude which he makes no effort to defend or justify with any argument or evidence. If, for example, the legal rights of the 1970s served to 'incorporate' and 'integrate' unions into the acceptance of 'capitalist growth criteria', it is difficult to understand why right-wing politicians and businessmen in Britain, Canada and elsewhere have been so eager to dismantle them (cf. Panitch and Swartz, 1985 for details of restrictive legislation in Canada in the 1980s).

Finally, Panitch suggests that corporatist arrangements will inevitably entail the management of industry along profitable and competitive lines, that is according to 'capitalist principles' (p.40), and that these requirements 'may be expected to conflict with' union demands. The only way for such conflicts to be avoided would be through the corruption of unions by 'capitalist growth criteria'. The implication of this passage is that a socialist government which sought to promote economic growth and to enhance workers' power whilst remaining within world capitalist markets would be doomed to failure. Why should this be the case? Panitch never clearly explains, but merely invites us to accept that economic growth regulated by 'capitalist principles' is obviously incompatible with workers' or unions' demands and interests. Now clearly it is incompatible with *some* of them because it would almost certainly entail work intensification, and possibly job or employment insecurity, and would not overturn capitalist exploitation. On the other hand it would probably result in rising living standards, and could lead to increases in union organisation, worker militancy and class consciousness. One could readily concede that such a mixture of outcomes would be fragile and subject to contradictions and erosion, but it might be perfectly rational for workers to judge that, on balance, it represented a positive if temporary set of gains. Yet this possibility is not entertained because it cuts across Panitch's capitalist growth/socialist transformation dichotomy, and violates his implicit notion that the interests of capital and labour are wholly antagonistic and zero-sum. In other words, one side's gain is assumed automatically to be the other's loss, and there is no conception of circumstances, such as survival of firms in recession, where the two sides may have joint interests.

Despite the plethora of 'facts' in his article, then, Panitch fails to provide evidence where it really counts. He simply *assumes* the State *necessarily* reproduces capitalism, *assumes* the nature of workers' interests is unproblematic, and *assumes* the effectivity for capital of corporatist structures in line with his functionalist mode of argument. Countervailing ideas are never seriously entertained: the idea of class struggle within the State is rejected by means of fallacious reasoning; the idea that labour movement organisations can and do make strategic choices about short- and long-term goals and interests never disturbs the preoccupation with wages and strikes; and the idea that corporatist structures could generate unintended and negative consequences for capital is gently mocked as a social-democratic delusion.

Relative Autonomy as Real Autonomy

Class struggle and the State

Many Marxists (myself included) would now argue that under most circumstances the capitalist State is not merely an instrument of the ruling class, and that its 'relative autonomy' from the economy provides labour, as well as capital, with the opportunity to influence state structure and policies in line with its own interests (cf. Jessop, 1982; Poulantzas, 1978; Urry, 1981; Clegg et al., 1986; McLennan, 1984; Offe, 1982). This idea is hardly new and forms the core of all liberal-pluralist theories of the State, as well as the basic operating ideology of many trade union leaders. Even within the history of Marxism, the strategy of using parliamentary democracy to effect a gradual shift in the balance of class power was strongly advocated by Eduard Bernstein at the turn of the century and became increasingly prominent in the writings of Karl Kautsky throughout the first three decades of the present century.

The rationale for this 'revolution' in Marxist theory derives in part from the accumulation of theoretical problems and difficulties within the corpus of 'classical Marxism', and the impact of the writings of Gramsci, which first became widely available in 1970 with the English translation of a selection of the Prison

Notebooks (see Chapter 3 above). These theoretical developments were intimately connected in myriad ways with the actual
development of authoritarian forms of socialism in Eastern
Europe and with the failure of social democracy and state
intervention in the West. The old certainties of 'orthodox Communism' came under mounting challenge, not least from within
the ranks of West European CPs, opening up a theoretical and
political space for the influx of new developments as well as the
older ideas of liberal pluralism and of Trotskyism.

Much of what contemporary Marxists have to say about the
capitalist State can be summarised under a number of broad
headings which unite a large number of intellectually and
politically disparate forces (Poulantzas, 1978; McLennan, 1984;
Jessop, 1982; Korpi, 1983; Urry, 1981; Zeitlin, 1985; Offe, 1982;
Clegg et al., 1986; Pierson, 1986). The basic premise of much of
this thinking is that the modern capitalist State does not inevitably, or necessarily, only reproduce a capitalist mode of production. There are powerful tendencies for it to do so, but in the final
analysis the State's reproduction of capitalism is contingent on
particular sets of circumstances.

Firstly, in any advanced capitalist society the actions and
policies of the capitalist State are often contradictory, i.e. the
pursuit of one objective directly conflicts with or hinders the
pursuit of another. In the realm of economic policy and industrial
relations numerous examples can be cited. The promotion of
trade union organisation through legal provisions may secure a
short-term reduction in conflict as part of a political exchange
between State and unions, but in the longer term it may provide
more workers with the resources to conduct conflict against their
employer. State incomes policies may briefly restrict the rate of
increase in money earnings (and even, occasionally, in real
earnings) but in Britain such policies have normally disintegrated
in a wave of large and disruptive strikes, as in 1969-70, 1974 and
1978-9. The future programme of any Labour government will
involve a simultaneous commitment to modernise the manufacturing sector (leading to increased unemployment as labour is
displaced by capital) and to restore full employment. The
promotion of public sector employment and job security will
conflict with the restoration of public sector pay losses relative to
the private sector, unless there is to be a phenomenal increase in
State expenditure (see Kelly, 1987c). These contradictions are
not peripheral, but are central to the State's functioning and
therefore call into question the idea of State policies as *necessarily*

functional for 'capital'. State policies may 'dampen' one problem
only to exacerbate another, or may fail to solve either pole of a
given contradiction (cf. Offe, 1982).

Secondly, the idea of the State as an agent of 'capital' becomes
increasingly difficult to employ as one looks more closely at
capital's interests under 'normal' conditions. Beyond a set of
general interests—preservation of national sovereignty, sound
money, law and order and the like—'the' interests of capital
begin to take on different forms, as Strinati (1982) has demonstrated in the field of industrial relations. Throughout the 1960s
and 1970s the various branches of the British state apparatus
were torn between two strategies for resolving a number of
industrial relations problems: a voluntary reformist strategy
based on union-management exchange and consensus, and a
repressive strategy designed to curb trade union power through
law. The 1980s recession has thrown up similar dilemmas with
ruling class fractions alternating between coercion and consent in
a range of countries (cf. Panitch and Swartz, 1985 on Canada,
and Lansbury and Davis, 1987 on Australia). To ask which of
these strategies best served 'the interests of capital' is to ask a
misconceived, perhaps impossible question. According to Strinati
(1982), the large, profitable US multinationals in Britain were
strong advocates of voluntary reform since they had the resources
to afford substantial concessions to their moderately well-
organised unions. By contrast many British motor and engineering capitalists, faced with highly competitive markets, declining
profit rates, new and costly investment projects, and powerful
shop steward organisation, perceived no gain from a strategy of
reforms and called expressly for state curbs on union power. In
other words a policy that suited the interests of one group of
capitalists would be deemed a failure by another group.

Thirdly, the State is to be understood as an ensemble of
institutions with their own histories and traditions, which have
'real' effects in their own right. These institutions are not simply
ciphers for interests that lie elsewhere but are staffed by functionaries whose power is wielded for a variety of personal, group
and class objectives. The long-standing struggle over industrial
relations law, between parliament and judiciary, is one that
stretches back over a century when parliament first enacted the
legalisation of trade unions only to find its 'intentions' being
narrowly interpreted and distorted by a reactionary judiciary.
Indeed much of the history of industrial relations law in Britain
can be read as an intra-class struggle between different branches

of the state apparatus. In the field of incomes policy, it is well known that the senior civil servants at the Department of Employment tended to favour such policies far more than their neo-classical and monetarist colleagues at the Treasury. It also emerges from an analysis of the actual institutions of particular states that capitalist states differ significantly in their internal balance of forces, and in the range of interests that these forces may represent. Britain's position as a world financial centre is reflected in the indirect influence of the City through the powerful Treasury Department. Strictly speaking therefore we should speak not of 'the' capitalist State, as if all states were alike, but of specific capitalist states in different countries.

Fourthly, a given capitalist state does not sit, as it were, above society, free from the conflicts and contradictions to be found in the economy or in civil society. As Poulantzas (1978) wrote, 'Today less than ever is the State an ivory tower isolated from the popular masses. Their struggles constantly traverse the State, even when they are not physically present in its apparatuses (p.257). The rise to office of social democratic parties with a substantial working-class base (which is essentially a post-war phenomenon—see Therborn 1983) has carried into the State at least some workers' aspirations, particularly in the areas of social policy. The organisation into trade unions of more and more public sector workers, coupled with the growing size of the state labour force, has transformed the conflicts of public sector industrial relations into forms of class struggle within the State. And the increasingly effective organisation of single-issue campaign groups within multi-party democracies, where voters can be swayed by party stances on such issues, has compelled an enhanced degree of State receptivity to such campaigns.

Fifth, because of the growing strength of organised labour in almost every advanced capitalist economy, measured by increases in union density and by social democratic/socialist/communist electoral performance (or what Korpi, 1983 and Korpi & Shalev, 1980 refer to as labour's 'power resources'), capitalist states have been obliged to make a series of concessions to workers' demands even when these have inflicted costs on capital (Simon, 1982). For as Gramsci wrote,

> Undoubtedly the fact of hegemony presupposes that account be taken of the interests and the tendencies of the groups over which hegemony is to be exercised, and that a compromise equilibrium should be formed—in other words that the leading group should make sacrifices of an economic-corporate kind (1971, p.161).

Finally, several contemporary writers have been at pains to stress the open-ended and unpredictable consequences of state policies, and to undermine the image of the State as an omniscient, rational agent calmly and mechanically computing a regular calculus of class interests. Zeitlin (1985) and in particular Elster (1985) have stressed that one of Marx's central insights was the idea of the unintended consequences of action. For example, state policies designed to 'incorporate' labour may end up strengthening trade unions and demoralising capitalists.

This general approach to the capitalist state has become increasingly influential amongst Marxist theoreticians and its influence can be traced in a variety of recent studies of labour-state relations in the advanced capitalist countries, which have sought to document and analyse labour's use of the 'capitalist' state (Clegg et al., 1986; Higgins, 1985; Korpi, 1983; Prior and Purdy, 1979; Hindess, 1983; Purdy, 1981). It is therefore worth examining these studies more closely in order to appreciate some of the theoretical and political implications of this approach, before proceeding with a critique.

Evidence for the 'class struggle' theory of the State

Firstly, comparative and historical research by Cameron (1984) and Therborn (1984a, 1986) has established a number of important conclusions on the effects of labour's use of the State in the advanced capitalist countries. In countries such as Sweden, Austria and Norway, 'corporatist', or 'neo-corporatist' relations between labour and the State have been established over many years, and in practice this has meant the following: i) wage bargaining has been highly centralised and regulated by 'peak' organisations of labour, capital and, sometimes, the State; ii) labour federations have under-utilised their market power derived from high union density by restraining wage demands and controlling strikes; iii) in exchange they have sought a series of state policies on union rights, full employment and social expenditure. Similar forms of 'political exchange' have occurred in other countries such as Italy and the UK, and more recently Australia, but have generally been more short-lived for a variety of reasons to be explored shortly.

Countries with these characteristics have witnessed on average lower levels of unemployment between 1965 and 1982, as well as lower strike levels and slower rates of increase in money earnings. There are several non-corporatist countries, such as Japan and

Switzerland, which also have low unemployment—a fact which shows that there are various routes to low unemployment, of which corporatist arrangements are one (Cameron, 1984; Therborn, 1986, esp. pp.98-101). Whilst labour quiescence on the earnings and strike fronts has made little impact on the distribution of wealth and income between labour and capital, it does seem to have been associated with higher levels of social spending as a percentage of GDP (Cameron, 1984, p.172; Therborn, 1984a; Stephens, 1979).

More recently the Swedish Social Democratic Party has legislated a diluted version of an LO proposal to establish wage-earner funds in Swedish industry, administered by regional boards of trade unionists. The original proposal was that company profits in excess of the specified limit were paid into a fund which would, over a period of time, eventually become the major owner of Swedish investment capital and whose controllers would be in a position to direct the business strategies of the major Swedish corporations. Supporters of this 'Swedish parliamentary road to socialism' have argued that the enactment of the wage-earner fund proposals, even in weakened form, provides further proof that the 'capitalist state' can be wrested from capital and used to promote the interests of labour (Cameron, 1984) or even the transition to socialism (Korpi, 1983; Stephens, 1979).

Second, it has been argued that such 'corporatist policies' are both viable and effective, because of the long-term growth in labour's 'power resources' compared to those of capital. Before 1965 there were only five capitalist countries in which socialist communist and social democratic parties or coalitions had achieved an absolute majority of all votes cast in a free election—Australia, New Zealand, Czechoslovakia (1946), Norway (1945) Sweden (1936). In the two decades since then labour movement parties have achieved absolute majorities again in Sweden (four times) and Norway (once), but also in Austria, Finland, France Greece, Portugal and Spain (Therborn, 1984a). (Exactly what meaning can be attached to such evidence is a moot point in the light of government performance in France, Greece and Spain. Trade union organisation showed an even stronger upward trajectory, rising in 18 out of 23 OECD countries in the post-war period and culminating in an all-time peak of trade union density in the late 1970s. Therborn (1984a) also noted that there were Communist Parties with a substantial mass base and electoral appeal in seven of the 23 OECD countries (Italy, Portugal France, Greece, Iceland, Finland and Japan), and significan

CPs in three others (Spain, Sweden and Luxembourg) (see also Chapter 4 above, where it was noted that some of these parties have suffered electoral reverses in the 1980s). It is argued that this growth in labour's power resources has not been matched by a corresponding growth in the resources of capital, largely because of labour's increasing ability to secure its interests through the State as against those of capital.

A third defence of labour's effective use of state power is based on legislation. The world strike wave of the late 1960s and early 1970s generated a spate of labour legislation in almost every capitalist country. In *Britain* the Labour Party repealed the repressive sections of the Industrial Relations Act and established rights to paid release for union training and limited protection against unfair dismissal. Health and safety representatives were empowered to discuss a range of issues with management. Rights to information for collective bargaining purposes were extended, and employers were obliged to issue advance notice of substantial redundancies. Legislation on picketing, strikes and the 'closed shop' was tightened in favour of trade union organisation. Similar or more extensive rights were embodied in the Work Safety Law (1973), the Security of Employment Law (1974) and the Law on Joint Determination (1976) in *Sweden*. In *France* the 1968 Grenelle agreements were subsequently enshrined in a series of laws that provided unions with rights to organise at the workplace, collect dues, hold meetings and attend relevant education and training programmes without loss of pay. In *West Germany* the 1972 Works Constitution Law extended the formal rights of the Works Councils and granted legal recognition to trade unionism at the workplace. In *Italy* the Labour Statutes of 1970 established trade union rights to organise, hold meetings and elect *delegati* (shop stewards) at the place of work whom the employer was obliged to recognise and discuss with. Similar legislative gains were made in *Norway* and *Austria*. Less forceful arguments can be based on the records of the social democratic governments of the 1980s, who have often extended the legal rights granted earlier in areas such as union facilities and the powers of health and safety representatives (see Goetschy and Rojot, 1987, on France; Lansbury and Davis, 1987, on Australia).

Finally, it has been argued that a number of trends in labour movement policy point towards the increased likelihood of labour movement action through the State. The Harvard European studies (Gourevitch et al., 1984; Lange et al., 1982) documented the significant shifts in labour movement policies consequent on the slow-down in post-war economic growth and the beginning of recession. At the most general level they detected a shift in emphasis from distribution politics towards production politics as union leaderships sought to influence the investment and production decisions of large corporations—decisions that were beginning to result in growing unemployment amongst their memberships. If one expression of this policy shift was a renewal of interest in industrial democracy at the level of the enterprise (see Chapter 8), another was an increased willingness by union leaders to participate in corporatist arrangements in order to try and regulate national economic conditions.

Theoretical critique and political logic

For many Marxists this approach to the State laid the foundation for an alternative road, a 'Third Way' to power, based neither on the social democratic view of the State as pluralist and neutral nor on the Leninist instrumentalist or capital-logic positions. In practice this meant avoiding on the one hand the most right-wing variants of the social-democratic parliamentary road to socialism, and on the other the apocalyptic insurrectionary path of the revolutionary groups (Claudin, 1977, 1978; Poulantzas, 1978; Miliband, 1983). Insofar as the former strategy is generally known as 'reformist' and the latter 'revolutionary', then the logic of this third approach to the State and to politics is to question, if not obliterate, the distinction between reform and revolution (cf. Mercer 1980). But to castigate two theoretical positions, and their associated political strategies, does not in itself illuminate any alternative and this indeed is the failing of many Marxist writers, exemplified most clearly by Ralph Miliband. Miliband has rightly criticised orthodox Leninists and capital-logic theorists for downplaying the significance and power of parliament, but has been equally sharp in his attacks on contemporary neo-Gramscians for underestimating the coercive apparatus of the State and the economic constraints on its actions. Yet no distinctive, third approach has yet emerged from his numerous essays (see Miliband, 1982, 1983; and likewise Claudin, 1977, 1978).

If it is pushed to its logical end-point the 'class-struggle' or 'neo-Gramscian' view of the State begins to lose its Marxist character altogether and either comes to resemble the traditional pluralist theory of the neutral State buffered by interest groups or holding the ring as a putative national interest, or else dissolves into a series of specific propositions about particular states, state institutions and state policies far removed from general theoretical discourse. The trajectory of Hindess and his associates (Cutler et al., 1977, 1978; Hindess, 1983) provides one instance of the first development, whilst Zeitlin's (1985) emphasis on historical specificity in the study of capitalist states provides an example of the second.

It must also be said that the type of evidence adduced in favour of the 'democratic road to socialism' is often ambivalent. Even Cameron (1984) admits that 'maintaining near-full employment hardly constitutes the first step in the transformation of a capitalist economy to socialism', though he adds that this is nevertheless 'a very significant achievement' (p.174). Other critics have disputed the significance of the legal rights obtained by workers and unions in the 1970s and pointed out that some of them actually offer very little protection to workers or enhancement of union power. The unfair dismissal legislation is one example, where under current British law workers have a right to compensation for unfair dismissal but not to reinstatement. Some of these points, however, confuse the general and the particular. It may be the case that a particular piece of legislation proves to be badly drafted or inadequate in practice, or that a social policy reform has unintended negative effects on income redistribution. But the principal claim of this approach to the State is not that every labour-inspired reform will usher in socialism, but that reforms can promote some of the short-term interests of workers within capitalism whilst simultaneously shifting the balance of power in favour of labour and against capital.

This brings us to the third point, and one that is prominent in Korpi's arguments, namely the question of labour's power resources vis-a-vis capital. We may accept (as I do) that trade union density and socialist/Labour party support are good measures of labour's power resources, but are we justified in claiming (as Korpi does) that these resources have a long-run tendency to rise? And does it therefore follow that the *balance* of power resources will increasingly favour labour over capital? Empirical evidence certainly confirms a secular upward trend in union density (though there are notable exceptions such as the USA), but socialist/Labour voting patterns are more varied (see Tables 4.3, 4.4 above). But why should an increase in labour's power resources *not* be matched by a corresponding increase in the resources of capital? After all, many writers have documented the growing concentration, centralisation and internationalisation of capital in the post-war period (cf. Enderwick, 1985 on Britain). Surely these processes provide sections of capital with increased mobility and therefore increased power resources vis-a-vis labour? So even if we accept that in a given country there is a long-run increase in labour's power resources, it does not follow that the balance of power shifts in labour's favour, because the power resources of capital may increase as much, if not more, than those of labour.

Fourth, the claim that the contradictory character of capital's interests and of state policies can be exploited and turned to labour's advantage needs to be qualified. Contradictions can cut two ways and they can hinder organised labour's use of the State, as well as facilitating it. Pontusson (1984) for example noted that throughout the 1970s the Swedish Social Democrats largely maintained their commitment to economic growth and efficiency, particularly in Sweden's key export-oriented manufacturing firms. But the emerging world recession and the capital-intensive nature of advanced production served to reduce the manufacturing labour force, whilst the already high tax levels seemed to prohibit any compensatory rise in public spending to curb the growing level of unemployment. A British Labour government assuming office in the 1990s will face equally conflicting demands on its portfolio of public spending: job creation, amelioration of low pay, modernisation of manufacturing industry. The contradictory character of state policy in a modern capitalist economy causes difficulty therefore not only for capital but also for labour.

Finally, even if we accept that sections of capital often have different interests and often find it difficult to create a common front against labour, need this always be the case? Strinati (1982), for instance, has shown how the incoherence and ambiguities of British state intervention in industrial relations since 1960 can be traced back to the conflicting interests of different sections of capital, and their consequent inability to forge a common programme unifying their general interests. Faced with divisions amongst capitalists it is said that the State enjoys a degree of relative autonomy which labour can deploy in order to promote *its* interests. Attractive though the argument sounds, it does rest on one very important assumption, namely that the specific and divisive interests of different sections of capital will be more salient for them than any general unifying interest. Given the divisions among British capitalists over government economic and industrial relations policies, and the existence of several representative organisations of capital (CBI, IOD,

NASM etc.), it is tempting to accept such an assumption as almost self-evidently true. But what needs to be considered is not only the current level of capitalist unity and organisation, but the level of unity likely to emerge in the face of a radical government programme directed at the roots of capitalist power.

Under these conditions capitalists might respond in one of three ways, with exit, voice, or loyalty, as described by Hirschman (1970). They might 'exit', shifting capital, production facilities and personnel out of the country and move to more hospitable surroundings (or threaten to do so). They might remain to exercise 'voice', defending and promoting their general interests over and above their specific, different interests. In other words a clearly perceived external, common threat could unify capital against labour. Thirdly, they might remain active in Britain and superficially 'loyal' to its state.

Evidence from Sweden, where the government has introduced a diluted form of wage-earner funds, provides confusing evidence on capitalist reaction to radical economic policy. When the wage-earner fund proposals were being debated in parliament the effect on capital was to reinforce an already existing high degree of unity, witnessed in the largest demonstration by employers the country had ever seen (Sarlvik, 1984). Faced with such opposition, and with uncertainty in their own ranks, the Social Democrats retreated by diluting their original proposals (Pontusson, 1987). Once the proposal became law, employers were then concerned to maximise profits in order to offset the impact of the payroll and profits taxes, but some felt constrained by Sweden's centralised bargaining arrangements: some firms faced acute skill shortages and wanted the freedom to raise skilled workers' wages, but other less profitable firms wanted exemption from these profit-squeezing wage levels (Lash, 1985). The result has been a breach in employer bargaining solidarity as firms have sought to pursue their own sectional interests. The other consequence has been an unprecedented volume of capital export as Swedish employers try to 'exit' from an increasingly inhospitable political climate (Pontusson, 1987).

In other words, one effect of radical policies by a socialist government may be to intensify the economic constraints on the State, identified by 'instrumentalists' as inimical to such policies. It is also possible to argue that in Britain such policies would generate political opposition inside the State, from the judiciary and the civil service (as has happened with even mildly reformist Labour governments). These facts raise a major and as yet unanswered question about the capacity of labour movements to use the state apparatus for their own ends, and in particular for the large-scale abolition of private ownership of the means of production. Whether, as instrumentalists maintain, there are limits beyond which socialist governments would be prevented from passing by economic and political pressure, and just where those limits are, remain open questions.

Would the 'Swedish road to socialism' work in Britain?

It has been argued that the type of strategy mapped by theorists such as Korpi and Stephens, and pursued by the Swedish labour movement, still has much to recommend it as a possible model for the British labour movement, and one way of examining its viability is in the form of a question about capital, not labour, namely what incentive is there for capitalists to cooperate with or tolerate a programme of radical reforms instigated by labour? In Sweden there are several reasons for believing that (at least until recently) the incentive to cooperate (to be 'loyal') has outweighed the incentive to protest (exercise 'voice') or to 'exit'.

First, Swedish capital has faced a powerful trade union organisation for many decades, measured by union density which stood at 65 per cent in 1970 and 85 per cent in 1980 (Gourevitch et al., 1984, p.345). Secondly, the Swedish LO has enjoyed considerably more power than its British counterpart for over 40 years because of its constitutional right to intervene in a wide range of disputes, and because of its strategic role in centralised negotiations with the employers' confederation. The discipline of the LO has meant that its threats to take industrial action carry rather more weight than do similar statements from the British TUC. Thirdly, employers have lived under Social Democratic governments (either majority or coalition) since 1932 and have come to regard SAP electoral success as an enduring feature of their environment (though the Party was out of office from 1976 until 1982). Fourthly, the high degree of employer organisation has meant that any capitalist strategy could be pursued with relatively little risk of disunity. Although such organisation could have facilitated a united stand against labour, in practice it has been used to ensure that favourable agreements with LO are both signed and implemented. (Having said that, Sweden has recently witnessed an unusual degree of fragmentation in its bargaining arrangements, with several major groups of employers breaking away to bargain separately with unions. This fact, coupled with the radicalism of the LO's wage-earner funds proposal, has placed a question mark beside the continued viability of the 'Swedish road'—see Lash, 1985; Lash and Urry, 1987, pp.238-52). Finally, Swedish capital, particularly in manufacturing and extraction, is highly concentrated (a fact that underpins SAF centralisation), heavily oriented to world markets because of the tiny domestic market, and predominantly national rather than multinational (Ingham, 1974). Its considerable involvement in world markets means that Swedish capital is under intense pressure to remain competitive, a fact that is recognised and accepted by the LO. Historically employers have sought to promote productivity growth through a strategy of cooperation, both because of labour's capacity to damage their interests and because of the LO's willingness to cooperate. The national character of Swedish capital has meant that the opportunity to 'exit' overseas, rather than confront organised labour, has not been so readily available as for say British or American capital. As a result of these factors Swedish capital has had powerful incentives to cooperate with labour.

In Hirschman's terms the incentive for Swedish capital to practise 'loyalty' has outweighed the advantages of 'voice' and the limited possibilities of 'exit'. It is this pattern of incentives, itself a product of Sweden's historical development, its economic structure and the organisational forms of labour and capital, that helps us understand and appreciate the viability of the Swedish labour movement's strategy.

To what extent do similar incentives exist for British capital to cooperate with organised labour? Firstly, trade union density is considerably less than in Sweden, though at approximately 50 per cent it is still above the levels in France, West Germany, Italy, Netherlands, Canada, the USA and Japan. Secondly, the British TUC is considerably weaker than the Swedish LO, a fact that has become painfully clear since 1979. Since the Conservative election victory of that year the TUC has organised several poorly-attended Days of Action against government policy (1980-82); has failed to secure greater influence in the affairs of its affiliates (1980-81); failed to mobilise sufficient trade union members to vote Labour in 1983 and 1987; and has seen its policy of non-cooperation with anti-union legislation destroyed by two powerful affiliates (AUEW, EETPU). The British trade unions are not as disciplined in collective action as their Swedish counterparts, and lack the centralised collective bargaining that might sustain such discipline.

Thirdly, British employers are not as well organised as their Swedish counterparts. Though most large companies belong to the CBI, the US and other multinationals in Britain are significant exceptions. Like the TUC, the CBI lacks any involvement in centralised bargaining that could provide it with authority over its affiliated membership. These properties of organised labour and capital mean that each party will be aware of the limited ability of the other to enter an agreement and make it stick with its members. Since both parties will be anxious to avoid association with an ineffective agreement, and their membership's criticism, both will be wary of such agreements and have less incentive to enter them than would otherwise be the case (see Grant and Sargent, 1987, Chap.6).

Fourthly, the British political system is rather more volatile than the Swedish, especially as it has now become *de facto* a three party system, and the Labour Party has been electorally much less successful than the Swedish Social Democrats. Consequently, any government pressure on employers to cooperate with organised labour can to some degree be safely resisted in the belief that a new government, with different policies, will shortly arrive on the scene (as with CBI opposition to the Bullock Report in 1977).

Last, but by no means least, capital in Britain is considerably more diversified by national origin and international outlets than in Sweden. In 1981 almost 20 per cent of British industrial output came from foreign-owned enterprises (Fine and Harris, 1985; p.107), and Britain is one of the world's most important host nations for foreign investment, third in importance after the USA and Canada (Enderwick, 1985, p.14). On the other hand British capital provides an enormous quantity of foreign investment, comprising just under 12 per cent of direct investment abroad in 1975 and placing Britain second only to the USA in the league table of internationalised capitalist nations (Enderwick, 1985, p.11). During the 1980s recession, even more foreign capital has entered Britain, with Japan starting to make an impact, whilst more British capital has moved overseas.

What this means is that for 'capital in Britain' taken as a whole, the incentive to cooperate with organised labour is considerably weakened by the availability of the 'exit' option. Foreign capital can be withdrawn, or its planned entry decelerated; British capital can run down British operations and/or concentrate expansion overseas. On the other hand, these same facts *could* cut the other way, for if British firms derive a shrinking

share of total profits from their British operations then they may
reason that the gains from resisting a radical Labour programme
would be minimal since their lucrative foreign operations would
remain unaffected by British developments.

On the whole it would appear that the structural features of
Swedish economy and society that have facilitated the 'Swedish
road to socialism' are present to a much lesser extent in Britain
and this fact could well offset the advantages, shared with
Sweden, of a single workers' party and a single union federation.
Moreover it is difficult to see how these structural properties of
the British economic, political and industrial relations systems
could readily be altered. On the whole, therefore, it would, at
present, be extremely difficult to transpose the 'Swedish road to
socialism' into the very different context of Britain.

The Australian Accord

In 1987 the Australian Labour Party (ALP) won its third election
victory in five years and announced that its Accord with the
Australian Congress of Trade Unions (ACTU) would continue.
As the Accord bears some resemblance to the British Social
Contract of 1974-79, and is far more modest in its aims than the
policies of Swedish Labour, it will become an increasing focus of
attention in Britain. In essence, the Accord is a prices and
incomes policy in which the ACTU accepts central wage determination. The government hopes to bring down unemployment
through a variety of fiscal and labour market measures whilst
curbing and reducing inflation. In addition the Accord stipulated
a range of legal rights for workers, in areas such as health and
safety, redundancy and retraining, and it also promised redis-
tributive tax changes, price controls, increases in social security,
and an enhanced role for organised labour in macro-economic
policy-making through new planning institutions (ALP-ACTU,
1983; Lansbury and Davis, 1987). One of the attractions of the
Accord for some British socialists is that it has not split the labour
movement like the 1970s Social Contract in Britain, which led to
a wave of strikes in 1978-79, and an election defeat for the Labour
government. Moreover at a time when unemployment is still in
double (percentage) figures in Britain, having begun to fall only
slowly in 1986, Australian unemployment has dropped from
9.9% in 1983 to 7.8% in 1986 and inflation has also fallen, from
11% in 1983 to 4% in 1985 (Lansbury and Davis, 1987). There

has also been some redistribution of taxes and some improvements in social security.

In a period when social democratic governments across Europe have been retreating on their election promises, and provoking confrontations with their working-class supporters (in Greece, France, Spain and Italy), even the very modest achievements of the Australian movement can begin to look impressive. But the achievements *have* been modest: no serious incursion has been made or even proposed into the strategic decision-making or prerogatives of big capital. Moreover there have been significant costs involved in the Accord: public sector workers suffered real wage cuts despite taking industrial action (Gardener, 1986); the system of wage indexation to the consumer price index only just kept other wage-earners up with inflation (Petridis, 1987); and union leaders in manufacturing have been highly critical of the restructuring and shake out that has hit manufacturing industry with little or no union influence in decision-making (e.g. Halfpenny, 1985). The ACTU has now pushed for more local collective bargaining to 'top up' the national awards and allow more flexibility in wage levels.

The Australian movement has basically sustained a prices and incomes policy for four years (where British labour managed only three years in the 1970s Social Contract), but there is no sign of any distinctively socialist element in the Accord, such as effective planning mechanisms or challenges to capital's prerogatives or rights of ownership (O'Lincoln, 1985). The durability of the Accord rests partly on the fact that average earnings have kept up with inflation whilst unemployment has been cut (during the British Social Contract real earnings fell during 1976 and 1977, whilst unemployment rose: see Kelly, 1987c). But it is also due to the longstanding willingness of Australian labour to rely on federal and state arbitration bodies to resolve wage disputes. These bodies have come to play a major role in Australian wage determination, and the type of shop steward-led bargaining found in Britain is much less common in Australia (Lansbury and Davis, 1987; Deery and Plowman, 1985, Chaps.5,8,9). Britain has no equivalent machinery for determining wages, but does have a much more powerful shop stewards' movement that has in the past undermined incomes policies agreed between the TUC and Labour government (see Kelly, 1987c). So even if we thought there *was* radical potential in the Australian Accord (and the evidence to date on that score is feeble—as Beilharz, 1986, argues, contrary to Clegg et al., 1986), the more decentralised union movement and industrial relations system in Britain provide a very inhospitable climate for such an initiative.

Conclusion

For the reasons given earlier, above all the contradictions of state policy and the unification of capital in the face of a radical economic programme, the 'democratic road to socialism' will prove neither smooth nor gradual if it proves possible at all. A gradual accumulation of labour's resources *could*, under certain conditions, facilitate a far-reaching programme of radical reforms and could even begin to challenge capitalist power in the economy. This could be done, for instance, in a country such as Sweden, where there is almost complete union organisation; the hegemony of a single socialist party; a high degree of trade union unity; political disunity amongst the bourgeoisie; a long-standing pacifist tradition; and fragmentation among the employers.

Britain possesses few of these attributes, and it is difficult to foresee its acquiring them in the near future. It therefore does not follow that because the Swedish labour movement has used the State to bring their economy to the brink of socialism that British labour can do the same. Its labour organisations, employers, state and political traditions are too different to facilitate such an easy transfer of ideas and practices.

All the available evidence suggests that the capacity of orga-nised labour in Britain to use the State as an effective instrument of socialist transformation is limited. A left government-trade unionist alliance could certainly legislate and implement a wide range of radical reforms, and in that sense conduct class struggle through the State as neo-Gramscians have advocated. But as these measures progressively challenged the prerogatives and interests of capital, so the 'relative autonomy' of the state would contract. Internal opposition from other branches of the state apparatus would intensify, and external constraints from the capitalist economy would grip the government in an ever-tightening vice. More and more the State would indeed come to resemble an instrument of the ruling class, raising the un-answered question of whether there is any set of conditions that would permit a peaceful and democratic road to socialism.

10

The State of the Labour Movement

What is the state of the labour movement in Britain and elsewhere after eight years of recession and mass unemployment? Eric Hobsbawm, whose 1978 Marx Memorial lecture initiated a wide-ranging and continuing debate on British labour's 'forward march', was even less optimistic in 1981 than three years earlier:

> Nobody can seriously deny that the British labour movement today is in a considerable mess. It is in a state of deeper crisis and confusion than was easily foreseeable even three years ago (Hobsbawm, 1981, p.167).

And in the wake of the 1984-85 miners' strike he dismissed the idea that the unions hadn't done all that badly as 'baloney', declaring it was obvious that in the past six years they had taken a 'good few beatings' (Hobsbawm, 1985a, p.7). Hinton, writing a few years earlier, adopted a similar perspective:

> The difficulties experienced by the labour movement since its high point in 1945 appear to mark, not a temporary interruption to the forward march of labour, but the disintegration of a particular pattern of working class institutions and ideology which had previously given substance to the very conception of a 'forward march' (Hinton, 1983, p.ix).

According to the influential writer Stuart Hall, '. . . the crisis of the capitalist system and the crisis of the working-class movement are proceeding together, in tandem, mirroring and feeding off one another' (Hall, 1982b, p.17).

Some writers foresaw the trade unions being pushed even further, into a type of business unionism, epitomised by the 'no-strike' deals of the Electricians (EETPU) (Adeney and Lloyd, 1986, Chap.14; Bassett, 1986), a process recently described as the 'Americanisation of British trade unions' (Hain, 1986). More recently the Communist Party's Industrial Organiser Peter Carter wrote that

> . . . there is a crisis of consciousness that runs very deep throughout the unions. The crisis has its origins in the history and development of trade unionism in Britain, which was linked to a perspective which saw the improvement of wages and conditions as the main function of unions (Carter, 1986, p.12).

Nor have such thoughts been confined to the intellectual pessimists of Eurocommunism, for Tony Cliff of the far-left Socialist Workers' Party was writing as long ago as 1979 about the downturn in industrial struggle and its exposure of an underlying crisis in workers' organisation, leadership and ideology (Cliff, 1979). For the SWP it was the decline of independent shopfloor organisation under the impact of reformist, Broad Left leaderships which had left the working class defenceless in the face of Thatcher's 'ruling-class offensive' (Beecham, 1981).

For some writers the 1984-85 miners' strike reinforced their analyses, as it constituted 'the last of an old wave of struggles' (Coates, 1985, p.22). According to Adeney and Lloyd (1986), 'the strike had turned the bulk of the leaders and activists away from policies which were, explicitly or implicitly, revolutionary' (p.278). Yet this rather gloomy prognosis for the left has not gone unchallenged and even the TUC, despite its overtures to a 'new realism', was moved to observe that 'unions have, in practice, stood up extraordinarily well to the onslaught' (TUC, 1984, para.9). Recent surveys of trade union organisation in recession appear to have lent weight to this view. According to Batstone, 'on some counts moves to "put the unions in their place" appear to have been fairly limited in intent or consequence' (1984, p.258)—a finding reinforced by his more recent survey (Batstone and Gourlay, 1986), and by the much more comprehensive data in Millward and Stevens (1986). Indeed, the miners' strike has produced a further flurry of attacks on the 'pessimism' of Hobsbawm and his allies, with strike supporters claiming it showed 'the working class is very much alive and kicking' (Freeman, 1985, p.50), and revealed to workers 'not the *past* of the labour movement but its *future*' (Socialist Action, 1985, p.13).

Similar speculation has occurred in almost every other capitalist country, but has been particularly pronounced where union
density has either fallen dramatically or is currently very low, e.g.
France, USA. Indeed the parlous state of American trade
unionism and its continued decline through the early 1980s'
economic recovery has led to speculation about its terminal
demise (cf. Lipset, 1986; Troy, 1986). Other writers have looked
ahead to the decline of manufacturing industry and the growth of
service employment and discerned an increasingly inhospitable
environment for union organisation (Muller-Jentsch, 1986; Offe,
1985).

There is little agreement amongst commentators about the
most appropriate criteria for measuring the state of the labour
movement. Some have used strike statistics, others have looked at
wages, and some have tried to get behind these data by examining union organisation at the workplace (Batstone, 1984; Batstone and Gourlay, 1986). Nor is there any agreement over
appropriate time-scales, and different commentators have
adopted a range of short and long-term perspectives.

What I propose to do is divide this chapter in two and begin
with the case *for* the claim that the Western (and principally the
British) labour movement is at a watershed in its history and
faces a profound crisis. In the second part of the chapter I shall
consider the case against this proposition, and then draw some
conclusions.

Unions in Recession: the Parameters of Crisis

The most striking index of the crisis of trade unionism in
recession is the decline in union membership and density shown
in Table 10.1 for Britain.

Between 1979 and 1985 the unions lost approximately 2.5
million members, a drop of 19% against the recent peak of 1979.
If we treat the TUC unions separately the drop was slightly
greater at 21%. Trade union density still stood at 49.5% in 1985
when measured against the employed population, but if we add
in the unemployed then density falls to 43%, reflecting the low
level of trade union membership amongst those out of work
(Carruth and Disney, 1986; Kelly, 1987d). Some critics have
suggested that even this figure is an exaggeration. They have
pointed out the unreliable nature of membership returns particu-

Table 10.1 Trade union and TUC membership and density in the United Kingdom[1] 1970–86

Year	Trade Union Membership (000s)	TUC Membership (000s)	Trade Union[2] Density A (%)	Trade Union[3] Density B (%)
1970	11178	10002	49.9	48.6
1975	12026	11036	53.2	50.7
1979	13289	12173	57.3	54.1
1980	12947	11601	57.9	52.6
1981	12106	11006	56.1	49.4
1982	11593	10510	55.0	47.9
1983	11236	10082	53.2	46.4
1984	10994	9855	51.2	44.5
1985	10716	9586	49.5	43.0
1986	—	9243	—	—

Sources: Department of Employment Gazette 95 (2), February 1987, Table 1, p.85; *TUC Reports* 1976-86; *TUC Bulletin* 15, July 1987, p.4

1. Includes Northern Ireland.
2. Total trade union membership divided by civilian employees in employment.
3. Total trade union membership divided by civilian employees plus the unemployed.

larly in unions such as the AEU where as many as 30% of its 'membership' may not have paid their dues for over six months (Bassett, 1986, p.41)

Nor is this experience peculiar to Britain. Many commentators have remarked on the decline of trade union membership and density in a range of European countries, and above all in America (Leadbeater and Lloyd, 1987, pp.102-3; Muller-Jentsch, 1986). According to Bradley and Gelb the density of trade unionism has declined 'in all industrial countries except Denmark and Norway' (1986, p.14).

A second casualty of the recession has been the political wing of the labour movement. I described the electoral performance of the Labour Party in an earlier chapter (5). Though its 1987 vote was an improvement over the previous General Election (when only 39% of trade unionists voted Labour), the percentage Labour vote was less than the level of 1924 (33%) and well below the peak periods of the 1940s and 1966 when almost 50% of the electorate voted Labour.

Thirdly, there has been a substantial decline in the number of strikes, though the number of days lost has fluctuated wildly and shown no obvious trend in any direction.

Table 10.2   British strike statistics 1975-86

Year	Number of strikes	Working days lost (000s)
1975	2,332	6,012
1976	2,034	3,284
1977	2,737	10,142
1978	2,498	9,405
1979	2,125	29,474
1980	1,348	11,964
1981	1,344	4,266
1982	1,538	5,313
1983	1,364	3,754
1984	1,221	27,135
1985	903	6,402
1986	1,074	1,920

Source: Department of Employment Gazette 95 (9),
September 1987, Table 2, p467.

In the 1970s the annual strike frequency never once fell below 2,000; in the 1980s it has never been *above* 2,000, and has once (to date) fallen below 1,000.

The 1985 figure of 903 strikes was the lowest annual total since 1938, and the decline in strikes has frequently been cited as *prima facie* evidence of the weakening of trade unions. More importantly, the decline between 1984 and 1985 suggests that the ballot provisions in the Trade Union Act (1984), effective from September 1984, may have contributed to a further fall in the strike totals following the first stage of their collapse in 1980. Another factor specific to 1984-5 could well have been the crumbling of the miners' strike and the ensuing demoralisation of many other workers. Indeed throughout the 1980s it has been argued that unions have been striking less effectively as well as less frequently (Coates and Topham, 1986). A series of unions have gone down to defeat despite prolonged industrial action, including the civil servants (1981), health workers and train drivers (1982), telecommunications workers and printers (1983), miners (1984-5), teachers (1985-7), and printers again (1986-7).

Fourthly, trade union bargaining power has arguably been eroded both by mass unemployment and by a series of legal measures in the Employment Acts of 1980 and 1982, and the Trade Union Act of 1984, with a further round of measures promised in the Employment Bill (1987) and due to become law in 1988. The closed shop has been attacked; various forms of secondary industrial action have been outlawed; picketing has been subjected to closer regulation; the definition of a trade dispute has been narrowed; ballots have been imposed before official strikes if unions are to retain immunity; injunctions against unions have been readily granted by the courts; and the penalties for breaches of the law or contempt of court have been draconian, with fines running into hundreds of thousands of pounds (see Wedderburn, 1986 for details).

Fifthly, it is argued that unions have been faced with profound changes of attitude amongst their membership, symbolised most graphically by their support for Tory legislation on ballots, and by their willingness to cross other workers' picket lines (cf. Bradley and Gelb, 1986, pp.15, 16). Trade union leaders have found it hard to mobilise opposition to government legislation on ballots, despite their defiant speeches, because opinion poll data has repeatedly shown widespread support for the increased use of secret ballots as a form of consultation and decision-making in unions (Roiser and Little, 1986). When the TUC backed down from outright opposition to the legislation on ballots and simply drew the line at refusing to accept state funds for their conduct, that line was also demolished. At the 1985 TUC Congress, engineering union leaders rejected the TUC line with the 12:1 backing of their members, consulted through a secret ballot. The electricians' leaders backed them up, and with several financially hard-pressed unions waiting in the wings to take government money, the last semblance of union opposition to government legislation finally crumbled.

Rank-and-file workers have proved equally rebellious when faced with strike calls. Most Nottinghamshire miners refused to join the 1984-5 miners' strike and many then formed a breakaway union, the UDM; many journalists refused to boycott Rupert Murdoch's Wapping plant, as did haulage drivers belonging to the TGWU; the same union watched a possible strike in 1984 fall apart as dockers insisted on a return to work; power station workers refused (for the most part) to support the miners' strike with industrial action, though in some stations there were fierce arguments (see Adeney and Lloyd's account of Didcot power station, 1986, pp.149-51); a number of white-collar unions, principally the CPSA and NALGO, lost several thousand members who resigned in protest at their union leadership's support for the miners. All in all these pieces of evidence have been taken as signs of a sea-change in workers' attitudes, against traditional forms of union organisation and action.

Sixthly, there have been sharp divisions within the trade union movement following the Government's virtual refusal to talk to trade union leaders in the manner to which they had grown accustomed in the 1970s.

One influential wing of the movement talked of the need for a 'new realism' about the prospects for trade unions in a cold climate and urged unions to think more seriously about collaboration with employers. Taken to its extreme this (and similar) injunctions has issued in the politics of the EETPU, with its aggressive refusal to support the miners, its antagonism to the mainstream policies of the TUC, and its willingness to enter new-style agreements with employers (see Bassett, 1986 for the most detailed, though uncritical, account of the EETPU).

The EETPU's 'philosophy' is built on two interlocking premises: that workers and employers have a common interest in the performance of their firm, and that conflicts of interest should be pursued through negotiation and arbitration, not through strikes. From these premises, the EETPU has pioneered a package of measures which offers the employer flexibility in production, cooperation in productivity improvements, a no-strike clause in procedural agreements and the use of pendulum arbitration (in which the arbitrator must award either the employer's last offer or the union's final demand—he cannot award a compromise settlement). In return (at least in the full package) the union receives exclusive negotiating rights in a single-union deal, a limited amount of worker participation in decision-making, and single status terms and conditions of employment for all workers, blue- and white-collar. Though deals of this type are presently thin on the ground (the so-called 'no-strike' deals probably cover no more than 20,000 workers) they have become the focus of widespread and heated discussion because of the principles that are at stake.

Seventh, trade unions have faced a veritable barrage of new or revamped employer practices all designed in one way or another to promote employee involvement in the enterprise. Company newsletters, briefing groups, quality circles, autonomous work groups, joint consultation, profit-related pay and profit-sharing are the most well-known (see Batstone, 1984; Millward and Stevens 1986; Bradley and Gelb, 1986; Kelly, 1982a, 1985; Fogarty and Brooks, 1986; Leadbeater and Lloyd, 1987). By linking elements of workers' pay to company performance, providing information about company performance and encouraging workers to contribute their own ideas for its improvement, the hope is that conflicts of interest can be weakened. Clearly, schemes of this kind, if successful, would pose a considerable threat to the role and possibly the very existence of trade unions. As many of these practices have been developed and applied in America, it is worth looking more closely at the US scenario.

Labour and industrial relations in America: Britain's future?

American trade union density has been declining for over thirty years, and is now one of the lowest in the advanced capitalist world.

Table 10.3 American trade union membership and density 1945–84

Year	Membership (000s)	Density (%)
1945	12254	30.4
1950	14294	31.6
1953	16310	32.5
1965	18269	30.1
1975	22207	28.9
1984	18306	19.4

Source: Troy, 1986, Table 2.

Moreover, the rate of decline has accelerated since the mid-1970s, before the great recession, and has continued unabated despite the recovery in the US economy after 1982. One popular explanation offered for this trend is the shift in employment composition as well-organised manufacturing industry declines rapidly, whilst the poorly organised service sector expands. But as Lipset (1986) has pointed out, whilst these employment trends are almost universal in the advanced capitalist world, few countries have experienced union decline as deeply and for as long as the USA. Perhaps more telling is that the union share of manufacturing workers has also been falling, and in the elections held to certify (or decertify) a union as a bargaining agent, more and more workers have rejected the offer of trade unionism, or thrown out (decertified) an existing union (Lipset, 1986; Dickens and Leonard, 1985). Attitude surveys have shown widespread scepticism amongst non-union workers about the likely effectiveness of a trade union in their own workplace, and not surprisingly, therefore, 70% of the unorganised US workforce say they would not join a union even if they had the opportunity (Kochan et al., 1986, Chap.8).

Perhaps a major (though not the only) factor in the decline of American trade unionism has been the growing opposition of US employers, a fact that may well be linked to worker attitudes. As international trade expanded and competition intensified in the 1970s and 1980s manufacturers found the constraints of trade unionism increasingly onerous. Detailed work rules and seniority clauses inhibited productivity improvements through labour flexibility between jobs; the widespread use of cost-of-living adjustments in pay contracts sent labour costs rapidly upwards as inflation took off in the 1970s; and employers increasingly resented union resistance to change and union workplace power (see Piore and Sabel, 1984; Freeman, 1987).

The result of all this was threefold: first, a concerted attempt to defeat unions in recognition ballots by the increased deployment of union-busting consultants coupled with an enhanced willingness to violate the electoral laws (Freeman, 1987; Lawler, 1984); second, the rundown of manufacturing plants in the well-organised North-Eastern States, and the start-up of new plants in the anti-union Southern States, such as Texas (Piore and Sabel, 1984); third, and perhaps most significantly, the development of a set of managerial practices designed to eliminate the perceived need for trade unions altogether.

US multinationals such as IBM, Texas Instruments, Hewlett Packard and others have for many years pioneered a sophisticated union avoidance strategy: recruits are carefully screened; pay and conditions are generally very good; extensive training and career development is provided and encouraged; internal grievance machinery has been installed, with some companies even appointing 'advocates' to pursue employee grievances in lieu of a trade union; and staff associations or company unions are sometimes found (see Beaumont, 1987, Chap.5; Bassett, 1986, Chap.10; IMF, 1987). US manufacturing firms have supplemented many of these changes in personnel policies with changes in work organisation: in the face of increasingly volatile and uncertain product markets, some firms have begun to move away from the rigidities of long assembly lines and mass production, to more flexible forms of work organisation, based around enlarged individual work stations or flexible work groups (Kelly, 1982a, 1985; Piore and Sabel, 1984). Indeed some analysts have discerned in these policies of 'flexible specialisation' the rebirth of craft traditions of work long since submerged beneath mass production (Piore and Sabel, 1984). Finally, about 7,000 smaller American companies have begun to experiment with employee share ownership schemes, in which individuals (not groups, or unions) are offered varying amounts of company stock (Klein, 1987). The generic purpose of these various schemes is to tie workers into their plants, enhancing their commitment to the performance of 'their' company, whilst removing the incentive for workers to demand independent representation. In some firms, unions have been kept out at considerable cost, whilst in organised firms, the fear of some labour officials is that unions will simply wither away and become less and less relevant to workers and their needs.

The spread of US multinationals to Britain, and the adoption of some of their practices, such as quality circles, flexible work practices, and employee share ownership, therefore holds out the prospect of long-term union decline in Britain on the American pattern (cf. Bradley and Gelb, 1986).

For all these reasons, then—the decline in union membership and Labour voting, the withering away and defeats of strikes, the encroachments of law, the new practices of employers, and changes in the attitudes and behaviour of the working class—the British labour movement is said by many commentators to be in a state of acute crisis.

Unions in Recession: Resilience and Stability

There is clearly some truth in many of the observations and evidence used to sustain the thesis of a labour movement in crisis.

But before accepting such a conclusion there are several major questions that need to be asked. Despite the problems of the 1980s, are there areas or issues in which labour movements have either held their own or made advances? Without an assessment of both the weaknesses *and* the strengths of organised labour no balanced appraisal is possible. We also need to consider the causes of the problems faced by unions and parties: are they short-term cyclical problems that will be eased with economic recovery or are they the products of long-term, secular trends in the economy that will continue despite economic growth? How severe are the problems faced by labour movements, compared with the past and with other countries? And will the changes in occupational structure, employer practices and legislation actually have the effects that some people believe and intend? Only when these questions have been posed and answered can we arrive at an informed and balanced assessment of the state of the contemporary labour movement. In this section I want to review conflicting evidence, and to argue that despite eight years of recession, the British trade union movement and many of its European counterparts are in remarkably good shape. The British movement clearly faces some big problems but these are not sufficiently widespread, serious or novel to warrant talk of a crisis or watershed. Let us begin with trade union membership.

Trade union membership

That British trade union membership has fallen during the recession is a fact so obvious that it hardly needs stating (see Table 10.1, above) and apart from minor quibbles about the accuracy of trade union returns, the broad trend is beyond dispute. With one or two exceptions the same can be said of every other trade union movement in the advanced capitalist world. But if we are interested in the power of trade unionism, then it is not the absolute level of membership that we need to consider, but the proportion of workers organised in unions. Since the employed workforce has shrunk in almost every advanced capitalist country with the rise in unemployment, then it is clearly possible that some trade union movements have continued to organise the same (or even a higher) proportion of a declining workforce. And this is exactly what has happened, as the following table shows.

The most striking feature of this table is that it refutes the widely-repeated claim that trade unions are in decline across the

Table 10.4 Trade union density in 17 advanced capitalist countries 1979-85

Country	Density 1979 (%)	Density 1985 (%)	Change 1979-85 (% points)
Denmark	86	98	+12
Belgium	77	84	+7
Sweden	89	95	+6
Ireland	49	51	+2
Austria	59	61	+2
Norway	60	61	+1
Canada	36	37	+1
Finland	84	85	+1
West Germany	42	42	0
France	28	28	0
Switzerland	36	35	−1
Australia	58	57	−1
Japan	32	29	−3
Italy	51	45	−6
Netherlands	43	37	−6
United Kingdom	58	52	−6
USA	25	18	−7

Source: Freeman, 1987, Exhibit 1.

whole of the advanced capitalist world. Trade union experience of recession has been highly variable, with eight countries showing a rise in density, seven showing a decline, and two recording no change between 1979 and 1985.

If we concentrate on Britain as one of the countries with declining union density, then the question we must ask is how serious is this situation? Is it a portent of a secular decline in trade unionism as seen in the USA where union density has fallen almost every year since 1954 and is now below 20%? Or is it merely a cyclical phenomenon associated with recession so that with economic recovery we will also see a resurgence of trade union growth? A useful way of putting the membership loss into historical perspective is to compare the current figures with those from previous major recessions that followed sustained periods of union growth. A comparison with the 1929-32 recession is therefore inappropriate because this followed a long period of declining union membership and militancy. The recession of

270

1920-23 is a better comparison with the present period because like today it marked the end of a steep upward curve in union growth and strike rates.

Table 10.5 British trade union membership 1910-24

Year	Membership (000s)	Density (%)
1910	2565	14.6
1915	4354	24.1
1918	6533	35.7
1919	7926	43.1
1920	8348	45.2
1921	6633	35.8
1922	5626	31.6
1923	5429	30.2
1924	5544	30.6

Source: Bain et al., 1972.

Trade union membership peaked at almost 8.5 millions in 1920, a density level of 45.2% that would not be reached again until 1948. And in the thirteen years from 1920 until the turning point of 1933 trade union membership declined in all but two of those years.

What is striking however is the *rate* of membership loss measured against the peak of 1920, a year which marked the culmination of ten years of spectacular growth. In just three years (1920-33) trade unions lost almost 35% of their membership. In the earlier recession of the 1890s, trade unions fared even worse, losing almost 40% of their membership in the years 1890-93. But in the comparable three years of the current recession (1979-82) unions lost proportionately fewer members, just 13% (the figure for TUC unions was 14%).

Let us put it another way: if trade unions today had lost members at the same *rate* as in 1920-23 then their membership figure for 1982 would have been just over 8.5 millions. In fact it stood at twelve millions. Why did union membership fall more steeply in the 1920-22 recession than in the current recession? Part of the explanation is that unemployment rose much faster and to a higher level in the earlier period, from 3.9% in 1920 to

16.9% in 1921, and 14.3% in 1922. By contrast unemployment between 1979 and 1981 rose from 5.5% to 10.4% (Cronin, 1979, Tables B9, B10; *D E Gazette*, various issues).

But this can only be *part* of the explanation, because the loss of trade union members (three millions, 1920-24) far outstripped the fall in employment (approximately two millions) over the same period. The result was that in the years 1920-24 trade union density fell by almost *fifteen* percentage points, whereas it fell just under *eight* percentage points in the four years 1979-83 (see Table 10.1, Col. 4).

Another factor may be the *stability* of union membership today compared with the past. In previous recessions it seems that quite a number of employers tried to get rid of unions from their workplaces, and that many workers may have dropped out of membership. But contemporary evidence shows that hardly any employers have tried to remove trade unions from their workplaces in the recent recession (Millward and Stevens, 1986, pp.52-3, 66-9). At the same time few workers will have dropped out of membership because of the pervasiveness of deduction of union dues at source ('check-off'). According to Millward and Stevens, 80% of workplaces with recognised manual unions and 82% with recognised non-manual unions operated the check-off, and the number of workplaces with check-off has increased during the recession (1986, pp.92-3). The bulk of recent membership loss has occurred in the private manufacturing sector because of the disproportionate closure or rundown of large well-organised plants.

British trade union membership has therefore held up reasonably well compared with previous recessions and union density in Britain is still higher than in most West European countries despite its faster rate of decline since 1979.

Trade union finance

Several writers have cited the financial difficulties of some unions as a further index of crisis, a problem that is obviously and intimately connected with trends in union membership. Approximately 80% of union income derives from member subscriptions, and the largest single item of union expenditure (c.75%) is union administration. It would seem reasonable to suppose that unions with declining memberships, and whose administrations were naturally reluctant to cut their own jobs, would provide a perfect recipe for grave financial difficulties. In practice, however, this is far from being the case, and union finances have in fact remained remarkably sound, as the following table shows.

Table 10.6 Numbers of large unions with expenditure in excess of income 1960-85

Year	Excess expenditure	Excess income
1960	9	30
1970	16	23
1975	2	24
1977	0	26
1978	1	25
1979	1	26
1980	5	21
1981	4	22
1982	2	22
1983	1	22
1984	1	20
1985	4	20

Sources: Latta, 1972; *Certification Office, Annual Reports.*

Expenditure:income ratios for *all* unions as a whole rose steadily throughout the 1960s, peaking at 96% in 1970, but then fell to 82% in 1976, rose again to 93% in 1980, and dropped back below 90% thereafter (see Willman and Morris, 1987).

A close inspection of large unions with financial deficits in at least one year shows three broad sets of causes: firstly, there were unions which embarked on very protracted, large and costly strikes (NALGO 1979; NUT 1980; ISTC 1980; NGA 1980; CPSA 1981; POEU 1983; NUM 1985; NUT 1985); secondly, there were unions which experienced a rapid and substantial rise in benefit payments (AUEW 1981, 1984; ASB 1982; NGA 1981); thirdly, there were unions which failed to increase membership subscriptions quickly enough to offset a sudden, rapid fall in numbers and/or a rise in costs (UCATT 1978, 1980; SCPS 1980; ASTMS 1981; CPSA 1982; NUPE 1985; AEU 1985). Indeed one interesting feature of the recession has been the capacity of British unions to force their membership income upwards in the face of declining numbers (see Table 10.7). On the other hand, it

Table 10.7 Membership trends and membership income: all trade
unions 1975-85

Year	Membership income (£'000)	Increase on previous year (%)	Membership change on previous year (%)
1975	100800	—	—
1976	130243	+29.2	+4.1
1977	151637	+16.4	+4.8
1978	170993	+12.8	+2.6
1979	198025	+15.8	+1.2
1980	230719	+16.5	−4.4
1981	284457	+23.3	−2.6
1982	298114	+ 4.8	−4.6
1983	310123[1]	+ 4.0	−3.8
1984	327631	+ 5.6	−1.9
1985	358588	+ 9.4	−2.2

Source: *Certification Office Annual Reports*, 1976-86.

1. This figure excludes the NUM.

should be noted that a significant number of very small unions
have not survived the recession and have been forced to merge
with larger unions.

The financial solvency of unions in recession can be partly
explained by real rises in subscription levels, since the average
contribution per member has grown from 0.31% of average
earnings in 1979 to 0.35% in 1984 (Willman and Morris, 1987,
Table 4). It is also the result of rising real earnings of union
members (see below) so that growing subscription rates are
translated into steadily rising real incomes for unions.

Wages, earnings and strikes

One of the most intriguing features of the recession has been the
capacity of trade unions through collective bargaining to achieve
rates of pay rise equal to or greater than the rate of price increase.
The average earnings index for the whole economy (according to
D E Gazette figures) remained equal to or above the Retail Price
Index throughout 1978, and then dipped several percentage
points below the RPI in the second half of 1979. From late 1979
until the middle of 1981 average earnings increases generally

exceeded the rate of inflation. The latter half of 1981 witnessed price rises overtaking the growth in average earnings, but for the next five years (1982-87) the earnings curve remained above the prices curve.

It is true that, for the whole economy, productivity rose significantly between early 1980 and late 1981, as the economy crashed. But during this crash, both productivity *and* output fell, so the productivity growth in 1981-82 was growth from an unusually low point. Thereafter the rate of annual productivity increase had fallen back and remained consistently lower than the rate of money earnings increase at between 2.5 and 4%. At the same time unit labour costs are rising faster in Britain than in many other OECD countries (though their rate of increase is less than in the 1970s: see TUC *Economic Review 1986*, paras 2.12-2.14, 4.15-4.17). Therefore whilst Britain's price and cost competitiveness is improving compared to the 1970s, other countries are improving as fast if not faster.

If we therefore take the earnings figures for the whole economy then on *average* workers in recession have not done too badly, suffering real pay cuts only in 1979 and 1981, but experiencing real pay rises between 1982 and 1987. And if we compare Britain with other countries, 'real wages for those fortunate enough to keep their jobs have risen much faster in the UK since 1979 than in any other major western country' (Rowthorn and Grahl, 1986, p.26).

If we break down these figures into different economic sectors then a rather more complicated picture starts to emerge. In general the average annual earnings rise in manufacturing industry has exceeded those in the public sector services, where government has been largely successful in holding down pay rises at or sometimes below the rate of inflation (Beaumont, 1987, p.165; Fogarty and Brooks, 1986, p.136). As a result many of the most bitter strikes of the 1980s have been fought by public sector employees over wages—steel, coal, water, civil service, health service, education.

The fact that many groups of employees have secured real pay rises during several years of recession is not in itself proof of the efficacy and vitality of trade unionism. Employers may have been anxious to compensate workers who remained after redundancies and closures for higher levels of effort. Though the results of this additional effort have yet to materialise in productivity figures it is possible that potential productivity rises are being concealed by low levels of output and product demand. Alternatively, employers may be rewarding the past (and future) cooperation of a more highly skilled and experienced workforce. Another interpretation is that changes in working practices have produced upgrading, and therefore earnings rises, for many workers. Or it may be that employers are having to keep wage rises up to a 'going rate' in order to retain and/or attract the skilled labour which is still, in some industries and regions, in short supply. Finally it may be the case that the recovery in manufacturing profit rates and volume since 1982-83 has allowed employers to be more generous in pay settlements than they might otherwise have been. Indeed for several years the volume of profit in British commercial and manufacturing companies has been rising significantly faster than wages, so that even where workers' incomes have been rising, the incomes of capitalists have been rising even faster thanks to a higher rate of exploitation of labour.

Nevertheless, whatever the motives for employers to agree on rises in basic pay at or above the rate of inflation, it is difficult to sustain the idea that a trade union movement whose members have received such rises is in the throes of a deep crisis. And it is interesting to note that *union* criteria for pay rises—increases in the cost of living, and comparisons with other groups of workers—are still widely cited by employers, even in the depths of recession, suggesting that union bargaining power may not have fallen as much as people have thought (cf. Millward and Stevens, 1986, pp.246-7).

It is certainly the case that the number of strikes has declined since 1979, and that 'secondary' industrial action is now very rare because of the draconian fines meted out to the NGA in the *Stockport Messenger* dispute. Indeed employers do seem more willing to go to the courts for injunctions to prevent secondary action or to force unions to hold a pre-strike ballot. But all previous evidence suggests that the strike pattern is strongly cyclical: strike frequency rises during economic booms, peaks on the threshold of recession, declines as recession bites and unemployment rises, only to rise again with economic recovery and the growth of trade union membership. This has been the pattern as far back as 1888 and there are no grounds for thinking it is about to change, and that strikes are a thing of the past (see Chapter 5, above; and Screpanti, 1987; Cronin, 1979).

Working-class political parties

If we turn to Labour Party voting then it is true that the decline

Table 10.8 Manufacturing employment and votes for workers' parties in 11 capitalist countries 1966-83

Country	Change in manufacturing employment 1966-83 (% points)	Change in social democratic and communist vote 1966-83 (% points)	Manufacturing employment as % total civilian employment 1981	Social democratic and communist vote 1966 (% total)
UK	−33.2	−19.4	26.4	28.3
Belgium	−30.8	−6.3	24.7	27.5
Netherlands	−25.7	+5.1	21.1	30.2
Denmark	−24.4	−4.6	21.3	34.8
Switzerland	−19.9	+0.1	32.0	26.5
Sweden	−18.8	−2.0	23.3	51.2
W. Germany	−16.2	−1.1	33.6	43.1
Austria	−14.3	+5.2	29.7	48.2
France	−14.0	+12.2	25.1	53.6
Italy	+5.3	−0.1	26.1	41.3
Finland	+17.5	−7.7	26.1	40.7

Sources: Employment data from Rowthorn, 1987, Tables 1.2, 1.3; voting data from von Beyme, 1985, Tables 2.3, 2.5.

in the core working class in manufacturing has gone hand in hand with a decline in the Labour vote (and a similar phenomenon has occurred in Belgium). And several countries with a more modest decline in manufacturing employment have witnessed only small falls in the combined social democratic and communist vote, as Table 10.8 shows.

Other things being equal it seems reasonable to suppose that the political parties which grew with the industrial working class would decline with them, but in practice matters are not so straightforward. First there are four countries in which manufacturing employment fell, but the proportion of votes for workers' parties rose, between 1966 and 1983, viz. Netherlands, Switzerland, Austria and France. Second, in two countries, Italy and Finland, where a growth of manufacturing employment might have been expected to result in a rising vote for workers' parties, the opposite happened, particularly in Finland. Third, if we examine the scale of voting decline it is clear that the losses of the British Labour Party are much too substantial to be explained by employment shifts: its loss of almost 20% of its 1966 peak vote is a disaster unmatched by any other large workers' party in the table. Fourth, although several countries with a substantial manufacturing base in 1981 showed high levels of voting for workers' parties, in particular Germany and Austria, it is also clear that most of these capitalist countries had broadly similar occupational structures in 1981, with about one-quarter of their workforce in manufacturing. Yet on this common substrate workers' parties attracted anywhere between 26.5% and 53.6% of votes in the early 1980s. So although industrial workers have traditionally formed the core of support for social democratic and communist parties, and will almost certainly continue to do so, it is quite wrong to believe that the decline of the manufacturing workforce entails the decline of working class based parties. For both the spread of trade unionism and the proletarianisation of some white-collar work are counteracting tendencies which can, and have, offset the shrinkage of the traditional core of the working class.

Trade unions and public opinion

That the Thatcher government has attempted to weaken trade unions and blacken their image is clear enough, but how successful has it been? It is not easy to measure the public standing of trade unions, but one source of data is the Gallup answers to the question whether unions are 'a good or a bad thing'. Responses to this annual poll show that approximately two-thirds of the adult population regard unions as 'a good thing', although there was a slow and uneven decline in union popularity between the 1960s and the late 1970s. It is large strikes or strike waves that appear to depress union popularity, as in 1972 (only 55% said unions were a good thing), 1974 (54%), 1975 (51%), 1977 (53%) and 1979 (51%). Paradoxically, the decline of strikes under the Thatcher government has displaced unions from the public consciousness, and since 1981 their popularity (measured by the Gallup polls) has risen to its highest level for twenty-two years (Gallup Political Index, 1985, 1986, 1987; Fogarty and Brooks, 1986, p.88).

One source of information about workers' attitudes to one aspect of their union's activity was provided by the results of the political fund ballots, in which all 38 unions with an existing fund won the overwhelming support of their members for its continuation. But the complexity of public opinion is shown by the Tory election victories in 1983 and 1987.

Taken as a whole the evidence on public opinion about trade unions does not confirm the existence of any simple and major drift to the right. But nor does it suggest that all the talk of attitude change in response to 'Thatcherism' can be dismissed as so much hot air.

Employers and the State—a 'new' American-style industrial relations?

But haven't employers moved to adopt and implement a range of new practices—share participation, 'flexibility' etc.—designed to erode union organisations such as the closed shop, and to cement employee loyalty to their firms? And what of the strike defeats suffered by well-organised groups of workers such as the printers and the miners? Don't these indicate a serious decline in trade union power compared with the 1970s?

Evidence on the scale, and more important the effects, of new employment practices is mixed. Some of them have been exaggerated out of all proportion: the so-called 'no-strike' deals probably cover no more than about 20,000 workers, less than 0.4% of the British manufacturing workforce, and are unlikely to spread because of union resistance and employer uncertainty (Sherman, 1986). Their main effect is likely to be an ideological contribution to that section of public opinion hostile to strikes. Other measures, such as single-union agreements, may actually benefit workers by reducing the incidence of sectional disputes over jobs and membership (though they can be damaging if introduced without consultation and agreement).

It is probably the case that 'flexibility' and 'productivity agreements' *have* spread through industry since 1978, and that in many firms working practices have been altered, particularly with the introduction of new technology. Whilst these changes have almost certainly been associated with job loss, especially in manufacturing industry, and have probably contributed to rises in labour productivity, there is no evidence that they have damaged union organisation. In any case it is a mistake to assume that the break-up of 'restrictive practices' or worker controls based on job demarcations necessarily diminishes workers' power at the point of production. New systems of labour flexibility often require extensive cooperation from workers in moving from job to job, and if conditions permit, this cooperation can be withheld from the employer and used as a power resource in bargaining to extract concessions. In this regard it is interesting to note that the American proponents of the 'flexible specialisation thesis' have been very careful *not* to predict the industrial relations consequences of changes in work organisation, and have simply noted they are likely to weaken unions in some contexts, but not others (Piore and Sabel, 1984, Chap.9).

Other new initiatives are much more widespread. Britain probably now has about eight million people who own shares, thanks to the government's sell-off of large, public corporations such as British Telecom, British Airways and Rolls Royce. Company-based share ownership schemes have also spread rapidly: in 1980 just 13% of workplaces were part of a company with such a scheme, but by 1984 the figure had risen to 23% (Millward and Stevens, 1986, p.259). The proportion of the total workforce actually participating in these schemes rose less spectacularly, from 5% to 7%.

The same survey of industrial relations also documented the proportions of establishments with 'new', non-bargaining institutions of industrial relations. Joint consultative committees existed in 34% of establishments, the same figure as for 1980, though many of these committees came into being or were re-activated in the late 1970s (Millward and Stevens, 1986, Table 6.1). More employers than in 1980 (35% as compared with 24%) reported various new initiatives to increase 'employee involvement'.

What effect do these changes in institutions have on workers' attitudes and behaviour? Too many people have jumped to the conclusion that the growth of 'joint consultation' and 'share ownership', for instance, necessarily indicates profound shifts in worker attitudes towards the firm, away from a conflictual and towards a cooperative or harmonious view. Whilst many employers and their supporters undoubtedly intend and would like this to happen, hard and reliable evidence for it is virtually non-existent, as even proponents of wider share ownership have admitted (Bradley and Gelb, 1986, pp.74-5). Detailed studies of joint consultative committees in operation have shown that their effects are highly variable. In many cases they have no impact on collective bargaining and trade union-management relations, though in a few cases they may do so (Cressey, Eldridge and MacInnes, 1985). In other words even if workers do cooperate with employers on production matters they are still as likely as before to come into conflict over wages; benefits and the other issues normally processed through bargaining.

Although some British employers have initiated various forms of institutional change to enhance employee commitment to their firms, interviews with managers in 72 large corporations suggest that very few expect any such attitude or behaviour changes to be profound and long-term. Most expect that as the economy recovers, so will trade union power (IMS, 1986, pp.74-5, 84-5). Evidence from America, where unions have engaged in widespread 'concession bargaining', suggests that few enduring changes in attitude are likely to result because workers and their unions have received very little in return for their concessions. A study of 210 concession bargains in 1982 showed that unions received a quid pro quo for agreed wage reductions, job losses and new work practices in only 52 cases. Only in 31 cases (15% of the total) did any workers receive guarantees of employment security, and future earnings rises were agreed in only 9% of cases (Kochan et al., 1986, pp.116-9). It would be unrealistic to expect major changes in worker attitudes on the basis of such meagre returns for substantial concessions.

The type of workplace organisation required for effective industrial action has enjoyed mixed fortunes during the recession. On the one hand the closed shop has been the most obvious victim of Tory legislation, with the number of workers covered by closed shop arrangements falling by over a million between 1980 and 1984 (Millward and Stevens, 1986, p.107). On the other hand the number of shop stewards and full-time lay representatives has remained unchanged over the same period, with a rise in the number of public sector stewards offsetting their predictable decline in manufacturing (Millward and Stevens, 1986, p.84). Particular examples of overt 'union-bashing' or confrontation with unions are not hard to find—MacGregor at the Coal Board, and Murdoch at Wapping, are the most recent and prominent cases. But we must go beyond particular cases and situations and ask just how widespread and systematic the British 'employers offensive' has been.

Overt attacks on trade union organisation and facilities, and dramatic restrictions on the scope of collective bargaining, have been concentrated in three types of firm. First, in the State trading sector and parts of the public sector services we have witnessed major confrontations in every year of Thatcher's two governments, as tight controls on public spending have been enforced and labour 'shaken out': BL (1979), British Steel (1980), Civil Service (1981), NHS (1982), British Rail (1982-83), Water Boards (1982), coal mining (1981, 1984-85), teachers (1985-86) and the newly-privatised British Telecom (1987). Secondly, a minority of private manufacturers who have been especially hard hit by recession and seen their market share eroded by more efficient competitors have also tried to restrict union rights and unilaterally alter working practices (Batstone, 1984). Thirdly, in some low-paying firms in the services sector there has been growing contempt for Wages Council orders and a rise in the number of firms failing to comply with their wage rates (Pond, 1983).

The other side of the coin is that in most sectors of manufacturing and in parts of the public sector, such as some local authorities, employers have not pursued strategies of overt confrontation. They have continued their existing bargaining and consultative arrangements with trade unions and have preferred to introduce change through negotiation rather than unilateral imposition (Millward and Stevens, 1986, pp.64-9). They have also been willing to reach pay settlements above the rate of inflation, partly because profits are booming, and also in order to attract skilled workers who are now in short supply in key areas of work (electronics engineering) or in certain parts of the country (South East). For their part unions have largely felt they had no choice because of their firm's weak competitive position; others have cooperated in such change over many years and were not therefore being asked to do anything radically new in recession. Consequently many employers have faced a fairly cooperative trade union movement and have therefore had no incentive to launch an offensive against shop stewards or collective bargaining. This is not to say that unions have been docile in respect of changes to work practices, but only that the resistance they have offered has rarely been so effective or on such a large scale as to force the employer into a wholesale attack on union organisation.

The results of government legislation have been equally mixed, confounding those who believed unions would suffer enormous damage as a result of the Employment Acts (1980, 1982) and the Trade Union Act (1984). Gauging the precise effects of legislation in the 1980s is extremely difficult for several reasons: first the number of claims for damages, or injunctions sought against secondary industrial action or picketing could be an inaccurate measure as it cannot tell us about threats to use the law which never materialised in legal action. Second, the law may have a more subtle effect on the parties by altering their expectations and their tactics without the appearance of any formal threats. Third, it is difficult to disentangle the impact of adverse product markets, mass unemployment and other factors from purely legal changes. Strike frequency, for instance, fell in 1980 as the recession began to bite, and fell again in 1984 as the pre-strike balloting provisions came into effect. But was the 1984 strike total depressed by legislation or by the discouragement effect of the disintegrating miners' strike?

One area in which some judgements can be made is the use of ballots in union decision-making, specifically to test support for the closed shop, to decide on official strike action and on whether unions should retain political funds, and to elect voting members of union executives. The most eloquent proof of the failure of these measures to live up to their architects' expectations is the passage of the Employment Bill (1987) which undoes or amends previous legislation in all these areas. The reason it does so can be gleaned from data on the results of these four types of ballots. According to ACAS (1986) 77% of the pre-strike ballots held between 1984 and 1986 recorded support for industrial action, whilst 82% of the closed shop ballots up to the end of 1986 went in the union's favour. All 38 unions with political funds voted overwhelmingly to retain them, and the ballots to elect union executives have failed to produce a widespread swing to the right. It is almost certainly this pattern of results which has led the government to introduce further legal measures against trade unions.

The picture in America is rather different, as we saw earlier, but it would be quite wrong to infer that American practices are likely to be repeated in Britain with the same effects. The trajectory of American trade unionism is almost unparalleled in the advanced capitalist world, and only the Japanese unions have managed to decline as consistently and for as long as the Americans (Bamber and Lansbury, 1987, Table A17). The violent hostility of American employers to trade unions has few parallels in Britain, and the US legal regime is markedly more hostile to unions and to union recognition than in Britain. Finally, it remains the case that British (and most European) workers can reasonably expect to elect a pro-labour government at some time in their lives, whereas American workers have proved unable to sustain an independent workers' party that could challenge the two bourgeois parties. Of all the countries one could use to illustrate Britain's future, America is undoubtedly the worst and most inappropriate example.

Before concluding this chapter it is worth dwelling at some length on the most recent and comprehensive analysis of labour movement crisis, because it has brought together a large number of often disparate themes.

Disorganised Capitalism?

The End of Organized Capitalism (Lash and Urry, 1987) is a work of extraordinary scope, ranging over the histories of five major capitalist countries, and analysing processes as diverse as deindustrialisation, spatial relocation and deurbanisation. In essence the book argues that an historical era of organised capitalism is drawing to a close. That era was characterised *inter alia* by the mass production of goods in large plants in large urban centres, by spatially and occupationally homogeneous labour movements dominated by core, industrial workers, and by societies in which the capital-labour relationship and class inequality played a dominant role. For a variety of reasons, this era is now giving way to disorganised capitalism in which: (i) the core industrial working class is in decline. In 1955, 48% of the British workforce was employed in industry (manufacturing, construction, mining and utilities), but by 1984 the figure had slumped to 34% (Rowthorn, 1987). Since 1979 the manufacturing workforce has fallen by one-quarter from 7.13 millions to 5.11 millions (1987). Meanwhile public sector employment, another traditional heartland of trade unionism, is stagnant, with falls in the trading corporations (cars, steel, coal, railways), civil service and education just about offset by a rise in the health service. The big growth in employment has come in the poorly-unionised private services sector (Fogarty and Brooks, 1986). Moreover whilst the number of manual workers fell from 14 to 12 millions between 1948 and 1979, the number of white-collar workers rose from 6.25 to 11.5 millions (Bain and Price, 1983); (ii) manufacturing facilities have become smaller, and have increasingly been concentrated in small towns and rural areas. In 1974 there were 18,002 factories employing between 20 and 49 workers, and 1,018 with over 1,000 workers. By 1983 the number of small factories had fallen 10% to 16,126, but the number of large factories had dropped by 42%, to just 589 (Harman, 1986). London and the conurbations have lost an enormous amount of manufacturing industry: in 1960 they contained 45% of manufacturing employment, but by 1981 this figure had fallen below 33%. Conversely, small towns and rural areas increased their share of these jobs, from 27% in 1960 to 38% in 1981 (Fothergill et al., 1987); (iii) large cities are losing population to small towns and rural areas, and established occupational communities are disintegrating; (iv) the workforce is becoming increasingly divided between a reasonably secure, well-paid core and a less-secure, lower-paid periphery. In Atkinsons's model of the fully flexible firm, a wide range of functions will be sub-contracted or carried out by casual, part-time or temporary workers, whilst the essential core of activities will be performed by its full-time workforce. Evidence shows that large manufacturing firms in Britain are moving unevenly to different forms of flexibility: the number of part-time workers has been rising for some years, and now stands at 4.4 millions, about 21% of the employed workforce (Kelly, 1987c), and spread across the economy as a whole, these developments could produce deep fissures in the working class (IMS, 1986; Leadbeater, 1987); (v) trade unions are in decline.

The major implication of 'disorganisation' is that a particular type of labour movement and its associated modes of action are disappearing. The labour movement under disorganised capital-ism still exists and still engages in conflict (*pace* Gorz, 1982), but compared with the past it will be more fragmented and divided, because of the spatial dispersion of the workforce and the increased heterogeneity of the organised working class. Its capa-city to develop and sustain class consciousness, and to pursue class as opposed to merely sectional interests, will henceforth decline (cf. also Lash, 1985; Bauman, 1987; and Muller-Jentsch, 1986 and Touraine, 1986 who advance similar arguments for West Germany and France).

The End of Organized Capitalism rightly points to a series of transformations in capital, labour and the State that have gathered pace since the 1970s, and the existence of many of the trends it identifies is beyond dispute. But the argument also implies, quite wrongly, that these trends are secular: they are not short-term products of recession that will be reversed once an economic recovery is under way. If we return to the 1930s it becomes clear that many of the factors that are today supposed to herald the decline of class politics were also present then. In the 1930s Depression the traditional heartlands of the industrial working class, in steel, coal, textiles and shipbuilding, went into major decline; new industries sprang up in the Midlands and the South, many on greenfield sites with unorganised labour forces; craft or batch production was giving way to the mass production of consumer durables; population was moving from the depressed periphery of Britain into the boom towns of the Midlands and the South; workers were increasingly moving into new suburban estates; some employers were attempting to consolidate new patterns of industrial relations through national bargaining; and trade unions faced the daunting task of organising new groups of

mi-skilled production workers in towns and cities where the
bour movement had traditionally been weak. With the benefit
 hindsight we can see that these far-reaching transformations
d not have the negative effects on working-class organisation
d politics that Lash and Urry believe they will have in the
80s. But if no such effects were observed in the 1930s why
ould they be expected today?

Secondly, the 1930s experience suggests that many of the
ends identified by Lash and Urry may be reversible. Part of
eir argument hinges on the growth of new manufacturing
ants on greenfield sites with 'green' labour forces lacking any
dition of militancy, and often located in small towns. But this
scription would apply to many British factories in the 1920s
d 1930s, which only became organised during or after the War,
d which later became centres of workplace organisation and
ilitancy (cf. Exell, 1981 on the creation of trade unionism in the
wley car plants in the 1930s). Greenfield sites and green labour
rces do not remain green for ever, and unless it can be shown
at there is something qualitatively different about the new
anufacturing plants of the 1970s and 1980s (and Lash and Urry
ve not shown this) there is every reason to believe that in time
ese new facilities too will be organised by trade unions. Similar
guments can be made about small firms and small towns: many
 the small towns in the South East whose industrial base is
panding are fast becoming medium-sized towns as their
pulation grows—e.g. Basingstoke, Reading, Milton Keynes.

In any case, and this is the third point, the impact of
anufacturing decline and relocation can easily be exaggerated.
sh and Urry make the point that whilst 67% of manufacturing
ants with over 1,000 employees experienced a manual workers'
ike in 1979, the figure for establishments with under 10
ployees was just 2% (1987, p.107), and the implication is that
e decline in average manufacturing establishment size is work-
g against industrial militancy. But to concentrate solely on the
ry largest plants is misleading, because the militancy of
edium-sized plants (500-999 workers) is virtually identical to
at of the large plants (1,000+) (See Daniel and Millward, 1983,
ble IX.4, Row 1). If we combine these two categories of
tablishment and examine their relative significance over time,
 find the following: in 1974 these medium and large establish-
ents comprised 6.4% of British factories with more than 20
ployees, but contained 44.6% of the manufacturing workforce.
 1983 these factories made up 5% of the total and contained

43.3% of the workforce (figures calculated from data in Harman 1986, p.6). This is hardly a stunning decline, and it shows tha the falling trend amongst large plants has been considerabl exaggerated (cf. also Gordon, 1988 on similar trends in the US

Equally exaggerated have been the claims for class de alignment in voting patterns, where Lash and Urry relied heavil on the arguments of Crewe and his colleagues. Class de alignment was measured by first dividing the workforce int manual and non-manual, and by assuming that they will vo respectively for parties of the Left and Right. The more manua workers vote for right-wing parties, the more class de-alignmen is said to have taken place, which is reasonable enough. But o the measure employed by Lash and Urry (the Alford index) cla de-alignment also occurs if non-manual workers vote for the lef So when white-collar workers join trade unions, engage i industrial militancy and vote for the left, this, according to Las and Urry, represents the decline of class voting and clas consciousness. This result is so bizarre as to cast grave doubt o the way in which Lash and Urry have conceptualised an measured voting trends. Moreover, through relying on a crud two-way division of voters into manual and non-manual, the have lumped together into the latter category routine clerica workers and company directors. By dividing the workforce mor finely into five skill/occupational bands, Heath et al. (1985) hav shown that social class still exerts a major influence on votin patterns, even in Britain where as we showed earlier the Labou Party has performed abysmally by the standards of worker parties elsewhere.

It is nonetheless true that the core industrial working class ha declined, both absolutely and relatively, in almost all capitali countries, and whilst economic recovery might lead to som expansion of the industrial workforce it is unlikely to act as major counterweight against what does seem to be a secula downward trend. We showed earlier that the decline of th industrial working class has not been translated into a ubiquitou decline in the electoral fortunes of workers' parties (Table 10 above). Moreover, it is worth putting the decline of manufactur ing into historical perspective. In Britain the manufacturin workforce comprised 26.4% of civilian employment in 198 (Rowthorn, 1987, p.5). On the threshold of the 1968-74 worl strike wave, the Italian workforce contained 25.8% of manufac turing workers, the French 28.7%, the Canadian 23.9%, th Swedish 31.2%, the Australian 28.6% (Rowthorn, 1987, Tabl

.3). In other words the world strike wave at the end of the
post-war boom was conducted by working classes whose indust-
ial composition was very similar to that of the British workforce
oday.

It is true that in the long run it is the private services sector
vhich is most likely to experience employment growth, and the
veakness of trade unionism amongst such workers has been used
o suggest that unions face a bleak future. But it is important not
o exaggerate the effect of this trend or to assume that unions will
ake no appropriate action in meeting it. The growth of white-
collar employment, for instance, has been responded to with
great energy and skill by unions such as ASTMS (now merged
vith TASS to form MSF), and where white-collar union density
tood at 33% in 1948, it had reached 44% by 1979. Secondly,
vithin the services sector as a whole rates of unionisation are
ighly uneven. In hotels and retail distribution national union
lensity was under 20% in 1979, but in banking, insurance and
inance it stood at 54.8% in the same year. Thirdly, the trend for
ervices capital to become more concentrated, through growth of
verage establishment size—hyperstores for instance—and
hrough mergers between firms, is likely to concentrate a rising
proportion of the services labour force in large firms which have
raditionally been easier to organise (cf. *Labour Research*, Nov.
986, p.3 on concentration in the contract cleaning industry). So
even if many service establishments (workplaces) do remain
mall they are increasingly likely to belong to a large chain of
establishments whose national workforce is substantial (see
Table 10.9 below)

Table 10.9 Employment in selected service sector firms 1986

Firm	UK Employees
Sainsbury's	64,007
Tesco	60,781
Marks & Spencer	56,444
Trust House Forte	55,400
Boots	55,311
ASDA-MFI	41,182
McDonalds	15,000

Sources: *Labour Research*, June 1986, p.12; July 1986, p.20; December 1986, p.14.

A similar point can be made about part-time workers who clearly do pose problems for trade unions which have tradition- ally preferred to organise full-time workers in large establish- ments; but again the problem should not be exaggerated. In the health service, for instance, union density amongst part-time employees is only slightly lower than among full-time employees, suggesting that where there is social interaction between full- and part-timers in large establishments and/or large bargaining units, and where union recruitment is taken seriously, part-timers can be successfully recruited (Bain and Price, 1983). Problems with part-time workers are more likely to occur in smaller establish- ments, or in small bargaining units.

It should also be noted that government action can and does have a significant impact on the willingness of employers to recognise and bargain with trade unions, as was shown during both World Wars and in the 1970s. This can be seen even more clearly when we compare the growth patterns of Canadian and American trade unions. With similar types of legislation both movements recorded similar trends in membership until the mid-1960s, when Canadian law was altered in directions favour- able to labour. Thereafter Canadian union density rose from around 30% to almost 40%, whilst US density declined to below 20% (Freeman, 1987; Beaumont, 1987, pp.49-50). There is every reason to suppose that a pro-trade union government will again be elected in Britain and that its policies will facilitate union growth in many sectors of the economy.

Finally the talk of 'new' worker attitudes, and the problems of organising workers with new, individualistic preferences and outlooks, needs to be placed in historical perspective. Through- out its history the British trade union movement has repeatedly confronted groups of workers whom it was widely said could never be organised. In the 1860s and 1870s the semiskilled factory workers were 'beyond organisation'. Irish immigrant labourers were thought to have no interest in unions. Women workers were too interested in domestic life to bother with unions. Clerical workers in the early part of this century were petit- bourgeois, and hostile to the rest of the working class. Workers in the new mass production industries of the South and Midlands that sprang up in the 1930s were money-orientated and out for themselves. Scientists and technicians in the 1960s were profes- sionals who would never join trade unions. Managers in the 1970s were considered beyond the scope of unions because of their loyalty to their firms.

At each successive period of restructuring of the working class trade unions have successfully surmounted the barriers erected by their critics, and have organised workers who were tradition- ally hostile to or uninterested in unions. The sophisticated employment practices of many large, non-union firms have been designed to minimise the incentives (and raise the costs) for such workers to join unions at all. But sooner or later competitive pressures will lead many of these firms to erode their employees' rights and expectations, and the cost-benefit ratio of unionising will shift in the unions' favour. The fear that unions will be unable to meet the new challenges of the 1980s and 1990s is therefore quite groundless and in the longer term trade union membership will continue its upward trend.

Conclusions

In general, and with some notable exceptions, British trade unions have weathered the recession remarkably well. Mem- bership and density have declined, but less than in previous recessions; workplace organisation has remained largely intact and is still expanding in the public sector; union finances are fairly sound; real wages for many of those in work have increased since 1981; and unions were completely successful in the political fund ballots despite the alleged unpopularity of the unions' political voice.

Those who believe in a crisis of the labour movement have made a series of analytical errors. They have mistaken short-term cyclical trends, such as the decline in union membership, strike frequency and bargaining power, for long-term, secular trends. All previous evidence suggests that these three indicators will rise again as the economy moves out of recession, and those who think otherwise have provided no convincing grounds for their beliefs. The scale of some trends, such as the 'no-strike' deals or the decline of strike-prone manufacturing plants, has been exagger- ated. More widespread or durable trends, such as the growth in joint consultative committees, or worker share-ownership, have been analysed as determinants of new attitudes amongst workers and trade unions, a proposition for which there is hardly any convincing and reliable evidence. In other cases pertinent evi- dence has simply been ignored altogether. The claim that workers have become increasingly dissatisfied with their unions and with union political links to Labour is contradicted by opinion poll data and by the overwhelming success of the trade union political fund ballots.

The claim that many of the problems of the labour movement are the inevitable products of economic restructuring and long-term shifts in working-class composition is frequently made but rarely backed up with hard evidence. The fact is that labour movement responses to these uniform changes are highly variable across countries, and there are simply no grounds for stating that union membership decline or falling Labour support are the inexorable end-products of changes in the composition of the working class.

PART THREE

Conclusions

11
Conclusions

Trade Unions, Class Consciousness and Socialist Strategy

The classical Marxist analyses of trade unionism were concerned with two principal questions: under what conditions would the majority of workers become politically class conscious, and what role would trade unions composed of such workers play in the transition to socialism? Marx and Engels correctly argued that the capitalist mode of production would always conjure into being a working class which would then organise itself into trade unions and into political parties based on socialism. With a few notable exceptions (such as the USA) these predictions have been amply vindicated and trade unions and workers' parties have put down roots and grown in almost every capitalist country. But despite these facts, and despite the ubiquitous character of industrial conflict between labour and capital, socialist transition in the advanced capitalist countries has yet to be achieved. Neither workers' class consciousness nor trade union action and policy has developed in the way that Marx and Engels foresaw.

The classical Marxist tradition offered two further preconditions for socialist advance, one of which at least remains undisputed even today. The necessity for an independent working-class political party was derived by Engels and Lenin from their accurate observation that most trade union action was designed to improve workers' terms and conditions of employment within capitalism. Yet the unintended consequence of union bargaining with employers was to provide workers with less and less incentive to overthrow an economic system from which they could clearly extract some benefits, in order to take an historical 'leap in the dark', into socialism. Consequently, the classical Marxists stressed a second precondition for socialist advance in the form of periodic economic crises. These would inflict so much damage to workers' conditions of life and employment that the propaganda of revolutionary socialism would start to find a highly receptive audience. At the close of the First World War the economic crisis—political party couplet seemed sufficient to understand the revolutionary wave that was then sweeping across Europe. But the failure of socialist advance in the wake of the economic crises of the 1930s and the 1960s-80s forced the need for rethinking. We can now see that Lenin's insistence on the need for an independent revolutionary party was only a partial theoretical answer to the question of what determines the development of political class consciousness. The same criticism can be made of Trotsky whose stark picture of a world poised between socialism and barbarism looked increasingly anachronistic as the post-war economic boom gathered pace. Even less convincing was his schematic vision of a revolutionary proletariat repeatedly held back and demobilised only by the treachery of its leaders (see Chapter 7).

From the corpus of classical Marxism it was possible to discern two distinct attempts to construct a *strategy* through which trade unions and political parties could enhance the class consciousness of workers and advance towards socialism. One tradition, starting with Luxemburg, emphasised the mobilisation of workers in struggle, in what might be called (following Gramsci) a 'war of maneouvre'. Luxemburg rightly pointed out that many individual strikes have little impact on the consciousness of their participants as they are normally limited affairs of short duration fought over local, economic issues. But during a *wave* of strikes, when there is an unusually high level of worker mobilisation, a different set of events is brought into play. Characteristically, there will be pressure on the capitalist state to intervene so as to restore law and order and protect capitalist profits and investments against the encroachments of labour militancy. State intervention, particularly if it takes a partisan and repressive form directed against labour, is likely to polarise society around the two major social classes, and temporarily elevate questions of class identity, interests and power to the centre of the political stage. Under such conditions organised labour has the opportunity to effect a major shift in the balance of power against capital.

Luxemburg's theory of strike waves is the most compelling and insightful attempt by any Marxist to analyse the dynamics of political class consciousness. It insists that the radicalising potential of industrial militancy is highly circumscribed to those historical periods marked by strike waves which trigger off a particular set of reactions by employers and the capitalist state. Outside of such periods and such reactions there is no reason to expect that strikes and strike waves will radicalise large numbers of workers. Luxemburg's theory therefore has the supreme virtue of being testable against empirical evidence.

The analysis of strikes and class consciousness in Chapter 5 showed that for three British strike waves (1915-22, 1968-74, 1977-79) the pattern of outcomes for class consciousness was consistent with Luxemburg's argument. The greater scale of worker mobilisation, strikes and state repression at the end of the First World War helped produce a dramatic upsurge of political class consciousness amongst workers, despite the fact that most of the strikes at this period were 'simply' wage disputes. The events of 1968-74 involved fewer workers and days lost and less overt and repressive state intervention.

Nevertheless, this period also witnessed some leftward shifts in political attitudes, the re-emergence of the political strike, an upsurge of factory occupations, marked shifts to the left in TUC and Labour Party policies, a growth of the far left and the consolidation of a new balance of power in additional legal rights and institutional reforms at the workplace (such as shop steward facilities, training etc.). Close examination of the empirical evidence suggests that whilst 1977-79 was a close approximation to 'pure' economistic militancy, 1968-74 was not.

Thus whilst it is wrong to argue that almost any strike can radicalise workers, it is equally wrong to follow Lenin's claim of 1902 that economic militancy can have no impact on political class consciousness. The central point about Luxemburg's theory is that it is the scale of mobilisation and ruling-class reaction that determine the impact of strikes on political class consciousness, *not* the initial demands of the strikers. A wave of 'purely' economic strikes (as in 1915-22) can have a dramatic effect on workers' class consciousness provided the other components specified in Luxemburg's theory are in place.

If Luxemburg's mass strike theory loosely corresponds to a Gramscian 'war of manoeuvre', then the second strategy for socialist advance through trade union action corresponds much more clearly to a 'war of position'. Although there are many variants of this strategy the core proposition is that trade union advance towards socialism consists of a process of encroaching control over capitalist prerogatives (Chapters 8, 9). In this view labour and capital have sufficient interests in common, and sufficient power to damage one another very seriously, to make it both feasible and sensible for the parties to negotiate wide-ranging compromises. At enterprise level, through various forms of 'industrial democracy', workers and their representatives have insisted on being involved in key economic decisions. Likewise, at the level of the State, labour and capital would negotiate agreements giving workers influence over major decisions. In return workers would be expected to guarantee at least some of the interests of capital, for otherwise no agreement would be possible. So workers might agree to accept technical change, to abide by disputes procedures, or to restrain pay demands, to give just three examples.

The calculation is that in the long run workers will be the net beneficiaries of such exchanges as their accumulating power resources (trade union membership and organisation, political party support etc.) shift the terms of the exchange in labour's favour. At the same time the gradual expansion of workers' involvement in decision-making will develop in them a sense of their own power and of their interests in taking over the 'commanding heights of the economy'. The Swedish labour movement has often been held up as an example of this type of strategy in action, and there has been some discussion about its feasibility for Britain.

In principle this type of strategy could well prove feasible, and the charge that it *necessarily* entails the 'incorporation' of labour has been examined and rejected. Nevertheless, any strategy of encroaching control does confront difficulties in the form of capital's mobility, as well as the limitations of economic reform of enterprises within a competitive economy regulated by profit. Moreover, in the case of Britain the institutional conditions required to sustain an enduring exchange between labour and capital are largely absent. The 'Swedish road to socialism' rests on a highly centralised system of national collective bargaining between the peak federations of labour (LO) and capital (SAF). The federations in turn enjoy considerable power over their affiliate members, and exercise their functions in a political system notable for a string of Social Democratic electoral victories. This fact has provided labour with a powerful resource and capital with a compelling incentive to cooperate with labour in sustaining a system of 'political exchange'. At the same time the dependency of the tiny Swedish economy on exports and competitiveness in world markets has given labour an incentive to cooperate with capital in productivity growth and technical change.

Unfortunately, these institutional conditions are largely absent from Britain, where the system of collective bargaining remains highly fragmented, the central federations (TUC and CBI) very weak, the political system volatile, and the economy both open and internationalised. Nor is it possible to foresee any way in which these conditions could be changed to approximate more closely to those in Sweden.

Consequently, this second road to socialism, based on encroaching control over capitalist prerogatives and institutions, is best regarded as inappropriate for Britain. There is little point in merely wishing that things were different, or hoping that somehow things will change, because in all probability they won't. A socialist strategy for the trade unions in Britain will therefore be forced to rely on the outcomes of periodic worker mobilisation in strikes, as envisaged by Luxemburg.

Marxism and its Critics

The claim that workers' struggles can develop political class consciousness and comprise a major element in a transition to socialism is not without its critics, both Marxist and non-Marxist. Although earlier parts of this book have dealt with a host of specific objections to particular claims, it is worth stepping back a little at this point and reflecting on some of the larger objections to Marxist arguments of this type. Broadly speaking, there are three serious objections that merit examination and rebuttal.

The non-revolutionary character of trade unions and of workers' interests

Pluralist writers have reacted sharply to the idea that unions contain the germs or embryos of any wider, political class consciousness:

> What I find so objectionable as well as invalid in the Marxist view is its implicit contempt for 'pure and simple' trade unionism. Trade unions, by doggedly sticking to their immediate ends and refusing to

be captured and exploited by any political party, have gradually transformed society. Only not according to the sacred text or the dialectical laws (Flanders, 1970, p.59)

More recently, Crouch (1982), whilst noting the strengths of Marxist inquiry, summarised its central weakness in these terms:

> To construct an entire theory of trade unionism around a non-existent phenomenon—the revolutionary working class—is to produce something of limited usefulness in understanding the real day-to-day choices of trade unions and their members. But that is what Marxist sociology has chosen to do (Crouch, 1982, pp.219-20).

Crouch is by no means alone in rejecting Marx's belief in the revolutionary working class. Other British sociologists, such as Mann (1973), adopted a similar position many years ago, whilst the French ex-Marxist André Gorz bid farewell to the working class on the grounds that 'working-class demands have turned into consumerist mass demands' (Gorz, 1982, p.40). The persistent belief that the working class remained in essence a revolutionary agency despite many appearances to the contrary was in Gorz's view merely a sign of the baleful influence of Hegelian Marxism, not a tribute to the revolutionary fidelity of Marxists.

These writers imply that to show that workers through trade unions 'only' struggle to satisfy their basic material interests in pay and conditions of employment is *ipso facto* to prove the non-existence of a revolutionary working class. There are three grounds for believing this argument to be invalid. First, it is wholly unrealistic to expect the majority of workers to be mobilised in struggle on anything other than their basic material interests. Second, this fact is wholly consistent with the likelihood of workers becoming class conscious because their material interests can be shown to be incompatible with the major features of capitalist economies. And third, the pursuit of such material interests can help to create conditions of economic and political crisis in which a transition to socialism becomes more probable.

The trade union emphasis on wages is not an expression of a 'crisis of consciousness' (Carter, 1986, p.12) but a product of the material circumstances of most workers and of the particular historical development of class relations in Britain. In 1981 Pond (1983) estimated that 25% of the British workforce were low-paid, i.e. earned less than £85 per week (a figure equal to two-thirds of median adult male earnings). Above these workers, but below the average weekly earnings for the whole economy (£190 per week in 1986) are the majority of manual workers in manufacturing as well as manual and some non-manual employees in the public sector and in private services. Even though these workers are better off than the most lowly-paid, they still experience economic problems as their family income will often fluctuate because of changes in overtime working, shift patterns, bonus pay, part-time hours worked by some members of the family, and job insecurity.

Moreover, many workers in Britain, particularly if they belong to trade unions, have come to expect that their standard of living will rise each year, and annual pay bargaining (as opposed to two- or three-year pay deals) therefore remains deeply rooted in the British system of industrial relations. For the same reason cost of living continues to feature as one of the most salient and widely used arguments in defence of pay rises (Millward and Stevens, 1986, Tables 9.17, 9.18). So long as there is some level of inflation in the economy, eroding the value of workers' incomes, the pressure for cost of living rises will rightly continue to be very powerful.

In addition, many workers expect that as their firms become more efficient and increase their sales and profits, then they will share in the proceeds of this economic growth, and will rightly insist on the justice and equity of their demands to do so. Finally, many workers will be influenced in their pay demands by the types of pay rise gained by other *similar* groups of workers, or the current levels of pay enjoyed by those groups. Most workers compare themselves with people doing similar jobs, not with the low paid. Skilled engineers do not feel well off just because they earn more than hairdressers, but judge their earnings by comparison with rates paid to engineers in neighbouring firms, and in the light of the employer's ability to pay.

It can moreover be shown that workers do have an objective interest in eliminating a mode of production based on the private ownership of the means of production and the pursuit of profit. It is, of course, very fashionable to dismiss the concept of 'objective interest' as '. . . little more than an arbitary attribution, . . . by the analyst, to a certain category of social agents' (Laclau and Mouffe, 1985, p.83). Although the concept of objective interest has been abused, that does not make it worthless. Let us take the familiar argument that most workers are highly motivated to obtain high and steadily rising earnings, job security, and an optimum degree of job satisfaction based on the exercise of skill and self-direction. The salience of these preferences is beyond dispute, having been confirmed in many attitude surveys, and manifested in collective bargaining and strike demands (cf. Wright, 1985, p.249; Kochan et al., 1986, p.210). Marxists would argue that these preferences cannot be satisfactorily met for the majority of workers throughout their lives in a predominantly capitalist economy. The pressure of economic competition will force firms to try and raise continually the productivity of labour, periodically necessitating redundancy for workers 'surplus to requirements'. The decline of particular branches of industry will render obsolete particular skills and displace workers onto the labour market. Periodic recessions will affect large numbers of workers in this way in the private sector whilst similar problems (albeit to a lesser degree) will be felt by state employees. In other words the inevitability of industrial restructuring by individual firms, and of periodic economic crises, in a society where no agency has the incentive as well as the power to promote 'full employment', will conflict with workers' own preferences for job and income security. If we define 'full employment' as a level of unemployment below 2 per cent, then even the wealthy capitalist economy of Great Britain has achieved full employment in only thirteen out of twenty-six peacetime years this century. Consequently, it can be argued that workers have an interest in a type of economic system from which unplanned restructuring and periodic crisis have been eliminated (cf. also E.M. Wood, 1986, Chap.12). That workers may actually think otherwise is a contradiction in their own thought which Marxists are perfectly entitled to point out.

What then needs to be shown is that there are conditions under which people would support socialist measures. Once again Laclau and Mouffe (1985) have objected to this type of question. They maintain that Marxists have looked for guarantees of class consciousness in the endogenous development of the capitalist economy and its labour process, and its production of a homogenised and deskilled working class. Although Braverman (1974) has argued in this fashion, very few Marxists have been prepared to follow him, and most labour process theorists have either avoided the issue of class consciousness altogether, or advanced far more complex models of its determination (Kelly, 1987a). Whilst Laclau and Mouffe are right to criticise Braverman's reasoning, they are wrong to regard him as representative of all Marxists, and to ignore those who argue that class consciousness is most likely to develop in the course of class struggle.

Normally workers inhabit a world that is heavily constrained and seemingly very difficult to change, and they therefore choose courses of action, and economic and political goals, which appear to have some reasonable chance of success: redundancy compensation rather than the guaranteed right to work for example. Only under conditions of political crisis (usually associated with economic crisis) is the 'givenness' and 'immutability' of the social world likely to be questioned. Under such conditions the contingency and mutability of institutions becomes more apparent, and the range of political choices available to workers may expand. Workers may therefore become more receptive to ideas of radical change, previously discounted (if they were considered at all) on the grounds of impracticability. It is this line of reasoning that leads Marxists to a particular interest in periods of crisis as they provide favourable conditions for the growth of class consciousness. This counterfactual argument is a perfectly legitimate one because it can specify conditions under which predicted changes in consciousness should occur. In other words, it is an argument which, in principle, can be tested and refuted (cf. Balbus, 1971).

Given that workers are most likely to participate in trade union actions over basic material interests, and given that these interests are incompatible with capitalism, a transition to socialism becomes feasible for two reasons: because of the unintended consequences of industrial militancy and because of the logic of trade union political action. Assuming that industrial militancy, particularly in strike waves, has a damaging effect on profits, discourages investment and contributes to unemployment, workers will almost certainly turn to political involvement to correct these unintended effects of their own actions (Crouch, 1982, Chap.6). Hence over the years trade unions have become increasingly involved in macro-economic policy as a way of reducing unemployment. But this involvement has a logic of its own which pushes trade unions into ever more detailed and extensive regulation of private economic activity and business decisions—on training, output, investment and so on. As one set of measures proves ineffective or disappointing then workers and union strategists are forced to consider additional and often more radical ways of controlling private capital. Hence, starting from the observation that workers and trade unions 'merely' struggle over basic economic issues, it is possible to show that such struggles do have an anti-capitalist potential, one that can be realised under the conditions specified by Luxemburg.

The benefits of capitalism and the costs of socialist transition

Even if all of the above was accepted, it could still be argued that a rational worker would never 'opt' for socialism, because, as Przeworski put it, 'the process of transition must involve a deterioration of the material conditions of workers' (Przeworski 1986, p.180; cf. also Elster, 1985, p.530). And Crouch (1982) made a similar point when he observed that *if* workers had nothing to lose but their chains, then opting for socialism would be rational; but as workers actually derive substantial benefits under capitalism then any such venture would be costly and thus foolhardy.

There are three counters to this objection. First, the argument assumes that in a revolutionary or crisis situation where socialist transition was 'on the agenda', opting for socialism carries net costs, whilst remaining within capitalism does not. But it would be just as rational to assume that a working class which refused the socialist option and remained with capitalism would suffer net costs as well. This might happen because such a refusal could signal working-class weakness to the employers and to state functionaries and thereby encourage them to instigate assaults on workers' hitherto protected material interests and conditions. Nor is this scenario mere speculation, for it depicts exactly what happened to the Italian and Chilean labour movements when both refused to embark on the costly road of socialist transition. In 1922 Italy fell to the fascists, and in 1973 Chile fell under a military dictatorship.

Secondly, if it were true that rational workers were averse to the costs involved in radical change, it is not obvious why any workers ever go on strike. For economists have repeatedly proved that even a successful wage strike lasting more than a few days will almost certainly cost workers more in lost wages than they can hope to recoup through a higher pay settlement. If workers are so rational, and are concerned only with their immediate material interests, as Przeworski (1986) argues, why do they ever strike? Since we know that workers do strike, and that many do it repeatedly, then they cannot be deterred by rational calculations of short-term material self-interest.

The third objection to this account of material self-interest is that it assumes workers could have sufficient information to enable them to reach an informed judgement about the costs and benefits of different courses of action. But in an economic and political crisis such decision-making will occur under conditions of acute uncertainty, making it difficult, if not impossible, to calculate the net costs and benefits of various courses of action. Consequently, workers are likely to be influenced by a host of other factors—moral and emotional appeals, the attributes of labour leaders, the attitudes of fellow workers etc. (cf. Waddington, 1987; Hartley et al., 1983 on decision-making by strikers).

The achievement of a unified class conscious majority

A final objection to the arguments advanced in this book would question the likelihood of the majority of workers ever becoming fully class conscious in the Marxist sense. Surely, it could be argued, the evidence from strike waves discussed in Chapter 5 shows that under such conditions it is only a minority of workers who are radicalised, whilst the majority continue to be preoccupied with their own local or sectional interests, as discussed in Chapter 6 (cf. Laclau and Mouffe, 1985).

Allied to this argument is the view that the organised working class is becoming increasingly complex and differentiated in its occupational structure. Where once the trade union movement was a relatively homogeneous body of mostly male full-time manual workers in heavy industry, it now consists of a wide range of occupational groups—miners and managers, seafarers and scientists. Half the trade unions are affiliated to the Labour Party, but many of the white-collar and civil service unions are not. Women and ethnic minorities now comprise substantial minorities of trade unionists, as do part-time workers (again, mostly women). Surely, this increased differentiation of the labour movement renders the achievement of a unified, politically conscious proletariat close to impossible?

I think it is correct to say that the majority of workers are unlikely to attain class consciousness in the full Marxist sense, but it is wrong to conclude (as do Laclau and Mouffe, 1985) that this invalidates the socialist project. For the reality of that project is that it will be carried through by a coalition of forces, with organised workers at its heart. This coalition will be composed of a small minority of class conscious activists, but a large majority of people motivated by varying mixtures of self-interest (as workers, consumers, environmentalists, women, gays, pacifists, etc.) and progressive values. Some labour movements, such as those in Sweden or Italy, may be able to construct class-conscious majorities, but the fragmented nature of trade unions and industrial relations makes this an extremely difficult task in Britain. Fox (1985) put this view very well when he said:

304

> Members of a group conscious of workplace conflict with their
> employers might well . . . see other groups similarly placed. They
> might . . . help them with funds. A very few might take the further
> considerable step of abstracting from these experiences and interna-
> lising general concepts of structural class conflict . . . [and] they
> might be regarded as having full working-class consciousness in the
> Marxist sense. In situations and periods of special grievance, excite-
> ment, or frustration, they might command the ear of their fellows
> who, while not internalising the analysis in any committed sense
> would find that it spoke to their mood . . . Suitably intense and
> prolonged, a situation of this kind is as much as revolutionaries can
> hope for. If successful revolutions depended on mass understanding-
> . . . the world would have seen few indeed (Fox, 1985, p.122).

It is to those periods of 'special grievance', marked by waves of
strikes and industrial conflict, that socialists must look for the
seeds of radicalisation, and for the forces that will shift the
balance of power decisively and finally against capital. Trade
unions will play an essential role in this process as the principal
agents of working-class mobilisation, but, as Marxists have
always recognised, the unions must work in tandem with a mass
socialist political party, something that Britain conspicuously
lacks. One of our major hopes for the immediate future must
therefore be that such a party emerges from the radicalisation
brought about by the next wave of strikes to hit the British
economy. Once that happens the full fruits of militant trade
unionism can then be reaped.

References

Abbreviations

MECW: Marx-Engels Collected Works, London, Lawrence & Wishart, 1975. (Where possible reference to the works of Marx and Engels is to this edition).

Lenin CW: Lenin's Collected Works, 4th English Edition, Moscow, Progress, 1960-70.

(P): Pamphlet

Date of publication is as in the bracket following author's name, except where reference is made to a different edition (such as MECW). *Place of publication* is London unless otherwise shown.

Aaronovitch, S. (1981) *The Road From Thatcherism*, Lawrence & Wishart.

ACAS, *Annual Reports* (various years) Advisory Conciliation and Arbitration Service.

Adeney, M. and Lloyd, J. (1986) *The Miners' Strike 1984-5: loss without limit*, Routledge and Kegan Paul.

Aglietta, M. (1979) *A Theory of Capitalist Regulation: the US experience*, New Left Books.

Albrow, M. (1970) *Bureaucracy*, Macmillan.

Allen, T. et al. (1978) 'The recession: capitalist offensive and the working class', *Revolutionary Communist Papers*, 3, July.

Allen, V.L. (1981) *The Militancy of British Miners*, Moor Press.

ALP-ACTU (1983) *Statement of Accord Between the Australian Labor Party and the Australian Council of Trade Unions Regarding Economic Policy*, Australia, ALP, ACTU.

Althusser, L. (1979a) 'Contradiction and overdetermination'. In Althusser, L., *For Marx*, Verso.

Althusser, L. (1979b) 'The materialist dialectic'. In Althusser, L., *For Marx*, Verso.

Anderson, P. (1967) 'The limits and possibilities of trade union action' In Blackburn, R. and Cockburn, A. (eds) *The Incompatibles: Trade Union Militancy and the Consensus*, Penguin.

Anderson, P. (1976) *Considerations on Western Marxism*, Verso.

Andrews, A. (1983) 'NHS: lessons of '82 key to coming struggles' *Workers' Socialist Review*, *3*, April/May.

APEX (n.d.) *Industrial Democracy?: Evidence to the Committee of Inquiry on Industrial Democracy*, APEX.

Armstrong, P., Glyn, A. and Harrison, J. (1984) *Capitalism Since World War 11*, Fontana.

AUEW (1976) *An Investigation Into The Scope of Industrial Democracy* AUEW.

Bain, G., Bacon, R. and Pimlott, J. (1972), 'The labour force'. In Halsey A., (ed), *Trends in British Society Since 1900*, Macmillan.

Bain, G. and Price, R. (1983) 'Union growth: dimensions, determinant and destiny'. In Bain, G. (ed), *Industrial Relations in Britain*, Oxford Blackwell.

Balbus, I., (1971) 'The concept of "interest" in pluralist and Marxian analysis', *Politics and Society*, *1 (2)*.

Ballentine, A., (1986) *An investigation to ascertain the validity of the assertion that the period since 1951 has seen an increase in sectionalism within the trade union movement*, London School of Economics, MSc thesis.

Bamber, G. and Lansbury, R. (eds) (1987) *International and Comparative Industrial Relations*, Allen & Unwin.

Bambery, C. (1985) 'Marx and Engels and the unions', *International Socialism*, *2:26*.

Banda, M. (1972) *Marxism or Rank-and-File-ism?*, Socialist Labour League (P).

Barker, C. (1972) *The Power Game*, Pluto Press (P).

Barratt-Brown, M., Coates, K. and Topham, T. (1975) 'Workers control versus "revolutionary" theory', *Socialist Register 1975*, Merlin

Bassett, P. (1986) *Strike Free: New Industrial Relations in Britain*, Macmil lan.

Batstone, E. (1984) *Working Order*, Oxford: Blackwell.

Batstone, E. and Davis, P. (1976) *Industrial Democracy: European Experi ence*, HMSO.

Batstone, E., Boraston, I. and Frenkel, S. (1977) *Shop Stewards in Action* Oxford: Blackwell.

Batstone, E., Ferner, A. and Terry, M. (1983) *Unions on the Board* Oxford: Blackwell.

Batstone, E. and Gourlay, S. (1986) *Unions, Unemployment and Innovation* Oxford: Blackwell.

Bauman, Z. (1987) 'Fighting the wrong shadow', *New Statesman*, 25 Sept.

Beale, J. (1983) *Getting It Together: Women as Trade Unionists*, Pluto Press.

Bean, R. (1985) *Comparative Industrial Relations*, Croom Helm.

Beaumont, P.B. (1987) *The Decline of Trade Union Organisation*, Croom Helm.

Beecham, D. (1981) 'Updating the downturn: the class struggle under the Tories', *International Socialism*, 2:14.

Beecham, D. (1984) 'How far has rank and file organisation been weakened and incorporated?', *International Socialism*, 2:23.

Beilharz, P. (1986) 'The Australian Left: beyond Labourism?', *Socialist Register 1985/86*, Merlin.

Bell, G., et al. (1977) *The Battle of Grunwick: View from the Left*, Socialist Challenge (P).

Bernstein, E. (1909) *Evolutionary Socialism* (first publ. 1902), ILP.

Beyme, K. von (1980) *Challenge to Power: trade unions and industrial relations in capitalist countries*, Sage.

Beyme, K. von (1985) *Political Parties in Western Democracies*, Gower.

Beynon, H. (1984) *Working for Ford*, Penguin.

Birchall, I. (1981) *'The Smallest Mass Party in the World': Building the Socialist Workers Party 1951-1979*, Socialist Workers Party (P).

Blumberg, P. (1968) *Industrial Democracy*, Constable.

Blumler, J. and Ewbank, A. (1970) 'Trade unionists, the mass media and unofficial strikes', *British Journal of Industrial Relations*, 8(1).

Bonner, S.E. (1981) *A Revolutionary For Our Times: Rosa Luxemburg*, Pluto Press.

Boraston, I., Clegg, H. and Rimmer, M. (1975) *Workplace and Union*, Heinemann.

Bordiga, A. (1920a) 'Towards the establishment of workers' councils in Italy'. In Gramsci, A. (1977), *Selections from Political Writings 1910-1920*, Lawrence & Wishart.

Bordiga, A. (1920b) 'Seize power or seize the factory?' In ibid.

Boston, S. (1987) *Women Workers and the Trade Unions*. 2nd edition, Lawrence & Wishart.

Bradley, K. and Gelb, A. (1986) *Share Ownership for Employees*, Public Policy Centre.

Brannen, P. et al. (1976) *The Worker Directors*, Hutchinson.

Brannen, P. (1983) 'Worker directors: an approach to analysis'. In Crouch, C. and Heller, F. (eds), *The International Yearbook of Organisational Democracy*, Vol.1, Wiley.

Branson, N. (1985) *History of the Communist Party of Great Britain 1927-1941*, Lawrence & Wishart.

Braverman, H. (1974) *Labor and Monopoly Capital*, New York: Monthly Review Press.

Brecher, J. (1972) *Strike!* Boston, Mass.: South End Press.

Brindle, D. (1987) 'Unloved and underpaid', *Marxism Today*, 31 (6), June.

British & Irish Communist Organisation (1984) *A Striking Contrast: Scargill & Gormley*, Belfast, BICO (P).

Bullock, P., and Yaffe, D. (1975) 'Inflation, the crisis and the postwar boom', *Revolutionary Communist*, 3/4, November.

Burawoy, M. (1979) *Manufacturing Consent*, Chicago: University of Chicago Press.

308

Burgess, K. (1980) *The Challenge of Labour*, Croom Helm.

Butler, D. and Sloman, A. (1980) *British Political Facts 1900-1979*, Macmillan.

Callinicos, A. (1982) 'The rank and file movement today', *International Socialism, 2:17.*

Callinicos, A. (1983a) *The Revolutionary Road to Socialism*, Socialist Workers Party.

Callinicos, A. (1983b) *The Revolutionary Ideas of Karl Marx*, Bookmarks.

Callinicos, A. and Simons, M. (1985) *The Great Strike: the Miners' Strike of 1984-5 and Its Lessons*, Socialist Workers Party.

Cameron, D.R. (1984) 'Social democracy, corporatism, labour quiescence, and the representation of economic interest in advanced capitalist society'. In Goldthrope, J.H. (ed), *Order and Conflict in Contemporary Capitalism*, Oxford: Clarendon Press.

Campbell, B. (1982) 'Women: not what they bargained for', *Marxism Today, 26(3)*, March.

Campbell, B. (1986) 'Proletarian patriarchs and the real radicals'. In Seddon, V. (ed), *The Cutting Edge: Women and the Pit Strike*, Lawrence & Wishart.

Carew, A. (1976) *Democracy and Government in European Trade Unions*, Allen & Unwin.

Carruth, A. and Disney, R. (1986) *Where Have Two Million Trade Union Members Gone?*, LSE, mimeo.

Carter, P (1981) Chapter (untitled) in Hobsbawm, E., *The Forward March of Labour Halted?*, Verso.

Carter, P. (1985) 'Striking the right note', *Marxism Today 29(3)*, March.

Carter, P. (1986) *Trade Unions: the New Reality. The Communist View*, CPGB (P).

Certification Officer, *Annual Reports*, Certification Office

Chernyayev, A.S. et al. (1980) *The International Working-class Movement, Volume 1: the Origins of the Proletariat and its Evolution as a Revolutionary Class*, Moscow: Progress Publishers.

Clarke, T. (1977) 'Industrial democracy: the institutionalised suppression of industrial conflict'. In Clarke, T. and Clements, L. (eds.), *Trade Unions Under Capitalism*, Fontana.

Claudin, F. (1977) 'Democracy and dictatorship in Lenin and Kautsky', *New Left Review, 106*, Nov/Dec.

Claudin, F. (1978) *Eurocommunism and Socialism*, New Left Books.

Clay, T. (1987) *Nurses: Power and Politics*, Heinemann.

Clegg, H.A., Killick, A.J. and Adams, R. (1961) *Trade Union Officers*, Oxford: Blackwell.

Clegg, H.A. (1976) *Trade Unionism Under Collective Bargaining*, Oxford: Blackwell

Clegg, S., Boreham, P. and Dow, G. (1986) *Class, Politics and the Economy*, Routledge and Kegan Paul.

Clements, L. (1977) 'Reference groups and trade union consciousness'. In Clarke, T. and Clements, L. (eds.), *Trade Unions Under Capitalism*, Fontana.

Cliff, T. (1970) *The Employers' Offensive: Productivity Deals and How to Fight Them*, Pluto.

Cliff, T. (1971) 'The bureaucracy today', *International Socialism, 1:48*.

Cliff, T. (1975a) *Lenin*, Vol.1, Pluto.

Cliff, T. (1975b) *The Crisis: Social Contract or Socialism*, Pluto.

Cliff, T. (1979) 'The balance of class forces in recent years', *International Socialism, 2:6*.

Cliff, T. (1983) *Rosa Luxemburg*, 2nd edition, Bookmarks.

Cliff, T. (1985) 'Patterns of mass strike', *International Socialism, 2:29*.

Cliff, T. and Gluckstein, D. (1986) *Marxism and Trade Union Struggle: the General Strike of 1926*, Bookmarks.

Coates, D. (1975) *The Labour Party and the Struggle for Socialism*, Cambridge: University Press.

Coates, D. (1980) *Labour in Power?*, Longman.

Coates, K. (1976) 'Some questions and some answers'. In Coates, K. (ed.) *The New Worker Cooperatives*. Nottingham, Spokesman.

Coates, K. (1977) *A Reply to Arthur Scargill*. Institute for Workers' Control, Pamphlet 56 (P)

Coates, K. (1985) 'The new age of trade unionism', *New Socialist, 31*, Oct.

Coates, K. and Topham, T. (1974) *The New Unionism*, Penguin.

Coates, K. and Topham, T. (1980) *Trade Unions in Britain*, Nottingham: Spokesman.

Coates, K. and Topham, T. (1986) *Trade Unions and Politics*, Oxford: Blackwell.

Colletti, L. (1977) 'Lenin's "State and Revolution" '. In Blackburn, R. (ed.), *Revolution and Class Struggle*, Fontana.

Cockburn, C. (1987) *Women, Trade Unions and Political Parties*, Fabian Research Series 349 (P).

Communist International Third (1980) *Theses Resolutions and Manifestos of the First Four Congresses of the Third International* (edited by Hessel, B.), Ink Links.

Cooley, M. (1980) *Architect or Bee? The Human/Technology Relationship*, Slough: Langley Technical Services.

Coote, A. and Kellner, P. (1981) *Hear This Brother! women workers and trade union power*, New Statesman (P).

Coote, A. and Campbell, B. (1987) *Sweet Freedom: the Struggle for Women's Liberation*. 2nd edition, Oxford: Blackwell.

CPGB (1976) *Evidence to the Committee of Inquiry on Industrial Democracy*, Communist Party.

CPGB (1977) *The British Road to Socialism*, Communist Party (P).

Cressey, P. and MacInnes, J. (1980) 'Voting for Ford', *Capital & Class, 11*.

Cressey, P. and MacInnes, J. (1985) *Just Managing*, Milton Keynes: Open University Press.

Crewe, I. (1982) 'The Labour Party and the electorate'. In Kavanagh, D. (ed.), *The Politics of the Labour Party*, Allen & Unwin.

Crewe, I. (1983) 'The disturbing truth behind Labour's rout', *Guardian*, 13 June.

310

Cronin, J.E. (1979) *Industrial Conflict in Modern Britain*, Croom Helm.

Cronin, J.E. (1984) *Labour and Society in Britain 1918-1979*, Batsford Academic.

Crouch, C. (1982) *Trade Unions: the Logic of Collective Action*, Fontana.

Crouch, C. (1983) 'Industrial relations'. In Griffith, J. (ed.), *Socialism in a Cold Climate*, Unwin.

Cutler, A., et al. (1977) *Marx's Capital and Capitalism Today*, Vol. 1 Macmillan.

Cutler, A. et al. (1978) *Marx's Capital and Capitalism Today*, Vol. 2 Macmillan.

Dahrendorf, R. (1959) *Class and Class Conflict in Industrial Society*, Routledge Kegan Paul.

Daniel, W.W. (1987) *Workplace Industrial Relations and Technical Change* Pinter/PSI.

Daniel, W.W. and Millward, N. (1983) *Workplace Industrial Relations in Britain*, Heinemann.

Davis, M. (1986) *Prisoners of the American Dream*, Verso.

Deason, J. (1975) 'The broad left in the AUEW', *International Socialism 1:79*.

Deason, J. (1980) *Defend our Unions*, 3rd edn., Rank and File Defend our Unions Committee (P).

Deery, S. and Plowman, D. (1985) *Australian Industrial Relations*. 2nd edition, Sydney: McGraw Hill.

Dickens, W.T. and Leonard, J.S. (1985) 'Accounting for the decline in union membership, 1950-1980', *Industrial and Labor Relations Review 38(3)*.

Draper, H. (1978) *Karl Marx's Theory of Revolution: Vol 2: The Politics of Social Classes*, New York: Monthly Review Press.

Dunleavy, P. & O'Leary, B. (1987) *Theories of the State: the politics of liberal democracy*, Macmillan.

Durcan, J., McCarthy, W. and Redman, G. (1983) *Strikes in Post-War Britain*, Allen & Unwin.

Eaton, J. and Gill, C. (1983) *The Trade Union Directory*, 2nd edition, Pluto

Eccles, T. (1981) *Under New Management*, Pan.

Edelstein, J.D. and Warner, M. (1979) *Comparative Union Democracy Organization and Opposition in British and American Unions*, New Brunswick, NJ: Transaction Books.

Edwards, C. and Heery, E. (1986) 'The incorporation of workplace trade unionism?', *Sociology, 19(3)*.

Edwards, P.K. (1983) 'The pattern of collective industrial action'. In Bain, G. (ed.), *Industrial Relations in Britain*, Oxford: Blackwell.

Edwards, R.C. (1979) *Contested Terrain: the Transformation of the Workplace in the Twentieth Century*, New York: Basic Books.

EETPU (1976) *Evidence to the Committee of Inquiry on Industrial Democracy* EETPU.

Elster, J. (1985) *Making Sense of Marx*, Cambridge: University Press.

Enderwick, P. (1985) *Multinational Business and Labour*, Croom Helm.

Engels, F. (1845) *The Condition of the Working Class in England*, in *MECW, 4*.

Engels, F. (1850) 'The English Ten Hours Bill', in *MECW, 10*.

Engels, F. (1852) 'Revolution and Counter Revolution in Germany', in *MECW, 11*.

Engels, F. (1874) 'The English elections', in Marx, K. and Engels, F., *Articles on Britain*, Moscow: Progress, 1975.

Engels, F. (1881) 'Trades unions,' in ibid.

Engels, F. (1885) 'England in 1845 and 1885', in ibid.

Engels, F. (1890) 'May 4 in London', in ibid.

Engineers Charter (1980) *What's Gone Wrong in Engineering? The Case for Change in the AUEW*, Engineers Charter (P).

England, J. (1981) 'Shop stewards in Transport House', *Industrial Relations Journal, 12(5)*.

Erd, R. and Scherrer, C. (1985) 'Unions—caught between structural competition and temporary solidarity: a critique of contemporary Marxist analysis of trade unions in Germany', *British Journal of Industrial Relations, 23(1)*.

Ernest Bevin Society (1984) *The Pit Strike in Perspective*, Ernest Bevin Society (P).

Exell, A. (1981) *The Politics of the Production Line: Autobiography of an Oxford Car Worker*, History workshop Journal (P).

Fernbach, D. (1974) 'Introduction'. In Marx, K., *The First International and After*, Penguin.

Fine, B. et al. (1984) *Class Politics: an Answer to its Critics*, Conference of Socialist Economists (P).

Fine, B. and Harris, L. (1985) *The Peculiarities of the British Economy*, Lawrence & Wishart.

Flanders, A. (1970) 'What are trade unions for?' In Flanders, A., *Management and Trade Unions*, Faber and Faber.

Fogarty, M. and Brooks, D. (1986) *Trade Unions and British Industrial Development*, Policy Studies Institute.

Foot, P. (1977) *Why You Should Be a Socialist*, Socialist Workers Party (P).

Foster, J. and Woolfson, C. (1986) *The Politics of the UCS Work-In*, Lawrence & Wishart.

Fothergill, S. et al. (1987) 'The de-industrialisation of the city'. In Martin, R. and Rowthorn, B. (eds), *The Geography of De-industrialisation*, Macmillan.

Fox, A. (1973) 'Industrial relations: a social critique of pluralist ideology'. In Child, J. (ed), *Man and Organisation*, Allen & Unwin.

Fox, A. (1985) *History and Heritage: the Social Origins of the British Industrial Relations System*, Allen & Unwin.

Freeman, M. (1984) *Taking Control: a Handbook for Trade Unionists*, Junius Publications.

Freeman, M. (1985) *Our Day Will Come: the Miners' Fight for Jobs*, Junius Publications (P).

Freeman, R. (1987) *Economic Performance and Industrial Relations Institutions*.

312

Lecture at the London School of Economics, 11 March, Exhibit 1.

Fryer, R.H. (1979) 'British trade unions and the cuts', *Capital & Class, 8.*

Fuller, K. (1985) *Radical Aristocrats: London Busworkers from the 1880s to the 1980s*, Lawrence & Wishart.

Gallie, D. (1983) *Social Inequality and Class Radicalism in France and Britain*, Cambridge: University Press.

Gardner, M (1986) 'Australian trade unionism in 1985', *Journal of Industrial Relations, 28(1).*

Geary, D. (1981) *European Labour Protest 1848-1939*, Croom Helm.

Geary, R. (1986) *Policing Industrial Disputes: 1893 to 1985*, Methuen.

Geras, N. (1976) *The Legacy of Rosa Luxemburg*, New Left Books.

Geras, N. (1987) 'Post-Marxism?', *New Left Review, 163*, May/June.

Gilhespy, D. et al. (1986) *Socialist Enterprise: Reclaiming the Economy*, Nottingham: Spokesman/New Socialist.

Gill, K. (1981) Chapter (untitled) in Hobsbawm, E., *The Forward March of Labour Halted?* (edited by Jacques, M. and Mulhern, F.), Verso.

Glyn, A. (1978) *Capitalist Crisis: Tribune's 'Alternative Strategy' or Socialist Plan*, Militant (P).

Glyn, A. and Harrison, J. (1980) *The British Economic Disaster*, Pluto.

Glyn, A. and Sutcliffe, B. (1972) *British Capitalism, Workers and the Profits Squeeze*, Penguin.

GMWU (1976) *Industrial Democracy: GMWU policy statement*, General & Municipal Workers' Union.

Goetschy, J. and Rojot, J. (1987) 'France'. In Bamber, G.J. and Lansbury, R.D. (eds), *International and Comparative Industrial Relations*, Allen & Unwin.

Goldthorpe, J.H. (ed.) (1984) *Order and Conflict in Contemporary Capitalism*, Oxford: Clarendon.

Gordon, D., Edwards, R. and Reich, M. (1982) *Segmented Work, Divided Workers: the Historical Transformation of Labor in the United States*, Cambridge: University Press.

Gordon, D. (1987) 'The global economy: new edifice or crumbling foundations?', *New Left Review, 166*, Nov-Dec.

Gorz, A. (1982) *Farewell to the Working Class*, Pluto.

Goulding, A. (1975) 'The building industry: background to a rank and file movement', *International Socialism, 1:75.*

Gourevitch, P. et al. (1984) *Unions and Economic Crisis: Britain, West Germany and Sweden*, Allen & Unwin.

Gramsci, A. and Togliatti, P. (1919a) 'Workers' democracy', in Gramsci, A., *Selections From Political Writings 1910-1920*, Lawrence & Wishart (1977).

Gramsci, A. (1919b) 'The conquest of the state', in ibid.

Gramsci, A. (1919c) 'The development of the revolution', in ibid.

Gramsci, A. (1919d) 'To the workshop delegates of the FIAT Centro and Brevetti plants', in ibid.

Gramsci, A. (1919e) 'Unions and councils', in ibid.

Gramsci, A. (1919f) 'Trade unions and the dictatorship', in ibid.

Gramsci, A. (1919g) 'Syndicalism and the councils', in ibid.

Gramsci, A. (1919h) 'Towards the Communist International', in ibid.

Gramsci, A. (1920a) 'The factory council', in ibid.

Gramsci, A. (1920b) 'Unions and councils', in ibid.

Gramsci, A. (1920c) 'Two revolutions', in ibid.

Gramsci, A. (1920d) 'The Turin factory councils movement', in ibid.

Gramsci, A. (1921a) 'Workers' control', in Gramsci, A., *Selections From Political Writings 1921-1926* (1978), Lawrence & Wishart.

Gramsci, A. (1921b) 'Officialdom', in ibid.

Gramsci, A. (1921c) 'Masses and leaders', in ibid.

Gramsci, A. (1923a) 'What is to be done?', in ibid.

Gramsci, A. (1923b) 'Our trade union strategy', in ibid.

Gramsci, A. (1926), 'Once again on the organic capacities of the working class', in ibid.

Gramsci, A. (1971) 'Some theoretical and practical aspects of "Economism". Political struggle and military war. Analysis of situations. Relations of forces.' In Gramsci, A., *Selections From the Prison Notebooks* (1971), Lawrence & Wishart.

Grant, W. and Sargent, J. (1987) *Business and Politics in Britain*, Macmillan.

Green, F. and Sutcliffe, B. (1987) *The Profit System: the Economics of Capitalism*, Penguin.

Green Paper (1987) *Trade Unions and Their Members*, HMSO.

Gregory, D. & Atkinson, J. (1986) 'A flexible future: Britain's dual labour force', *Marxism Today, 30(4)*, April.

Griffith, J. (1985) *The Politics of the Judiciary*, 2nd edn., Fontana.

Guerin, D. (1979) *100 Years of Labor in the USA*, Ink Links.

Hain, P. (1986) *Political Strikes: the State and Trade Unionism in Britain*, Penguin.

Halfpenny, J. (1985) 'The effectiveness of the Accord', *Journal of Industrial Relations, 27(2)*.

Hall, S. (1977a) 'The "political" and the "economic" in Marx's theory of classes'. In Hunt, A. (ed.), *Class and Class Structure*, Lawrence & Wishart.

Hall, S. (1977b) 'Rethinking the "base-and-superstructure" metaphor'. In Bloomfield, J. (ed.), *Class Hegemony and Party*, Lawrence & Wishart.

Hall, S. (1982) 'A long haul', *Marxism Today, 26(11)*, November.

Hall, S. and Jacques, M., eds. (1983) *The Politics of Thatcherism*, Lawrence & Wishart.

Hallas, D. (1977) 'The CP, the SWP and the rank and file movement', *International Socialism, 1:95*.

Hallas, D. (1979) *Trotsky's Marxism*, Pluto.

Hallas, D. (1980) 'Trade unionists and revolution: a response to Richard Hyman', *International Socialism, 2:8*.

Hallas, D. and Harman, C. (1981) *Days of Hope: the General Strike of 1926*, Socialists Unlimited (P).

Hammarstrom, O. (1987) 'Sweden'. In Bamber, G.J. and Lansbury, R.D. (eds), *International and Comparative Industrial Relations*, Allen & Unwin.

Hammond, T.T. (1957) *Lenin on Trade Unions and Revolution 1893-1917*, New York: Columbia University Press.

Harding, N. (1983) *Lenin's Political Thought*, Macmillan.

Harman, C. (1985a) *The Miners' Strike and the Struggle for Socialism*, Socialist Workers Party (P).

Harman, C. (1985b) '1984 and the shape of things to come', *International Socialism, 2:29*.

Harman, C. (1986) 'The working class after the recession', *International Socialism, 2:33*.

Harris, L. (1985) 'British capital: manufacturing, finance and multinational corporations'. In Coates, D. et al. (eds), *A Socialist Anatomy of Britain*, Oxford: Polity Press.

Harrison, R. (1981) Chapter (untitled), in Hobsbawm, E., *The Forward March of Labour Halted?*, Verso.

Hartley, J., Kelly, J. and Nicholson, N. (1983) *Steel Strike*, Batsford Academic.

Heath, A., Jowell, R. and Curtice, J. (1985) *How Britain Votes*, Pergammon Press.

Heery, E. and Kelly, J. (1988) *Union Women: a Survey of Women Full-time Officials*, LSE, Department of Industrial Relations, mimeo.

Held, D. (1983) 'Central perspectives on the modern state'. In Held, D. et al. (eds), *States & Societies*, Oxford: Martin Robertson.

Higgins, W. (1985) 'Political unionism and the corporatist thesis', *Economic & Industrial Democracy, 6(4)*.

Hill, S. (1981) *Competition and Control at Work*, Heinemann.

Hindess, B. (1983) *Parliamentary Democracy and Socialist Politics*, Routledge and Kegan Paul.

Hinton, J. (1973) *The First Shop Stewards' Movement*, Allen & Unwin.

Hinton, J. (1983) *Labour and Socialism: a History of the British Labour Movement 1867-1974*, Brighton: Wheatsheaf.

Hirschman, A. (1970) *Exit, Voice and Loyalty*, Cambridge, Mass: Harvard University Press.

Hirst, P. (1981) 'On struggle in the enterprise'. In Prior, M. (ed.), *The Popular and the Political*, Routledge and Kegan Paul.

Hoare, Q. and Nowell-Smith, G. (1971) 'Introduction'. In Gramsci, A., *Selections from the Prison Notebooks*, Lawrence & Wishart.

Hobsbawm, E. (1981) *The Forward March of Labour Halted?*, Verso.

Hobsbawm, E. (1984) 'The 1970s: syndicalism without syndicalists?'. In Hobsbawm, E., *Worlds of Labour*, Weidenfeld and Nicholson.

Hobsbawm, E. (1985a) 'The retreat into extremism', *Marxism Today, 29(4)*, April.

Hobsbawm, E. (1985b) 'Fifty years of people's fronts'. In Fyrth, J. (ed) *Britain, Fascism and the Popular Front*, Lawrence & Wishart.

Hodgson, G. (1975) *Trotsky and Fatalistic Marxism*, Nottingham: Spokesman.

Hodgson, G. (1984) *The Democratic Economy*, Penguin.

Houston, R. (1984) 'The POEU Broad Left'. In Socialist Organiser, *The Broad Lefts: what they are and what they must become*, Socialist Organiser Alliance (P).

Hughes, J. (1981) *Britain in Crisis: de-industrialisation and how to fight it*, Nottingham: Spokesman.

Hutt, A. (1975) *British Trade Unionism*, Lawrence & Wishart.

Hyman, R. (1971) *Marxism and the Sociology of Trade Unionism*, Pluto (P).

Hyman, R. (1974) 'Workers' control and revolutionary theory', *Socialist Register, 1974*, Merlin.

Hyman, R. (1975) *Industrial Relations: a Marxist introduction*, Macmillan.

Hyman, R. (1979) 'The politics of workplace trade unionism: recent tendencies and some problems for theory', *Capital & Class, 8*.

Hyman, R. (1980) 'British trade unionism: postwar trends and future prospects', *International Socialism, 2:8*.

Hyman, R. (1983) 'Trade unions: structure, policies and politics'. In Bain, G. (ed.), *Industrial Relations in Britain*, Oxford: Blackwell.

Hyman, R. (1984a) *Strikes*. 3rd edition, Fontana.

Hyman, R. (1984b) 'Wooing the working class'. In Curran, J. (ed.), *The Future of the Left*, Oxford: Polity Press.

Hyman, R. (1985) 'Class struggle and the trade union movement'. In Coates, D., Johnston, G. and Bush, R. (eds.), *A Socialist Anatomy of Britain*, Oxford: Polity Press.

Hyman, R. (1987) 'Rank-and-file movements and workplace organisation, 1914-39'. In Wrigley, C. (ed), *A History of British Industrial Relations, Vol II 1914-1939*, Brighton: Wheatsheaf.

Hyman, R. and Elger, T. (1981) 'Job controls, the employers' offensive and alternative strategies', *Capital & Class, 15*.

IDS (1984) *Vredeling and The Fifth*. Study 313, May. Incomes Data Services Ltd.

IMF (1987) *The IBM File*, Geneva: International Metalworkers Federation.

IMG (1980) *Lessons of the Steel Strike and the Fight to Kick out the Tories*, International Marxist Group (P).

IMS (1986) *Changing Working Patterns*, Sussex: Institute of Manpower Studies.

Ingham, G. (1974) *Strikes and Industrial Conflict*, Macmillan.

ISTC (1980) *New Deal for Steel*, Iron & Steel Trades Confederation.

Jeffery, K. and Hennessy, P. (1983) *States of Emergency: British Governments and Strike Breaking since 1919*, Routledge and Kegan Paul.

Jefferys, S. (1979) 'Striking into the 80s — modern British trade unionism, its limits and potential', *International Socialism, 2:5*.

Jefferys, S. (1981) Chapter (untitled) in Hobsbawm, E., *The Forward March of Labour Halted?*, Verso.

Jessop, B. (1982) *The Capitalist State*, Oxford: Martin Robertson.

Joll, J. (1977) *Gramsci*, Fontana.

Jones, J. (1970) *The Right to Participate: Key to Industrial Progress*, Transport & General Workers Union (P).

Kautsky, K. (1983) *Selected Political Writings*, (edited by Goode, P.), Macmillan.

Kautsky, K. (1910) 'The mass strike', in ibid.

Keenan, J. (1984) *Scargill's Strike*, Belfast: British & Irish Communist Organisation (P).

Kellner, P. (1987) 'Two nations born from one vote', *The Independent*, 13 June.

Kelly, J. (1982a) *Scientific Management, Job Redesign and Work Performance*, Academic Press.

Kelly, J. (1982b) 'Useful work and useless toil', *Marxism Today, 26(8)*, August.

Kelly, J. (1984) *Trade Union Officials: a Study of Union Behaviour, Power and Ideology*, Submission to the Economic and Social Research Council.

Kelly, J. (1985) 'Management's redesign of work: labour process, labour markets and product markets'. In Knights, D., et al. (eds), *Job Redesign*, Gower.

Kelly, J. (1987a) 'The Labour Process and Working Class Consciousness', paper delivered to the 4th Aston-UMIST Labour Process Conference, Manchester.

Kelly, J. (1987b) 'Trade unions through the recession 1980-84', *British Journal of Industrial Relations, 25(2)*.

Kelly, J. (1987c) *Labour and the Unions*, Verso (P).

Kelly, J. (1987d) *The Measurement and Meaning of Trade Union Density*, LSE, Department of Industrial Relations, Mimeo.

Kelly, J. and Heery, E. (in preparation) *Working For The Union: British Trade Union Officers*.

Khromov, S.S. et al., (eds) (1983) *The International Working Class Movement, Volume 3: Revolutionary Battles of the Early 20th Century*. Moscow: Progress.

Kilpatrick, A. and Lawson, T (1980) 'On the nature of industrial decline in the UK', *Cambridge Journal of Economics, 4*.

Kitching, G. (1983) *Rethinking Socialism*, Methuen.

Klein, K.J. (1987) 'Employee stock ownership and employee attitudes: a test of three models', *Journal of Applied Psychology (Monograph), 72(3)*.

Klugmann, J. (1969) *History of the Communist Party of Great Britain Vol 1: Formation and Early Years 1919-1924*, Lawrence & Wishart.

Kochan, T.A., Katz, H. C. and McKersie, R.B. (1986) *The Transformation of American Industrial Relations*, New York: Basic Books.

Korpi, W. (1983) *The Democratic Class Struggle*, Routledge and Kegan Paul.

Korpi, W. and Shalev, M. (1980) 'Strikes, power and politics in the Western nations 1900-1976', *Political Power and Social Theory, Vol 1*, Greenwich, Conn: JAI Press.

Krasso, N. (1967) 'Trotsky's Marxism', *New Left Review, 44*.

Labour Party (1985) *NEC Report*, Labour Party.

Laclau, E. and Mouffe, C. (1981) 'Socialist strategy: where next?', *Marxism Today, 24(1)*, Jan.

Laclau, E. and Mouffe, C. (1985) *Hegemony and Socialist Strategy*, Verso.

Lane, T. (1974) *The Union Makes Us Strong*, Arrow Books.

Lane, T. (1982) 'The unions: caught on an ebb tide', *Marxism Today*, 26 (9), Sept.

Lane, T. (1986) 'Economic democracy: are the trade unions equipped?', *Industrial Relations Journal, 17(4)*.

Lane, T. and Roberts, K. (1971) *Strike at Pilkingtons*, Fontana.

Lange, P. et al. (1982) *Unions, Change and Crisis: French and Italian Union Strategy and the Political Economy, 1945-1980*, Allen & Unwin.

Lansbury, R.D. and Davis, E. (1987) 'Australia'. In Bamber, G.J. and Lansbury R.D. (eds), *International and Comparative Industrial Relations*, Allen & Unwin.

Lash, S. (1984) *The Militant Worker*, Heinemann.

Lash, S. (1985) 'The end of neo-corporatism? The breakdown of centralised bargaining in Sweden', *British Journal of Industrial Relations, 23(2)*.

Lash, S. and Urry, J. (1987) *The End of Organized Capitalism*, Oxford: Polity Press.

Latta, G. (1972) 'Trade union finance', *British Journal of Industrial Relations, 10(3)*.

Lawler, J.J. (1984) 'The influence of management consultants on the outcome of union certification elections', *Indusirial and Labor Relations Review, 38(1)*.

LCC (1981) *Trade Unions and Socialism*, Labour Coordinating Committee.

Leadbeater, C. (1987) 'In the land of the dispossessed', *Marxism Today, 31(4)*.

Leadbeater, C. and Lloyd, J. (1987) *In Search of Work*, Penguin.

Lenin, V.I. (1896) 'Draft and explanation of a programme for the Social Democratic Party', *CW 2*.

Lenin, V.I. (1899) 'On strikes', *CW 4*.

Lenin, V.I. (1902) 'What is to be done?', *CW 5*.

Lenin, V.I. (1905) 'The reorganisation of the party', *CW 10*.

Lenin, V.I. (1906) 'A tactical platform for the Unity congress of the RSDLP', *CW 10*.

Lenin, V.I. (1907a) 'Draft resolutions for the third Conference of the RSDLP', *CW 10*.

Lenin, V.I. (1907b) 'Preface' to the collection *Twelve Years, CW 13*.

Lenin, V.I. (1908) 'Trade union neutrality', *CW 13*.

Lenin, V.I. (1910) 'The lessons of the revolution', *CW 16*.

Lenin, V.I. (1912) 'In America', *CW 36*.

Lenin, V.I. (1913) 'In Britain', *CW 19*.

Lenin, V.I. (1915) 'Karl Marx', *CW 21*.

Lenin, V.I. (1916) 'Imperialism and the split in socialism', *CW 23*.

Lenin, V.I. (1917a) 'Lecture on the 1905 revolution', *CW 23*.

Lenin, V.I. (1917b) 'The state and revolution', *CW 25*.

Lenin, V.I. (1920a) 'Theses on the fundamental tasks of the Second Congress of the Communist International', *CW 31*.

Lenin, V.I. (1920b) 'The trade unions, the present situation and Trotsky's mistakes', *CW 32.*

Lenin, V.I. (1920c) ' "Left-wing" Communism: an infantile disorder', *CW 31.*

Lenin, V.I. (1970) *On Trade Unions*, Moscow: Progress Publishers.

Lipset, S. (1986) 'North American labor movements: a comparative perspective'. In Lipset, S. (ed), *Unions in Transition*, San Francisco: Institute For Contemporary Studies.

Lozovsky, A. (1935) *Marx and the Trade Unions*, New York: International Publishers.

Lukacs, G. (1970) *Lenin: a Study of the Unity of his Thought*, New Left Books.

Lukacs, G. (1971) *History and Class Consciousness*, Merlin.

Luxemburg, R. (1900) 'Reform or revolution?' In Luxemburg, R., *Rosa Luxemburg Speaks* (ed. Waters, M.A.), New York: Pathfinder Press, 1970.

Luxemburg, R. (1904) 'Organisational question of social democracy'. In ibid.

Luxemburg, R. (1906) 'The mass strike, the political party and the trade unions'. In ibid.

Luxemburg, R. (1918) 'The Russian revolution'. In ibid.

Lyddon, D. (1977) 'British Leyland: the shop stewards and participation', *International Socialism, 1:102.*

McCarthy, W. and Parker, S. (1968) *Shop Stewards and Workshop Relations*, HMSO, Donovan Commission Research Paper 10.

McIlroy, J. (1984) *Strike!*, Pluto Press.

MacIntyre, S. (1986) *A Proletarian Science: Marxism in Britain, 1917-1933*, Lawrence & Wishart.

MacKintosh, M. and Wainwright, H. (eds) (1987) *A Taste of Power: the politics of local economics*, Verso.

McLellan, D. (1980) *Marxism After Marx*, Macmillan.

McLennan, G. (1984) 'Capitalist state or democratic polity? Recent developments in Marxist and pluralist theory'. In McLennan, G. et al. (eds) *The Idea of the Modern State*, Milton Keynes: Open University Press.

Mandel, E. (1971) *The Formation of the Economic Thought of Karl Marx*, New Left Books.

Mandel, E. (1973) 'The debate on workers' control'. In Hunnius, G. et al. (eds), *Workers' Control*. New York: Vintage Books.

Mandel, E. (1978) *From Stalinism to Eurocommunism*, New Left Books.

Mandel, E. (1979) *Trotsky: a Study in the Dynamics of his Thought*, New Left Books.

Mann, M. (1973) *Consciousness and Action Among the Western Working Class*, Macmillan.

Marx, K. (1845) 'The Holy Family'. *MECW 4.*

Marx, K. (1847) 'The Poverty of Philosophy'. *MECW 6.*

Marx, K. (1849) 'Wage labour and capital'. *MECW 9.*

Marx, K. (1852) 'The Chartists'. *MECW 11.*

Marx, K. (1853) 'Chartism'. *MECW 12.*

Marx, K. (1855) 'The crisis in England'. *MECW 14.*

Marx, K. (1859) 'Preface' to 'A Contribution to a Critique of Political Economy'. In Marx, K. and Engels, F., *Selected Works in Three Volumes, Vol One*, Moscow: Progress, 1969.

Marx, K. (1864) 'Inaugural Address of the International Working Men's Association'. In Marx, K., *The First International and After*, ed. D. Fernbach, Penguin, 1974.

Marx, K. (1865) 'Wages, Price and Profit'. In Marx, K. and Engels, F., *Selected Works* (Moscow: Progress), Vol.2, 1969.

Marx, K. (1887) *Capital. Vol 1*, Lawrence & Wishart, 1974.

Marx, K. (1974) *The First International and After* (edited D. Fernbach), Penguin.

Marx, K. and Engels, F. (1845) 'The German Ideology', *MECW 5.*

Marx, K. and Engels, F. (1848) 'The Communist Manifesto'. *MECW 6.*

Marx, K. and Engels, F. (1871) 'Resolution of the London Conference on Working-class Political Action'. In Marx, K., *The First International and After*, Penguin 1974.

Marx, K. and Engels, F. (1975) *Selected Correspondence*. Moscow, Progress.

Mavrakis, K. (1976) *On Trotskyism*, Routledge and Kegan Paul.

Mayhew, K. (1979) 'Economists and strikes', *Oxford Bulletin of Economics and Statistics, 41.*

Mercer, C. (1980) 'Revolutions, reforms or reformulations? Marxist discourse on democracy'. In Hunt, A. (ed), *Marxism and Democracy*, Lawrence & Wishart.

Miliband, R. (1969) *The State in Capitalist Society*, Quartet.

Miliband, R. (1973) *Parliamentary Socialism*, Merlin.

Miliband, R. (1977) *Marxism and Politics*, Oxford: University Press.

Miliband, R. (1982) *Capitalist Democracy in Britain*, Oxford: University Press.

Miliband, R. (1983) *Class Power and State Power*, Verso.

Miliband, R. et al. (eds) (1986) *Socialist Register 1985/86: Social Democracy and after*, Merlin.

Militant (1980) *AUEW: the Case for a Fighting Socialist Leadership*, Militant (P).

Militant (1981?) *A Fighting Programme for the NUR*, Militant (P).

Millward, N. and Stevens, M. (1986) *British Workplace Industrial Relations 1980–1984*, Gower.

Montague, K. (1979) *Going On Strike*, Rank and File (P).

Moorhouse, H. (1978) 'The Marxist theory of the labour aristocracy', *Social History, 3(1).*

Mouffe, C. (1979) 'Hegemony and ideology in Gramsci'. In Mouffe, C. (ed.), *Gramsci and Marxist theory*, Routledge and Kegan Paul.

Muller-Jentsch, W. (1985) 'Trade unions as intermediary organizations', *Economic and Industrial Democracy, 6(1).*

Muller-Jentsch, W. (1986) 'Labour conflicts and class struggles', in

Jacobi, O. et al. (eds), *Technological Change, Rationalisation and Industrial Relations*, Croom Helm.

Nagliatti, A. (1974) 'Towards a rank and file movement', *International Socialism, 1:66*.

Nettl, J.P. (1969) *Rosa Luxemburg*, Abridged edition, Oxford: University Press.

Nichols, T. (1986) *The British Worker Question*, Routledge and Kegan Paul.

Nichols, T. and Beynon, H. (1977) *Living with Capitalism*, Routledge and Kegan Paul.

Offe, C. (1975) 'Theses on the theory of the state'. In Offe, C., *Contradictions of the Welfare State* (1984), Hutchinson.

Offe, C. (1982) 'Reflections on the welfare state and the future of socialism. An interview' In Offe, C., *Contradictions of the Welfare State*, Hutchinson, 1984.

Offe, C. (1985) *Disorganized Capitalism*, Oxford: Polity Press.

Offe, C. and Wiesenthal, H. (1980) 'Two logics of collective action'. In Zeitlin, M. (ed), *Political Power and Social Theory, Vol. 1*. Greenwich Conn: JAI Press. Reprinted in Offe, C., *Disorganized Capitalism* (1985), Oxford: Polity Press.

Ogden, S. (1982) 'Trade unions, industrial democracy and collective bargaining, *Sociology, 16(4)*.

O'Lincoln, T. (1985) *Into The Mainstream: the Decline of Australian Communism*, Westgate, NSW: Stained Wattle Press.

Olson, M. (1965) *The Logic of Collective Action*, Cambridge, Mass: Harvard University Press.

Panitch, L. (1976) *Social Democracy and Industrial Militancy*, Cambridge: University Press.

Panitch, L. (1978) 'The importance of workers' control for revolutionary change', *Monthly Review, 29(10)*.

Panitch, L. (1981) 'Trade unions and the capitalist state', *New Left Review, 125*, Jan-Feb.

Panitch, L. (1986) 'The impasse of social democratic politics', *Socialist Register 1985/86*, Merlin.

Panitch, L. and Swartz, D. (1985) *From Consent to Coercion: the Assault on Trade Union Freedoms*, Toronto: Garamond Press.

Parker, S. (1974) *Workplace Industrial Relations, 1972*, HMSO.

Parker, S. (1975) *Workplace Industrial Relations, 1973*. HMSO.

Parker, S. (1975a) 'Meriden and workers' control', *Revolutionary Communist, 1*, Jan.

Partridge, B. (1978) 'The activities of shop stewards', *Industrial Relations Journal, 8(4)*.

Peak, S. (1984) *Troops in Strikes*, Cobden Trust.

Pearce, B. (1959) 'Some past rank-and-file movements'. In Woodhouse, M. and Pearce, B., *Essays on the History of Communism in Britain*, New Park Publications, 1975.

Peterson, R.B. and Tracy, L. (1985) 'Problem solving in American collective bargaining: a review and assessment'. In Lipsky, D. (ed.), *Advances in Industrial and Labor Relations, Vol 2*, Greenwich, Conn: JAI Press.

Petridis, A. (1987) 'Wage policy and wage determination 1986', *Journal of Industrial Relations, 29(1)*.

Phillips, A. (1983) *Hidden Hands: Women and Economic Policies*, Pluto Press.

Pierson, C. (1986) *Marxist Theory and Democratic Politics*, Cambridge: Polity Press.

Piore, M.J. and Sabel, C.F. (1984) *The Second Industrial Divide: Possibilities for Prosperity*, New York: Basic Books.

Pirani, S. (1985) 'Stalinism and the miners strike', *Labour Review, 8(9)*, April.

Polan, A.J. (1984) *Lenin and the End of Politics*, Methuen.

Pond, C. (1983) 'Wages councils, the unorganised and the low paid'. In Bain, G. (ed), *Industrial Relations in Britain*, Oxford: Blackwell.

Pontusson, J. (1984) 'Behind and beyond Social Democracy in Sweden', *New Left Review, 143*, Jan-Feb.

Pontusson, J. (1987) 'Radicalization and retreat in Swedish Social Democracy', *New Left Review, 165*, Sept-Oct.

Poulantzas, N. (1972) 'The problem of the capitalist state'. In Blackburn, R. (ed), *Ideology and Social Science*, Fontana.

Poulantzas, N. (1978) *State, Power, Socialism*, Verso.

Prior, M. and Purdy, D. (1979) *Out of the Ghetto*, Nottingham: Spokesman.

Przeworski, A. (1977) 'Proletariat into a class: the process of class formation from Karl Kautsky's *The Class Struggle* to recent controversies', *Politics and Society, 7(4)*.

Przeworski, A. (1980) 'Social democracy as a historical phenomenon', *New Left Review, 122*, July-Aug.

Przeworski, A. (1986) 'Material interests, class compromise and the transition to socialism'. In Przeworski, A., *Capitalism and Social Democracy*, Cambridge: University Press, reprinted in Roemer, J. (ed.), *Analytical Marxism*, Cambridge: University Press.

Purdy, D. (1981) 'The social contract and socialist policy'. In Prior, M. (ed.), *The Popular and the Political*, Routledge and Kegan Paul.

Ramsay, H. (1983) 'Evolution or cycle? worker participation in the 1970s and 1980s'. In Crouch, C. and Heller, F. (eds), *International Yearbook of Organizational Democracy, Vol 1.*, Wiley.

RCP (1984) *Preparing For Power: the Programme of the Revolutionary Communist Party*, Junius Publications (P).

RCP (1987) *The Red Front: a Platform for Working Class Unity*, Junius Publications (P).

Real Steel News (1980) *Steelworkers' Power: the Steel Strike and How We Could Have Won It*, Socialists Unlimited (P).

Reed, D. and Adamson, O. (1985) *Miners' Strike 1984-1985: People Versus State*, Larkin Publications.

Reid, J. (1985) 'What Scargill means', *New Society*, 17 Jan.

Regini, M. (1984) 'The conditions for political exchange: how concertation emerged and collapsed in Italy and Great Britain'. In Goldthorpe, J.H. (ed.), *Order and Conflict in Contemporary Capitalism*, Oxford: Clarendon Press.

Report of the Committee of Inquiry on Industrial Democracy (Bullock Report) (1977) HMSO, Cmnd. 6706.

Richards, F. (1975) 'The International Socialists and centrism: the re-emergence of economism', *Revolutionary Communist, 1*.

Richards, F. (1984) *The Miners' Next Step*, Junius Publications (P).

Roberts, B.C. (1956) *Trade Union Government and Administration in Great Britain*, LSE/G. Bell and Sons.

Roberts, G. (1976) 'The strategy of rank and filism', *Marxism Today, 20(12)*, Dec.

Robertson, N. and Sams, K. (1978) 'Research note: on the work pattern of union officers', *Industrial Relations Journal, 9(1)*.

Roddy, K. and McHugh, K (1985) *The DHSS Shiftworkers' Dispute at Newcastle Central Office and Washington Child Benefit Centre*, Newcastle Central Office CPSA (P).

Roiser, M. and Little, T. (1986) 'Public opinion, trades unions and industrial relations', *Journal of Occupational Psychology, 59(3)*.

Rowthorn, B. (1980) 'Marx's theory of wages'. In Rowthorn, B., *Capitalism Conflict and Inflation*, Lawrence & Wishart.

Rowthorn, B. (1987) 'De-industrialisation in Britain'. In Martin, R. and Rowthorn, B (eds), *The Geography of De-industrialisation*, Macmillan.

Rowthorn, B. and Grahl, J. (1986) 'Dodging the taxing questions', *Marxism Today, 30(11)*

Royal Commission on Trade Unions and Employers Associations (1968) (Donovan Report), HMSO.

Rustin, M. (1985) 'Workers' plans and industrial democracy'. In Rustin, M., *For A Pluralist Socialism*, Verso.

Sabel, C. (1982) *Work and Politics: the Division of Labor in Industry*, Cambridge: University Press.

Salvadori, M. (1979) *Karl Kautsky and the Socialist Revolution 1880-1938*, New Left Books.

Sarlvik, K. (1984) *The Swedish Wage-Earner Funds*, MSc thesis, Political Sociology, London School of Economics.

Scargill, A. (1975) 'The new unionism', *New Left Review, 92*, July-August.

Scargill, A. et al. (1978) *A Debate on Workers' Control*, Nottingham: Institute for Workers' Control, Pamphlet 64 (P).

Scargill, A. and Kahn, P. (1980) *The Myth of Workers' Control*, Universities of Leeds and Nottingham: Occasional Papers in Industrial Relations (P).

Scase, R. (1977) *Social Democracy in Capitalist Society*, Croom Helm.

Schuller, T. and Robertson, D. (1983) 'How representatives allocate their time: shop steward activity and membership contact', *British Journal of Industrial Relations, 21(3)*.

Screpanti, E. (1987) 'Long cycles in strike activity: an empirical investigation', *British Journal of Industrial Relations, 25(1)*.

Selbourne, D. (1985) *Against Socialist Illusion*, Macmillan.

Shalev, M. (1978) 'Lies damned lies and statistics: the measurement of trends in industrial conflict'. In Crouch, C. and Pizzorno, A. (eds), *The Resurgence of Class Conflict in Western Europe Since 1968, Vol. 1*, Macmillan.

Shaw, M. (1978) 'The making of a party', *Socialist Register 1978*, Merlin.

Sherman, B. (1986) *The State of the Unions*, Wiley.

Shipley, P. (1976) *Revolutionaries in Modern Britain*, Bodley Head.

Simon, H. A. (1976) *Administrative Behaviour*, 3rd edition, New York: Free Press.

Simon, R. (1982) *Gramsci's Political Thought: an Introduction*, Lawrence & Wishart.

Smith, C.T. et al. (1978) *Strikes in Britain*, HMSO, DE Manpower Paper 15.

Smith, S. (1981) 'Craft consciousness, class consciousness: Petrograd 1917', *History Workshop Journal, 11*.

Smith, S. (1983) *Red Petrograd: Revolution in the Factories 1917-18*, Cambridge: University Press.

Socialist Action (1985) *In Defence of the NUM*, Socialist Action (P).

Socialist Organiser (1985) *Starved, Battered, Defiant Magnificent Miners: the 1984-5 Strike*, Socialist Organiser, 219-220, March (P).

Spriano, P. (1975) *The Occupation of the Factories*, Pluto Press.

Stephens, J.D. (1979) *The Transition From Capitalism to Socialism*, Macmillan.

Stocking, D. (1978) 'Marxists and the trade unions', *Workers' Power, 7/8*, Autumn.

Storey, J. (1980) *The Challenge to Management Control*, Routledge and Kegan Paul.

Strinati, D. (1982) *Capitalism, the State and Industrial Relations*, Croom Helm.

Taafe, P. (1986) *Militant: What We Stand For*, Militant (P).

Taafe, P. et al. (1983) *The State, a warning to the labour movement*, Militant (P).

Taylor, R. (1980) *The Fifth Estate: Britain's Unions in the Modern World*, Pan.

Terry, M. (1983) 'Shop steward development and managerial strategies'. In Bain, G. (ed), *Industrial Relations in Britain*, Oxford: Blackwell.

Terry, M. (1986) 'How do we know if shop stewards are getting weaker?', *British Journal of Industrial Relations, 24(2)*, July.

TGWU (1978) *Industrial Democracy*, Transport & General Workers' Union (P).

Therborn, G. (1983) 'The rule of capital and the rise of democracy' (1977). In Held, D. et al. (eds), *States and Societies*, Oxford: Martin Robertson.

Therborn, G. (1984a) 'The prospects of labour and the transformation of

324

advanced capitalism', *New Left Review*, 145, May-June.

Therborn, G. (1984b) 'Britain left out'. In Curran, J. (ed.) *The Future of the Left*, Polity Press and New Socialist.

Therborn, G. (1986) *Why Some Peoples Are More Unemployed Than Others*, Verso.

Thompson, P., and Lewis, G. (1977) *The Revolution Unfinished? a Critique of Trotskyism*, Liverpool: Big Flame (P).

Thompson, P. and Bannon, E. (1985) *Working the System: the shopfloor and new technology*, Pluto.

Thornett, A. (1983) 'What happened to the stewards' movement?', *Workers' Socialist Review*, 3, April/May.

Togliatti, P. (1979a) 'Leninism in the theory and practice of Gramsci'. In Togliatti, P., *On Gramsci and Other Writings*, Lawrence & Wishart, 1979.

Togliatti, P. (1979b) 'The Communist policy of national unity'. In ibid.

Tomlinson, J. (1982) *The Unequal Struggle? British Socialism and the Capitalist Enterprise*, Methuen.

Tornquist, D. (1973) 'Workers' management: the intrinsic issues'. In Hunnius, G. et al. (eds), *Workers' Control*, New York: Vintage Books.

Topham, T. (1983) 'The role of trade unions'. In Topham, T. (ed.), *Planning the Planners: How to Control the Recovery*, Nottingham: Spokesman.

Touraine, A. (1986) 'Unionism as a social movement'. In Lipset, S. (ed.), *Unions in Transition*, San Francisco: Institute For Contemporary Studies.

Towers, B., Cox, D. and Chell, E. (1987) *Worker Directors in Private Manufacturing Industry in Great Britain*, Department of Employment Research Paper 29.

Treu, T. (1983) 'Collective bargaining and union participation in economic policy: the case of Italy'. In Crouch, C. and Heller, F. (eds), *The International Yearbook of Organizational Democracy, Vol 1*. Wiley.

Trotsky, L. (1919) 'French socialism of today'. In Trotsky, L., *The First Five Years of the Communist International. Vol 1.*, New Park, 1973.

Trotsky, L. (1921a) 'Theses on the international situation and the tasks of the Comintern'. In ibid.

Trotsky, L. (1921b) 'Report on the world economic crisis and the new tasks of the Communist International'. In ibid.

Trotsky, L. (1921c) 'Summary speech'. In ibid.

Trotsky, L. (1922) 'The fifth anniversary of the October Revolution and the Fourth World Congress of the Communist International'. In Trotsky, L., *The First Five Years of the Communist International, Vol 2*, New Park, 1974.

Trotsky, L. (1924) 'The working class in the nineteenth century'. In Trotsky, L., *Writings on Britain, Vol. 1* (edited by R. Chappell and A. Clinton), New Park, 1974.

Trotsky, L. (1926a) 'Where is Britain Going?' In Trotsky, L., *Writings on Britain, Vol. 2* (edited R. Chappell and A. Clinton) New Park, 1974.

Trotsky, L. (1926b) 'Notes on the situation in Britain 1925-26'. In ibid.

Trotsky, L. (1929a) 'The errors in principle of syndicalism'. In *Leon Trotsky on the Trade Unions*, New York: Pathfinder, 1975 (P).

Trotsky, L. (1929b) 'Communism and syndicalism'. In ibid (P).

Trotsky, L. (1931a) 'Questions of perspective'. In Trotsky, L., *Writings on Britain, Vol. 3* (edited R. Chappell and A. Clinton), New Park, 1974.

Trotsky, L. (1931b) 'Workers' control of production'. In Trotsky, L., *The Struggle Against Fascism in Germany*, Penguin, 1975.

Trotsky, L. (1932-3) *The History of the Russian Revolution*, Pluto Press, 1977.

Trotsky, L. (1933a) 'The first British Trotskyists'. In Trotsky, L. *Writings on Britain, Vol. 3*, New Park, 1974.

Trotsky, L. (1933b) 'The ILP and the New International'. In ibid.

Trotsky, L. (1935) 'The middle of the road'. In ibid.

Trotsky, L. (1938a) 'Discussion with a CIO organiser'. In *Leon Trotsky on the Trade Unions*, New York: Pathfinder, 1975 (P).

Trotsky, L. (1938b) *The Death Agony of Capitalism and the Tasks of the Fourth International (The Transitional Program)*, New York: Pathfinder, 1970 (P).

Trotksy, L. (1938c) 'Discussion on the Transitional Program'. In *Writings of Leon Trotsky 1938-39* (1st edition), New York: Merit Publishers, 1969.

Trotsky, L. (1940) 'Trade unions in the epoch of imperialist decay'. In *Leon Trotsky on the Trade Unions*, New York: Pathfinder, 1975 (P).

Trotsky, L. (1975) *The Struggle Against Fascism in Germany*, Penguin.

Troy, L. (1986) 'The rise and fall of American trade unions: the labor movement from FDR to RR'. In Lipset, S. (ed.), *Unions in Transition*, San Francisco: Institute For Contemporary Studies.

TUC *Congress Reports*.

TUC (1979) *Industrial Democracy*, Trades Union Congress.

TUC (1984) *TUC Strategy*, Trades Union Congress.

TUC (1985) *TUC Strategy: Union Finance and Administration*. Unpublished document, June.

TUC-LPLC (1982) *Economic Planning and Industrial Democracy*, TUC-Labour Party Liaison Committee.

TUC-LPLC (1983) *Partners in Rebuilding Britain*, TUC-Labour Party Liaison Committee.

TUC-LPLC (1985) *A New Partnership, A New Britain*, TUC-Labour Party Liaison Committee.

TUC-LPLC (1986) *People at Work: New Rights, New Responsibilities*, TUC-Labour Party Liaison Committee.

TUC-LPLC (1987) *Work to Win*, TUC-Labour Party Liaison Committee.

Undy, R. et al. (1981) *Change in Trade Unions*, Hutchinson.

Undy, R. and Martin, R. (1984) *Ballots and Trade Union Democracy*, Oxford: Blackwell.

Urry, J. (1981) *The Anatomy of Capitalist Societies*, Macmillan.

Waddington, D. (1987) *Trouble Brewing: a Social Psychological Analysis of the Ansell's Brewery Dispute*, Aldershot: Avebury.

Wainwright, H. and Elliott, D. (1982) *The Lucas Plan: a New Trade Unionism in the Making?*, Allison & Busby.

Webb, S. and Webb, B. (1902) *Industrial Democracy*, Longmans Green.

Wedderburn, Lord (1986) *The Worker and the Law*, 3rd edition, Penguin.

Weekes, B. et al. (1975) *Industrial Relations and the Limits of Law*, Oxford: Blackwell.

Weir, A. & McIntosh, M. (1982) 'Towards a wages strategy for women', *Feminist Review, 10*.

Westergaard, J. (1984) 'The once and future class'. In Curran, J. (ed), *The Future of the Left*, New Socialist/Polity Press.

Wheeler, H. (1987) 'Management — labour relations in the USA'. In Bamber, G. J. and Lansbury, R. D. (eds), *International and Comparative Industrial Relations*, Allen & Unwin.

White, M. (1981) *Case Studies of Shorter Working Time*, Policy Studies Institute, Report 597.

Williams, G.A. (1975) *Proletarian Order: Antonio Gramsci, Factory Councils and the Origins of Communism in Italy 1911–1921*, Pluto.

Williams, R. and Steward, F. (1985) 'New technology agreements: an assessment', *Industrial Relations Journal, 16*.

Willman, P. and Morris T. (1987) *The Finances of UK Trade Unions 1975 – 1985*, London Business School, mimeo.

Winchester, D. (1983) 'Industrial relations in the public sector'. In Bain, G. (ed.), *Industrial Relations in Britain*, Oxford: Blackwell.

Wood, E.M. (1986) *The Retreat From Class*, Verso.

Wood, S. (1986) 'The cooperative labor strategy in the US auto industry', *Economic and Industrial Democracy, 7*.

Workers' Power (1978) 'Against the capitalist offensive: the political strategy for a rank and file movement', *Workers' Power, 7/8*, Autumn.

Workers' Power (1984) *The Road to Working-Class Power*, Workers' Power (P).

WRP (1985) *Lessons From the Miners' Strike: the Struggle for Power*, Workers Revolutionary Party (P).

Wright, E.O. (1985) *Classes*, Verso.

Zagladin, V.V. et al. (1981) *The International Working-Class Movement, Volume 2: The Working-class Movement in the Period of Transition to Imperialism (1871-1904)*. Moscow: Progress.

Zeitlin, J. (1985) 'Shop floor bargaining and the state: a contradictory relationship'. In Tolliday, S. and Zeitlin, J. (eds), *Shopfloor Bargaining and the State*, Cambridge: University Press.

Index

328